Spying through a Glass Darkly

Spyin

Spying through a Glass Darkly

American Espionage against the Soviet Union, 1945–1946

David Alvarez and Eduard Mark

University Press of Kansas

Published by the University Press of Kansas (Lawrence, Kansas 66045), which was
organized by the Kansas Board of Regents and is operated and funded by Emporia State
University, Fort Hays State University, Kansas State University, Pittsburg State University,
the University of Kansas, and Wichita State University

Library of Congress Cataloging-in-Publication Data

Alvarez, David J. and Mark, Eduard Maximilian / Spying through a glass darkly :
American espionage against the Soviet Union, 1945–1946
Includes bibliographical references and index
ISBN 9780700621927 (cloth : acid-free paper)
ISBN 9780700621972 (ebook)
United States—Foreign relations—Soviet Union | Soviet Union—Foreign relations—
United States | Espionage, American—Soviet Union—History | Intelligence service—
United States—History—20th century | United States. War Department. Strategic
Services Unit—History | United States—Foreign relations—1945–1953
E183.8.S65 A555 2016
327.7304709/044—dc23
2015032188

British Library Cataloguing in Publication Data is available.

Printed in the United States of America

10 9 8 7 6 5 4 3 2 1

In memory of
J. Garry Clifford
(1942–2014),
who thought I could be a historian

Contents

Preface

For now we see through a glass, darkly.

1 Corinthians, 13:12

With the exception of the U.S. Civil War and World War II, perhaps no period in American history has generated as much research as the Cold War, particularly the early years of that period. The attention is well deserved. The antagonism between the United States and its allies and the Soviet Union and its allies significantly influenced the political, diplomatic, military, economic, scientific, and cultural history of much of the second half of the twentieth century. Given the impact of the Cold War—an impact not always felicitous for the world and its inhabitants—historians have expended much energy and imagination to understand how the conflict began, investigating the possible contributions of political ideologies, economic systems, national security interests, domestic politics, religion, race, culture, and gender.

In their determination to develop a comprehensive understanding of the origins of the Cold War, historians have neglected one element: intelligence. A student seeking to understand the role of espionage in shaping U.S. suspicions toward the USSR in the critical period 1945–1946 would be hard pressed to find detailed information beyond references to Alger Hiss, Whittaker Chambers, Elizabeth Bentley, and the "atom bomb spies," all examples of *Soviet* espionage against the United States. But what of American espionage? Typically, accounts of the early Cold War simply ignore American intelligence operations. The first volume of the authoritative *Cambridge History of the Cold War* is devoted entirely to "Origins," but nowhere does it discuss espionage. Intelligence appears in a single essay in the second volume, "Crises and Détente," but this essay has nothing to say about American clandestine activities before 1948. In their surveys and monographs respected historians of the Cold War, such as Melvyn Leffler and John Lewis Gaddis, scarcely mention intelligence. The periodical literature is no more helpful. Over their fifteen-year histories the two leading journals in the field, the *Journal of Cold War Studies* and *Cold War History*, have together published scarcely a dozen articles on intelligence subjects, and most of these concern topics from the later Cold War. The handful of articles dealing with the immediate post–World War II period invariably deal with the intelligence operations of the Soviet Union and its East European client states, such as Poland and Czechoslovakia.

The disinclination to investigate intelligence operations in the early Cold War has led to certain gaps in accounts of that period. One example may illuminate the problem. No historian has done more to illuminate American diplomacy in that period than Melvyn Leffler, but he has not cast his light into some of the darker corners of Washington's foreign policy. In *The Specter of Communism: The United States and the Origins of the Cold War, 1917–1953*, for example, Professor Leffler makes no mention of American intelligence operations in his discussion of the years 1945–1946. He is, however, puzzled that by early 1946 President Harry S. Truman seem "predisposed" to a tougher policy toward the Soviet Union and that the president and his advisers discounted such indicators of Moscow's efforts at accommodation and flexibility as the demobilization of the Red Army, free elections in Hungary and Czechoslovakia, and the establishment of representative governments in Austria and Finland. He is hard pressed to explain this American posture except by reference to intangibles such as personal predispositions, ideological biases, or "immense fears" of Soviet intentions and capabilities. It escapes Professor Leffler's notice—as well as that of other distinguished historians of the early Cold War—that in the first year of peace American policy makers may have been receiving secret intelligence reports from Europe that challenged or counterbalanced reports of Soviet demobilization or Russian flexibility in Eastern Europe. American policy makers may have had immense fears because secret intelligence gave them serious cause to be fearful.

Indifference to American intelligence operations in the early Cold War has led historians to overlook the activity—indeed the very existence—of the Strategic Services Unit (SSU), an espionage service that played an important role in the evolution of U.S. policy toward the Soviet Union in the early postwar period. Established in the War Department from the remnants of the Office of Strategic Services (OSS), America's wartime intelligence service abolished by presidential order in October 1945, SSU represented the country's clandestine intelligence capability in the first year of peace. Understaffed and underresourced, SSU nevertheless ran clandestine collection operations to uncover the capabilities and intentions of the Soviet Union, a political entity so opaque that Winston Churchill famously described it as "a riddle wrapped in a mystery inside an enigma." These operations were important to Washington's policy making since not only the White House, but also the State Department and the War and Navy Departments, depended on SSU for secret information concerning Soviet affairs.

The story of the Strategic Services Unit and its operations remains untold. Even among specialists the organization has received little attention. Intelligence historians have described the postwar political battles in Washington that accompanied the demise of OSS and the eventual appearance, two years later, of the Central Intelligence Agency (CIA), but they have largely ignored the organization that struggled to maintain the country's clandestine intelligence capabilities while these political battles raged. In its thirty-year history, *Intelligence and National Security*, the premier journal in the field, has published hundreds of articles on all aspects and periods of intelligence history, but only eighteen of those articles even mention, let alone feature, the Strategic Services Unit. The most comprehensive history of U.S. intelligence through the Cold War, Christopher Andrew's *For the President's Eyes Only: Secret Intelligence and the American Presidency from Washington to Bush*, mentions SSU in only a single sentence and does not discuss U.S. human intelligence operations in the months immediately following the end of World War II. In his *Cloak and Dollar: A History of American Secret Intelligence*, Rhodri Jeffreys-Jones makes no reference at all to SSU or to clandestine operations in the first year of peace. Tim Weiner's *Legacy of Ashes: The History of the CIA* devotes 10 pages (out of 702 pages) to the years 1945–1946, but he limits his discussion to the bureaucratic battles over the end of OSS and the beginning of CIA. He refers to SSU in only two sentences and does not describe any of its operations. For such authors it is as if the history of American espionage was interrupted between 1945 and 1947. The handful of specialist monographs have not filled the gap. Most, such as Peter Grose's *Operation Rollback: America's Secret War behind the Iron Curtain*, ignore the immediate postwar period and focus not on espionage but on special operations to arm anti-Soviet partisans and spread anticommunist propaganda. The few with an espionage focus—*Battleground Berlin: CIA vs KGB in the Cold War* by David Murphy, Sergei Kondrashev, and George Bailey is an example—treat SSU operations in only a few pages as part of a longer historical arc or a focus on a particular locale.

It is apparent that in histories of the Cold War as well as histories of intelligence the role of American espionage, especially agent operations, in the period immediately following World War II remains unexplored territory. This book is an effort to map that territory for the first time by surveying the history of the Strategic Services Unit and providing details of its operations in Europe, particularly those aimed at collecting information on the Soviet

Union. These operations—many revealed for the first time—illuminate a secret war of espionage, disinformation, kidnappings, and political subversion that broke out soon after the surrender of Germany. More importantly, the "spy stories" will reveal the quantity and quality of information collected by SSU and other American intelligence services and disseminated to policy makers in Washington and elsewhere. Any effort to understand the attitudes and responses of those policy makers will remain incomplete without a consideration of that information and the organizations that provided it.

The genesis of this book was a casual conversation over coffee during the annual meeting of the Society for Historians of American Foreign Relations in Washington, D.C., in 2003. It was only several months after that coffee break that the idea for a book on American intelligence in the early Cold War moved from casual banter to serious action: from "Someone should write a book" to "We should write a book." Over the following ten years the project proceeded in fits and starts, often interrupted by the demands of other projects or commitments and then, most seriously, by the unexpected death of one of the authors, Eduard Mark. This terrible loss raised questions about the completion of the book, questions that eventually were answered by a resolution to see the project through, if only as a testament to his memory.

This project could not have been begun, let alone completed, without the encouragement and assistance of many individuals. The authors owe a special debt to veterans of the Office of Strategic Services and the Strategic Services Unit, some of whom are no longer with us, who recalled their service in Europe after the Second World War and patiently answered questions about American and Russian clandestine operations in that period: Karl Abt, Tennent Bagley, Richard Cutler, Albert Materazzi, James McCargar, Hugh Montgomery, Thomas Polgar, Harry Rositzke, Peter Sichel, and Hans Wynberg. Many colleagues in academe and the larger community of intelligence historians in Europe and the United States offered advice and generously shared the fruits of their own research: Christopher Adam, Matthew Aid, Duncan Bare, Jeffrey Barlow, Siegfried Beer, Steve Budiansky, Jonathan Clemente, Ralph Erskine, Peer Henrik Hansen, Igor Lukes, Tamas Meszerics, Kevin Ruffner, Mark Stout, and Michael Warner.

My wife, Donna Kelley, endured yet another book with her usual patience, aplomb, and good humor. I have promised her that this is the last one and that she can permanently reclaim the dining room table. Without her encouragement and understanding this book and so much else in my life would have remained incomplete.

My friend and coauthor, Eduard Mark, passed away in the middle of the project and in the midst of a distinguished career as a historian of the Cold

War. A remarkable talent, who published major articles in the *American Historical Review*, *Journal of American History*, and *Foreign Affairs*, Eduard brought to the study of the Cold War a prodigious appetite for research, an insightful and critical intelligence, and a willingness to challenge—one might say an enthusiasm for challenging—conventional academic wisdom and embrace academic controversy. The historical profession will feel his loss as much as his friends and family.

David Alvarez
Abiquiu, New Mexico

Spying through a Glass Darkly

CHAPTER ONE

On the Precipice of Peace

At the end of the Second World War the United States deployed an intelligence apparatus that was—with the possible exception of the secret services of the Soviet Union—unrivaled among the belligerents in its size and reach. That reach extended from the mountains of Afghanistan to the beaches of Zanzibar as thousands of men and women, working in a myriad of agencies, scrutinized newspapers, magazines, and trade journals in dozens of languages; monitored foreign radio broadcasts; intercepted the communications of governments, businesses, and private citizens; interviewed travelers and refugees; interrogated prisoners of war; purloined documents from guarded buildings; and recruited a legion of informants ranging from cooks and cleaners to generals and cabinet ministers. Remarkably, this apparatus had been created during the war virtually from scratch. Despite more than a century and a half of national experience, participation in many wars and military interventions, and exposure to various domestic and international crises, the United States had been slow to establish standing professional espionage services to inform and guide political and military leaders. Presidents and generals, reflecting a broader national revulsion against the skullduggery and intrigue associated more with European absolutism than American republicanism, preferred to rely on ad hoc organizations, assembled and deployed when the need for information arose and then disbanded once the need had passed. This approach ensured that the country's experience with intelligence organizations was decidedly mixed. In some cases, such as the Lewis and Clark reconnaissance mission to the Pacific coast in 1804–1806, the nation was adequately served by temporary arrangements, but more frequently, particularly in times of war, the deficiencies of improvisation and amateurism quickly became apparent to national leaders desperate for accurate and timely information.

A permanent peacetime intelligence office first appeared in 1882 when the navy created the Office of Naval Intelligence (ONI). The army followed suit by establishing the Military Intelligence Division (MID) in 1885. Poorly staffed and inadequately funded, these service organizations shunned anything smacking of espionage and limited their activities to collecting maps, photographs, and newspaper articles of military interest and collating the reports of the handful of army and navy officers who were attached to certain

American embassies. After America's entry into the First World War on 6 April 1917, ONI and MID increased significantly in size and expanded their activities to include modest ventures into secret operations, such as communications intelligence (comint), the interception and decryption of the secret communications of other governments. After the armistice in November 1918, however, staffing and operations returned to the modest levels of prewar practice.[1]

In the two decades following the First World War the United States claimed the status of a great power but maintained the intelligence resources of a minor power. Although the mediocrity of American intelligence organizations in the period 1918–1941 is often exaggerated and many of the problems that constrained their efforts also afflicted the secret services of other countries, there is no question that in the interwar years American intelligence capabilities were limited.[2] There was no central organization responsible for collecting, evaluating, and disseminating to policy makers foreign political, economic, and military information. By tacit agreement, intelligence tasks were apportioned among various government departments. The State Department claimed a monopoly on foreign political and economic information, while coverage of military developments overseas fell to the Military Intelligence Division and the Office of Naval Intelligence. Counterespionage, the pursuit of foreign spies on American soil, was largely the bailiwick of the Federal Bureau of Investigation (FBI), although the military services, particularly the navy, occasionally made forays into this area. Cooperation among these agencies was rare, and there was little effort to coordinate operations. The dissemination of information was compartmentalized, with reports moving up vertically in an organization but rarely laterally to other organizations. The State Department, for example, did not distribute embassy cables or dispatches to army or navy intelligence offices, which, in any case, exhibited little interest in political or economic reporting from abroad. MID reports circulated within the War Department, but they rarely passed to either the State Department or the Navy Department until the late 1930s, when military intelligence officers began to share with their counterparts in State and Navy some of the foreign diplomatic messages intercepted and decrypted by army code breakers.

Toward the end of the 1930s, as the world moved closer to another global war, American policy makers still relied on small, underresourced organizations capable of pursuing only a narrow range of intelligence activities. In 1938, for example, the Military Intelligence Division, the organization responsible for collecting and distributing information on the organization, deployments, and capabilities of the world's armies, employed only sixty-nine people. MID's Intelligence Branch, the section directly concerned with the collection and evaluation of intelligence, numbered as few as eight officers. That year the army's Signal Intelligence Service, the specialized and highly secretive unit charged with intercepting and decrypting foreign diplomatic and military communications, had a staff of barely two dozen. When Germany opened a European war by invading Poland on 1 September 1939, the Office of Naval Intelligence had only sixty-three people in its Washington headquarters. Of the seventeen naval attachés serving in American embassies, ONI's eyes and ears abroad, only nine were in Europe.[3]

Intelligence units were modest in stature as well as size. Within their parent organizations, intelligence offices and their staffs were marginalized, receiving little attention and less respect. In no government department or military service was intelligence work a separate career path. Personnel usually rotated through brief tours in intelligence before returning to more mainstream assignments. The work still carried a whiff of dishonor and disrepute for its supposed recourse to thievery, blackmail, bribery, and other unsavory practices. Particularly in the armed services, ambitious and capable officers, believing intelligence assignments would tarnish their reputations and retard their careers, sought to avoid such posts. The resulting paucity of experienced personnel combined with a weak professional identity and narrow definitions of institutional mission to constrain efforts to obtain information. Most of these efforts centered on American embassies where diplomats and the army and navy attachés represented the collection end of the intelligence process. The emphasis was on acquiring information from open sources such as newspapers, journals, personal observation, and contacts with foreign colleagues. There was little effort at clandestine espionage, that is, the recruitment and control of secret informants who were cajoled or suborned to provide confidential information. The State Department strictly eschewed espionage as an unseemly and unprofessional activity that, if exposed, would discredit American diplomats, embarrass the United States government, and poison relations with foreign governments. The army and the navy were hardly more enthusiastic about spying, and during the 1930s neither had a clandestine espionage service, although the navy briefly experimented with recruiting spies in China. In the army, commanders consistently opposed the employment of secret agents as unethical or unnecessary. Recalling the state of MID collection efforts in the 1930s, General George C. Marshall, the army chief of staff during World War II, acknowledged that intelligence was "little more than what a military attaché could learn at a dinner, more or less, over the coffee cups."[4] For its part, ONI actively discouraged its representatives from recruiting informants, and in 1933 it circulated an order that required each naval attaché to employ "only such means as are consonant with his official position and the diplomatic relations that he bears to the government which receives him as naval attaché." A separate directive specifically warned the attachés against employing "immoral women" as agents, primly observing that "a woman that will sell herself is usually willing to sell her employer."[5] Such directives did little to encourage an aggressive approach to intelligence collection. On 1 September 1939 the American naval attaché in Berlin, ONI's sole representative inside Nazi Germany, had no clandestine informants and collected information solely from open sources: newspaper articles, official briefings at the German naval ministry, conversations with colleagues in the local attaché community, and officially organized and supervised trips beyond the capital. That year the director of naval intelligence admitted that "a real undercover foreign intelligence service, equipped and able to carry on espionage, counterespionage, etc. does not exist."[6]

By increasing the demand in Washington for information while exposing the limited ability of existing practices to satisfy that demand, the outbreak of the European war stimulated a modest expansion in American intelligence capabilities and efforts. Even before Japan's surprise attack on American military installations at Pearl Harbor, Hawaii, on 7 December 1941 catapulted the United States into what had become a global war, both the army and navy had begun—albeit slowly—to reconsider their hostility toward clandestine intelligence operations. In August 1941, for example, MID dispatched a retired officer to the Far East to survey the potential for establishing espionage networks in the region. This officer's encouraging report reached Washington four weeks before Pearl Harbor, too late for MID to act upon it before Japan attacked.[7] The navy also recognized the need to expand its intelligence program to include clandestine collection. In the summer of 1940, ONI established a Special Intelligence Section to recruit and run secret agents abroad. It was, however, a modest effort. The headquarters staff for the new section consisted of a retired naval officer recalled to active duty and a clerk. After more than a year of effort the unit had managed to recruit only a handful of sources in Latin America, the Far East, and the Middle East.[8] In the months before Pearl Harbor both the army and the navy discovered the price of their neglect of informant networks, which, to the dismay of MID and ONI, could not simply be wished into existence when required. While the services grappled with the problems of constructing such networks from scratch, they took steps to improve foreign intelligence collection in the short term by expanding significantly their attaché systems; sending training, liaison, and observer missions to the armed services of many belligerent and neutral countries; and augmenting their communications intelligence units.[9] With operations expanding, there were tentative attempts to coordinate better the disparate activities of the State, War, and Navy Departments and the FBI. In the summer of 1939, State, MID, ONI, and FBI, prompted by President Franklin D. Roosevelt, had formed the Interdepartmental Intelligence Committee (IIC) to consider the government's intelligence and counterintelligence efforts, particularly in the Western Hemisphere. After a year of desultory discussions the committee concluded that the United States required a special organization devoted exclusively to clandestine foreign intelligence operations. There was, however, less agreement on who should control this organization. While fully expecting to influence the direction and priorities of the proposed clandestine service, neither the army nor the navy wanted to engage in actual espionage for fear that such operations might compromise the diplomatic status of their attachés abroad. The FBI refused to accept sole responsibility for espionage operations without sole authority to direct those operations, authority that the other members of the committee were loath to concede. For its part, the State Department, aghast at the mere thought of espionage, wanted nothing at all to do with spies and spying. President Roosevelt resolved the impasse by ordering, on 24 June 1940, a division of responsibilities. The FBI received responsibility for foreign intelligence work in Latin America, for which task it established a Special Intelligence Service (SIS), while MID and ONI covered the rest of the world. The State Department successfully protected its virtue, receiving no additional responsibilities beyond its traditional—and entirely above board—political reporting.[10]

Roosevelt's directive did little to remedy the lethargy, decentralization, and parochialism that seriously constrained the American intelligence effort. As much attitudinal as administrative in origin, these deficiencies could not be alleviated by new boxes and lines on organization charts. Jealous of their prerogatives and protective of their institutional interests, IIC members were reluctant to pursue any initiatives that might undermine their respective authorities, budgets, and statuses. Within a month of the president's directive, for example, MID was challenging the FBI's monopoly on Latin American intelligence operations, arguing that the new Special Intelligence Service should merely supplement, not replace, the collection activities of military attachés.[11] In such a bureaucratic environment, effective mechanisms for coordinating collection programs and sharing and collating intelligence reports across departmental lines remained elusive. Even more serious was the continued failure to accelerate—beyond the FBI's nascent and narrowly focused SIS—the expansion of clandestine collection capabilities.

The continuing disarray in the American intelligence community troubled those in the government, such as President Roosevelt, Secretary of War Henry Stimson, and Secretary of the Navy Frank Knox, who believed that war was creeping closer to the United States and that the country had to hasten its efforts to address the threat. Frustration and concern, particularly in the White House, stimulated additional organizational initiatives, the most important of which was a presidential directive on 11 July 1941 establishing a new office, the Coordinator of Information (COI). Responsible directly to the president, charged with collecting, analyzing, correlating, and disseminating to the White House and interested departments information concerning national security, and empowered to secure relevant material from other agencies or departments of the government, COI appeared over the opposition of its putative partners in the State, War, Navy, and Justice Departments. Vigilantly patrolling the boundaries of their organizational turf, these departments considered the new agency a threat to their institutional prerogatives and independence and feared subordination to a "super" intelligence agency. The president's selection of William J. Donovan to run COI did little to assuage their concerns. A much-decorated hero of the First World War, successful Wall Street attorney, prominent Republican, and assistant attorney general in President Calvin Coolidge's Justice Department, "Wild Bill" Donovan had previously been entrusted by Roosevelt with confidential political missions to Europe. Two trips to Britain in 1940 to survey that country's prospects against the Axis powers included extensive briefings by British authorities on the organization and activities of His Majesty's intelligence organizations. The British, their backs against the wall and desperate for any assistance from the United States, hoped to cultivate closer intelligence cooperation with Washington, but suspected that the Americans could contribute little to the relationship until they reformed and energized their fragmented and uncoordinated intelligence programs. These meetings—as the British probably intended—convinced Donovan that the United States required a larger and more centralized intelligence service to navigate through the political and military storms that were engulfing the world. He made it his mission to create and lead that service, and his advocacy, in the spring and summer of 1941, was a significant factor in Roosevelt's decision to establish COI.[12]

Scorned and distrusted by its sister agencies, COI struggled to find a place in the national security structure. Although the lack of an effective clandestine espionage capability remained the most serious deficiency in American intelligence, the new agency did little at first to remedy that defect. Donovan's plans may have included a clandestine service, but he moved slowly to implement those plans. Perhaps to assuage fears of a "secret police" lurking in the shadows of American government and disarm bureaucratic competitors protective of their operational turf, the COI director focused initially on mobilizing the resources of universities and research centers such as the Library of Congress to prepare and circulate to policy makers reports on political and economic issues arising from the war. In composing these reports, COI analysts would depend primarily on open sources, but would also incorporate information generated by the collection efforts of the army, navy, FBI, and State Department. Secondarily, Donovan expected his organization to assume a leading role in propaganda and psychological warfare, for which purposes it would again rely primarily on information provided by other parties.[13] COI's original mission, therefore, precluded any significant commitment to espionage operations. Furthermore, the political and organizational effort to launch a new agency and the bureaucratic competition for personnel, facilities, resources, and authorities so consumed the attention and energy of Donovan's fledgling intelligence service that, initially, it developed relatively few independent sources of information. In October 1941, however, Donovan's organization took its first, tentative steps into the clandestine world when MID and ONI, still leery of that seemingly sinister and dangerous world, agreed that COI should have full responsibility for espionage operations beyond the Western Hemisphere.[14] Donovan promptly created within COI an office for secret intelligence, but this unit had barely begun its work when the United States suddenly found itself at war.

By exposing the continuing deficiencies of American intelligence and embarrassing MID and ONI, the unanticipated Japanese attack on Pearl Harbor demonstrated that recent initiatives, such as the creation of IIC and COI, had done little to improve collection and dissemination practices. The Japanese attack also strengthened the resolve of those in Washington, including William Donovan, who were committed to thoroughly revamping the nation's intelligence apparatus. Entry into the war, however, simply set off another round of bureaucratic battles over control of intelligence programs, and the prospects for the Coordinator of Information were particularly uncertain. The armed services, which after Pearl Harbor were acutely sensitive to any suggestion that they were not up to the intelligence challenges of war, remained eager to abolish the upstart agency and distribute its functions among the military intelligence offices. For his part, William Donovan fought hard not only to protect COI but to significantly expand its role. In the spring of 1942, Donovan's organization began to move more aggressively into the area of clandestine collection operations, placing officers under State Department cover in American embassies and consulates in several neutral countries and co-opting traveling American businessmen and scholars. No one, however, not even the ambitious and energetic Wild Bill Donovan, could conjure spy networks from thin air. Progress was slow. As late as May 1942, there were still fewer than twenty-five COI representatives operating abroad.[15] To disarm his opponents in the military, who recoiled from the prospect of an independent civilian service insensitive to the needs and unresponsive to the direction of admirals and generals, and to establish a more secure political base, Donovan (with Roosevelt's support) agreed to place his organization under the Joint

Chiefs of Staff. Rechristened the Office of Strategic Services (OSS), the service theoretically was responsible for all intelligence collection, analysis, and dissemination, but in practice OSS fell short of Donovan's vision of a centralized national intelligence service. From its creation, interdepartmental rivalries and bureaucratic politics limited the scope of its mission and the range of its activities. The FBI managed to exclude OSS from any role in domestic counterintelligence and countersubversion. Teaming up with the Office of the Coordinator of Inter-American Affairs, an organization established by presidential directive in July 1941 to counteract Axis propaganda and commercial penetration in South America, the FBI also contrived to prohibit Donovan's people from operating in Latin America, which throughout the war remained the bailiwick of the Bureau's Special Intelligence Service. For their part, the army and navy successfully protected the autonomy of their respective intelligence services and successfully asserted exclusive control over communications intelligence programs, excluding OSS from any share of these most secret radio-intercept and code-breaking operations.

Undeterred by bureaucratic opponents, Donovan quickly turned the Office of Strategic Services into an intelligence organization that, at least in size and activity, was unprecedented in American history. At the height of the war OSS employed 12,995 personnel with almost 5,000 of these working in Europe alone. Most of these individuals worked quietly and safely at desks in Washington, London, Cairo, New Delhi, Chungking, and other cities around the globe, collating and evaluating reports from the field, translating newspapers and documents, administering programs and budgets, and performing the myriad tasks required to maintain a large bureaucracy and support field operations. Many of Donovan's men and women, however, worked closer to the edge on the "mean streets" of Europe, Asia, and Africa, recruiting and running secret agents, purloining papers from offices and hotel rooms, running guns and explosives to resistance groups, leading guerilla raids and sabotage missions, and generally practicing the dark arts of espionage and conspiracy at a level hitherto unimagined by any American save the most inventive writers of cheap thrillers. The result of this frenetic activity was a flood of political, military, economic, geographic, and social intelligence that informed decision makers to a degree unprecedented in American history. The most significant aspect of Donovan's empire, however, was not the size of its staff or the range of its activities. What principally distinguished the Office of Strategic Services from its predecessors and contemporaries in American intelligence history was its clandestinity. OSS was self-consciously a *secret* espionage service. Though thousands of its employees may have fought the war from desks in office buildings, OSS was in its heart and its imagination all about spies, covert operators, and secret missions, and it gave the United States a clandestine espionage capability that the country had never before enjoyed.[16]

The Office of Strategic Services represented only one element in a major expansion of American intelligence resources. During the war the army and navy significantly increased their collection efforts. The small prewar military offices that had relied largely on newspapers, magazines, and the observations of a handful of attachés for their view of the world evolved into large bureaucracies. By early 1943, for example, the Office of Naval Intelligence, which ten years earlier had scarcely more than a dozen representatives abroad, was receiving information from a worldwide reporting net that included twenty-nine naval attaché offices, twenty-two naval observer posts, and forty-three naval liaison missions, plus dozens of officers working as "shipping advisors" or "petroleum observers" in a swath of territory from South America to South Asia.[17] For all their growth, however, the military's information services continued to define their missions narrowly. Both the Military Intelligence Division and the Office of Naval Intelligence tended to focus on tactical intelligence in support of military operations. Order-of-battle intelligence—information about the size, location, organization, and capabilities of enemy forces—was the highest priority. Political, economic, and social developments—issues often central to wartime policy making—received less attention. The service intelligence organizations, moreover, still relied primarily on relatively overt methods: military attachés and observers; ground, sea, and air reconnaissance; aerial photography; interrogation of prisoners of war; and translation of captured enemy documents. The Office of Naval Intelligence had actually abandoned its nascent clandestine capabilities by transferring its small Special Intelligence Section to COI in the summer of 1941. For its part the army, after Pearl Harbor, made modest forays into the clandestine world. The army's Counterintelligence Corps, for example, occasionally went undercover to ferret out subversives, spies, and black market operators. More significantly, in the spring of 1942 the army quietly established a new unit, the Special Service Branch, to recruit and run secret informants. Major General George Strong, the assistant chief of staff for intelligence and a relentless opponent of William Donovan and all his works, refused to cede responsibility for clandestine espionage to COI or its successor, OSS. Convinced that Donovan was an unscrupulous empire builder and concerned that the military's intelligence requirements would lose priority in any organization controlled by Wild Bill, General Strong created the Special Service Branch to ensure that the army had its own spies. Known to initiates as "the Pond," this small and shadowy organization was so cloaked in secrecy that few people, even among intelligence insiders, knew of its existence. Under the direction of John "Frenchy" Grombach, a West Point graduate who left the regular army in 1928 to pursue a successful career in commercial radio, Pond representatives usually adopted the cover of businessmen as they recruited informants and built agent networks. The organization focused on Europe, and by the end of the war Grombach—who shared Strong's suspicion of and disdain toward Donovan—claimed to have clandestine sources reporting from several countries, including Hungary, Norway, Portugal, and Sweden.[18]

For the armed forces—and American decision makers in general—the richest information came not from spies or covert operators but from hundreds of men and women working with graph paper, pencils, dictionaries, and data-processing machines at desks in closely guarded buildings in the Virginia suburbs of Washington and along the capital's Nebraska Avenue. Before the war the military services had small communications intelligence units devoted to intercepting and decrypting the secret diplomatic, military, and naval messages of foreign powers. Shortages of personnel and resources, however, combined to limit their attention primarily to the codes and ciphers of Japan and secondarily to those of Germany, Italy, and Mexico. The solution of the machine cipher used by the Japanese foreign ministry for its most confidential communications—designated PURPLE by the Americans— was the greatest achievement of the code breakers before Pearl Harbor. At a time when American intelligence possessed not a single clandestine source inside Germany, Italy, or Japan, access to Japanese diplomatic messages provided the small circle of decision makers aware of this top secret program insight into the intentions not only of Japan but, through the reports of Tokyo's ambassadors in Berlin and Rome, of the other Axis powers. After Pearl Harbor the code-breaking units, the army's Signal Intelligence Service and the Navy's OP-20-G, significantly expanded their operational capabilities. By the end of the war, for example, the army service, now known as the Signal Security Agency, controlled eleven major and dozens of minor intercept stations that regularly monitored more than three hundred foreign commercial and government radio transmitters and thousands of military and diplomatic circuits. In June 1945 alone these stations intercepted 783,767 commercial, diplomatic, and military messages. At Arlington Hall, a one-time finishing school for young women, whose campus outside of Washington the army requisitioned as the headquarters of its communication intelligence service, hundreds of cryptanalysts cracked the diplomatic and military ciphers of some sixty governments—allied, enemy, and neutral—while linguists translated decrypted messages in twenty-five languages. The successes of the code breakers, one of the best-kept secrets of the war, provided unprecedented access to the intentions and activities of friendly, hostile, and neutral governments and represented the greatest achievement of wartime American intelligence.[19]

The wartime experience of organizational growth, resource expansion, and operational escalation left the United States at the end of the war with a tested intelligence capability that extended around the globe. This capability was distinguished not only by its reach but by the diversity of its sources. Never before had policy makers had so much information to guide their decisions. On 15 August 1945, the first day of peace, the intelligence available to policy makers in Washington would have included dispatches from American diplomats and military attachés in foreign capitals; decrypted diplomatic, military, and naval messages of dozens of governments; summaries of international press stories and radio broadcasts; interviews with refugees and prisoners of war; liaison reports from friendly foreign intelligence services; and the revelations of thousands of secret informants. These sources were so extensive and rich that, in the late summer of 1945, the United States appeared finally to have developed an intelligence capability commensurate with its status as a world power and one well positioned to allow policy makers to discern and address important political, economic, and security issues as they emerged on the postwar horizon. Unfortunately, appearances were deceiving. While impressive on paper, the intelligence structure after VJ (Victory over Japan) Day was seriously challenged by deleterious conditions that intelligence managers could not or would not alleviate. These conditions threatened to reverse the improvements in collection, analysis, and distribution achieved during the war and to return the United States to the intelligence desert of the prewar years.

William Donovan had not waited for the war to end to begin thinking about the peace. As early as the spring of 1943, the OSS director had begun speaking with his senior staff about intelligence requirements in the postwar world and the prospects for their service in that world. By the fall of 1944 these discussions had evolved into a draft proposal for a peacetime national intelligence organization that, not surprisingly, looked like a more empowered Office of Strategic Services. The proposal envisaged an independent agency, based largely on the organization and personnel of OSS, reporting directly to the president, who would appoint its director. A board composed of the secretaries of state, war, and navy and such other members as the president might designate would advise the director. The organization would control its own personnel and budget. Focusing on strategic intelligence to guide national decision makers, it would independently collect, analyze, and distribute intelligence. The collection function included espionage and counterintelligence. The military services would retain their intelligence units to service their special requirements, but the proposed national intelligence organization would coordinate their activities, as well as those of civilian agencies such as the FBI, and have access to the fruits of their efforts. The proposed service would have no police or domestic law enforcement powers.[20]

In October 1944, Donovan informally shared his proposal with the White House. Although some on the presidential staff were receptive, important presidential counselors received the report with skepticism. Harry Hopkins, the president's closest advisor, who personally disliked the flamboyant OSS chief, solicited the advice of now retired General George Strong, onetime chief of army intelligence and an implacable adversary of William Donovan. Strong fervently advised Hopkins to oppose the plan, arguing that the proposed postwar agency was unnecessary, cumbersome, and possibly dangerous. The president's budget director, Harold Smith, was also hostile, although his opposition probably reflected his concern for reducing rather than increasing postwar government departments and their expenses. While unhelpful, the hostility of senior advisors would not have mattered if the president himself had embraced Donovan's proposal, but he did not. Enervated by his deteriorating health, convinced that the American public would expect a smaller government after the war, and more than a little irritated by the importuning OSS director, Roosevelt gave Donovan no encouragement.[21] Blind to the warning signs, Donovan brashly pushed forward. On 12 November 1944 the OSS director officially submitted to the president his proposal for a postwar intelligence service and, rather presumptuously, appended for the president's signature a draft of an executive order establishing that service. Ignoring the draft executive order, Roosevelt circulated Donovan's proposal to his advisors and to the State, War, and Navy Departments for comment. The reaction, predictably, was hostile and marked the opening salvo in a political battle that, to the detriment of American intelligence, would continue to distract national security managers long after the death of Franklin Roosevelt and the end of the war.

The political conflict was engaged around four important issues. The first concerned what might be called the architecture of American intelligence. Military and political leaders disagreed about the size and shape of the country's peacetime intelligence capabilities. Some, including Harry S. Truman, who assumed the presidency upon the death of Franklin Roosevelt on 12 April 1945, and Francis Biddle, FDR's attorney general who remained in office in the first months of the new presidency, feared that a large secret intelligence and security apparatus posed a potential threat to the freedoms of American citizens. Others, such as the influential director of the Bureau of the Budget, Harold Smith, worried that a large postwar intelligence establishment would be an unnecessary drain on the government's finances as the nation returned to a peacetime economy. These civilian leaders easily convinced themselves that peace would significantly reduce the need for intelligence organizations and that modest capabilities would be sufficient for the country's needs. This attitude also allowed them to consider with equanimity a second issue that threatened the prospects for postwar intelligence: demobilization. After the war, Washington would face enormous political pressure to release from military service the millions of men and women who had been mobilized for war. Since the vast majority of intelligence personnel were in military service, the demands of demobilization would militate against maintaining anything but a modest postwar intelligence structure. The third issue concerned control. While profoundly sensitive to the impact of demobilization, an important group of skeptics, found largely among senior officers of the armed services, worried less about the size of postwar intelligence and more about who would control it. Perpetuating the military's wartime hostility toward OSS, these officers stoutly resisted any proposal for a powerful civilian national organization that might preempt existing army and navy intelligence units. They insisted that the only way to ensure that the army and navy received the intelligence they needed was to empower each of the services to collect its own information free from control or interference by outside authorities or organizations. The last issue of contention concerned targets. What kinds of intelligence would the United States require in the postwar world? Should intelligence programs concentrate on monitoring defeated enemies in order to prevent a resurgence of fascism and militarism or should efforts focus on other countries, including wartime allies, whose postwar political and economic interests might conflict with those of the United States? What methods—spies, communications intercepts, traditional diplomatic reporting, open sources—were best suited for covering postwar targets?

The first casualty of the intelligence war in Washington was the Office of Strategic Services; the second casualty was William Donovan. After submitting his plan for a postwar central intelligence organization to the White House, Donovan had departed for a tour of OSS facilities in Asia. In his absence from Washington, the enemies of his reorganization plan worked to ensure its demise. The armed services proposed an alternative plan in which the president would appoint a director of national intelligence whose budget and operations would be controlled by a "national intelligence authority" composed of representatives from the State, Navy, and War Departments. By stripping the director of independent authority and devolving operational, as opposed to purely advisory, functions to a committee of interested departments, none of which would forsake its independent intelligence capabilities, the military proposal was the antithesis of Donovan's vision of a centralized intelligence organization to which all service or departmental services would be subordinate.

The traveling OSS chief was kept apprised of developments at home through reports from his deputy, Brigadier General John Magruder. More attuned than his boss to the changing political climate in Washington, Magruder suggested that the military's plan for a joint intelligence authority might be the best deal for postwar intelligence they could get. Donovan, who blithely assumed that he would direct whatever intelligence organization emerged after the war, had no intention of subordinating himself to a committee. He dismissed his deputy's advice and remained confident that he could outmaneuver his enemies. Returning to Washington in mid-February 1945, Donovan found himself and his service the targets of sustained attacks by his political enemies. On 9 February Walter Trohan, the Washington correspondent for the vehemently anti–New Deal McCormick-Patterson newspaper chain, which included the large circulation *Chicago Tribune* and *Washington Times-Herald*, had published a long article revealing Donovan's postwar plans and accusing the OSS chief of plotting to create a powerful, Gestapo-like intelligence service to spy on Americans after the war. Since Trohan's account included word-for-word text from Donovan's proposal, it was clear that the proposal had been deliberately leaked to the journalist. The inflammatory article was merely the first in a series of hostile press stories that denigrated OSS as a corrupt, incompetent, and unnecessary agency and portrayed William Donovan as a power-mad New Dealer who would introduce the secret police into American life.[22]

Eventually, Donovan would respond to the press attacks by launching his own media campaign, unilaterally declassifying and sharing with sympathetic journalists hundreds of secret reports in an effort to educate the public concerning the work of OSS and its contributions to the war effort. He had faced down political enemies before and believed he could do so again, but this time he underestimated the strength of the opposition. The death of Franklin Roosevelt, moreover, seriously weakened Donovan's position. Although over the course of the war he had become somewhat disenchanted with "Wild Bill," Roosevelt understood the value of intelligence and was usually willing to give his OSS chief a sympathetic hearing. The new president, Harry S. Truman, knew little about Donovan and less about intelligence, but harbored a suspicion that the Office of Strategic Services represented a distasteful and disreputable element in wartime government that required very close watching. This suspicion probably intensified when, shortly after Roosevelt's death, Truman received a report on OSS prepared by Colonel Richard Park, a military aide in the White House. The report was a scathing indictment of OSS, accusing Donovan's agency of numerous improprieties and missteps ranging from reckless and unprofessional field operations to wild orgies among personnel at foreign stations. Park claimed that President Roosevelt had secretly commissioned the report and that the result reflected investigations conducted in various theaters of the war. In fact, the document represented an effort by Donovan's political enemies to undermine his credibility and derail his plans for a postwar intelligence service by impugning his direction of the Office of Strategic Services. The impetus for the report came not from Roosevelt but from John Grombach, the chief of the Pond, the army's small clandestine intelligence service, who had directed his agents to record every derogatory allegation, rumor, and item of gossip concerning OSS. Grombach, an ambitious intriguer who despised Donovan and feared that a civilian national intelligence agency would displace his own service, collected these stories in a memorandum that he passed to Colonel Park. The colonel simply reshaped Grombach's charges, added additional unsavory (and unverified) stories of OSS incompetence or corruption happily provided by the FBI, and presented the whole as the product of his independent investigation. Although it deliberately exaggerated certain events and circumstances, such as reports of OSS personnel hosting wild parties, and misrepresented others, such as the claim that an OSS operation to purloin documents from the Japanese legation in Lisbon compromised successful efforts to read Japan's ciphers, the Park report would not have comforted a new president who was already inclined to be suspicious of Donovan and his ambitions.[23]

Harry Truman was not so naïve as to believe that he could fulfill his presidential duties without access to information about the world, and he harbored no animus toward intelligence work in general. The future of postwar communications intelligence programs, for example, was never questioned in the White House, and neither the Signal Security Agency nor OP-20-G received the scrutiny reserved for OSS; indeed on 12 September 1945 the president readily approved without extended discussion a request from the secretaries of state, war, and navy to continue communications intelligence collaboration with Britain. Human intelligence programs and the control of those programs were the problems. Truman was open to a clandestine service, but aside from knowing he didn't want a service shaped and directed by William Donovan, he didn't know what kind of intelligence organization would be best suited for the postwar world. For advice he turned not to his intelligence chiefs, but to the Bureau of the Budget, which, by the summer of 1945, had begun planning for postwar demobilization and the liquidation of various agencies established to prosecute the war.

The Budget Bureau recommended the immediate dissolution of the Office of Strategic Services and the disposal of its organizational assets. Specifically wartime capabilities, such as paramilitary and propaganda units, would be terminated outright. The research and analysis branch, useful for its studies of long-term political and economic issues, would move, in much reduced form, into the State Department, while the remaining elements, mainly the clandestine espionage service, would move into the War Department for "salvage and liquidation."[24] The reference to "salvage" suggested that the Budget Bureau's planners anticipated that some, as yet undetermined, clandestine capabilities would be retained in the postwar world, albeit in a modest form appropriate for peacetime. The plan was an interim response to immediate requirements, particularly demobilization, and would serve until the government sorted out its peacetime requirements and structures. Truman accepted the Budget Bureau's recommendation, and on 20 September 1945, he signed Executive Order No. 9621 dissolving OSS and distributing its parts to the State and War Departments. That same day, the president sent William Donovan a brief and rather cool letter of dismissal masquerading as a letter of appreciation.[25]

Executive orders are not self-implementing, and this was apparent in the War Department's response to Truman's directive. Whatever the expectations of the White House, neither Robert Patterson, the secretary of war, nor John McCloy, the assistant secretary of war responsible for the newly arrived refugees from Wild Bill Donovan's secret world, was inclined simply to liquidate the assets of the intelligence and counterintelligence units, demobilize their personnel, and close the shop. Both believed deeply that America's need for timely and comprehensive information about the world did not end with the war and that the country's postwar security required a clandestine intelligence capability. While various government agencies, including their own, debated the precise scope and shape of such a capability, the secretary of war and his deputy were determined that the clandestine operators from OSS and their records, now designated the War Department's Strategic Services Unit (SSU), should be protected and nurtured as a separate unit rather than simply being absorbed into the army's military intelligence office. In their instructions to Brigadier General John Magruder, the newly designated director of SSU, Patterson and McCloy emphasized not only the termination of unnecessary activities and the demobilization of personnel, but also the preservation of important assets and the maintenance of programs that might prove useful in the future.[26]

This double-barreled mission seriously complicated the work of General Magruder. A professional army officer whose prewar career included service as military attaché in China and Switzerland and command of the War Department's Intelligence Division, Magruder had served in OSS as William

Donovan's principal deputy. He now faced the difficulty of pursuing two missions that were in tension with each other. To fulfill Truman's executive order he had the melancholy duty of supervising the disposal of the remaining OSS assets—bases, training establishments, equipment stores, archives, secret bank accounts, agent networks, liaison arrangements—while responding to the orders of his immediate superiors in the War Department to maintain a nascent foreign intelligence capability by preserving many of the very resources he was supposed to be liquidating.

Liquidation was the easy part of the assignment. Any number of people in Congress and the White House, for example, were eager to help General Magruder achieve this goal by reducing dramatically the funds available for the maintenance of an intelligence service. In the last months of the war, Congress had granted OSS a budget of $20 million for the fiscal year 1945–1946, a sum less than half that authorized for 1944–1945. With the Japanese surrender on 14 August 1945 the White House and Congress were eager to secure an immediate "peace dividend" by eliminating or reducing significantly the budgets of all war agencies.[27] The Office of Strategic Services was a particularly tempting target for economies. In September 1945 President Truman recommended to Congress a reduction in the $20 million earlier authorized for OSS to a new level of $10.5 million. He further recommended that the lower figure be used exclusively for expenses related to closing OSS. Eager to demonstrate its own frugality, Congress indicated that it was willing to reduce the president's suggested figures by an additional $2 million. Since by this time OSS had already spent or obligated almost one-third of the original $20 million, Magruder faced the prospect of maintaining SSU on a very thin diet for the remainder of the fiscal year.[28]

Manpower was an even bigger issue than money; indeed, the SSU director was losing people faster than he was losing dollars. It was a curious feature of America's secret world in the first months of peace that at the very time when intelligence managers were furiously maneuvering for advantage on the bureaucratic battlegrounds of Washington, their field armies were shrinking. Wartime staff levels simply could not be sustained. Most of the intelligence organizations were part of the military, and as such they experienced the same loss of personnel through demobilization as other military elements. The majority of operational planners, analysts, agent runners, interrogators, code breakers, document specialists, and photo interpreters wanted to return to civilian life as much as any infantryman, pilot, or seaman. As the United States made the transition from war to peace, the intelligence services positively hemorrhaged personnel.

No service, even the most successful, was immune. The army and navy code breakers were the elite of the intelligence community, and their contributions to the war effort were unmatched by other American services. Convinced that their intelligence product had amply demonstrated its importance and confident that their customers in the American government would insist on continuing their access to foreign communications after the war, senior communication intelligence managers anticipated an expansion of intercept and cryptanalytic operations in the postwar world. At Arlington Hall, for example, army officers visualized a peacetime network of sixteen fixed monitoring stations—five more than the wartime net—that would encircle the globe and establish American antennae as far afield as Reykjavik (Iceland), Cape Town (South Africa), Manila (Philippines), and Quito (Ecuador). These grandiose visions did not outlive the Japanese surrender. Like their counterparts in other American intelligence organizations, communications intelligence managers were soon in contraction mode: closing intercept stations, scaling back operations, and watching helplessly as hundreds of highly gifted and experienced cryptanalysts, intercept operators, and linguists returned to civilian life. Between September and December 1945 the combined strength of the army and navy comint services fell from 36,500 to 7,500 men and women, a reduction of almost 80 percent. In their most pessimistic projections of postwar staff levels, army code breakers had assumed in August 1945 that they would be able to hold on to at least 5,000 men and women for postwar operations. A year later their roster numbered fewer than 4,000 personnel. The navy's Communications Supplementary Activities (CSA)—as OP-20-G had been renamed in July 1945—went from 9,100 men and women in September 1945 to 3,000 in June 1946. In the four months following Japan's surrender, the navy closed ten of its sixteen radio intercept stations.[29] The impact on crucial code-breaking programs in the first year of peace was devastating. By July of 1946, for example, staff in the CSA section responsible for solving complex machine ciphers had declined from forty-three to seven, and three of the latter were scheduled to depart in August. The section commander wearily concluded, "So many have left or are soon to leave that it is difficult to continue functioning."[30]

No services were hit harder than the Office of Strategic Services and its successor, the Strategic Services Unit. At the end of the war William Donovan had presided over an intelligence empire whose outposts and operations were scattered around the globe. In the immediate postwar period the borders of that empire contracted significantly. Training schools, warehouses, safe houses, and other support facilities were closed, spy rings dissolved, communication networks shut down, and foreign intelligence stations deactivated or reduced in size. In September 1945, for instance, OSS had twenty-three bases in China, but by the end of October the number had fallen to eight, and that total would have been even lower if the U.S. Army's China

Theater Headquarters had not specifically requested the continuation of intelligence operations in the area until the end of the year.[31]

At its height, in 1944, OSS had employed 12,995 people. After VJ Day, demobilization quickly reduced that number. On 1 October 1945, when General Magruder assumed command of the newly rechristened Strategic Services Unit, the organization was down to 9,028. Three weeks later the number had been reduced to 7,640, including 2,879 staffers earmarked for separation from the unit before 1 November 1945. The general anticipated that by the end of the year his command would shrink to fewer than two thousand people. Foreign intelligence stations were decimated, with the European posts absorbing particularly debilitating blows. Some secret intelligence stations, such as those in Lisbon, Madrid, and Rome, were simply closed, while others struggled to survive with a corporal's guard of operators. By the end of 1945 the SSU mission in London, once the largest fiefdom in Donovan's domain, had lost 90 percent of its personnel. The staff of the station in Stockholm fell from fifty to six.[32]

Staff reductions had a deleterious impact on operations. Recalling the first months of peace, Colonel (later Lieutenant General) William Quinn, the executive officer of the Strategic Services Unit and subsequently its director, observed that "the intelligence collection effort more or less came to a standstill."[33] The OSS/SSU stations in Europe were particularly affected. Station chiefs repeatedly warned Washington that the loss of experienced personnel was compromising operations. As early as August 1945, for example, the Paris station informed headquarters that the "constant pressure" to retrench was forcing the unit to slow down and in some cases completely suspend collection programs. In September, the Vienna station, which only a month earlier had felt compelled to submit a memorandum begging headquarters to keep the newly opened Austrian office alive, flatly announced that it no longer had sufficient personnel to fulfill its intelligence mission. The following month Allen Dulles, whose wartime service for OSS in Switzerland made him America's most accomplished spymaster, resigned as chief of the German mission in part because he had concluded that his unit's capabilities were hopelessly compromised by cutbacks in funds and personnel. Time did not cure the ill. In early 1946 the European stations were still complaining about "acute" and "vexing" personnel shortages, and a senior SSU official had to explain to a War Department review panel that his service had very few deep-cover penetration agents because retrenchment prevented the recruitment of new sources.[34]

It was naïve of the intelligence services to assume that the end of the war would have little impact on their status and operations. Reductions in the scope and tempo of operations allowed reductions in personnel, and political leaders in Washington were eager to seize any opportunity to reduce the size and cost of government agencies and to satisfy constituents who wanted to "bring the boys [and girls] home." Most of these men and women were only too happy to go home and, unlike organizational managers, did not see personnel reductions as problematic. Many of the departing personnel were individuals whose skills and experience were seemingly ill-suited for a peace-time intelligence service, but more than a few were valuable staffers who would have contributed significantly to such a service. Under the "first in, first out" demobilization guidelines, the departures were heavily weighted toward those with the most experience. The talent drain was so severe that in early 1946 SSU managers concluded that only 30 percent of their service's clandestine officers could be considered first-class or highly professional, and one senior officer candidly acknowledged, "In the flood of personnel released in our past liquidations the great majority of our best intelligence personnel have left the organization." [35]

As the intelligence services struggled to retain sufficient staff to maintain a modicum of operational capacity, senior officials in Washington struggled over the structure within which those services would operate. On the day he signed the executive order abolishing the Office of Strategic Services, President Truman also signed a letter directing Secretary of State James F. Byrnes to establish an interdepartmental committee to develop, under State Department leadership, "a comprehensive and coordinated foreign intelligence program" for his approval.[36] The presidential directive set off several weeks of desultory meetings in which the usual bureaucratic actors, replaying scenes from the pre–Pearl Harbor struggle to coordinate U.S. intelligence, bickered over authorities, definitions, and responsibilities. The Bureau of the Budget, which no one had thought sufficiently informed or concerned to include in the prewar debates but which now interjected itself into the postwar discussions, preferred an approach that would avoid the need to create—and fund—new agencies; after all, in the immediate postwar period the Budget Bureau was in the business of closing, not opening, government agencies. Dismissive of "spies and intrigue" and "the development of new or special sources of information," the Budget Bureau advocated a focus on "really basic intelligence," a concept the bureau never bothered to define. Since basic intelligence was most useful at the point of decision or action, the intelligence function should be performed at the level of departments or even subdepartments. This was a call for extreme decentralization of intelligence, even within departments. Acknowledging that some intelligence might be required to guide decisions above the level of particular departments—say, at the presidential level—the bureau proposed that the State Department procure and develop such intelligence as well as supervise any "integrated

Government-wide programs" that should be required. Nowhere in its plan does the Budget Bureau discuss, or even identify, the methods by which "basic intelligence" might be collected. Given its aversion to "spies" and "special sources of information," it probably imagined an effort dependent primarily on open sources and traditional diplomatic reporting. The role, if any, of clandestine collection remained unaddressed.[37]

Aside from the fact that State could not decide what role, if any, it wanted to assume in a postwar intelligence structure, the Budget Bureau's plan received no support from other agencies. These agencies could not agree on a postwar intelligence structure but they could agree that, whatever the structure, they did not want the State Department at the top of it. The Federal Bureau of Investigation, which congratulated itself on its responsibility for wartime intelligence operations in South America, thought the national interest would best be served by expanding that responsibility to include the entire globe, thereby centralizing intelligence in a single agency, the FBI. Unfortunately for the FBI, no one else thought so, least of all President Truman, who believed the bureau staffing should be returned to prewar levels and its activities limited to U.S. territory.[38] For their part, in September 1945 the armed services advanced a "federal" approach that ensured that the military would have a significant, if not dominant, voice in postwar intelligence affairs. This approach allowed the services to retain their departmental intelligence units, such as the Office of Naval Intelligence, but provided for a "national intelligence authority" composed of the secretaries of state, war, and navy plus a representative of the Joint Chiefs of Staff. This group would coordinate all federal intelligence activities; address national intelligence issues that transcended particular department requirements or authorities; and direct a central intelligence organization that would perform services required by the national intelligence authority, including the direct collection of intelligence and the synthesis and dissemination of information collected by all relevant departments. This organization would be commanded by an individual appointed by the president on the recommendation of the national intelligence authority. A committee composed of the chiefs of the intelligence offices of the State, War, and Navy Departments would advise the commander of the central intelligence organization.[39]

Despite President Truman's directive of 20 September, Secretary Byrnes and his department had not taken a strong leadership role in the discussions over a postwar intelligence structure, partly because the military services were not inclined to subordinate their preferences to those of State and partly because Byrnes was distracted by other responsibilities, particularly his participation in the meetings of the Council of Foreign Ministers. Concerned by the lack of progress, Truman, in early November, decided to summon to the White House the secretaries of state, war, and navy to reiterate the importance of working together toward the creation of a "Central Intelligence Service." Although the White House meeting never occurred, the president's impatience was apparent, and the three secretaries now moved forward with greater purpose and alacrity. The reference to a central intelligence service also indicated that the president was inclined against the Budget Bureau's recommendation for decentralization within established departments. Although the State Department fought a rearguard action to defend its claims to dominance in the intelligence field, the military services and their preferences won out. On 7 January 1946, the secretaries of state, war, and navy sent the president a plan for the organization of postwar intelligence.[40] The plan was basically that proposed by the armed services the previous September. After slight revisions in the White House—and a futile last-minute intervention by Budget Bureau director Harold Smith on behalf of his agency's original proposal—Truman accepted the plan. On 22 January the president signed a directive designating the secretaries of state, war, and navy, plus one additional person to be selected by the president, as members of a National Intelligence Authority (NIA). The directive also created a Central Intelligence Group (CIG), under a director of central intelligence (DCI) to be named by the president, to assist the National Intelligence Authority. Composed of personnel from the Departments of State, War, and Navy, the Central Intelligence Group would perform various duties including the "correlation and evaluation of intelligence relating to the national security . . . and the appropriate dissemination within the Government of the resulting strategic and national policy intelligence." The presidential directive also stipulated that CIG perform for the NIA "services of common concern" to the three supervising departments, a euphemism understood by all to refer to clandestine espionage.[41] The ascendency of the armed forces was complete when two days later Truman appointed Rear Admiral Sidney Souers, the deputy director of naval intelligence, as the first director of central intelligence and Fleet Admiral William D. Leahy, the president's personal military adviser, as the White House representative on the National Intelligence Authority.

While a step in the direction of centralization, the Central Intelligence Group had no independent staff or budget, depending instead on the three departments represented on the NIA for personnel and funds. It also possessed no independent operational capabilities, again depending on the resources of other departments. To perform its coordinating functions, CIG had to rely on other agencies to share whatever information they collected, but the presidential directive was not clear as to whether the new entity had the authority to compel sharing. The army and navy communication intelligence units, for example, simply refused, on grounds of security, to share the results of their code-breaking programs. Most importantly, it was not clear how CIG, lacking a clandestine collection capability of its own, would perform those "services of common concern" that included espionage.

The Central Intelligence Group was an intelligence *office* but it was not an intelligence *service*, an organization with operational capabilities. To become the latter, CIG would have to acquire a clandestine element ready and willing to conduct foreign clandestine operations around the globe. Such organizations were not exactly thick on the ground in early postwar America; indeed, there was only one, the Strategic Services Unit. General John Magruder had anticipated CIG's problem and identified a solution. On 14 February 1946, three weeks after President Truman had established the new national intelligence structure, the SSU director, noting that "it was generally understood that the Central Intelligence Group would, as one of its major functions, operate a clandestine service for procurement of intelligence abroad," warned his superiors that it would be "inefficient" for the State, War, and Navy Departments to detail personnel for temporary assignment in such a service if and when suitable personnel became available. As an alternative, Magruder proposed that the new Central Intelligence Group accept control of the Strategic Services Unit, an experienced organization in being that was prepared, from day one, to provide the complete array of operational capabilities from administration, transportation, and communications to a worldwide system of intelligence stations and clandestine networks. Why go to the time and trouble of building a clandestine service, the general implied, when you could simply acquire one off the shelf.[42]

General Magruder's proposal made sense to Admiral Souers. On 19 February the director of central intelligence issued his first major order, Central Intelligence Group Directive No. 1, which established a special committee to investigate the resources, facilities, and operations of the Strategic Services Unit; identify those elements that should be preserved and continued in the national interest; and recommend who should assume responsibility for administering the preserved elements.[43] Under the chairmanship of Brigadier General Louis Fortier, a former military attaché to Yugoslavia, and composed of representatives from the State Department, the Office of Naval Intelligence, the War Department's Military Intelligence Division, and the office of Army Air Corps intelligence, the committee convened a series of meetings in February and March 1946 at which it received written and oral testimony from SSU's senior administrative and operational officers, including the chiefs of the Secret Intelligence (SI) and Counterintelligence (X-2) Divisions. General Magruder and his officers believed in the value of the Strategic Services Unit, and they clearly hoped to preserve it—and their jobs—but their testimony was surprisingly candid, noting the weaknesses as

well as the strengths, the failures as well as the successes, of their organization. They reviewed their efforts to maintain the nucleus of a clandestine service and described some of the programs that nucleus had initiated despite
mission uncertainty and resource shortfalls. Most importantly, Magruder
and his deputies argued that the United States required a clandestine service
devoted to national intelligence needs as opposed to the purely departmental
needs already served by such organizations as the Office of Naval Intelligence and the army's Military Intelligence Division. For its part, the Fortier
Committee discovered, perhaps to its surprise, that five months after the
dismissal of Wild Bill Donovan and the abolition of the Office of Strategic
Services the United States still had a clandestine intelligence service that,
despite organizational vicissitudes, was actually running operations in the
field and collecting intelligence.[44]

For all its difficulties, the Strategic Services Unit had survived as the
country's principal clandestine intelligence organization in the immediate
postwar period. While Washington officialdom dithered over the structure
and purposes of postwar intelligence, General Magruder, with the support of
Robert Patterson and John McCloy, had husbanded scarce resources, fended
off bureaucratic rivals, and maintained modest operational capabilities. If
William Donovan was the father of modern American intelligence, John Magruder was its savior, sheltering the flame of clandestine operations from the
crosswinds of budget cuts, demobilization, and interdepartmental politics.
When its director appeared before the Fortier Committee, SSU's principal
operational components were the Secret Intelligence Division (SI) responsible for collecting and processing foreign intelligence and the Counterintelligence Division (X-2) responsible for protecting the organization from
foreign intelligence penetration. Since SSU saw itself primarily as an intelligence service, SI was the heart of the organization. Whitney Shepardson,
who had been William Donovan's chief representative in wartime London
before returning to Washington to run all OSS clandestine intelligence operations, directed the division. In early 1946 SI employed 437 clerical and operational personnel in Washington and abroad.[45] At headquarters SI personnel
staffed a small office responsible for recruiting Americans for clandestine
work; three support offices that performed routine administrative tasks; an
operations section (O Branch) responsible for supervising foreign stations
and agent activities in the field; and a plans section (P Branch) charged with
establishing intelligence requirements, tasking field units with collection priorities, and processing the resulting intelligence intake.[46]

In theory all collection operations were pursuant to guidelines from P
Branch, which was divided into sections for political, economic, and tech-

nical intelligence. Government departments, such as State, War, and Navy, were supposed to indicate their intelligence requirements to P Branch, but, as Shepardson lamented, "this very rarely happens in spite of innumerable efforts on our part . . . to get such intelligence directives." Without direction from its customers, SI was largely left to its own devices, guessing what intelligence might be useful and identifying targets accordingly. The nearest approximation to departmental directives was the occasional responses of the Military Intelligence Division indicating what reports it found interesting and suggesting additional lines of inquiry.[47] In the months immediately following VJ Day, moreover, uncertainty about the future of the clandestine service inhibited P Branch, which was reluctant to consider future intelligence requirements, priorities, and programs without assurances that the service would survive beyond the next month. This initial passivity caused problems for the field stations, which, lacking guidance from headquarters, were left to wonder what they were supposed to do. In November 1945, for example, the station in Switzerland complained, "We are still without the indispensable directives which would permit us to concentrate on what is really significant. . . . It should not be impossible for S.I. Washington to send out to the field weekly or biweekly cables outlining the particular questions of priority interest in Washington." Without any guidance from headquarters, some operational units felt as if they had slipped entirely off Washington's radar screens. In its monthly progress report for October 1945, the Spanish desk of the SSU mission in France—which, in view of the withdrawal of American secret intelligence personnel from the Iberian peninsula as an economy measure, was responsible for collecting intelligence on Spain—noted wryly that yet another month had elapsed without any direction, support, or communication of any type from Washington.[48]

In the field raw intelligence was processed and distributed to local customers by P Branch's representative in the local SSU station before being forwarded to Washington headquarters. The SSU mission in the American occupation zone of Germany, for example, disseminated copies of its intelligence reports to the offices of the American military governor and his political advisor, the zonal commander of U.S. Army intelligence, its sister mission in Austria, and SSU stations in Britain, France, and Switzerland. The station in Paris passed reports to the local American embassy and the SSU units in Britain, Germany, and Austria. When intelligence reports reached Washington, they were distributed by headquarters P Branch to the army's Military Intelligence Service (formerly, Military Intelligence Division) and the Office of Naval Intelligence. As appropriate, reports would also go to the State Department, the Treasury Department, and the Alien Property Custodian. Initially, customers received the raw reports. Aside from grading the reliability of the source, P Branch made no effort to analyze or explain the information or draw conclusions from a particular report or series of reports.[49]

In early 1946, President Truman, annoyed and frustrated by the uncoordinated and undigested intelligence reports that flooded his desk each day, expressed a desire for a single document that would summarize the more important international developments as reported by intelligence sources. In response, the newly constituted National Intelligence Authority, on 8 February 1946, directed the Central Intelligence Group to produce a daily summary containing "factual statements of the significant developments in the field of intelligence and operations related to national security and to foreign events for the use of the President."[50] The reference to "factual statements"—as opposed to opinions or recommendations—reflected the State Department's concern to protect its claim to be the sole source of foreign policy advice for the president. CIG dissemination to the White House, therefore, remained descriptive rather than analytical or prescriptive. The first Daily Summary went to the White House on 15 February 1946. Almost immediately, the secretaries of state, war, and navy were added to the distribution list. Although CIG was supposed to coordinate the government's intelligence collection programs and produce "all source" reports, it did not have access to communications intelligence produced by the Army Security Agency and the navy's Communications Support Activity. The Daily Summary, therefore, did not include the intercepted communications of foreign governments. Such highly sensitive material went to the White House and a select group of senior officials in a separate instrument, the daily Diplomatic Summary, produced by the Army Security Agency. Additionally, the president received each day a summary published by the State Department addressing international affairs as reported by American embassies.[51]

At headquarters, SI field operations were supervised by regional divisions, which were further subdivided into country desks. In early 1946, for example, the Western Europe Division under Homer Hall had desks for France and Belgium; the Netherlands, Spain, and Portugal; and Switzerland and Italy. In three of these countries—Italy, Portugal, and Spain—SSU had no secret intelligence units, only X-2 (counterintelligence) offices. Positive intelligence concerning these three countries was collected occasionally by the X-2 personnel, but more frequently by SI units in neighboring states. Secret intelligence offices in Paris and Bern, for example, were active in providing coverage of the Iberian Peninsula. Richard Helms directed the Central Europe Division with its subunits for Germany and Austria. The German desk was also responsible for Czechoslovakia and Poland. When, eventually, the Soviet Union began to figure more prominently in intelligence calculations,

Helm's division assumed responsibility for the western part of the USSR (west of the Ural Mountains). The Southeast Europe Division covered Bulgaria, Greece, Hungary, Romania, and Yugoslavia. There were also small divisions for the Far East and Africa, but none for Latin America, which had been the wartime responsibility of the FBI and from which OSS had been excluded. Although the creation of the Central Intelligence Group in January 1946 effectively signaled the end of the FBI's Special Intelligence Service and its responsibility for South America, SSU seemed reluctant to abandon wartime arrangements.[52]

The operational divisions at headquarters loosely supervised the units in the field. In areas under U.S. military control, such as the American occupation zones in Austria and Germany, the field organizations were known as missions. A mission might exercise responsibility for SSU operations in neighboring areas. The German mission, for example, was responsible for a SSU unit in Czechoslovakia, while the Austrian mission also supervised operations in Hungary. The missions operated overtly or under very shallow cover as elements of the local military command. In other areas the SSU field units were known as stations. By March 1946, the European divisions at headquarters supervised stations in Britain, Belgium, Denmark, France, Holland, Italy, Norway, Poland, Portugal, Rumania, Spain, Sweden, and Switzerland.[53]

Unlike the missions, the stations were supposed to be entirely clandestine with personnel operating under official or nonofficial cover. The Strategic Services Unit, however, struggled to identify appropriate cover positions. Diplomatic or consular appointments represented the most promising official cover for SI station personnel, but such appointments required the cooperation of the State Department. During the war, OSS had often attached intelligence personnel to American embassies and consulates, although the interaction between diplomats and spies was not always smooth. SSU wanted to continue wartime practice, but the State Department demurred. While prepared to accept into its embassies X-2 personnel whose counterintelligence work included vetting visa and passport applicants, State was not eager to provide facilities for SI officers. In early 1946, Whitney Shepardson acknowledged that there were "very few" secret intelligence personnel working under diplomatic cover, and these were mainly in Switzerland and Turkey.[54] The situation did not soon improve. In June 1946 Homer Hall, the chief of SI's Western Europe Division, complained to a senior colleague that from the day of its creation SSU had had to beg the State Department for cooperation. The closure of American military installations around the world, which provided convenient cover for intelligence units, had made SSU even more dependent on the diplomats for cover positions. "Without the confidence and wholehearted cooperation of the State Department," Hall observed, "SSU will be so hampered in its functions that justification for its being will be extremely difficult to establish." Hall proposed the immediate appointment of a senior SSU officer, "a man of certain distinction," to liaise with State and facilitate an understanding between the two organizations. The goal was to place under diplomatic cover at least one SI officer in every American diplomatic mission.[55]

To SSU officers, the aloofness of the State Department must have seemed especially craven since the diplomats were perfectly happy to accept the work product of the very spies with whom they declined to associate. In one month alone, May 1946, for example, State received 899 intelligence reports from the Strategic Services Unit.[56] Some diplomatic missions, particularly those in the U.S. occupation zones in Austria and Germany, depended significantly on the political and economic information collected by local SSU teams. The diplomats, however, seemed to take this support for granted. Reviewing the scope of SSU's support to the diplomats, one senior intelligence officer noted dryly, "Letters of appreciation from State are hard to come by."[57]

The Strategic Services Unit's frustration might have turned to anger if it had known that, at the same time the State Department was rebuffing SSU's advances, the diplomats were embracing cooperation with another clandestine service. Building upon contacts initiated during the war, State had come to an arrangement with the army's Special Service Branch, the shadowy espionage unit better known as "the Pond" among the handful of high officials indoctrinated into its activities. The State Department allowed certain of its personnel at American embassies in Europe to act as communication channels for Pond operatives, most of whom worked under business or commercial cover. These operatives would pass their intelligence reports to one of these designated diplomats who, in turn, would transmit the reports to the State Department's Division of Foreign Activity Correlation in Washington for further dissemination among national security managers. Occasionally, a diplomat would move beyond the narrow communications role to collect information directly on behalf of the Pond, but these instances of clandestine activity by embassy officers were not common.[58] The State Department's favoritism toward the Special Service Branch to the disadvantage of the Strategic Services Unit probably reflected a concern to protect the professional integrity and autonomy of the diplomatic service. Unlike SSU, which sought to place and control its own officers inside embassies, the Pond sought no positions inside the diplomatic missions, remaining content merely to use a small portion of the time and energies of embassy personnel. Working with the Pond, State did not have to accept into the embassy family "outsiders" who did not share the ethos, culture, and mission of the diplomatic service and who might embarrass that service by their dangerous and disreputable activities.

That concern to maintain the exclusivity of the "club" was an important motive behind State's refusal to provide diplomatic cover positions to SSU is apparent in the terms of an agreement the two organizations eventually concluded in the late summer of 1946. The initiative came from Lieutenant General Hoyt Vandenberg, who had succeeded Admiral Souers as director of the Central Intelligence Group in June of that year. On 22 August, Vandenberg proposed to Dean Acheson, the undersecretary of state, certain "basic principles and ideas" concerning State Department support for CIG operations. Vandenberg suggested that a "conservative number" of intelligence personnel receive State Department positions abroad. State and CIG would agree on the qualifications required of these individuals, and State would have the right to interview the candidates to determine their suitability. Once approved, the successful candidates would receive training at State to prepare them for appointment to a particular embassy. Upon appointment, they would have embassy ranks and functions, but their true status as intelligence officers would be known to a minimum number of embassy staff, including the ambassador, who would have access to the officers' files. To assuage anxieties about compromising the embassy and upsetting relations with the host country, the intelligence operatives inside the embassy would refrain from running operations against local targets. Given the opportunity to participate in the selection, indoctrination, and supervision of SSU officers working undercover in its embassies—that is, given the opportunity to turn outsiders into insiders—State abandoned its opposition to such officers and accepted Vandenberg's proposal. By October 1946, by which time SSU had been closed and most of its clandestine operators integrated into the Central Intelligence Group, thirteen intelligence officers were receiving indoctrination from the State Department preparatory to deployment abroad in November.[59]

While preferring embassy positions for its officers, the Strategic Services Unit also used other covers. In the fall of 1945, for example, the chief of the SSU station in Prague posed as an official American investigator gathering evidence for war crimes trials. A predecessor had traveled around Czechoslovakia as part of an American army medical mission. Headquarters also worked to place more personnel under nonofficial cover, expecting that officers might pose as students, research professors, journalists, employees of American companies with offices abroad, or independent businessmen. In the spring of 1946, for instance, SSU formally discharged a serving case officer who then, by prearrangement with his former service, set up a trucking business that delivered materials to Hungary, Yugoslavia, and the Russian occupation zone in Austria. Though no longer an employee of the U.S. government, this individual continued to report to the SSU mission in Vienna and made his trucks available for clandestine operations.[60] Some organizations, though potentially rich in cover positions, were deemed inappropriate for intelligence purposes. As late as October 1946 headquarters prohibited the use for cover or recruitment purposes of the American Red Cross, the United Nations Relief and Rehabilitation Administration (UNRRA), and private philanthropic organizations, although there seems to have been no prohibition against the use of religious organizations, such as the Catholic Church and its personnel.[61] Cover identities of any type, however, were useless if individual officers were already known to be spies. Because of their wartime work in OSS, often in the same areas as their postwar assignment, many SSU field officers were well known to local police and security services, particularly in Switzerland, Sweden, Portugal, and Spain. Aware of this problem, SI Washington tried to introduce new personnel into the European stations, but this effort was seriously constrained by staff reductions required by demobilization. In early 1946 headquarters estimated that the identities of 85 percent of its field officers, no matter what their cover, had been compromised, an impossible situation for a clandestine service.[62]

In the first months of peace, demobilization and uncertainty concerning the structure and direction of American intelligence inhibited the development of systematic collection programs. Headquarters directives concerning intelligence requirements and priorities were few. Lacking guidance from Washington, field units in areas occupied by the U.S. Army (specifically the American zones of Germany and Austria) simply accepted assignments from the military governments and occupation authorities. In other areas, such as France and Switzerland, field units, left to their own devices, generally pursued targets of opportunity, although the pursuit was constrained by lack of personnel and resources. Not surprisingly, collection efforts were uneven across Europe. Stations with particularly ambitious and entrepreneurial chiefs, such as Homer Hall in Bern, ran many operations and flooded Washington headquarters with reports, while other stations, such as those in the Low Countries, launched few operations and did little more than liaise with the local intelligence and security services. Through 1946 foreign operations, whatever their origin or scope, were limited to intelligence and counterintelligence programs, since SSU had, as part of its general retrenchment, abandoned all covert paramilitary and propaganda activities.[63]

In addition to organizing and directing clandestine collection programs, the field stations were also responsible for maintaining contact with foreign intelligence and police agencies. During the war OSS had developed productive liaison arrangements with several foreign services, and SSU continued the connections after the war. In January 1946 SSU had confidential ties—of varying degrees of cooperation—with the intelligence and security services of Britain, Belgium, Czechoslovakia, Denmark, France, Italy, the Netherlands, Norway, Spain, Sweden, Switzerland, Thailand, and Turkey as well as contacts with the remnants of the wartime service controlled by the former government-in-exile of Poland.[64] At a time when its own collection efforts were constrained by demobilization and insufficient resources, SSU relied on its liaison partners to extend its reach into areas that were beyond the organizational capabilities of American intelligence. As we shall see, SSU happily supplemented its own sparse collection with information from the French on Eastern Europe, the Danes on Poland, the Swedes on the Baltic States, the Italians on Yugoslavia, and the British on just about everywhere.

The smaller services were particularly eager to cooperate with the Americans. Aware of their own limitations—and unaware of the organizational and budgetary problems afflicting their new American partners—these services expected to expand their intelligence reach and enhance their technical capabilities by connecting with a "rich uncle." One appraisal of liaison relations noted that the Danish, Dutch, and Swedish services in particular had "a definite Western bias" and were "enthusiastically" seeking collaboration.[65] Among these collaborators, Britain's Secret Intelligence Service (SIS) was by far the most important. During the war the United States and Britain had developed close intelligence liaison, particularly in the sensitive area of code breaking but also in clandestine espionage, counterintelligence, special operations, and disinformation, and both sides hoped to continue that relationship into the postwar world. The Anglo-American communications intelligence partnership made the transition from war to peace with scarcely an interruption mainly because the highly secret comint programs were never an important battlefield in the intelligence wars that wracked bureaucratic Washington in the summer of 1945. For these programs, whose importance was readily acknowledged by all, the question was not whether they would continue but at what level would they continue. The future of human clandestine programs—spies and covert operations—was more problematic. Uncertainties regarding the postwar prospects for American clandestine intelligence initially encouraged a certain reserve among SIS managers who watched the bureaucratic battles in Washington with more than a little consternation. The demise of their wartime partner, the Office of Strategic Services, without an assured successor agency was especially unsettling. British authorities were not prepared to share secrets with an American intelligence service until they were confident that the service would survive beyond the next month, thereby ensuring not only the security of those secrets but a reciprocal flow of American confidences. As early as 16 August 1945, the day after Japan's surrender, a senior SIS officer had confessed to Philip Horton, the head of the OSS intelligence unit in Paris, that the British service was hesitant to continue official exchanges in peacetime until the future of OSS and the stability of its personnel were assured. As late as January 1946, SIS officers were telling SSU representatives that despite a desire in London for close collaboration, formal agreements and exchanges were impossible until the uncertainties surrounding the future organization of American intelligence were resolved.[66]

Formal relations may have been impossible, but informal exchanges were not. After Japan's surrender SIS continued to pass intelligence "under the table" to OSS and its successor, SSU. With the creation of the Central Intelligence Group and the emergence of the Strategic Services Unit as a functioning espionage service the British were sufficiently assured of the long-term stability of American intelligence to reinvigorate the wartime partnership. By the spring of 1946 cooperation between SIS and SSU was so close that the American intelligence station in London did almost nothing but service the liaison arrangement. SIS reporting significantly augmented American collection efforts, particularly since the British service provided coverage of areas, such as the Middle East, where Washington had few, if any, intelligence assets. The partnership's focus, however, was Europe. In February 1946, for example, SSU received from SIS 117 intelligence reports. The reports covered fifteen countries, all in Europe. Although the intelligence exchange was supposedly reciprocal, initially the flow of information was largely from London to Washington. Uncertainty about the future of American intelligence, demobilization, and the transition from OSS to SSU disrupted American collection efforts, and the Americans just didn't have much to share. The SSU station in London, which collected no information on its own but received the intelligence product from sister stations in various European countries, acknowledged that at the beginning of 1946 the American output to the British remained "relatively small."[67]

As the Strategic Services Unit began to find its feet, the exchanges became more equal. In February 1946, SSU gave SIS 99 reports in return for the 117 it received. The following month the Americans received from the British 150 items (including information on economic conditions in the Soviet zone of Germany, the attitude of the Greek communist party toward proposed elections in their country, and the strength of pro-fascist movements in Italy), but offered 159 in return. The American contribution included reports on Russian wool and cotton deliveries to Yugoslavia (judged "of some value" by the Ministry of Economic Warfare in London), socialist overtures to Don Juan de Bourbón, the pretender to the Spanish throne (considered "of some interest" by the Foreign Office), and the strength of the Hungarian army (graded "C" by the War Office).[68]

The increased activity of the London station reflected a more general organizational vitality across SSU departments and units in the spring of 1946. Although resources, especially personnel, remained scarce, the service had survived the immediate dislocations of demobilization, regrouped around leaner headquarters and field units, and regained institutional confidence. In the field this renewed vitality was reflected in increasing levels of operational activity. In Washington it was evident in a more systematic effort to establish intelligence priorities and direct scarce resources against those targets.

This new energy was probably encouraged by developments in Washington in the spring of 1946 that stabilized the position of the service and affirmed its long-term prospects. On 14 March 1946, after weeks of testimony from SSU officers and visits to that organization's headquarters, the Fortier Committee issued a report supporting the continuation of the Strategic Services Unit. Asserting that "there is immediate need for the continued maintenance of foreign intelligence coverage throughout the world and for the implementation of clandestine and semi-clandestine operations in areas hitherto covered by SSU" and noting that "no other intelligence authority has been established with appropriate directions to perform . . . functions of the character of those performed by SSU," the Fortier Committee recommended that the War Department turn the service over to the Central Intelligence Group, where it should function "in selected and carefully defined fields of vital interest to the United States in which clandestine operations and planning for clandestine operations are deemed necessary."[69]

Admiral Souers accepted the recommendation of the Fortier Board, and over the next several months the Central Intelligence Group quietly absorbed most of the staff and resources of SSU. For security purposes intelligence managers tried to make it seem as if SSU had simply faded away without a successor. In June 1946 Colonel William Quinn, the former executive officer of SSU who had succeeded General Magruder as director of the unit in April 1946, informed the field stations that the service's SI and X-2 offices were abolished and that further use of those designations was prohibited. In their place a Foreign Security Reports Office was established that included an administrative office, planning and steering staff, training and dissemination offices, and branches for various regions of the world. Within each geographic branch a Foreign Reports Group would be responsible for positive intelligence and a Security Control Group would deal with counterintelligence.[70] The new arrangement lasted until 19 October 1946, when the Strategic Services Unit itself was liquidated and all personnel were dismissed. The reorganization was largely cosmetic. In fact, all SSU headquarters functions were simply assumed by a new element of CIG, the Office of Special Operations (OSO), which was charged with conducting "all organized Federal espionage and counterespionage operations outside the United States and its possessions for the collection of foreign intelligence information required for the national security."[71] In the field SSU stations morphed into so-called External Survey Detachments. Most SSU personnel were promptly reemployed in their former capacities by OSO.[72] When the National Security Act of 1947 dissolved the National Intelligence Authority and the Central Intelligence Group and established in their place the Central Intelligence Agency, most of the administrative and operational elements of OSO were absorbed by the new agency.

In the first six months of 1946 most of the immediate issues that had roiled the waters of American intelligence at the end of the war had been clarified if not completely resolved. Questions of structure and control had been addressed with the creation of the National Intelligence Authority and the Central Intelligence Group. The continuation of a peacetime clandestine espionage capability, at least on a modest scale, was assured by the incorporation of the Strategic Services Unit into the CIG. The negative effects of demobilization continued to be felt, but the intelligence services had accommodated themselves to the situation and could believe that the worst of the personnel losses were behind them. Perhaps surprisingly, targeting—the identification of those subjects and those countries that should receive attention from the services—would prove to be the most problematic of the issues that confronted intelligence managers in the first year of peace. It took some time for America's spies to decide on whom they should spy, but inevitably, and perhaps necessarily, their gaze turned toward the Soviet Union.

CHAPTER TWO

A Mystery in an Enigma

On 2 September 1945, the day Japanese representatives formally ended the Second World War by signing the surrender protocols aboard the U.S.S. *Missouri* in Tokyo Bay, the United States knew surprisingly little about the postwar capabilities and intentions of the Soviet Union and had little prospect of remedying that deficiency in the near future. This ignorance was a result of three factors: the peculiar nature of the wartime alliance that linked Britain, the Soviet Union, and the United States; the secretive and suspicious nature of the Soviet regime; and Washington's ambivalence toward overcoming that secrecy through aggressive intelligence operations.

Connections of language, culture, and history certainly facilitated a close wartime connection between the United States and Britain, but the necessity of fighting on common fronts in North Africa, Western Europe, and, to a lesser extent, Southeast Asia sealed the relationship. Among the various governments aligned with the wartime United Nations, the London–Washington axis was marked by a degree of confidence, consensus, and cooperation unprecedented in the history of alliances. Though never perfect and not infrequently unsettled by disagreements and misunderstandings, this partnership produced a dense and complex network of bilateral consultations, joint committees, and liaison exchanges that labored, not always with success, to integrate, or at least coordinate, the military and diplomatic operations of the two countries. The level of wartime cooperation was so complete that London and Washington withheld relatively few secrets from each other. In a very real sense the United States had little need to spy on Britain because it pretty much already knew most of what it wanted to know, and what it didn't know just wasn't worth the effort of discovery.

The relative trust and cooperation that connected London and Washington did not extend to Moscow. Geography and ideology conspired to discourage collaboration. On the eastern front the Soviet Union faced the Axis alone, linked to its putative allies only by tenuous supply lines across Arctic waters and Iranian deserts and mountains. In effect, the Russians fought a separate war with little reference to the wars in other theaters of operation. Despite the occasional "Big Three" diplomatic conference and exchanges of military and economic missions, there was nowhere near the degree of consultation and collaboration between the Soviet Union on the one hand and Britain and the United States on the other that characterized relations between the latter two countries. Moscow was not inclined to share experiences, plans, or information of any type with London and Washington. In the eyes of Josef Stalin and his confederates in the Kremlin, Britain, the United States, and all capitalist states were allies of convenience but were otherwise the natural and inevitable enemies of the Bolshevik Revolution and the "Soviet experiment." This ideological suspicion and hostility was, to some extent, reciprocated by elements in London and Washington—including elements in the intelligence community—who considered Stalin a ruthless tyrant and Soviet communism a real threat to the religious, social, and political values of liberal democracy. Even in the face of a common enemy, ideological tensions limited the free exchange of information between the western and eastern poles of the alliance, a condition reinforced by the visceral obsession with secrecy and security, manifested in the pervasive apparatus of a police state, which characterized the Soviet regime's approach to all matters.

If the United States desired accurate information concerning Moscow's diplomatic, economic, and military capabilities, intentions, and operations it would have to work to obtain it. This necessity placed a particular burden upon the intelligence services, a burden those organizations were ill-equipped to shoulder. When the United States entered the war, American intelligence had no clandestine sources inside the Soviet Union, but then it had at that time very few clandestine sources anywhere. For lack of alternatives, Washington policy makers relied upon traditional and relatively open sources. The State Department received regular reports from its political and economic officers at the U.S. embassy in Moscow, although it was not inclined to share such reports with the Office of Strategic Services and the War and Navy Departments. In the Russian capital the diplomats gathered information from interviews with notoriously close-mouthed government officials, conversations with journalists and foreign colleagues in the diplomatic community, and personal observations of life under the Stalinist regime. The Office of Strategic Services established a USSR division in its Research and Analysis Branch, but the analysts relied primarily upon information gleaned from press coverage of Soviet affairs; interviews with journalists, academics, refugees, and businessmen concerned with Russia; and perusal of communiques and reports released by the Soviet government. For their part, the military services relied almost exclusively upon the observations of the army and navy attachés attached to the Moscow embassy.

Open sources, such as public records, official pronouncements, and press reports, sometimes proved revealing. The question of postwar prospects for Soviet economic recovery, an issue that much preoccupied American policy makers in 1944–1945, was a case in point. Throughout the war and into the early postwar period there was a general perception that the Soviet Union, rich in natural resources and a large and increasingly educated population, would eventually become one of the world's leading economic powers. Many observers believed that the Soviet system with its command economy had an exceptionally strong capacity for economic development because resources could be allocated "rationally." In January 1946, for example, the Joint Intelligence Staff of the Joint Chiefs of Staff predicted that the Soviets were capable of raising living standards "while at the same time developing their economic capabilities and their latent military potential more rapidly than any other great power."[1]

While American observers generally thought that the long-term economic prospects of the Soviet Union were good, they also understood that the country's wartime losses had been severe. Less clear was the rate at which the USSR could be expected to recover from the war. The significance of this question derived in part from another: What use would the Soviet Union make of the strong geopolitical position it would enjoy when the fighting ended? Would Moscow use this position to advance an expansionist political and territorial agenda in Europe and the Middle East? Would, instead, the Soviets turn inward and focus on rebuilding an economy and society shattered by war? The expectation that Russia would emerge from the war gravely weakened and preoccupied with tasks of reconstruction was comforting to those concerned about Moscow's intentions. Not only would such a condition constrain any impulses toward expansionism, but it might also make Moscow, eager for Western economic support, amenable to Washington's preferences. During the war, some journalists, doing their bit for the common effort, encouraged this attitude in order to counteract doubts about Soviet plans. The influential commentator Quentin Reynolds struck a common note in 1944 when he wrote in his best-selling book, *The Curtain Rises*, "People in America who are still distrustful of the Soviet Union lose sight of the fact that this war is going to leave Russia in a horribly weakened condition." According to Reynolds, Russia was for some time going to be "a giant on crutches." For that reason Josef Stalin, the Soviet leader, would be "very easy to do business with" when the war was over.[2] Of course American officials knew that the USSR would not be absolutely dependent upon the United States, as even leading advocates of economic diplomacy, such as the ambassador in Moscow, W. Averell Harriman, conceded. Their confidence in future Russian moderation rather derived in large measure from the conviction that Soviet communism had changed. While the revolutionary spirit might linger in certain quarters of the Communist Party, Harriman advised Washington in early 1944, the thinking of Stalin and his advisers would be directed toward the consolidation and economic recovery of their country within its 1941 frontiers.[3] This perception offered grounds for hope that the prospect of postwar aid from the United States would have some effect on Soviet policy because it might hasten Russian recovery and spare the Kremlin what in American terms would have been a politically difficult choice between consumer goods and capital investment and equipment. This view penetrated the highest levels of American government. At the Yalta Conference, for instance, President Roosevelt pointedly declined to raise the issue of postwar aid for Russia, informing his senior aides, "I think it's very important that we hold this back and don't give them any promises of finance until we get what we want."[4]

The Soviets certainly wanted postwar financing from the United States. In January 1945 they asked for $6 billion in credits for the purchase of manufactured goods and industrial equipment. The question was whether they needed credits so much that they would adjust their postwar behavior significantly to obtain them. The tone of their request suggested that in their view the United States, soon to be faced with a crisis of overproduction, needed *them*. To understand the limits of economic diplomacy, policy makers in Washington needed intelligence concerning Russia's prospects for postwar recovery. They got that intelligence not from spies operating clandestinely in Moscow, but from academics working at desks in the backrooms of the Office of Strategic Services, who cast serious doubt on the proposition that Russia's need for American credits would give Washington a special leverage in postwar diplomacy.

For years financial circles had estimated that the USSR, thanks to the convicts who labored their lives away in the goldfields of the Kolyma, was a producer of gold second only to South Africa. There was, therefore, some consternation among diplomats and financial advisors when, at the Bretton Woods conference in the summer of 1944, the Russian delegation balked at the contribution of gold requested of the Soviet Union for the proposed International Monetary Fund. The Russians insisted that financing postwar reconstruction would require so much gold that the Soviet Union would be unable to deposit much of the precious metal with the International Monetary Fund for some years after the war.[5]

Shortly after the Soviets announced that they intended to use their gold for reconstruction, the Research and Analysis Branch of OSS undertook a study of what that announcement portended for the USSR's dependence on assistance from abroad. The study was the work of two of the branch's senior economists, Abram Bergson, perhaps the leading American expert on the Soviet economy, and Wassily Leontief, a future winner of the Nobel Prize. Their findings could not have been encouraging for those who saw credits as an instrument to influence Moscow's postwar behavior. The OSS economists calculated that, on the basis of publicly available statistics, the Soviet Union could recover fairly rapidly from the war without American financial assistance. Their report estimated that the USSR had suffered losses amounting to approximately $16 billion, or about 25 percent of its fixed capital. If the war ended in late 1944, Russia's national income could return to the level of 1940 by 1948, and what would have been the level of 1942, barring the German invasion, in 1950–1951. More importantly for policy makers, Bergson and Leontief concluded that the Soviets could reconstruct at this projected rate "entirely out of domestic resources without the aid of foreign loans or reparations." This they could do by exporting gold from their substantial stockpile of the metal. Even if they maintained an army of the size of 1938 (about 4 million men) living standards would reach the level of the immediate prewar period in the first year of reconstruction. Even annual foreign credits, say from the United States, in the amount of $3.5 billion for three years, or the equivalent in reparations, would accelerate reconstruction by only a few months. "Thus, the success of Russian reconstruction," the OSS report concluded, "will depend to a very limited degree on foreign loans."[6]

The report by Bergson and Leontief found an audience in the highest circles of the U.S. government. At the State Department the assistant secretary for economic affairs, Dean Acheson, read a copy and asked Charles Bohlen, the department's resident expert on the Soviet Union, for his comments. Bohlen replied that, while the paper might have projected too rapid a rate of postwar recovery for the Soviet Union, it was a useful corrective "to certain exaggerated opinions as to the degree of Soviet dependency on economic assistance from abroad in the postwar period as a possible means of political pressure." A senior State Department economist shared Bohlen's criticism but nonetheless concluded that the OSS report definitely showed that the United States in its dealings with Moscow would have less bargaining advantages than many presumed.[7] The State Department's Office of Research and Analysis endorsed the OSS report, as did the Joint Intelligence Committee of the Joint Chiefs of Staff. In January 1945 the report was presented to President Franklin Roosevelt and the director of war mobilization (and soon-to-be secretary of state), James F. Byrnes.[8]

The Office of Strategic Service's demonstration that the USSR would not need American aid to recover from the war did not end Washington's efforts to use the prospect of aid to influence Soviet behavior, but it likely influenced the way the efforts were made. The importance of economic diplomacy in dealings with the Soviet Union diminished, and policy makers scrambled for alternative instruments of persuasion. In the meantime, throughout 1945 and 1946, the approach was to dangle credits in front of the Soviets without any expectation of granting them in any significant amounts.[9] Credits certainly remained on the negotiating table if only for tactical purposes, but expectations of their efficacy as a bargaining chip were much reduced.

The issue of postwar credits demonstrated the potential utility of open sources, but intelligence managers did not fool themselves into thinking that newspaper reports and publicly released data would illuminate every corner of the Soviet edifice. Trying to understand a country characterized by obsessive security, pervasive surveillance, ingrained suspicion of foreigners, complete censorship, and strict restrictions on travel, observers discovered the limitations of open sources in a closed society. The challenge for American intelligence working to inform customers in Washington about what to expect from the Russian ally was to overcome these limitations and expand its sources on the Soviet Union.

The wartime desire for more and better information about the Soviet Union did not reflect an anti-Soviet bias that somehow presaged the later Cold War. To be sure, some American intelligence officials despised communism, harbored a visceral hostility toward the Soviet regime, and suspected that Stalin would use the war to expand Russian influence into as much of Europe as possible. For most of the war the military attaché's office in the Moscow embassy under Major Ivan Yeaton and his assistant (and eventual successor) Major John A. Michela, was a hotbed of anti-Soviet sentiments.[10] Inside the Office of Strategic Services similar sentiments characterized the circles around a few senior officers, particularly James Grafton Rogers, the chairman of the Planning Group, and Dewitt Clinton Poole, chief of the Foreign Nationalities Branch, and his deputy, John Wiley. For example, Rogers and his like-minded colleagues, convinced of Soviet perfidy, interpreted such initiatives as the formation in Moscow in July 1943 of the National Committee for a Free Germany, composed of captured German army officers and émigré German communists, not as a propaganda ploy but as a preparatory step toward a communist takeover of postwar Germany.[11] The professional fate of these individuals, however, suggests that anticommunism and fear of the USSR did not pervade the U.S. secret services and were not the primary motives behind wartime intelligence interest in the Soviet Union. Both Yeaton and Michela were recalled from Moscow when it became apparent that their anti-Soviet attitudes were poisoning U.S.-Soviet relations and prejudicing rather than assisting the collection of information. Both officers received appointments to the Russian section of the Military Intelligence Division (MID) in Washington, but their influence over the division's approach toward the Soviet Union was probably modest. By the last year of the war, Yeaton had been eased out of Russian affairs with a transfer to the Far East, where he became chief intelligence officer for the U.S. Army's China command. Michela remained in MID, but there is little evidence that his anti-

Soviet attitudes significantly influenced the work of the division; indeed, his hardline posture seemed to have strained his relations with his colleagues in army intelligence.[12] In the Office of Strategic Services the anti-Soviet faction, never large, had been reduced to a corporal's guard by 1944. Early that year, James Grafton Rogers, frustrated over the refusal of senior officers to accept his suspicions about the USSR, resigned from the service. His principal ally in OSS, Dewitt Clinton Poole, noticing a progressive decline in his influence and visibility in management circles, gave up his direction of the Foreign Nationalities Board and accepted a largely honorific appointment as special adviser to William Donovan. John Wiley continued to sound the alarm in OSS about the Soviet Union but found himself increasingly marginalized in the organization.[13]

Initially, intelligence interest in the Soviet Union reflected not hostility toward an ideological foe, but a concern to determine the country's ability to withstand the German invasion of 22 June 1941. Given the modest capabilities of American intelligence in the summer of 1941, Washington had to rely on reports from its embassy in Moscow, where the military attachés were especially pessimistic about the prospects for successful resistance. After America's entry into the war the intelligence focus remained for some time on Russia's ability to stay in the war and engage and distract Axis military power. The USSR Division of OSS's Research and Analysis Branch, for example, was preoccupied with agricultural, industrial, and energy production and Russia's capacity to mobilize the human, financial, and material resources necessary to maintain these activities at the levels required by large-scale war. The division generally eschewed speculation about political subjects, such as Moscow's long-term political ambitions, although in 1943 the analysts gradually began to include such topics in their considerations.[14]

During the war most of American intelligence activity in the USSR did not actually have the Soviet Union as its principal target. On the eastern front the Red Army, Navy, and Air Force were actively engaged against the military forces of Germany, Italy, Finland, Romania, and Hungary. The scale and tempo of combat in this arena of operations and the importance Berlin assigned to the war against the Soviet Union guaranteed that the eastern front would be an important laboratory to observe the latest tactics and equipment of the German military and other Axis forces. If accessible to London and Washington, evidence from this laboratory—in the form of battlefield observations, captured equipment, and information from deserters and prisoners-of-war—would improve the performance of the Western allies in their own military contests against the Axis on other fronts. Something as basic as the order of battle (OOB) of the German army and air force on the eastern front—the number, identity, and location of units—would be an immense aid. After all, if the Third and Seventh Panzer Divisions were known to be in the Ukraine, then American and British military planners would not have to worry about those divisions unexpectedly appearing in France. Since the USSR was a land and sea power in northern Asia and the north Pacific, Moscow was also potentially an important source of information concerning Japanese military and political affairs even though the Soviet Union was not at war with Japan.

Of course, U.S. intelligence also wanted as much information as possible about the order of battle, training, equipment, and tactics of the Red Army, Navy, and Air Force and the plans of the political and military leadership in Moscow. This interest was no necessary indicator of suspicion or hostility. American decision makers wanted equivalent information about British (or Australian or Canadian) political and military dispositions and pursued such information without any suggestion of hostility toward these partners. It was natural, if not actually necessary, for wartime allies to want to know about the capabilities and intentions of coalition members. The only difference between Washington's pursuit of information from London (or Canberra or Ottawa) and its pursuit of information from Moscow was that the latter source was much less open and forthcoming with its partners.

Deep Hibernation

For information of any type from inside the Soviet Union—aside from that available from open sources, such as the press—wartime U.S. intelligence relied primarily upon three sources: formal intelligence exchanges with Soviet representatives, intelligence exchanges with British colleagues, and the observations of Americans inside the country. After Pearl Harbor the American military services pursued, more or less consistently, a policy of encouraging an exchange of data, reports, and observations with their Russian counterparts. Over the course of the war the tempo and success of this effort rose and fell according to the vagaries of war and politics and the temperaments and diplomatic skills of the individuals involved in liaison contacts. In their degree of openness and comprehensiveness, however, the exchanges of information with the Soviets never approached the level of similar collaboration with the British. Most of the contacts occurred in Moscow and involved U.S. Army and Navy officers from the embassy or the American military mission and their Soviet counterparts. Efforts to establish direct liaison between intelligence services, particularly an initiative in late 1943 by William Donovan for an exchange of OSS-NKVD delegations between Moscow and Washington, came to naught, although a few items of information indirectly passed between the Russian and American espionage services through the military mission.[15] The military exchanges produced useful but limited intelligence, mainly concerning Axis tactics, equipment, order of battle, and operations on the eastern front, although after Germany's surrender the focus shifted to the Far East and Japan. Occasionally, however, liaison contacts generated intelligence about Soviet topics as the partners traded information about their own equipment and dispositions. Russian contributions ranged from the narrowly technical—a gift of a Red Army antitank rifle, data on Russian naval mines, an offer to allow the American military attaché to inspect Soviet tanks—to the more broadly operational—a summary of the composition of the Red Navy's northern and far eastern fleets.[16] The information, while welcomed by American liaison officers, was limited in quantity and strictly military in scope. At no time did the Russians allow a discussion of Moscow's political posture or plans or provide an insight into leadership thinking.

Parallel to American liaison contacts with the Soviet armed services, British military officers also exchanged information with their Russian counterparts. Initially, the Western allies did not share the product of their respective contacts with their eastern partner, but by 1943 British and American military intelligence services began to exchange information. In February 1944, for example, these services, frustrated by Moscow's reluctance to provide information concerning Soviet military organization and deployments along the eastern front, organized a week-long conference in London to develop a picture of the order of battle of the Red Army and Red Air Force. The meeting was so productive that the participants agreed to continue sharing information on the Soviet armed services, particularly intelligence obtained from Britain's reading of intercepted German radio communications on the eastern front. German army and air force radio traffic proved a rich source of information concerning the order of battle, tactics, and equipment of their Russian opponents.[17]

American citizens—diplomats, couriers, military attachés, personnel attached to military missions, Lend-Lease officials, representatives of war industries—occasionally had the opportunity to travel inside the Soviet Union. Though strictly limited in their itineraries and always under some degree of surveillance by Moscow's security services, these Americans had the opportunity to observe military bases, ports, transportation networks, and factories. Their reports "from the field" provided a welcome supplement to the more formal and structured conferences of official liaison officers and proved a useful, though limited, source of information from inside of the USSR. A two-week visit to Red Air Force bases and training schools by a representative of the Bell Aircraft Company, who spoke to more than 200 pilots and mechanics, probably provided better insight into the Soviet air force than any number of organization charts passed across conference room tables by Russian generals.[18] Personnel of the U.S. Lend-Lease program had the responsibility, as part of their job, to report on the capacities and operations of ports, railroads, and shipping facilities, while officers attached to the various American military missions had the opportunity to visit army camps and supply depots, naval shipyards, and air force bases. In the spring of 1945, for example, U.S. Navy personnel reported visits to an automobile assembly plant, a Red Air Force base, and several shipyards, where, among other opportunities, they had a chance to observe a Red Navy antisubmarine vessel. That summer, American diplomats from the Moscow embassy chronicled several trips into the interior of the Soviet Union, including a long rail journey across the country to Siberia.[19]

While these activities were not without value, the dependence upon liaison and travel revealed the woeful state of intelligence collection on the Soviet Union. An intelligence service that depends upon handouts from the target government and occasional and uncoordinated observations by travelers is a service that cannot effectively cover that target. During the war, the Office of Strategic Services and other military intelligence organizations were never able to expand their collection efforts. Noticeably absent from their collection repertoire were clandestine agents. The United States recruited no secret sources inside the country. This deficiency was not merely a testimony to the quality of the security and counterespionage organs of the Soviet regime, as accomplished as they were. The work of these organs was immeasurably eased by a real ambivalence among American authorities concerning the appropriateness of aggressive intelligence operations against the USSR. It was not that U.S. intelligence agencies could not recruit secret informants inside Russia; it was that there is no evidence that they even tried. In both Washington and Moscow American authorities were reluctant to pursue any initiatives that might alienate a notoriously suspicious and irascible ally. This reluctance extended beyond clandestine operations inside the USSR to include opposition to the mere presence of American intelligence organizations on Russian soil. As early as 11 December 1941, within a week of America's entry into the war, President Franklin Roosevelt rejected a proposal from William Donovan to send to the Soviet Union two operatives of the Coordinator of Information, the intelligence organization directed by Donovan. Subsequently, Donovan and COI's successor service, the Office of Strategic Services, for some time adopted toward the USSR a posture that one authority has characterized as "deep hibernation," limiting its initiatives to an unsuccessful proposal to station in Moscow a representative of the Research and Analysis Branch who would collect Soviet newspapers, magazines, and technical publications and an agreement with an American engineering firm working in Russia for the Lend-Lease Administration to provide information to OSS concerning Soviet defense construction projects.[20] Often it seemed that the OSS director could not decide whether the Soviet Union was an important intelligence target like Germany or a potential intelligence collaborator and partner like Britain. For their part, the military services were apparently no more enthusiastic about extending their intelligence activities into the Soviet Union. There is no evidence that either MID or ONI launched clandestine operations. Indeed, Major General John Deane, the influential chief of the U.S. military mission in Moscow, successfully opposed all plans to establish intelligence collection programs inside the country. In early 1944, for example, he vetoed a proposal from army intelligence to attach a single officer to the military mission, a veto that received the explicit endorsement of General George Marshall, the army chief of staff.[21]

An ambivalent attitude is not a consistent attitude, so while the de facto posture was to avoid clandestine espionage against the Soviet Union, there were occasional exceptions to that posture. Such exceptions were to be expected in an intelligence community that lacked formal guidelines, central direction and oversight, and interagency coordination. The result was a handful of operations that collected intelligence *about* the USSR but not *within* the USSR. In the spring of 1943, for example, the Stockholm station of the Office of Strategic Services began secretly receiving information from the military and naval attachés in Finland's embassy in the Swedish capital. Finland, though not at war with the United States, was an ally of Germany and fought the Russians on the eastern front. The attachés shared with OSS reports circulated by the Finnish intelligence service to its representatives abroad as well as information gleaned from their contacts in Finnish, German, and Swedish military circles. The intelligence concerned primarily Finnish political and military personalities and German military capabilities and operations on the eastern front. Occasionally, however, there were items relating to the Soviet Union, particularly Red Army and Navy deployments in the Baltic region, but Russian subjects were not the principal focus of this clandestine relationship and there is no evidence that OSS handlers in Stockholm tasked their sources to provide intelligence on the USSR. Apparently OSS was happy to receive Russian intelligence from the Finnish attachés but did not actively pursue it. In November 1944 the source was seriously compromised when the military attaché, the more important informant, fell under suspicion by his superiors and was removed from his post.[22]

Eavesdroppers

Communications intelligence provided the most significant exceptions to the "no clandestine collection" approach to intelligence about the Soviet

Union. After Pearl Harbor the army and navy code-breaking organizations had dramatically expanded their capabilities and operations. The army's wartime program was especially ambitious. After the Japanese attack had seemingly revealed serious deficiencies in the collection, analysis, and dissemination of information by U.S. intelligence, Secretary of War Henry Stimson had asked Alfred McCormack, a respected New York attorney who had been recommended by Assistant Secretary of War John McCloy, to propose reforms for the Signal Intelligence Service (SIS), the army's code-breaking unit. After a wide-ranging investigation of SIS, McCormack proffered a series of changes that focused on increasing the size of the organization, expanding its operations, and improving the processing of the product of these operations. Most importantly, he called for a redefinition of the service's mission. Previously, limited resources had forced the Signal Intelligence Service to define its mission in narrow terms. It would attack a small number of targets, selected because they were immediately relevant to American diplomatic and military concerns. McCormack wanted SIS to think big. In a global war, government agencies as diverse as the Treasury Department, the Commerce Department, and the State Department had to contribute to the war effort. In such a war the army's intelligence services would be called upon to support other departments by providing information on a range of political, economic, military, and social topics, hitherto considered beyond the purview of military intelligence. To fulfill this broad responsibility, McCormack argued, the War Department "must know as much as possible about the objectives, the psychology and the methods of our enemies and potential enemies (*and of our Allies as well*) in order to make the right decisions in military matters" (emphasis added). Total war required total intelligence, and the pursuit of total intelligence required an expansionist SIS that would take the communications of the entire world, not just four or five governments, as its purview.[23]

The Secretary of War and senior managers in military intelligence embraced McCormack's views and adopted his recommendations. In April 1942 the army directed SIS to expand its operations and aggressively attack the codes and ciphers of not only America's enemies, but also "all major neutral and allied powers." Colonel Carter Clarke, the representative inside SIS of the assistant chief of staff for intelligence and a career intelligence officer who would significantly influence the direction of American communications intelligence, reflected the new operational posture by insisting that "our primary task is to paint for our superiors as completely a realistic picture as possible of the activities 'behind the arras' of all those associated with and against us."[24] By the spring of 1942 "total coverage" of the world's communications had become the mission of the Signal Intelligence Service.

In practice the Signal Intelligence Service, later renamed the Signal Security Agency (SSA), never fully achieved its ambitions, though not for want of effort.[25] The code breakers at Arlington Hall, the wartime headquarters of SIS/SSA, never possessed the total resources necessary to ensure total coverage. Limited resources—personnel, materials, data processing equipment, and even office space—were distributed according to shifting priorities and unexpected opportunities. Some targets, depending on circumstances, received a lot of attention, while other targets received little or none. The strategic importance of Arlington Hall's first successes against Japanese Army cryptosystems in the spring of 1943, for example, justified the diversion of personnel and resources from other targets to exploit the opportunity. On the other hand, Arlington Hall delayed attacking the codes and ciphers of the Vatican until September 1943, when, after the Italian armistice and the occupation of Rome by German forces, encrypted Italian diplomatic traffic virtually disappeared from the airwaves and cryptanalysts and linguists could be shifted from the now idle Italian section to a newly formed Vatican section.[26] The goal of total coverage remained out of reach also because the codes and ciphers that protected the communications of some governments resisted all efforts to crack them. Wartime efforts to read the secret messages of the Vatican, Sweden, and the governments-in-exile of Poland and Norway, for example, were constrained by Arlington Hall's inability to solve the high-grade cryptosystems that protected those countries' most confidential communications.[27]

Despite such constraints, by 1943 the Signal Security Agency (as the army's communications intelligence service was now known) was actively working the diplomatic and military communications of more than thirty nations: enemy, neutral, and allied.[28] One of these countries was the Soviet Union. Soviet communications had not been an early wartime priority for American code breakers, and Arlington Hall had largely ignored the Soviet Union. Because of wartime censorship regulations that required foreign embassies and consulates in the United States to file with the U.S. government copies of every telegram they sent or received, the code breakers had, in the year following Pearl Harbor, collected thousands of encrypted Russian communications just as they had collected large numbers of Argentine, Portuguese, and Turkish communications, but unlike the dispatches of other governments, Moscow's messages sat unnoticed in Arlington Hall file cabinets. No one yet was trying to read Soviet communications. The only exception were the short enciphered radio messages broadcast on a daily schedule by weather stations in Siberia. Since these weather reports cast light on developing climate conditions in the north Pacific, they were useful for U.S. air and sea operations. In June 1942 the small section at Arlington Hall devoted to studying the ciphers of foreign meteorological services solved a simple Russian weather cipher. This success represented the first—and for some time the only—wartime effort by American cryptanalysts against Soviet codes and ciphers.[29] The inattention to Moscow's communications, however, would not last.

On 1 February 1943, Lieutenant Leonard Zubko, a Russian-speaking cryptanalyst from SSA's Japanese diplomatic section, and Gene Grabeel, a new civilian recruit only weeks away from teaching school in Virginia, established themselves behind two tables and several file cabinets in a corner of a large room occupied by Major Geoffrey Stevens, the British liaison officer at Arlington Hall, and discreetly—Stevens was to know nothing about their project—began to sort through the thousands of Russian messages collected but unstudied by American intelligence. The Signal Security Agency's new Russian section was open for business. The event received little notice beyond a brief entry in the weekly report of SSA's Department B-II, the Arlington Hall unit responsible for foreign code systems. A single line in the report for the week ending 6 February 1943 announced "Russian: This section activated during the past week."[30] Two weeks later, just as quietly and without explanation, the section was abruptly closed. Lieutenant Zubko left Arlington Hall and was assigned to an army air corps mission in China, while Gene Grabeel moved to the SSA's French section. Work on Russian ciphers remained in abeyance for several weeks until, in April 1943, the section was reconstituted under the leadership of Captain Ferdinand Coudert, a Russian-speaking officer whose family law firm had at one time represented the czarist government. Gene Grabeel returned from the French section to assist Coudert.

The creation of a Russian section at Arlington Hall has been ascribed to a concern within the Signal Security Agency that Stalin might secretly negotiate a separate peace with Germany and that warning of such perfidy might appear in Russian diplomatic traffic. Also, SSA had discovered from intercepted Japanese messages that Japan and Finland were collaborating successfully in an attack on Russian ciphers, and "this information was probably the immediate inspiration for SSA's examination of the Soviet telegrams."[31] According to this scenario, Arlington Hall had not only a reason to break Russian ciphers (fear of a separate peace), but also a reason to believe that an attack on those ciphers could be successful.

The scenario is superficially plausible. Recalling the Nazi-Soviet Nonaggression Treaty of August 1939 (the Molotov-Ribbentrop Pact) American intelligence was not fanciful in imagining that Stalin might abandon his allies and cut a deal with Hitler. Furthermore, it is apparent, though the details remain obscure, that in 1943 the Soviet Union and Germany (or elements in Germany) extended feelers on the subject of a separate peace. It is not clear, however, what and when American intelligence knew about these feelers. There is no evidence that the Signal Security Agency suspected German-Soviet contacts before the creation of the Russian section in February 1943; indeed, the evidence that SSA would consider most credible—intercepted diplomatic traffic—seemingly dismissed the possibility of such contacts. Throughout 1942 the Japanese ambassadors in Germany, Russia, and Italy, whose communications were read at Arlington Hall, consistently informed Tokyo—and American eavesdroppers—that there was no chance of an accommodation between Berlin and Moscow. The first indication that such assurances might be misplaced came in an intercepted message from the Japanese ambassador in Turkey, who informed his government on 29 January 1943 that his German counterpart in Ankara believed a compromise peace with the Soviet Union was possible. An editorial note appended to this item in the Magic Diplomatic Summary, the top-secret communications intelligence survey circulated daily to the highest American policy makers, indicated that this was the first evidence received by the code breakers of a German official expressing such a sentiment. Of course this was not evidence that German-Soviet contacts were actually occurring or that a compromise peace between the two countries was imminent, merely evidence that one German diplomat, distant from Berlin, thought such contacts might be possible. Though intercepted promptly by the Signal Security Agency, this message was not decrypted, translated, and disseminated until 7 March 1943, more than a month *after* SSA's decision to open a Russian section at Arlington Hall.[32]

It is also difficult to see how the decision to study Russian ciphers could have resulted from news that certain Axis powers, particularly Finland and Japan, were successfully collaborating against Soviet codes and ciphers. After all, SSA knew that the Axis powers were also attacking British cryptosystems, but this news did not compel Arlington Hall to create a British section. Furthermore, once again the timing is off. American intelligence learned of Axis communications intelligence collaboration against the Soviet Union by decrypting traffic between Tokyo and the Japanese military attaché in Helsinki. Because of delays in the solution of the Japanese attaché ciphers, many of these messages, though intercepted in 1942, were not decrypted and translated until 1944. Before the establishment of the Russian section the principal, if not only, insight into Axis progress against Moscow's cryptosystems was a brief summary of Japanese work against Soviet diplomatic ciphers. This Japanese message was translated on 29 January 1943, only two days before the activation of the Russian section at Arlington Hall. Given the notorious sluggishness of any bureaucracy, it is unlikely that two days was sufficient for the

SSA senior managers to receive the translated message, meet to consider the implications of this message, decide to respond by starting their own Russian program, and select Zubko and Grabeel to implement that decision. It is far more likely that the decision to attack Russian ciphers had been made before news of Axis work against the same target reached Arlington Hall.[33]

The decision to add the Soviet Union to the list of SSA's targets in February 1943—a decision that was made without consulting the White House or State Department—did not reflect an anti-Soviet animus. If the leadership of American communications intelligence was motivated by such animus, why did they wait until early 1943 to give organizational expression to it? Why weren't they actively attacking Moscow's communications in 1942 or 1941? In 1942 the code breakers solved the diplomatic and military codes and ciphers of a dozen countries including Colombia, Ecuador, and the Dominican Republic, but aside from the solution toward the end of the year of a single Siberian weather cipher they paid no attention to Soviet systems.[34] A cryptanalytic organization that devotes resources to minor South American powers but virtually ignores the USSR is not an organization obsessed with the Soviet menace. The Signal Security Agency opened a Russian section not because of visceral anticommunism or what the Axis was doing or what the Soviets were doing, but because the goal of the agency, as articulated by intelligence leaders such as Alfred McCormack and Carter Clarke, was to read the secret communications of *every* government in the world: allies, enemies, and neutrals.[35] An active cryptanalytic program presumed no hostility toward the targeted country. In this context SSA's decision to open a Russian section in February 1943 was no more anti-Soviet than its decision to open a Vatican section in September of that year was anti-Catholic.

Whatever its origins, the Russian section in 1943 was not an important unit, and Russian codes and ciphers were not priority targets at Arlington Hall. As late as June, Coudert and Grabeel remained the only staff, and the office was so resource-poor that it lacked even a Russian alphabet typewriter. Gradually additional personnel appeared, but by the end of that year the staff still numbered barely thirty, a roster only slightly larger than that of the unit working the ciphers of Near Eastern governments (Saudi Arabia, Iraq, Iran, and Afghanistan) but still smaller than such middling units as the Spanish-Portuguese and French-Swiss sections. Even the foreign weather ciphers section had more personnel.[36] On the other hand, Coudert began to draw upon support from OP-20-G, the U.S. Navy's communications intelligence service, which had established its own Russian program in July 1943. Like the army's effort, OP-20-G's program started small; a month after its creation the navy's Russian section had only five staffers, although it did possess that apparently rare commodity, a Russian-language typewriter.[37]

The code breakers began to register their first successes against Moscow's ciphers in early 1944. By July of that year Arlington Hall was able to read four Red Army cryptosystems, and by November it had added a fifth to its list of accomplishments. These achievements, while welcome, were modest. The number of solved systems represented a small proportion of the total in Russian service. By September 1944, for example, OP-20-G had identified twenty-one Red Army and Navy codes or ciphers in service on Far Eastern radio networks alone, while Arlington Hall was sorting out a number of systems that were used on diplomatic channels. The handful of readable codes and ciphers protected relatively low-grade radio traffic—mostly minor administrative matters such as veterinary reports, the shipment of vegetables, service orders for rolling stock, and, in one case, advice on good fishing spots—which possessed so little intelligence value that Arlington Hall did not bother to distribute any of the decrypted messages to its customers in the U.S. government. Two of the readable systems were no longer even used by the Russians after 1943 and so were mainly of historical interest. Success against Moscow's diplomatic communications, potentially the most important source of intelligence, remained elusive. As late as September 1945 no Russian diplomatic messages had been read by American intelligence.[38]

Communications intelligence did provide an oblique perspective on Soviet affairs. By the last year of the war Arlington Hall was able to read the diplomatic traffic of dozens of governments, many of whom had embassies in Moscow. By monitoring the communications of neutral and allied ambassadors in the Russian capital, American intelligence could eavesdrop on what others were observing about Soviet affairs. As will be seen, this surveillance occasionally illuminated Moscow's attitude toward such issues as the postwar government of Poland, but it was a poor substitute for direct access to Russian communications.

Polar Star

The second exception to the general aversion to wartime clandestine collection operations against the Soviet Union also involved communications intelligence. On 21 September 1944, the day Finland abandoned the Axis alliance by accepting an armistice with the Soviet Union, the entire Finnish military intelligence service loaded their files and families onto four small coastal steamers and sailed to Swedish ports in an operation code-named STELLA POLARIS. This mass defection, one of the most remarkable events in the intelligence history of the war, provided a potential windfall for the world's secret services since the enterprising Finns, rich in information but poor in patrons and monetary assets, promptly offered the contents of their files to any government willing to provide protection or payment. The market promised to be active since the Finnish service, though small, had a well-deserved reputation for effectiveness, particularly in communications intelligence. In an effort to advertise their wares, the Finns, hardly more than a week after their arrival in Sweden, met with officers from the American embassy and the OSS station in Stockholm. Colonel Reino Hallamaa, chief of the Finnish communications intelligence unit, promptly astounded his American audience by demonstrating that his service had broken the cipher used by the U.S. State Department for its most confidential communications. Now assured of his listeners' attention, Hallamaa next discussed his unit's success against Soviet cryptosystems, claiming to have broken more than a thousand Russian codes and ciphers. The Finnish colonel ended his presentation with a dramatic flourish, offering to sell to the United States all the Soviet cryptographic material in his service's possession and, as a special bonus, proposing to send the Finnish code breakers to the United States to work in American service.[39]

In Washington the initial response to Colonel Hallamaa's offer was mixed. As a result of a clandestine operation against the Japanese legation in Lisbon in 1943 that threatened Arlington Hall's successful program against Tokyo's communications, the Office of Strategic Services had agreed to avoid operations involving foreign ciphers.[40] Despite this prohibition, General Donovan could not resist the prospect of an intelligence windfall. On 10 October 1944, he notified the OSS station in Stockholm of his "complete approval and strongest support" for the acquisition of the Finns' cryptographic files.[41] The State Department was less enthusiastic. Preoccupied by the compromise of their most secure communications, the diplomats were more interested in finding out exactly what the Finns—and their former allies, the Germans and the Japanese—knew about American ciphers than in discovering what the Finns knew about Russian ciphers. The State Department's reticence only increased when, on 30 October, Acting Secretary of State Edward Stettinius received from General Donovan a copy of a dispatch from the OSS station chief in Stockholm, Wilho Tikander, cautioning against a hasty acceptance of Colonel Hallamaa's proposal. In this communication, Tikander reported that Finland was subject to increasing Soviet pressure because of what Moscow considered insufficient compliance with the armistice agreement of September. One Soviet complaint was that alleged Finnish war criminals were escaping arrest and prosecution. Tikander indicated that Hallamaa, who was now advertising for sale two hundred boxes of Russian cipher materials, was likely to appear on a list of war criminals and that his approach to the United States might well be an effort to attach himself to a powerful protector. The station chief also warned that U.S.-Soviet relations would be hostage to Hallamaa should the Finnish colonel threaten to reveal his transactions with American intelligence. While conceding that if in the future "real differences" developed with the Soviet Union the cryptographic material "would undoubtedly be of great value," Tikander judged the political risks inherent in the situation sufficient to counsel against purchasing the material at that time, although the OSS officer left open the possibility of acquiring the collection "on some more propitious occasion."[42] That was enough for the State Department. On 1 November, after a meeting between State Department and OSS representatives, Acting Secretary of State Stettinius concluded that it would be "inadvisable and improper" for the United States to have any connection with the Russian files in the possession of the Finns, although the State Department indicated to OSS that it would have no objection to acquiring the Soviet cryptographic items "when the present dangers of detection or exposure were no longer present."[43] Reluctantly, Donovan acquiesced, cabling Tikander: "Do not now undertake to secure or indicate interest in any Russian material now in the hands of your Finnish friends. There are impelling political reasons for this prohibition which must under no circumstances be violated."[44]

With Donovan's acquiescence OSS/Stockholm narrowly interpreted the prohibition to apply only to Russian cryptographic materials. The station continued to accept from the Finns other forms of intelligence, most of which related to conditions in Finland, such as Helsinki's compliance with the September 1944 armistice terms and the state of the postarmistice Finnish armed forces, but some of which concerned the Soviet Union, such as the Red Army's order of battle on the eastern front. In early December, however, the issue of Moscow's ciphers reemerged. On or about 1 December, Wilho Tikander informed Washington that the Finns had renewed their offer of Russian cryptographic materials. Believing the situation urgent, Tikander flew to Washington to consult with his superiors. While the State Department dithered, OSS decided. On 11 December General Donovan, apparently acting on his own authority after discussions with his Stockholm station chief, approved a message directing the OSS station in Sweden "to accept delivery immediately of the materials previously rejected" in return for a payment of 250,000 Swedish kroner, then the equivalent of $62,500. The materials were to be delivered to Washington by courier after they had been copied in Stockholm. News of the deal with the Finns was to be withheld from the American embassy in Stockholm and the State Department in Washington.[45] The OSS director's unilateral decision may have been a response to additional information from Stockholm that the Swedes were about to purchase the Finnish files. Donovan, who saw a precious intelligence prize slipping through his fingers, seems to have believed that the prohibition insisted upon by the State

Department was temporary rather than permanent and would be lifted once the political climate was less charged or if circumstances changed, although his insistence on hiding the purchase from the diplomats suggests he was not entirely certain these conditions had been met.

Unfortunately for Donovan, the secret could not be contained. Somehow, the American embassy in Stockholm got wind of the affair. On 14 December, the ambassador, Herschel Johnson, informed the State Department that OSS representatives in Sweden had been instructed by their headquarters to purchase the Russian cipher materials offered by the Finns and inquired if the State Department had been consulted. Not surprisingly, the State Department did not take this news well. James Dunn, the political advisor to the secretary of state, went immediately to OSS headquarters, where he sternly reminded Colonel Edward Buxton, Donovan's deputy, of the State Department's opposition to involvement with the Finnish market in Russian ciphers. Refusing to be intimidated, Buxton coolly replied that General Donovan was so convinced of the importance of the matter that he was willing to assume full responsibility for authorizing the purchase and was perfectly prepared to justify his decision to the president. Returning to the State Department without satisfaction, Dunn passed the ball to his boss. Edward Stettinius, now secretary of state, went to the White House to appeal to President Roosevelt. Whatever his arguments, Stettinius carried the day. On 23 December the president ordered Donovan to deliver the purchased materials to the Russian ambassador in Washington, an undoubtedly awkward encounter that occurred on 15 February 1945.[46] Presumably, OSS retained copies.

Much about the STELLA POLARIS affair remains obscure, including the exact contents of the purchase, their distribution within the American intelligence community, and their contribution to developing an intelligence picture of the Soviet Union in 1945. In addressing the first of these issues, historians have been inclined to depend upon a memorandum from William Donovan to Franklin Roosevelt, dated 11 December 1944, in which the OSS director informed the president that "our chief representative in Stockholm was able to obtain three diplomatic codes and one military through special sources of the Turkish government. We have made the necessary payments and have just turned over these codes to the State Department and the War Department." At the same time, the memorandum continued, OSS had learned that the Axis had "tampered" with certain State Department codes.[47] Presumably, the reference to the compromise of American codes has encouraged these historians to assume that Donovan is referring to the deal with the Finns in Stockholm. There are, however, five serious problems with this assumption. The most obvious is that Donovan says the codes were purchased from the Turks, not the Finns. The OSS director would hardly lie to the president about the source of the codes when the State Department certainly, and the president probably, were fully acquainted with the discussions with the Finns. Second, the memorandum does not identify the nationality of the codes in question, so there is no necessity to conclude that Donovan was speaking about Russian cryptographic systems. Third, the Finns did not have three Soviet diplomatic codes to sell. When Finland joined Germany in attacking the USSR in June 1941, Finnish security forces had occupied the Soviet consulate in Petsamo, a town in northern Finland. Although the staff of the consulate tried to burn their codes and ciphers, the Finns recovered all or part of four codebooks, three of which were used by Russian intelligence officers stationed at the consulate, but one of which was a system used by the Russian foreign ministry to communicate with its consulates, that is, a diplomatic code.[48] This captured item was the only Russian diplomatic code in the Finnish bag of cryptologic treats. Indeed, in November 1944, when Colonel Hallamaa opened negotiations with the Americans in Stockholm, the normally boastful Finn had admitted that his cryptanalysts had found Soviet diplomatic codes and ciphers impossible to crack. Fourth, Donovan wrote his memo to Roosevelt on 11 December, the same day the cable went out authorizing OSS Stockholm to close the deal with the Finns. On 11 December OSS had not yet taken possession of the Finnish cache, but on that date not only had the codes referred to by Donovan in his memo to the president been purchased, but they had already been delivered to the State and War Departments. Lastly, one military and three diplomatic codes by themselves would not have filled the two hundred boxes of Russian cryptographic documents that Colonel Hallamaa offered to OSS. Clearly, Donovan's memo is referring not to STELLA POLARIS, but to an entirely separate transaction with the Turks.

The records of the National Security Agency, a postwar successor to the Signal Security Agency, contain a long list of Soviet codes, ciphers, and other cryptographic materials under the heading "STELLA POLARIS/Source 267." This list may well represent copies of the collection OSS purchased and then returned to the Soviet embassy in February 1945. It is, however, impossible to determine from the list when these items reached various members of the American intelligence community. The official historians of the early American communications intelligence programs against the Soviet Union maintain that during the war Arlington Hall never received any Russian cryptographic materials from the Office of Strategic Services.[49] The report of Arlington Hall's "Special Problems [Russian] Section" for the fiscal year 1944–1945 does not mention Finnish material, although it explicitly acknowledges the use of material from Japanese sources. If the code breakers had received product from the STELLA POLARIS group, the annual report probably would have said so. An internal history of OP-20-G's Russian section makes no reference at all to OSS or the Finns. It is more likely that the Finnish files eventually reached American code breakers not via OSS, but much later via London. "Source 267" was the designation British intelligence assigned to materials obtained from the STELLA POLARIS group when, probably in the fall of 1945, MI6 developed a relationship with the expatriate Finns. In the spring of 1946, more than a year after the deal between Hallamaa and OSS, the British code-breaking organization, the Government Communications Headquarters (GCHQ), gave the Signal Security Agency copies of all the Russian codebooks and cipher materials the British had obtained from the Finns.[50]

If, as seems almost certain, Arlington Hall did not receive the STELLA POLARIS records until after the war, the acquisition would have largely duplicated material already in the code breakers' hands. As allies of Germany, Finnish code breakers collaborated closely with their German counterparts, especially against Russian communications. Exchanges of intercepted messages, decryptions, cipher keys, and code identifications were full and frequent. As a result, much of the content of Colonel Hallamaa's files found its way into German files, where, in turn, they were discovered by one of the most secret Anglo-American intelligence operations of the war. In 1945 British and American intelligence authorities established the Target Intelligence Committee (TICOM), a highly classified program that dispatched Anglo-American teams into the collapsing Third Reich to locate and remove to Britain the remnants of Germany's communications intelligence organizations and their files. The principal purpose of the program was to determine whether the Germans had discovered weaknesses in Allied communications security, but secondarily London and Washington hoped to benefit from German cryptanalytic successes against the communications of other countries, including the Soviet Union. In May and June 1945 TICOM teams scooped up personnel, records, and technical equipment from the code-breaking units of the German foreign ministry and the armed services high command as well as specialized units serving the German Army, Navy, and Air Force. The captured files included cryptographic materials received by the Germans from their Axis partners, particularly the Finns. TICOM Teams 3 and 6, for example, between them scooped up copies of all the items captured by the Finns as a result of their seizure of the Russian consulate at Petsamo.[51] Referring to the STELLA POLARIS collection, the leading authorities on the early "Russian Problem" at Arlington Hall note, "TICOM had already obtained all of this and more in their sweep through the German Sigint [signals intelligence] centers."[52]

Whatever their origin, purchase or capture, foreign materials did little to advance the American effort against Russian ciphers *during* the war. The modest successes registered by the Signal Security Agency and OP-20-G against low-grade Red Army and Navy cryptosystems were made without benefit of the German or Finnish records. The continued classification of postwar American and British communications intelligence records makes it difficult to determine the impact of the foreign materials *after* the war. The Finns, with one exception whose case will be considered below, were an increasingly problematic asset. By the spring of 1945, OSS counterintelligence (X-2), which was the only section inside Donovan's organization that had access to communications intelligence, had learned from German decrypts that the United States was not Colonel Hallamaa's only customer. The wily Finn had been selling the same code-breaking secrets, including files on his organization's successful solution of American ciphers, to other bidders, such as Germany and Japan. The loyalties of the Finns were further suspect when, in August 1945, OSS learned that Colonel Hallamaa had secretly signed an agreement with the French intelligence service, the Service de Documentation Extérieure et de Contre-espionnage (SDECE), that provided for the remaining elements of the émigré Finnish intelligence organization to relocate to France and enter French service. By the end of the war, the remnants of the STELLA POLARIS group, now working for French intelligence, were seen less as an intelligence source and more as a counterintelligence problem.[53]

The TICOM program, particularly the interrogation of captured German cryptanalysts, contributed more directly to postwar American and British code-breaking programs against the Soviet Union. As we have seen in chapter 1, the close wartime collaboration between SSA and OP-20-G on the one hand and GCHQ on the other continued, almost seamlessly, into the postwar period as a result of a directive from President Harry Truman, who also authorized his intelligence managers to "extend, modify or discontinue this collaboration, as determined to be in the best interests of the United States."[54] This presidential directive gave the code breakers carte blanche to identify targets of opportunity or necessity in the postwar world, and there was no question that the Soviet Union would be the most important target. Obviously, information concerning the capabilities and intentions of the Soviet Union after the defeat of the Axis would be of vital concern to policy makers in Washington. The opaqueness of the regime in Moscow meant that clandestine programs would be a necessary instrument for obtaining such information. With the goal of "total intelligence" American communications intelligence services had long before abandoned any scruples about reading the messages of friendly governments. Furthermore, after the war Russia was the only significant power, with the exception of Great Britain, whose communications remained inaccessible, making the USSR the principal obstacle to the goal of total intelligence. The Soviet Union would have been a major postwar communications intelligence target whether it was friendly, hostile, or indifferent toward the United States. This priority was evident in the decision by American intelligence managers, in July 1945, to respond positively to British overtures concerning active collaboration against Russian communications.[55] This decision was made without reference to the White House or State Department. Although the two countries had cooperated closely during the war in attacks against the communications of many other governments, collaboration initially did not extend to operations against the Soviet Union, a target that American and British code breakers had attacked independently until the British overtures.

The joint exploitation of TICOM products was an early feature of the new partnership, and some of these products significantly advanced the effort against Moscow's codes and ciphers. Although German code breakers had had no success against high-grade Soviet diplomatic ciphers, they had cracked many systems used by the Red Army, Navy, and Air Force. American and British cryptanalysts could learn from the experiences and files of their German counterparts. On one occasion in late May 1945 captured personnel from a German army communications intelligence unit that specialized in intercepting high-level Russian radio teleprinter traffic led TICOM Team 1 to the site in Bavaria where they had buried their equipment before surrendering to the advancing Americans. Under the eyes of their American and British captors, the Germans not only excavated more than one hundred boxes of gear, but actually set up their receivers on the spot and demonstrated their use. As Lieutenant Paul Whitaker, an American member of TICOM 1, reported with amazement, "They were intercepting Russian traffic right while we were there. And pretty soon they had shown us all we needed to see."[56]

Since much of the Soviet Union's civil and military communications moved across radio teleprinter circuits, TICOM Team 1's discovery was potentially an intelligence windfall. The Germans and their equipment were moved to Britain, where their knowledge was assimilated into British communications intelligence units that during the war had worked German radio teleprinter traffic (code-named FISH) and whose radio receivers now scanned the airwaves for Russian transmissions. In late July 1945, two planeloads of the German equipment arrived in the United States, the first fruits of the understanding reached earlier that month to cooperate against Russian communications.[57] Soon American and British intercept folders bulged with Russian teleprinter messages. The intercepted Russian traffic, code-named CAVIAR, included plaintext (i.e., unenciphered) commercial and civilian messages and encrypted military communications. American and British classification guidelines continue to shroud the CAVIAR program in secrecy, so it is difficult to determine the exact scope and nature of the information collected by the operation. The degree to which code breakers were able to solve the encryption that protected the military traffic that moved across the radio teleprinter channels remains uncertain. From what little is known, the bulk of the messages intercepted would appear, to the untutored eye, rather mundane: "everything from people announcing the birthday of a grandson to Communist Party messages about collective farm production," recalled an American analyst.[58] For secret services desperate for hard information from inside the USSR and lacking other sources, even mundane messages were an intelligence bonanza. Patiently collating and comparing pieces of information, American and British analysts were able over time to establish the organizational structure of various departments of the Soviet administration, including the important Ministries of Internal Affairs (MVD) and State Security (MGB); the location of Red Army, Air Force, MVD, and MGB bases and facilities; the identities and ranks of leading personalities in the civil and military administration; and details concerning MGB managed construction projects and labor camps.[59]

CAVIAR was the first in a series of cryptanalytic successes that would propel communication intelligence to the forefront of Anglo-American intelligence operations against the Soviet Union. In the spring of 1946 U.S. army code breakers, now organized as the Army Security Agency (ASA) though still working at Arlington Hall, solved a cipher machine used by the Red Army in the Far Eastern territories of the USSR. Code-named SAUTERNE, this program provided valuable insights into Soviet military facilities, order of battle, training, and supply in the Far East. Just as the SAUTERNE intelligence product came on line, British cryptanalysts solved another military cipher machine, code-named COLERIDGE by the code breakers, which the Red Army employed in European regions of the Soviet Union. Used by the Russians mainly for administrative matters, COLERIDGE provided a trove of information concerning Red Army order of battle, training, and logistics in an area central to the concerns of American and British military planners. Within a year of its solution, an American intelligence officer described COLERIDGE's contribution to coverage of the Soviet Union as "the most important, high-level system from which current intelligence may be produced." At about the same time as COLERIDGE went into production, Anglo-American cryptanalysts made their first break into a third Russian army cipher machine, code-named LONGFELLOW, although production of usable intelligence from this system did not begin until the spring of 1947.[60]

The Anglo-American partnership also scored important successes against Red Navy and Air Force communications. By 1947 cryptanalysts had solved several cipher systems used by naval units in the Black and Baltic Seas as well as the Pacific. By this time American code breakers were reading the traffic of Red Air Force commands in the Far East, and in 1947 they would solve the cipher system used by Red Air Force headquarters in Moscow to communicate with its subordinate commands in the Soviet Union and Eastern Europe.[61]

In the early postwar period U.S. intelligence services had no other source that came close to providing the window on Soviet affairs that the code breakers did. For all its importance, however, the value of communications intelligence was relative. In the first months of peace the Army Security Agency and its naval counterpart, OP-20-G, were the only elements of the American intelligence community systematically collecting intelligence on the Soviet Union. It was easy to seem fruitful when no one else was producing anything. Furthermore, for all its very real successes, communications intelligence still fell far short of providing a comprehensive perspective on the USSR. The window provided by the code breakers provided American policy makers a view of one or two rooms of the Soviet house, but never the entire structure. Communications intelligence coverage of the Soviet Union was heavily weighted toward military affairs and within that area further weighted toward administrative, organizational, and logistical matters. Other areas of Soviet activity remained in darkness. Throughout the period under study, Moscow's diplomatic ciphers were not broken, and the communications of the Russian Ministry of Foreign Affairs were not read by U.S. intelligence. Neither, apparently, were the ciphers that protected the communications of Stalin and the Communist Party leadership. When President Harry Truman dealt with the Soviet leader at the Big Three conference at Potsdam (July–August 1945) or American diplomats engaged their Russian counterparts at the newly organized United Nations or at the conferences of foreign ministers at London (September 1945), Moscow (December 1945), and Paris (April–June 1946), communications intelligence gave the American side no special insight into Soviet diplomatic goals or negotiating strategies.[62]

Continuous access to the ciphers that were read was precarious. Once code breakers had cracked a system they could not sit back and from then on simply decrypt the messages as they were intercepted. Even solved cryptosystems needed to be worked continuously. Most modern ciphers use a key to guide the enciphering/deciphering process, and cryptanalysts must recover the current key before they can begin decryption. Similarly, operators would set the internal mechanisms of their cipher machines, such as gears or rotors, in a particular sequence before enciphering messages. Without knowledge of the setting the receiver of the message could not untangle the message even if possessing an example of the cipher machine. Since keys and settings could change daily and different users could use different keys and settings, the job of decryption was a constant effort to identify settings and recover keys before any messages could be read even after the cipher had been "solved." In this effort American cryptanalysts were constrained by lack of personnel as ASA and OP-20-G experienced the effects of postwar demobilization. By the end of 1945 Arlington Hall's Russian section had lost one-third of its personnel.[63] The experience of OP-20-G's Russian section was equally debilitating. Since its establishment in July 1943, the section had grown slowly but steadily—August 1943, 5 personnel; April 1944, 29 personnel; February 1945, 73 personnel—but growth had accelerated after Germany's surrender freed up intercept operators and cryptanalysts for deployment against other targets, and by September 1945 OP-20-G had 243 people assigned to the Russian target. With demobilization, however, the roster declined significantly—December 1945, 149 personnel; March 1946, 114 personnel; May 1946, 96 personnel. In July 1946, the navy's Russian section reached its postwar low of 76 staffers.[64] Well beyond the middle of 1946 the impact of staff reductions was a recurring lament in the operational diaries of units involved in the Russian program. The monthly report for May 1946 by a team of U.S. naval cryptanalysts stated, "The principal feature of May was the rapid loss of personnel. So many left or are soon to leave that it is difficult to continue functioning." The following month was no better. "The most obvious change in June was the decrease in personnel," the code breakers lamented, adding that "there were on 28 June just ten persons covering (thinly) the same problems for which we once had forty-three."[65] The staff reductions caused by demobilization were especially untimely because they occurred at the very time that bodies were needed to exploit the entries into the SAUTERNE, CAVIAR, COLERIDGE, and LONGFELLOW systems. Inevitably, intelligence production suffered. In August 1946, for example, the naval cryptanalysts running the American end of CAVIAR reported ruefully that they "put to bed" the program because "lack of personnel forces us to temporarily abandon this project."[66]

Potentially, the value of the Soviet decrypts was further limited by security restrictions concerning their dissemination. Continuing classification of almost all Cold War communications intelligence records makes it very difficult to determine how and when ASA and OP-20-G distributed intelligence to its customers in the U.S. government and what the content of that intelligence was. Arlington Hall certainly distributed no intelligence from its Russian program before Japan's surrender because decrypts in hand were deemed of no intelligence value. OP-20-G circulated its first brief intelligence summaries—based largely on decryptions of low-grade Russian coast guard and freighter communications—in July 1945, but the summaries went only to the Office of Naval Intelligence and the army's G-2. At the end of 1945 Arlington Hall began to circulate reports, code-named TANAGER, based not on decrypted messages, but on traffic analysis of Russian military communications—information culled not from the content of the messages but from their external attributes, such as the identity of the sender and receiver and the frequency and length of communications. Apparently the army code breakers did not begin to distribute summaries of Russian military activity based on actual decrypts of Red Army messages until June 1947, three years after Arlington Hall's first solution of a Red Army cipher.[67]

It is even more difficult to determine who the customers for Russian messages were. No programs in the repertoire of the U.S. intelligence community were more secretive than communication intelligence programs, whose products were routinely withheld by Arlington Hall even from other members of the community let alone other departments of the United States government. Neither the Office of Strategic Services nor the Strategic Services Unit, for example, had knowledge of U.S. code-breaking operations or access to the results of such operations.[68] During the war, the Magic Diplomatic Summary, a daily intelligence newsletter based on decryptions of Axis, Allied, and neutral diplomatic traffic, circulated to the president, the secretaries of state, war, and navy, the directors of army and navy intelligence, and the Joint Chiefs of Staff. Presumably, senior aides of these officials also saw these summaries. After the war, this instrument, now known simply as the "Diplomatic Summary," continued to appear, with the same or perhaps longer distribution list. Whoever received the postwar summary—and we can't be sure that those who received it actually read the newsletter—would have learned from it little about Soviet affairs. A review of the summaries from the period 1 September 1945–30 April 1946 reveals that Russian topics rarely appeared in the Diplomatic Summary. This is not surprising since American cryptanalysts were not reading Moscow's diplomatic traffic during this period, but Russian topics rarely appeared even indirectly through the decrypted messages of third-party governments—for example, France, Turkey, Spain—whose diplomatic messages were read.[69] Thus, the one instrument for disseminating communications intelligence that we know went to the White House and the Departments of State, War, and Navy carried very little information on the Soviet Union well into the spring of 1946. Of course there may have been other instruments that have not yet emerged from the secrecy that, even today, surrounds the communication intelligence programs of the early Cold War, but it is unlikely that any such instruments would have carried much of interest until the spring of 1946, when the products of SAUTERNE, CAVIAR, and COLERIDGE first came online in any significant quantities.

The Primary Object of Concern

That communications intelligence, for all its limitations, was the best source of information on the Soviet Union in the first year of peace is testimony not to the superiority of these collection programs, but to the absence of alternative sources of information. The paucity of sources reflects, in large part, a paucity of interest and effort. Despite the claims by some historians that even before Germany's surrender American intelligence services were assiduously collecting information about the Soviet Union in what amounted to the opening salvos of the Cold War, these clandestine services turned surprisingly late toward the Russian target. As we shall see in later chapters, OSS and SSU stations in Europe, distracted by other priorities, did not seriously direct their attention toward the Soviet Union until late 1945, and the USSR did not become the first priority of the Strategic Services Unit until the spring of 1946. On VE Day the Office of Strategic Services had no element or unit responsible for collecting intelligence on the USSR, and it still had no such unit when it closed up shop on 30 September 1945. One OSS veteran familiar with the state of American coverage of Russia in the immediate postwar period recalled that "OSS probably didn't have one drawer of one file cabinet worth of clandestine intelligence on Soviet stuff."[70] Under the Strategic Services Unit the situation changed, though slowly. By February 1946 the Soviet Union was deemed worthy of a desk at Washington headquarters, albeit one in a section also responsible for Poland and all of Scandinavia. Even with a designated desk officer, the USSR still generated little operational energy. Another veteran of postwar Soviet operations noticed that when he reported for duty at SSU headquarters in March 1946 no one was very interested in the Soviet Union. Operational focus remained largely on the war and its aftermath: war criminals, SS and Gestapo fugitives, German scientists, Nazi assets. "Moscow was a distant prospect," this officer recalled. "Suspicion at the top in Washington had not yet hardened into hostility. No directives were coming down on Soviet requirements."[71] Apparently some officers were concerned by the lack of attention toward a great power about which little was known. In mid–March 1946, one such officer circulated in headquarters an "open memorandum" on the subject of intelligence coverage of the Soviet Union. Referring to a pervasive inclination inside SSU to avoid the issue of collection operations against Russia even when other government departments were begging for information about this target, the author complained that SSU only "casually" directed its foreign stations to report Russian items and that it had not established any units or machinery to conceive and direct specific operations. Russian materials received no special handling, and there was no effort to analyze the materials in order to prepare further directives to the field. The author closed his memorandum by recommending that "P" Branch, the headquarters element responsible for determining intelligence targets, identify clear objectives and priorities for Russian collection and that managers establish a separate Russian section to run expanded Soviet operations.[72] This memorandum with its appeal for someone in SSU to start paying attention to the USSR certainly does not reveal an intelligence effort single-minded and relentless in its obsession with the Soviet menace.

Apparently the author of the "open memorandum" was adept at reading the signs of the times because within a week of his appeal to focus attention on the Soviet Union, the Strategic Services Unit decided to do just that. It probably would have acted even without a chastising note from a presumptuous junior officer. As we shall see in later chapters, by the spring of 1946 SSU headquarters was receiving from its European stations an increasingly alarming flow of reports that raised suspicions concerning Moscow's intentions on a range of issues from the reconstruction of postwar governments in Eastern Europe to the demilitarization of German industry. These reports were evaluated against a backdrop of events that further fueled alarm in Washington. These events are well known to historians who have marked them as milestones on the road to the Cold War.

On 9 February 1946, in a speech that seemed to reaffirm the necessity of ideological warfare, Josef Stalin asserted the absolute incompatibility of capitalism and communism and implied that future wars were inevitable until communism replaced capitalism on the world scene. In Washington, most informed observers interpreted the Soviet leader's words as a rejection of peaceful coexistence and a call to extend communist ideology. Supreme Court Justice William O. Douglas captured the common reaction when he commented to Secretary of the Navy James Forrestal that Stalin's speech marked "the Declaration of World War III."[73] A week after Stalin's remarks, news broke of the arrest in Canada of twenty-two individuals charged with spying for the Soviet Union. Since most of those arrested were seeking the secrets of the atomic bomb program, the impression was that the Russians were threatening America's vital national security programs for their own nefarious purposes and that they were using local communists or communist sympathizers in those programs to advance those purposes. The following week the State Department received a long telegram from George Kennan, the chargé d'affaires in the U.S. embassy in Moscow, in which the experienced American diplomat reported that the Soviets, rejecting the possibility of coexistence between the capitalist and communist worlds, would work relentlessly in the postwar period to strengthen the communist camp, particularly the power of the Soviet Union, while weakening the capitalist powers. Since the theme of capitalist hostility and encirclement justified their totalitarian rule, Stalin and his associates would be unmoved by gestures of conciliation or accommodation, but they could be influenced by the threat of force.[74] On March 5, in a speech at Westminster College in Fulton, Missouri, Winston Churchill, by then a cultural icon of fortitude and foresight, echoed Kennan's view of the Soviet Union as a totalitarian, expansionist power by referring to an "iron curtain" that divided Europe from the Baltic to the Adriatic Seas, behind which curtain Moscow was intent upon extending its power through client governments established by ruthless and undemocratic means.[75]

Churchill's rhetorical flourishes, as well as those of Stalin and Kennan, could not easily be dismissed when Soviet actions seemingly gave them credence. In a case of uncanny coincidence, on the same day that Churchill appeared at Westminster College, Soviet armored columns appeared on the roads leading to Teheran, the capital of Iran. Under interallied agreements during the recent war American, British, and Russian troops had occupied portions of Iran to ensure the security of oil fields and Lend-Lease transit routes into the Soviet Union. The Soviet Union, however, did not honor the agreement to withdraw all foreign forces by 2 March 1946, retaining forces in the region of Azerbaijan where they facilitated the creation of a pro-Soviet "autonomous government," perhaps in preparation for the region's incorporation into the USSR. On March 5 the American consulate in Tabriz, the principal city of Azerbaijan, reported that Red Army units were moving south into Iran proper. In conjunction with reported Red Army concentrations in the Balkans as Moscow pressured Turkey for major political and territorial concessions before renewing an earlier treaty of friendship and neutrality, the Russian troop movements in northern Iran suggested to observers in Washington that Stalin was intent upon using military force to extend Soviet influence.[76] Although both the Turkish and Iranian crises were settled without conflict, the experience elevated the Soviet Union to the top of everyone's threat list.

On 25 March 1946, William Maddox, the chief of P branch, alerted Whitney Shepardson, the chief of the secret intelligence branch (SI), the office responsible for running clandestine collection operations, to the new priorities. Maddox opened his directive with a rationale for the new emphases:

An estimate of the prevailing world situation leads inevitably to the conclusion that the primary object of national concern in the foreign sphere arises today and in the foreseeable future from the activities of the Soviet Union, and of other governments and political organizations which tend to assist in the fulfillment of its purposes. No other threat to our national security and interests, or to the international legal order which we are committed to uphold, approaches in dimension or in imminence that which is latent in the policies and actions of the USSR and its assorted allies.[77]

Revealing a concern that the Strategic Services Unit was still insufficiently concerned with the Soviet threat, Maddox insisted that the organization's resources must now be directed "with unequivocal emphasis" toward the Soviet Union and that this new priority "needs to be repeated again and again" for the benefit of SSU's clandestine operators in the foreign stations, lest they allow their attention to shift toward other targets. After rather condescendingly reminding the chief of secret intelligence that the capabilities and intentions of a totalitarian dictatorship are best revealed at the seat of that government, in this case Moscow, the P branch director then glibly enjoined Shepardson to accelerate "the solution of the operational problems involved" in penetrating leadership circles in the Russian capital. In the meantime, Maddox suggested helpfully, SI might pursue opportunities to observe Russian capabilities and intentions through operations along the periphery of the Soviet Union.[78]

Spies, Defectors, and Émigrés

Whitney Shepardson, who had run clandestine intelligence operations against Hitler's Germany, did not need to be reminded of the "operational problems involved" in spying on leadership circles in a dictatorship. In the case of the Soviet Union the problems were especially formidable. By the summer of 1946, fully three months after the Soviet Union became the priority target, the Strategic Services Unit still had only four general sources, aside from open sources such as the Russian press, purporting to provide information from inside the USSR: (1) refugees, POWs, and defectors, (2) anti-Soviet émigré organizations, (3) recruited informants, and (4) foreign liaison. These four sources were already available at the time that P branch elevated the Soviet Union to the highest priority. Since P branch's directive, SI had struggled to expand its collection net, with recruited agents proving particularly elusive.[79]

The sources were of uneven quality. The least reliable were the émigré organizations composed of anti-Soviet "White Russians" (as opposed to "Red" Russians) who had fled their homeland after the Bolshevik Revolution or the Russian Civil War. Many of these émigrés had gravitated to France, where they became a special interest of SSU's Paris station. Although most had not stepped foot inside the Soviet Union for twenty years, they purported to maintain close, though necessarily secret even from their

American friends, connections with their home country, which alleged connections produced a steady stream of reports on political and economic conditions inside Russia, the morale and dispositions of the Red Army, and the strength of anticommunist resistance in the Soviet Union. "Virtually no value" was the judgment of SSU headquarters on such reports, which were deeply colored by the anti-Soviet biases of the émigrés and which contained "virtually no factual information" on any subject of interest to American intelligence, such as Soviet industrial and agricultural production.[80] The testimony of defectors, deserters, refugees, and returning prisoners of war was marginally more useful, but by the summer of 1946 the number of such individuals arriving from the east with recent experiences and fresh observations was declining. Defectors were very few in the first year of peace, scarcely more than a couple, and their motives and authenticity were always suspect. One such individual was Wadim Denisoff, who claimed to have served as an intelligence officer in the Red Navy before defecting to Germany at the onset of the German invasion of the Soviet Union and then, after VE Day, offering his services to the United States. Denisoff offered information on the organization and operations of Russian naval intelligence, at least as these subjects appeared before June 1941. An evaluation of his testimony noted that "he is cooperative, but he is obviously trying to play up his own importance in order to better his position."[81] A second case involved an engineer who commanded a Soviet technical survey team in occupied Austria that was, among other things, concerned with locating and recruiting Austrian scientists for atomic research in Russia. A Jew, he contacted SSU through Austrian relatives with a view to emigrating to Palestine. The would-be defector offered to provide general information about life in the Soviet Union, but declined to reveal anything about his work in Austria from fear of being labeled a traitor. Convinced still that the engineer possessed useful information—after all, Russian defectors were not knocking on American doors every day—the Vienna station made arrangements to evacuate him to Rome for debriefing before moving him on to Palestine. Headquarters, however, canceled the project from a concern that the engineer was a false defector and part of a Soviet ruse to penetrate American intelligence or embarrass the United States.[82] Deserters from the Red Army appeared in greater numbers and represented a potentially useful source on Russian military affairs, particularly order-of-battle topics. Surprisingly, it appears that, at least in the first year of peace, the worth of these Russian soldiers was underappreciated by some elements of the U.S. government. As late as June 1946, three months after SSU had made the USSR the priority target, the U.S. Army's Counterintelligence Corps complained that American military police and border control units in occupied Austria and Germany were picking up Red Army deserters and returning them to Russian authorities without any effort to extract useful information from them.[83]

By the summer of 1946 the Strategic Services Unit was directly running only three agents with credible claims of access to information from within the USSR. Only one was Russian. The first, known only as the "Regular Polish Source," was an agent of the counterintelligence unit of SSU's Stockholm station. Rather surprisingly, this unit ran its source so secretly that SSU headquarters in Washington knew almost nothing about him beyond the hint that he was using surviving networks of the wartime Polish intelligence service. From this source SSU Stockholm had received information concerning military districts inside the USSR and maps of airfields in Russian-controlled Latvia.[84] The second agent was a former Finnish naval intelligence officer, Jukka Mäkelä, who had fled to Sweden with the STELLA POLARIS group. Code-named MAKI, this officer, who was married to an American, had volunteered his services to the OSS station in Stockholm in March 1945 in the hope of relocation to the United States and a job with U.S. naval intelligence. In pursuit of this dream—concerning which his OSS handlers remained noncommittal—Mäkelä provided copies of documents from the extensive intelligence files brought to Sweden by the STELLA POLARIS group. Many of these documents concerned Soviet matters, particularly the dispositions of the Red Navy's Baltic fleet, a subject on which the Finnish officer was an expert. This source temporarily dried up when Mäkelä, disappointed that he had not been offered a job with American naval intelligence in Washington, decided to cast his lot with the group of Finns who entered French service in August 1945. One authority on STELLA POLARIS has argued that MAKI continued to serve American interests after his departure for France by leaving behind in Stockholm a trove of documents concerning the Soviet Union from Finnish intelligence archives. This claim in unconvincing since some of the documents in question, such as the order of battle of the Red Baltic Fleet in November 1945, could not have been left behind for American intelligence since their information postdates Mäkelä's departure for France.[85] It is more likely that a foreign intelligence service, probably the Swedish, provided these materials. Fortunately for American intelligence, SSU reestablished contact with MAKI in Paris in February 1946, and the Finn, forgetting his earlier disillusionment, returned to American service. This time around, SSU, by then aware that the Finns had shopped their intelligence, including their knowledge of American ciphers, to any number of customers and concerned that the remnants of Colonel Hallamaa's organization had been penetrated by Russian intelligence, considered the STELLA POLARIS group a target in its own right. Now reporting to SSU's counterintelligence officers, Mäkelä provided inside information concerning his colleagues' work for SDECE, the French foreign intelligence service, and Anglo-French collaboration on various Soviet operations, activities London and Paris had intended to keep secret from Washington. MAKI also passed along Russian items collected by SDECE or copied from the STELLA PO-LARIS files that Colonel Hallamaa had brought from Sweden to France, although by the spring of 1946 the most marketable materials from this archive had been shopped to any number of intelligence services, and what remained in a collection that left Finland in September 1944 was increasingly of mainly historical interest.[86] It is testimony to how empty of Soviet product U.S. intelligence shelves were that SSU was thrilled to receive from their Finnish agent in February 1946 a list of Russian admirals that Mäkelä had compiled before Finland's surrender and a list, also compiled before the surrender, of Russian military radio call signs.[87] Since Finland had signed an armistice with the Soviet Union in September 1944, these lists were at least seventeen months old—hardly current intelligence.

The third unilateral source, and the only Russian, was both the most promising and the most problematic. In early 1946 an individual claiming to be an officer in the Soviet army contacted American military intelligence in Berlin through a Russian émigré, Michael Tscherbinine, who held a minor post in the local office of the U.S. Army's criminal investigation service. Army intelligence, apparently unsure as to how to handle the Russians on its doorstep, sent Tscherbinine and his friend to tell their story to the Berlin station of the Strategic Services Unit. It was quite a story. To the astonishment of his American listeners, the Soviet officer announced that he was the representative of a clandestine group of anticommunist officers in the Red Army. Known as the "Freedom Loving Folk" (FLF), this group, which included generals, was centered in Moscow but had cells in Leningrad, Odessa, Kiev, and Tiflis as well as outposts in Bulgaria, Czechoslovakia, and Yugoslavia. The FLF had decided to contact the United States and offer their collaboration in an effort to undermine the Stalinist regime. Several officers had been sent into Western Europe to establish contact, but they never returned and were never heard from again. The surprise visitor announced that he had been sent to Berlin by the FLF with an offer of services. In return for financial support and the clandestine evacuation of some of it members to the United States, where they would work with SSU headquarters to plan operations against the USSR, the organization would put its resources at the disposal of American intelligence to collect political, military, and economic information inside the Soviet Union.[88]

The Russian officer, now code-named LONDONDERRY, next surfaces in April 1946, when for reasons unknown (the available records are fragmentary and unclear about the chronology and much else concerning this operation), he has become an agent of the SSU mission in Vienna, which gave him cash for operational expenses—$23,000 in the first six months—and furnished a private villa, complete with document forging facilities, for his use when he visited the Austrian capital. LONDONDERRY's appearance was a godsend to SSU/Vienna. All things Russian were the new priorities, and in the spring of 1946 the station was under increasing pressure from the U.S. Army to provide accurate intelligence concerning Red Army and Air Force strengths and dispositions not only in the Russian occupation zone in Austria but also in Czechoslovakia and Hungary. At the same time the station's efforts to collect intelligence in those areas were not prospering, and it was compelled to inform Washington that the flow of information from the east, never very strong, was drying up.[89] Vienna immediately directed LONDONDERRY to mobilize the clandestine organization he represented, now designated the PAREGORIC network, to focus on Red Army and Air Force order-of-battle intelligence. PAREGORIC came through with flying colors. Within two weeks of launching the new operation, Alfred Ulmer, the chief of secret intelligence in Vienna, was ecstatic. "We have received more good, reliable Lambda [Russian] intelligence from Londonderry in the last fourteen days than we have from all other sources in the last ten months," Ulmer informed Colonel William Quinn, the SSU director, on 22 April, describing his new source as "by far the most important acquisition of this organization I have seen since the war ended."[90] And the best was yet to come. By July SSU was anticipating that well-placed PAREGORIC elements would very soon "report on more or less high-level personalities and activities in the military headquarters departments in Moscow."[91] It all seemed too good to be true.

For some in the Strategic Services Unit, it *was* too good to be true. While the Vienna office swooned over their new agent (who was now designated LISTER), SSU's Berlin Operations Base (BOB) worried. There was, for one thing, the matter of LISTER's backstory. In his early contacts with American intelligence the Russian officer had said that the Freedom Loving Folk had been active inside the Soviet Union since 1937, but in later conversations in Berlin, to which he had been sent by Vienna station on a special mission, he said that the organization had been established in 1944. Also, the agent had earlier described the FLF as a centralized organization with a clandestine chain of command, but in later testimony he downplayed the degree of organization, maintaining that the group was held together by common ideas and goals rather than a central command structure.

Then there was the matter of LISTER's curious operational behavior. In September 1946, he had arrived in Berlin, traveling with forged Soviet travel documents prepared by SSU/Vienna, on a mission to contact three associates from the PAREGORIC group. To communicate with Berlin Base the agent would meet a "cutout" or third party—"will have a newspaper visible in left coat pocket"—at one of Berlin's commuter train stations and identify himself with an agreed-upon recognition phrase. The meeting did not go well. LISTER announced that he required new travel documents because the travel papers prepared by Vienna were completely unsatisfactory, although apparently he had found them acceptable when he received them in Austria. When asked by the cutout about the plan to contact three associates in Berlin, the Russian retorted that he probably could not identify one, let alone, three friends in the former German capital, and that anyway he had decided unilaterally to change the plan. He now intended to visit the headquarters of the Soviet Military Administration for Germany located in the Berlin neighborhood of Karlshorst, where he would determine the current organizational arrangements and procure as many recent documents as he could. Having earlier offered SSU the facilities of his organization to establish espionage networks in Czechoslovakia, LISTER now asked the cutout if American intelligence had agent nets inside Poland, and assured him that the PAREGORIC group could set up such a network if one was needed. If accepted—apparently they were not—these offers would have allowed FLF to control much of the intelligence coming from Czechoslovakia and Poland. After his meeting with SSU's cutout, LISTER, apparently no longer concerned about the mortal danger to which he was allegedly exposed by poorly forged identity and travel documents, was observed entering Red Army headquarters at Karlshorst and then departing, in civilian clothes, in a Red Army staff car with a Red Army driver.[92]

Finally, there was the matter of the intelligence LISTER was passing to his American controllers. At first glance the information was rich, but it seemed so mainly in comparison to the scanty intelligence available before the Russian officer appeared on the doorstep. Something, after all, is always better than nothing. The intelligence was also narrowly focused on the dispositions of the Red Army in the Soviet zone of Austria. While order-of-battle information was always welcome, especially by the U.S. army, what the Strategic Services Unit was after was strategic political, military, and economic information from the heart of Stalin's regime. The PAREGORIC network held out the promise of such intelligence, but the source was slow in achieving that promise. Ultimately, SSU hoped to deal directly with the organization's core leadership, referred to as "GHQ," but contact with that leadership proved elusive. LISTER, for example, claimed that he could not provide details of FLF's organization and membership without the permission of its top leaders, code-named variously PASTEUR and OLDSTERS by the Americans, but whenever the Russian officer returned to FLF's clandestine headquarters, those leaders were always unaccountably absent.

While complaining that "GHQ itself has not paid off" and acknowledging the possibility that the claims of LISTER might be "smoke," SSU/Austria advised Washington to be patient since it could take months, even years, to build a secure and effective espionage net. SSU/Germany, however, was less sanguine. Berlin Base now suspected that Michael Tscherbinine, the individual who had introduced LISTER to U.S. intelligence, was a Russian agent, and BOB suggested to Washington that LISTER might be part of a Russian disinformation operation. Without the declassification of the entire LISTER/PAREGORIC file—available documentation ends in the late summer of 1946—it is impossible to know with certainty if Berlin's suspicions were correct, but circumstantial evidence suggests they were. Beyond LISTER's claims, no evidence has ever surfaced of an anti-Soviet resistance organization active in the 1940s and centered on the Red Army's officer corps with cells in major Russian cities and including generals among its membership. Given the efficiency of Stalin's security apparatus, the very idea is preposterous. The operation, moreover, bears an uncanny similarity to known cases of Soviet deception and disinformation. In 1921, in a five-year operation that came to be known as "The Trust," an agent of the Soviet intelligence service, the OGPU, arrived in Paris posing as an emissary of an anti-Bolshevik underground movement inside the Soviet Union called the Monarchist Organization of Central Russia. Trafficking in false intelligence, this organization—wholly the brainchild of Soviet intelligence—attracted the attention and sometimes the support not only of anti-Bolshevik émigré associations in Western Europe but also of the intelligence services of Britain, France, Finland, Poland, and the Baltic States.[93] After World War II, the Soviet services would launch several deception operations that lured Western intelligence services into supporting notional resistance groups in the Baltic States and Poland. The most famous such deception was the "WiN" affair in which, in 1949, the secret service of communist Poland, guided by its Soviet mentors, sent to the West an agent purporting to represent "Freedom and Independence," an anticommunist resistance movement in Poland known by its acronym WiN. The real WiN had been wiped out by communist security forces by 1947, but the resurrected organization, wholly controlled by the Polish and Soviet services, attracted the support of Western intelligence agencies, particularly the Central Intelligence Agency, the successor to SSU, which poured millions of dollars into supporting a notional resistance organization.[94]

The parallels between PAREGORIC and other known Soviet deception operations—the unannounced emissary, the large but previously unnoticed resistance organization inside the USSR, a shadowy leadership that could never be tied down, the promise of high-level intelligence from inside the

Soviet empire—are hard to ignore. If PAREGORIC was indeed the operational cousin of the Trust and WiN, then it was probably the most serious American intelligence debacle of the early Cold War.

A Little Help from Friends

By the summer of 1946 the Strategic Services Unit's most prolific source of information on the Soviet Union was neither refugees, nor émigrés, nor controlled agents, but rather liaison with friendly intelligence services. Much of the information SSU received about Russia was collected by someone else. As we have seen, the wartime Office of Strategic Services had developed during the war cooperative relationships with the intelligence services of many European governments, including those temporarily in exile in the United Kingdom. The Strategic Services Unit inherited these relationships and actively cultivated them in the early postwar period. At the time SSU was not the only service seeking to penetrate the Soviet Union, and rather quickly these other services discovered the benefits of collaboration with the United States.

Within a month of Germany's surrender the Direction Générale des Etudes et Recherches (DGER), the French foreign intelligence service, had approached the Paris station of the Office of Strategic Services about sharing information concerning the Soviet Union and Soviet-occupied areas of Europe as well as information regarding German and Austrian territories occupied by American and French troops. Although Philip Horton, the chief of station, believed that the two services had reached an agreement only in principle, the French promptly began passing Russian items to their American friends. Horton sent this material to the OSS mission in Germany, where he assumed they were directed to the unit's "Russian Section" for dissemination to its customers in the U.S. occupation authority.[95] The OSS chief in Paris, however, seriously misunderstood the state of his service's organization in the former Third Reich. The personnel for OSS/Germany did not arrive in the country until June 7, just days before Horton began receiving information from the DGER. As we shall see (chapter 3), OSS/Germany took some time to find their operational footing, and when they did the Soviet Union was not an immediate priority. In June 1945, OSS/Germany had no Russian desk and no Russian operations, and it wouldn't have either for some time. Given these circumstances, it is likely that the DGER reports on the USSR forwarded by Philip Horton to OSS/Germany in the summer of 1945 circulated no further than a file cabinet in the mission's headquarters in Wiesbaden.

Initially, the arrangement with the DGER was rather one-sided. Horton was prepared to select items concerning Russia, as they came in to OSS/ France, for transmittal to the French, but such items were not exactly thick on the ground. The DGER continued to press for more active collaboration. In a series of meetings in August 1945 the French service's Russian section shared with Philip Horton some of their operational plans concerning the Soviet Union. The French intended to focus their long-term collection efforts on Russia's military preparedness and war potential, particularly industrial capacity, transportation networks, and Red Army dispositions. Political intelligence would be a secondary concern. In attacking these targets, French intelligence would rely little on traditional espionage. The DGER estimated that 95 percent of their agents in Russia and Russian-occupied areas were double agents working for the Russians, and the French suspected that the same was true of the agent networks of other secret services. The DGER, instead, intended to invest heavily in communications intelligence, which allegedly had already paid dividends in terms of intercepted Russian messages. The French pressed the OSS representative in Paris for an outline of American operational planning concerning the Soviet Union and suggested an exchange of communications intelligence material. Throughout these conversations Horton remained noncommittal and declined to discuss OSS plans for Russia, mainly because he was unaware of any such plans.[96]

Undeterred by the lack of reciprocity, the DGER continued to pass Russian material to OSS, and after that organization's demise, to SSU. The largesse, however, was not complete. The French, who were also collaborating on Russian operations with Britain's Secret Intelligence Service, withheld from the Americans some of the product of their collection efforts as well as the extent of their cooperation with the British. Fortunately, OSS had developed a back-channel connection to the head of the DGER's Russian desk, and by August 1945 this officer, perhaps because of his pro-American attitudes or perhaps because of an intrigue in the internecine warfare that afflicted the French intelligence services, was passing reports to American intelligence outside of normal liaison channels.[97] Code-named HAMPSHIRE/ BARTON, this material included the product of French communications intelligence operations against the Soviet Union. Philip Horton had predicted that HAMPSHIRE/BARTON would become a significant source of information on Soviet affairs, but early enthusiasm soon waned. On 15 October 1945, SSU notified its station chief in Paris that headquarters' opinion concerning the accuracy of the material was "quite unfavorable." By the summer of 1946 skepticism about French operations against the Soviet target was pervasive; one evaluation dismissed such efforts as "almost worthless."[98] With the integrity of their best French source on the Soviet Union under question, SSU adopted an increasingly reserved attitude toward the French service and turned to more reliable partners.

During the war, no liaison relationship had been closer than that with the British intelligence services, and after the war London was concerned to maintain that relationship particularly in the area of Russian affairs. As we have seen, in the summer of 1945 British code breakers at the Government Communications Headquarters had approached their American counterparts at the Army Security Agency about cooperating against Soviet communications, and the Secret Intelligence Service was not far behind in contacting OSS. By mid-August 1945 Philip Horton had had several conversations in Paris with Commander Wilfred "Biffy" Dunderdale, a legendary SIS officer who at the time ran a shadowy organization known as the Special Liaison Center (SLC). Dunderdale was primarily interested in discussing Russia. While insisting that official conversations with OSS were unlikely until the postwar status of the American service was clarified, the British officer made it clear to Horton that SIS considered cooperation against Soviet intelligence targets as both possible and desirable. At their meetings in the summer of 1945 Dunderdale explained his belief that traditional agent networks would not work against the Soviet target and that collection would have to focus on technical means, such as communications intelligence. He also tried to elicit from Horton some idea of the quantity and quality of Russian materials collected by OSS. Wild Bill Donovan's representative in Paris may have found it curious that the SIS officer's appraisal of viable collection methods against the Soviet Union echoed appraisals he was concurrently hearing from French intelligence officers—unbeknownst to Horton the British and French were already cooperating against Russian targets and keeping that cooperation from the Americans—but whatever his curiosity, he remained prudently noncommittal and deflected Dunderdale's inquiries about U.S. intelligence plans concerning the Soviet Union without admitting that he was not aware of any such plans.[99]

The head of the Special Liaison Center insisted that until SSU's future was on a firm footing, Anglo-American exchanges of information in Paris would have to remain unofficial and "under the table," but no such concern constrained SLC's parent organization in London.[100] By the end of 1945 the Secret Intelligence Service was passing to the SSU station in London significant amounts of information in four general categories. Under the designation BULKINGTON, the British provided economic reports from around the world. A second series, code-named COVENTRY, contained political reports concerning various European countries. These reports were considered so sensitive, probably because of their source(s), that SIS placed stringent restrictions on their circulation. SSU was specifically enjoined from disseminating COVENTRY intelligence to other departments of the U.S. government. HARBURY designated a special series on Russian topics based on all-source reporting, including press and open radio broadcasts. Under the designator HARTSHILL, SSU received from its British counterpart reports on political and economic activity in specific countries. Both HAR-BURY and HARTSHILL reports were highly classified, although not at the level of the COVENTRY material.[101]

One prominent student of early Cold War intelligence, noting that in December 1945 SSU's London station had seventy-three staffers and that these personnel were processing an increasing number of reports from SIS, particularly Russian items, has argued that the British service and its shared reporting practically propped up SSU as it struggled to maintain its organizational existence in late 1945.[102] There can be little doubt that SIS was an important helpmate for U.S. intelligence, especially in the transition from OSS to SSU when American collection programs were weak; indeed, well into 1946 the relationship was decidedly one-sided, with SSU/London acknowledging that the American contribution to the relationship remained "relatively small."[103] It is possible, however, to exaggerate the impact of this liaison relationship upon American collection efforts, particularly those targeted against the Soviet Union. The seventy-three individuals working in SSU's London office in December 1945 represented a declining work force that was a mere remnant of wartime force levels. By February 1946 the station's staff had been reduced to "a purely holding minimum," and by the following month an additional sixteen staffers had departed, allowing the station to vacate an entire floor of its premises at 71 Grosvenor Square and return seven truckloads of furnishings to U.S. Army warehouses. Only one of the remaining officers handled liaison with SIS, although this individual was assisted by five support staff.[104] If the size of the SSU station was an indicator of the importance of the liaison relationship—it wasn't—then that relationship was waning rather than waxing in early 1946.

Most of the material passed by SIS to its American friends—one survey by SSU estimated more than 90 percent of the total—came not from clandestine sources but from open sources such as newspapers and open radio broadcasts.[105] Russian topics, furthermore, were numerous but not predominant in the early Anglo-American exchanges. In February 1946, for example, HARBURY reports, the series devoted exclusively to Soviet matters, represented less than half (42%) of the reports passed by SIS to SSU, and most of these dealt with Russian activities in Poland rather than political, military, or economic affairs inside the Soviet Union. That month none of the top-grade COVENTRY reports—the most sensitive materials shared with the Americans—dealt directly with the USSR (code-named LAMBDA), although a handful of COVENTRY items from Austria might have concerned the Soviet zone of occupation.[106]

Whatever their subject, British intelligence reports could have had little impact in Washington if no one was reading them. When accepting material from SIS, the Strategic Services Unit conscientiously applied the security restrictions insisted upon by the British service, with the result that in the first months of peace, the best of that material never left SSU's offices. Only in early December 1945 did General John Magruder, perhaps acting without the knowledge of SIS, inform the chiefs of army, air corps, and navy intelligence that SSU received through British liaison highly sensitive intelligence reports designated COVENTRY. The SSU director explained that due to an understanding with London this material had hitherto not been circulated outside of SSU, but he now wondered if the three military intelligence chiefs might be interested in reading some of the more interesting COVENTRY reports. Since the material was too sensitive for inclusion in interdepartmental mail, messengers would deliver the reports, none of which could be placed in regular department files.[107] Whatever the reaction in London to Magruder's decision to share British secrets with other American intelligence authorities, the reaction of those authorities was immediate. The chief of army intelligence, General Clayton Bissell, promptly informed Secretary of War Robert Patterson, Magruder's superior, that SSU had been withholding important intelligence from other departments of the U.S. government that required such information to perform their responsibilities. In a curt missive ordering Magruder to furnish army intelligence "any and all" information received by SSU from *any* source, on 18 December Patterson reminded the SSU director that General Bissell was responsible for keeping the secretary of war, the army staff, and various military commands completely informed of the international situation and that by keeping information to itself SSU was compromising the ability of army intelligence to perform its duty.[108] General Magruder did not require further direction; the next day he sent a packet of COVENTRY reports to General Bissell. Hoping to mend fences and knowing that army intelligence would be interested in any material concerning the Soviet military, the SSU director prudently included in this first delivery a file of British reports on the Red Army. By April 1946 the circulation list for COVENTRY reports had been lengthened to include the secretary of state and the director of the Central Intelligence Group.[109]

Though no substitute for the British connection, liaison with the espionage services of smaller European powers proved a useful source of information, particularly regarding the Soviet Union, in the early postwar period. Forced by limited resources to focus their collection efforts, such services often developed good coverage of particular regions, such as the Baltic or the Balkans, where American capabilities were limited. By associating with larger and richer intelligence organizations, the smaller national services extended their own reach and gained access to resources in material, technology, and communications that improved their operational capabilities. During the war OSS had established cooperative relationships with more than a dozen foreign services, and these connections continued to pay dividends after the defeat of the Axis. As early as November 1944, by which time Italy had abandoned Germany and realigned itself with the Allied powers, the Italian military intelligence service had offered, in return for a financial subsidy, to place its clandestine networks in Bulgaria at the service of OSS, an offer that would have been hard to refuse when the Red Army, upon occupying Bulgaria, expelled OSS personnel from the country.[110]

Among the smaller services, the Swedes and the Danes worked most closely with the Americans against the Soviet target. Even before the end of the war the Swedish intelligence service had begun to make overtures to their American counterpart. These early gestures included limited cooperation on the operational level, most significantly in a joint operation to place listening devices in the homes and offices of Japanese diplomats in Stockholm.[111] Contacts intensified in the summer of 1945 with the Swedes the more eager participant in the exchanges. In July, Swedish intelligence officers revealed to OSS officers in Stockholm that in the postwar period their service intended to concentrate on the USSR. Since the Russians were alert to the threat of Swedish espionage operations along their Baltic sea and land frontiers, the Swedes planned to attack the Russian target from a direction where they were least expected: the Balkans. In both the Baltic and Balkans agents would operate under the cover of large Swedish industrial and commercial firms that had offices in those regions. As a result of early operations in the Balkans a substantial amount of intelligence had accumulated in a Swedish intelligence center in Bern, Switzerland, but the Swedes lacked a secure channel for forwarding this material to Stockholm. If OSS would facilitate the passage of a special courier between the Swiss and Swedish capitals and provide information on Red Army dispositions in Europe, the Swedes would share whatever military and economic intelligence they collected on the Soviet Union.[112] An arrangement must have been concluded because by August 1945 the Swedish service was passing to OSS intelligence on the Red Army and Air Force, such as a survey of air bases in the area of the Barents and White Seas. Collaboration intensified as time passed and the Soviet Union began to loom larger on the American intelligence horizon. By the spring of 1946 the Swedes were routinely passing Russian intelligence items to the United States, and the chief of Swedish military intelligence had visited Germany to consult with senior officers of the Strategic Services Unit and U.S. Army intelligence. By the summer of that year the partners were planning an operation to use female agents to penetrate the Soviet embassy in Stockholm.[113]

While focusing their limited resources on Poland and the Russian zone of occupied Germany, the small Danish intelligence service also directly attacked the Soviet target. The day after Germany's surrender, the Red Army, preceded by an aerial bombardment, had invaded and occupied Bornholm, a Danish island occupied during the war by a German garrison. Located in the center of the Baltic Sea, some distance from Denmark proper, the island was well placed to monitor shipping and naval movements in a region that included an important maritime frontier of the Soviet Union. Not surprisingly, the Danish intelligence service was quite interested in what the Russians were up to on Bornholm. The service's many sources on the island provided information on the organization, disposition, and equipment of the occupying forces. One source, an interpreter for Russian naval officers, reported on living conditions, morale, and training in the Red Navy. The Danes also closely monitored Soviet naval activity in the Baltic Sea and the Arctic Ocean, noting ship movements and the deployment of new naval vessels, while collecting, often in close-up, photos of Red Navy units, their armaments, and communication arrays. Copenhagen happily shared its Russian material with American intelligence, and by February 1946 senior American and Danish intelligence officers had twice met to discuss common concerns.[114]

The various sources of Russian information available to the Strategic Services Unit in the summer of 1946 were more or less useful, but none was a substitute for agents inside the Soviet Union directly recruited and controlled by SSU. The absence of such agents—excepting LISTER, whose bona fides remained uncertain—seriously undermined American efforts to understand Moscow's motives, capabilities, and intentions, a deficiency of which American intelligence was well aware by the summer of 1946. To overcome this deficiency, a review of SSU collection assets concluded that "an adequate SSU program for the procurement of secret intelligence on the USSR must be based on the employment of entirely new operational methods and sources."[115] In short, SSU had to contrive entirely new collection programs unconnected with any of its current arrangements or operations. Toward this end the organization pursued two paths. The first was the brainchild of Henry Sutton, an officer at SSU's Berlin Base who specialized in "tourist missions," the dispatch of agents, invariably German nationals, into the Soviet zone of occupation in Germany on short-term collection missions while ostensibly on personal, family, or commercial business. Sutton proposed to apply the same method to the USSR. He realized, of course, that sending and recovering agents across the Russian border was not quite the same thing as sending Germans from the American zone of Germany into the Soviet zone of Germany. For one thing, Russians willing and able to move back and forth between the Soviet Union and Berlin or Paris or Vienna on behalf of American intelligence were not crowding the anterooms of American intelligence offices. Sutton understood that several fundamental questions required answers before his operational plan, code-named ALADDIN, could be implemented. What types of people—age, nationality, occupational background—should be employed in the operation? In what places and by what methods could such individuals be located and recruited? What kinds of cover—seamen, peasants, businessmen, intellectuals, journalists—would prove efficacious in protecting the agents? At what points and by what methods could the Soviet frontier be crossed, a problem compounded by the fact that, at least in Europe, the frontier must be approached through countries, such as Poland, under Russian control? How would agents live in the Soviet Union? What police and travel controls would be in place, and what identity, residential, and employment documents would be required of inhabitants of the USSR? How would the agents communicate with their controllers? To answer such questions, Sutton proposed sending to Europe senior operational personnel to establish a research office and channels for identifying and questioning people with recent personal or professional experience with the Soviet Union, particularly diplomats, journalists, and others who resided in the country. This office would also survey friendly foreign intelligence services and exploit the experiences and knowledge of former members of the German intelligence community. The operation would also require European facilities for training and clandestine communications and a workshop for creating disguises and concealment devices and forging documents. Facilities, personnel, and operations should be administratively subordinate to one of SSU's European stations but should shelter under a separate and suitably innocuous cover designation—Sutton proposed "Survey of Foreign Administrative Procedures" as a cover name.[116]

The subsequent evolution of Project ALADDIN (if any) remains classified, but it is apparent that Henry Sutton's proposal to send agents into the Soviet Union was a long-term plan. It would take time, certainly months, to identify, recruit, and train suitable personnel, prepare support facilities, and develop operational methods. It might be a year or more before the project was fully functioning, but in the meantime the Soviet Union remained the top priority of American intelligence, and government departments—State, War, Navy, Treasury, Commerce, to say nothing of the White House—continued to clamor for information concerning the USSR. The Strategic Services Unit required short-term solutions to the Russian problem while its long-term solutions had time to develop.

Enter the Ukrainians

At the end of the war Moscow ruled a multinational and multiethnic empire. Some of the components of that empire, such as the Baltic States, had been independent before the war, while others, including the Ukraine and Georgia, had only dreamed of independence. Never sympathetic to what Lenin scornfully dismissed as "bourgeois nationalism" (unless that nationalism was of the Russian variety), heavy-handed Soviet control had inadvertently nourished among some of the subject nationalities a fierce opposition that persisted despite ruthless measures of repression that killed, incarcerated, or displaced hundreds of thousands of people. Anti-Soviet sentiments in some areas, particularly Ukraine, Belorussia, and the Baltic States, were so strong that when Germany invaded the Soviet Union in June 1941 the invaders were often greeted as liberators by a population prepared to support the war against the hated masters in Moscow. This support tended to diminish quickly with exposure to German occupation and the realization that Hitler was no more sympathetic to the nationalist aspirations of subject peoples than Stalin, although nationalist and anti-Semitic diehards served and fought in SS and auxiliary police formations until the bitter end.

With Germany's surrender and the reestablishment of Moscow's control, the Soviet borderlands became a witch's brew of mutually antagonistic political movements of many persuasions. Along a broad arc running from the Baltic to the Black Sea there were nationalist anticommunist movements, some still favoring Nazism, though most probably preferred freedom from both German and Russian domination. A few of these groups, particularly in the Baltic and Ukraine, turned to armed resistance against the Red Army and other organs of Soviet control. Even before the end of the war the Office of Strategic Services had been aware of the nationalist groups and their intelligence potential, but had declined opportunities to establish connections. In the spring of 1945, for example, Michael Kedia, a Georgian nationalist who had worked for German intelligence, approached OSS about collaboration against the Soviet Union and offered the support of 100 of his wartime colleagues who were "most active in anti-Russian activities."[117] The offer was declined. "He was not," an OSS officer reported about Kedia, "a suitable person to be used for current intelligence objectives. His fanatical anti-communism, which amounted to a strong desire to see an early war between Russia and the US . . . rendered it essential for security reasons that no commitments be made to him and that contact be held to a minimum."[118] As late as February 1946, the chief of intelligence for SSU Germany could still assure Washington of his approval of the decision by his counterpart in Prague to avoid contact with "troublesome" anti-Russian groups such as the Georgians and Ukrainians.[119] As the demand for Russian intelligence increased in Washington in the spring and summer of 1946, however, and American intelligence struggled to develop sources inside the USSR, the Strategic Services Unit wondered if the nationalist resistance movements might be an aid in that struggle.

The first contact came in April 1946, although it originated several months earlier when SSU was seeking intelligence not from the Soviet Union, but from Germany. In August 1945, Father Eduard Gehrmann, a priest who had worked for many years in the Vatican's nunciature (embassy) in Berlin, sought American assistance in returning to the German capital from which he and the rest of the nunciature's staff had fled to escape Allied bombing. From his refuge in postwar Austria, Father Gehrmann had provided the Office of Strategic Services with information concerning religious conditions and personalities in Germany, and the good priest offered to continue to serve as an informant should OSS facilitate his return to his homeland. OSS agreed, but the plan collapsed when the Catholic bishop of Berlin, Johann Konrad von Preysing, refused to accept the priest as one of the city's clergy.[120]

Disappointed but ever obliging, Gehrmann suggested to his OSS handlers that Monsignor Ivo Zeiger, a cleric well placed at the Vatican and since the late fall of 1945 the chief of a special mission sent by Pope Pius XII to assess the condition and needs of the Catholic Church in the ruins of the Third Reich, might be a good person to approach for information about the various regions of Germany. The referral proved productive because Monsignor Zeiger, almost certainly with the knowledge of his superiors inside the Vatican, agreed to pass to U.S. intelligence information collected from the Big Four occupation zones by the papal special mission, which received the code name WESTMORELAND.[121] At some point in their relationship with the papal official, probably February or March 1946, SSU seems to have asked him about priests who might be in a position to help the United States with information from Eastern Europe. Monsignor Zeiger recommended as a useful contact a young Ukrainian priest, a Father Dyacisin, who had served briefly with the papal mission to Germany before returning to the Vatican. When contacted in Rome, Father Dyacisin, who had connections with the Ukrainian diaspora, turned aside American approaches, saying that he was too well known to accept a clandestine mission, but he suggested the Americans speak with Bishop John Bucko, the director of the Ukrainian Institute, a college in Rome dedicated to the preparation of young men for the priesthood in the Ukrainian Greek Catholic Church.[122]

The Strategic Services Unit first contacted Bishop Bucko on 22 April 1946 when Zsolt Aradi, an officer who specialized in Vatican affairs, called on the prelate in Rome. The course of the conversation revealed that SSU, having established the Soviet Union as a priority barely a month earlier, was interested in exploring the espionage potential of the Ukrainian nationalists but was new to the subject. It is clear from the record of the conversation that SSU at the time had no relationship with the Ukrainians and had not previously been using them for intelligence or paramilitary purposes. Indeed, Bucko, surprised by the appearance on his doorstep of a representative of the United States government, complained that the Americans had previously expressed very little interest in the activities of the Ukrainian resistance movement. At subsequent meetings Aradi patiently cultivated the bishop until, in early May 1946, Bucko agreed to lend his support to operations to infiltrate agents into the Soviet Union and introduced the American agent to Ivan Bilanych, a young priest studying at the Ukrainian Institute, who volunteered to undertake a clandestine mission into the Ukraine, an operation later code-named MORPHINE. As a preliminary to his infiltration, Father Bilanych traveled to Salzburg, Austria, under SSU auspices in June 1946, but there the trail of declassified documents ends, and there is no further evidence of the fate of the priest or MORPHINE.[123]

In the summer and fall of 1946 the Strategic Services Unit laid the groundwork for collaboration with the Ukrainians. Though long aware in a general way that resistance groups in the Ukraine and the Baltic were fighting the Russians, neither SSU nor its predecessor, OSS, had had dealings with such groups, so SSU was surprisingly uninformed about the size, location, and operations of such groups. As late as August headquarters was still compiling information about anti-Soviet Ukrainian groups and asking its European stations to contribute whatever they knew about these groups.[124] In 1946 the Strategic Services Unit was interested in the Ukrainians only as intelligence sources. At that time there was no intention of using separatist groups to undermine the political integrity and internal stability of the USSR, although in 1948 these more ambitious goals would be embraced by SSU's successor service, the Central Intelligence Agency.[125] The Ukrainians, hoping to attach themselves to a rich and powerful patron, were eager to fill whatever role the United States cast for them. In July 1946, for example, a representative of the Ukrainian armed resistance (known by its Ukrainian acronym, UPA) approached the SSU station in Bern, Switzerland, with an offer to provide information on conditions in Soviet-dominated Eastern Europe and on Russian intelligence agents and operations in Switzerland in return for a monthly subsidy and immediate cash to purchase radios, cameras, and office supplies. At the same time SSU was in discussions with representatives of the Ukrainian Supreme Liberation Council (UHVR) concerning collaboration on intelligence-gathering operations.[126]

By midsummer of 1946 SSU had initiated two operations with the Ukrainians. Operation BELLADONNA aimed to collect information on Red

Army and Air Force dispositions by dispatching Ukrainians from Germany into the western Soviet Union, while Operation LYNX sought to identify Soviet intelligence networks in Germany. The Strategic Services Unit launched these operations despite certain reservations concerning its new ally. The American service realized that it was accepting a partnership in which it knew relatively little about its partner. It wasn't even certain about how many partners it had since the Ukrainian resistance included several organizations, some with overlapping memberships. Colonel William Quinn, the director of SSU, was especially leery of committing his organization to an open-ended collaboration, and he urged his staff to investigate the history, reliability, and motivations of the various Ukrainian groups before "major steps are taken to exploit them for intelligence purposes."[127] Additionally, these notoriously anti-Soviet groups were obvious targets for penetration by Russian intelligence and as such posed a potential security threat to any American service that chose to collaborate with them.

Also worrisome was the rather unsavory past of these groups and their leaders. Some had espoused political and racial views that barely distinguished them from the Nazis; some had engaged in terrorist activities before the war; and some had actively collaborated with the Nazis during the war in Russia and had been linked to atrocities on the eastern front. Mykola Lebed, the "foreign minister" of UHVR, had been convicted for his involvement in the assassination of the Polish minister of the interior in 1934. Stefan Bandera, a prominent personality in the Ukrainian diaspora and the leader of the largest force in the armed resistance, was a likely candidate for a war crimes trial for his activities alongside the Germans in the early months of the fighting on the eastern front. Myron Matvieyko, a senior security officer in the resistance movement and the point man for the movement in its operational contacts with SSU, had been an agent for German military intelligence and may well have become a double agent working for the Soviets against the Americans after the war.[128]

Finally, SSU was under no illusions concerning the motives of the Ukrainians. The Americans were well aware that their new partners had their own political agenda, national independence, which was at the time no part of American plans. They would try to manipulate their connection with U.S. intelligence to advance that agenda. Of course this was an issue in SSU's relations with any anti-Soviet émigré groups. Such groups had an interest in presenting the USSR in the most negative light and cultivating American hostility and fear concerning Soviet activities and intentions. These biases could poison any intelligence reports they shared with U.S. intelligence agencies. In August 1946, SSU headquarters warned its mission in Germany that "these White Russians and Ukrainians have but one aim and that is to create dissension between us and the Russians."[129] Two months later, Colonel Quinn reminded his officers that the Ukrainians were only interested in acquiring allies in their struggle against the Soviet Union. "Their leaders," the SSU director added, "create the impression that their cause is just, that their past record is a clean one, that there exists a strong resistance movement in the Soviet Ukraine, that they have excellent intelligence services leading directly into the USSR, and that they are backed by an efficient organization." Quinn noted that the veracity of these claims remained an open question, although another claim, that the movement was democratic, was demonstrably false.[130]

American concerns proved well founded. In January 1947, only nine months after SSU's first contacts with the Ukrainians, Harry Rositzke, a senior officer on the Soviet desk, was warning his superiors against the continued use of the Ukrainians. The following month the Office of Special Operations (OSO—formerly the Secret Intelligence Branch of SSU before the latter's liquidation in October 1946) was reassessing its connections with the Ukrainians. This reassessment had nothing to do with the checkered background of the resistance or the notoriety of many of its leading personalities, some of whom OSO protected against Russian efforts to locate and extradite them for war crimes. The concerns of the Office of Special Operations were purely practical; the Ukrainians simply did not live up to their early promise. The results of the BELLADONNA and LYNX operations were disappointing. OSO concluded that "intelligence derived from such Ukrainian groups is [not] worth the time and effort which would necessarily have to be expended on such a project. Experience has shown that information from such organizations has been both low-grade and ideologically biased."[131] Doubts were fueled by the refusal of the Ukrainians to reveal the identities of their sources and the locations of their networks, an attitude that led the Americans to question the existence of such networks and suspect their supposed partners of duplicity. In May 1947 OSO recommended severing contacts with the Ukrainians, and overseas stations gradually dropped their contacts, although many of these connections were subsequently picked up by the U.S. Army's Counterintelligence Corps and, a few years later, the Central Intelligence Agency.[132]

Although OSS and SSU had been relatively slow to turn their attention toward the USSR, by the spring of 1946 the Soviet Union was the highest priority for America's clandestine service. Unfortunately, capabilities fell far short of interest. In the first year of peace, the United States had no reliable sources, communications intelligence excepted, reporting from inside Russia. For the information increasingly demanded by its customers, American intelligence would have to look elsewhere. Unable to collect information *in* Russia, the secret services had no choice but to collect information *about* Russia wherever such information was available. Reflecting the adage, "If you want to hunt ducks, go to where the ducks are," American intelligence went to where the Russians were. The hunt took them first to Germany.

CHAPTER THREE

Signs and Portents: Germany

It took some time for American intelligence to establish itself in the ruins of the Third Reich. The Office of Strategic Services, Washington's principal source of clandestine information, was surprisingly slow off the mark. German authorities signed the instrument of surrender on 7 May 1945, but William Donovan waited until the following month before appointing Allen Dulles, the chief of the OSS station in Bern, to direct his organization's activities in postwar Germany, and he did not formally approve and circulate the postwar mission directive for the OSS contingent in Germany until August. From neutral Switzerland Dulles had run successful clandestine operations into several European countries, including Germany, and in the last weeks of the conflict had secretly brokered the surrender of German forces in northern Italy. A jovial, pipe-smoking raconteur with an appetite for fine wine, beautiful women, and secret operations, Dulles had emerged from the war as America's premier spymaster, and his appointment as chief of the newly constituted OSS mission in Germany affirmed the centrality of that mission in Donovan's plans for postwar intelligence activities. The director of the Office of Strategic Services may have expected the intelligence war in Germany to continue after the guns fell silent, but the delay in appointing Dulles, who did not actually take up his new post until early July, suggests that Donovan did not anticipate any immediate engagements in that secret war.

Dulles arrived in Germany to find his fledgling OSS mission ensconced in the premises of the Henkel champagne company on the outskirts of Wiesbaden. A popular prewar spa, Wiesbaden had suffered relatively little damage during the war, and the offices, garages, and storerooms of the Henkel firm were intact. Personnel were comfortably billeted in private residences requisitioned from their owners. Many of the secret intelligence officers found housing in the "Horned Rabbit Club," a villa so named by its American occupants because one of its rooms prominently featured the mounted head of a rabbit to which the taxidermist had affixed a set of miniature antlers. From Wiesbaden the mission sent teams to establish outposts in Berlin, Heidelberg, Munich, and other cities in the American zone of occupation.[1]

At first OSS Germany struggled to find its legs. During the war the Office of Strategic Services had recruited few sources inside Germany. The best agent had been Fritz Kolbe, an anti-Nazi official in the Germany foreign ministry who offered his services to Allen Dulles in Switzerland in August 1943. Code-named "George Wood," Kolbe often carried the foreign ministry's diplomatic pouch to Bern, a cover that allowed him to bring out of Germany duplicates of foreign ministry documents, including the cables of German representatives abroad.[2] In the last months of the European war Donovan's service had run some agents—mainly German émigrés—into the collapsing Third Reich, but these operations were modest in scope and scale, and the results were sparse.[3] On Victory in Europe (VE) Day American intelligence had no significant networks and few reliable contacts inside the country, so the members of the Horned Rabbit Club had to start largely from scratch.

Effective intelligence coverage of a target cannot be conjured from thin air. For much of the summer of 1945 the OSS mission was preoccupied with the administrative minutiae of finding, furnishing, and staffing suitable premises in various cities, establishing secure communications, determining intelligence priorities, developing collection programs, identifying potential sources, and completing a hundred other tasks that are necessary for the creation of an intelligence apparatus. The process was further complicated when in July Washington headquarters decided to organize European operations in three clusters centered on the British, French, and German missions. Under this arrangement Wiesbaden assumed supervisory responsibility for the nascent OSS stations in Czechoslovakia, Denmark, the Netherlands, and Norway.[4] Struggling to open their own intelligence shop and understand their immediate neighborhood, Dulles and his team unexpectedly found themselves running several "foreign" franchises.

Organizational distractions were exacerbated by uncertainties concerning future staff levels. It was difficult to make considered judgments about the scope and nature of intelligence activities in Germany without a clear sense of how many people and what skill sets would be available. Unfortunately, in the summer of 1945 OSS headquarters, increasingly distracted by the emerging threats to its postwar survival, could provide no assurances concerning staffing because questions concerning the future direction and organization of American intelligence remained unresolved. The problem became even more acute after the Japanese surrender in August 1945 when OSS supervisors in Washington and the various field units had to absorb the impact on staffing of peacetime demobilization and the loss of many of their most experienced officers. Of course the problem was not unique to OSS, and some of the American secret services were buffeted more than others. The U.S. Army's Counterintelligence Corps (CIC), the largest American intelligence organization in Germany in the months following VE Day, was especially hard hit by demobilization. To replace the loss of experienced personnel who departed for home and civilian life at the first opportunity, CIC was compelled to lower its recruitment and training standards. Not surprisingly, operational effectiveness was compromised, and in the early postwar period CIC was hard-pressed to fulfill its security and counterespionage mission in Germany and elsewhere. Conditions did not improve with time. As late as 1947 the army concluded that 20 percent of its counterintelligence officers in Germany were totally unqualified for their duties.[5] The Office of Strategic Services did not escape the storm. Even before the end of the war Donovan and his senior advisers had grappled with the problem of maintaining capabilities with significantly fewer resources. The closure of OSS in the fall of 1945 and the pressure upon its successor agency, the Strategic Services Unit (SSU), to liquidate or consolidate activities turned a worrisome problem into a serious personnel crisis in America's principal clandestine espionage service. The crisis affected all the overseas units, but the impact on operations in Germany was particularly serious. In early October Allen Dulles, whose appointment just months before seemingly affirmed the centrality of the German intelligence mission in America's postwar intelligence scheme, resigned, noting that the depletion of his new command seriously compromised the mission's ability to perform its tasks. His successor, Lieutenant Colonel William Suhling, was no more sanguine, warning Washington in his first report that personnel issues were the principal problem facing the German mission.[6]

The problem was not just numbers. Poor morale, pervasive lethargy, and lax discipline plagued American occupation forces in the months following the German surrender, and the OSS/SSU outposts in Germany did not entirely escape the malaise. In an unusually frank appraisal, Lieutenant Colonel Suhling bluntly warned Washington in October that "the morale of the unit is at extremely low ebb."[7] Some intelligence staffers, counting the days to the end of their service and their repatriation home, felt little incentive to exert themselves and worked to the book and the clock. Others, who may have hoped to continue in peace the work they had found interesting and important in war, concluded that their commitment, energy, and skills went unappreciated and unrewarded by Washington bureaucrats, who seemingly exhibited little interest and less expertise in foreign intelligence. Yet others, abusing their access to military post exchanges and other U.S. government stores, subordinated their official responsibilities to more lucrative activities in the black markets of postwar Germany.

Corruption fueled by a flourishing black market was common across occupied Germany, and the vice significantly compromised the early efforts of the OSS/SSU mission. The base in Berlin was so affected that General Lucius Clay, the military governor of the American zone, complained to Allen Dulles, "How the hell can you expect those guys to catch spies when they can't smell the stink under their own noses?"[8] In the once grand capital of the Third Reich, now devastated physically, socially, and economically, cigarettes, watches, liquor, soap, and foodstuffs such as chocolate and canned meat were highly prized. Such items were readily available in U.S. Army post exchanges and quartermaster depots, and enterprising GIs could literally make a fortune by buying (or stealing) these commodities and then reselling them on the street. On the Berlin black market ten packs of cigarettes, which an American soldier could obtain for 50 cents in a PX, had the purchasing power of $100. A cheap Mickey Mouse watch might be worth as much as $500.

Few could resist the temptation of easy money, and the eager entrepreneurs included officers and enlisted men assigned to the OSS/SSU base. In September 1945 detectives from the army's Criminal Investigation Division arrested at the Munich airport an officer assigned to OSS Berlin and the commander of the OSS detachment in Munich on charges of smuggling. In their baggage the investigators found 138 Swiss watches destined for the black market.[9] In October, while welcoming Peter Sichel, his replacement as commander of the secret intelligence (SI) section of the Berlin base, Richard Helms noted that his driver, an enlisted man, was worth hundreds of thousands of dollars as a result of black market activities. Helms warned his successor, "You're going to have to get rid of all these people, because otherwise you are never going to be able to run an intelligence unit."[10] The new SI chief did not have to wait long for confirmation of this warning. At a luncheon organized by the SI staff to celebrate his arrival in Berlin, Sichel was dumbfounded when the officer who would be his deputy offered to buy his watch off his wrist for $1,500.[11]

Confusion over organizational mission proved another complication. Should OSS/Germany collect strategic political, economic, and military intelligence for the use of Washington policy makers or should the mission serve local customers by gathering information concerning conditions inside Germany for the use of the U.S. Army theater commands and other occupation authorities? If the latter, should coverage extend beyond the American zone of occupation to include the British, French, and Russian zones? Should more extensive coverage include countries bordering on Germany, such as Poland? Should intelligence collectors rely on relatively open sources such as newspapers, public opinion surveys, and interviews with refugees or should they seek to establish clandestine networks of informants? The answers to these questions would have significant consequences for the organization and

operation of American espionage in postwar Central Europe, but unequivocal responses eluded intelligence authorities for months after the German
surrender.

OSS (and, later, SSU) managers in Washington, distracted by bureaucratic battles over the shape and direction of postwar intelligence and uncertain about the short-term survival of their own service, provided little
direction to their representatives in Europe. Pleas from the field for guidance concerning target priorities and headquarters' expectations went unanswered. Lacking assurances concerning their future and guidance concerning
intelligence targets and requirements, field stations were largely left to their
own devices, and more often than not enterprising officers simply attacked
targets of opportunity without reference to any intelligence program or plan.
In the American zone of occupied Germany, military authorities rushed to
fill the vacuum in intelligence policy. Responsible for denazifying and demil-
itarizing German society; maintaining law and order and reestablishing basic
services in a war-devastated territory; supervising the emergence of political
movements, labor unions, voluntary associations, and other elements of civil
society; protecting American forces from diehard Nazi fanatics; and coordinating their activities with their British, French, and Russian counterparts,
American occupation authorities required detailed information about political, economic, and social conditions inside Germany. The army's own local
intelligence capabilities, the spy catchers of the Counterintelligence Corps
and the G-2 order-of-battle specialists, document analysts, and interrogators
attached to the theater commands and individual army units, were inadequate in terms of training or experience for the task. On the other hand, the
OSS/SSU mission and its bases, administratively and logistically linked to
the local army command structure, prepared by training and experience for
broadly based clandestine intelligence collection, and burdened by few competing assignments from Washington, were present and available for the job.

During the summer of 1945, as OSS Germany found its organizational
footing and launched its first operations, Dulles and his mission focused on
serving the intelligence requirements of the American occupation authorities. The most pressing requirement concerned the residual threat posed by
fugitive Nazis, especially civilian and military leadership elements (many of
whom were on automatic arrest lists as suspected war criminals), members
of the defeated regime's security and intelligence services, and underground
groups of fanatic Hitler loyalists who might resist the occupation by sabotage,
assassination, and guerilla warfare. As early as 1944, Nazi leaders had begun
organizing a guerilla force, although they seemed initially to have imagined
an organization that would complement the regular army by harassing the
advancing Allied forces rather than an armed underground movement that

would continue the struggle in a postwar Germany. These "Werwolfs" were especially active on the eastern front as the Red Army moved into Germany, and they continued their resistance, on a sporadic and more or less organized level, even after the fall of Berlin. In the months following the German capitulation the Russians remained particular targets, and snipers and saboteurs harassed Red Army personnel and facilities across the Soviet zone of occupation. The American, British, and French zones also experienced terrorist or anti-occupation actions ranging from pro-Nazi graffiti to the murder of Germans collaborating with the victors. While few in number, the incidents seriously preoccupied Allied authorities in all four occupation zones, and intelligence officials deployed scarce resources to identify and neutralize pockets of Nazi or neo-Nazi resistance.[12]

Throughout the autumn of 1945 the suppression of pro-Nazi underground groups and the apprehension of fugitive Nazi officials remained a high priority for American intelligence in Germany, and as late as the following spring American and British counterintelligence units were still cooperating on large-scale operations to penetrate and neutralize these targets. In the months following VE Day the army's Counterintelligence Corps, ostensibly responsible for protecting the army from sabotage, subversion, and penetration by foreign espionage agencies, spent more time in Germany chasing war criminals and other Nazi fugitives than chasing spies. Describing CIC's priorities in early postwar Germany, an official history of the corps noted, "During the first 6 months of occupation duty, CIC personnel spent most of their time conducting wholesale roundups and interrogating individuals on various 'wanted' lists."[13] The army's spy catchers were also diverted to the denazification program that sought to purge Nazi party members from surviving civil, financial, labor, and educational organizations. The task of vetting tens of thousands of German officials was enormous—in the summer of 1945 more than 30,000 Germans were dismissed from public employment in the American zone—and left CIC with little time and few resources for counterintelligence work.[14]

Nazi fugitives and internal security were no less a preoccupation of OSS/ SSU. Prodded by a Washington headquarters convinced that German intelligence services would go underground, presumably to prepare a fascist revival, X-2 (counterintelligence) branch representatives in Germany placed the suppression of the elusive Werwolf organization, the capture of Nazi police and intelligence officials, and the neutralization of surviving German intelligence networks at the top of their list of priorities.[15] Nazis also topped the "to do" list of SI (secret intelligence) branch. An SI officer, transferred from the Heidelberg intelligence unit in October 1945 to command SSU clandestine operations in Berlin, recalled, "Our priority targets at that time were the same as the ones I had in Heidelberg: identify high level personnel from the German intelligence and security service, high party officials as well as SS officials, to basically ascertain if a 'werewolf' [*sic*] organization was in existence and apprehend such personnel who were identified."[16]

Resources not committed to locating Nazi miscreants were devoted to educating American occupation authorities about the land and people they now administered. These authorities were often woefully ignorant of conditions in their areas of responsibility. When, for example, American representatives, pushing against Russian obstructionism, finally established themselves in their allotted sector of Berlin in July 1945, the realization that they had absolutely no knowledge of political, economic, or social conditions in the city compelled them reluctantly to accept without question the municipal administration and legislation established by the Russians since their capture of the city two months earlier.[17] To remedy such embarrassing intelligence deficiencies in Berlin and throughout the American zone of occupation, the military government relied on the bases established by OSS in Berlin, Bremen, Kassel, Heidelberg, and Munich.

Suburban News

From the start, OSS (later SSU) Germany shaped its intelligence collection programs to meet the needs of its local customers, the myriad army commands and military and civilian offices that composed the occupation government. Early operations were modest in scope and emphasized what one intelligence professional contemptuously dismissed as "suburban news items": school openings; rehabilitation of factories; clearance of debris; food prices and economic conditions; activities of local political, business, and religious notables; meetings of nascent political movements, cooperative organizations, and labor unions; and public attitudes toward the occupation.[18] Such mundane topics seemed a far cry from the more glamorous political and military targets of wartime espionage. The intelligence summaries produced by the occupation administration capture the tenor of reporting in the first months of peace. Intelligence updates disseminated in late July by U.S. headquarters in Berlin, for example, included items on the chlorination of the city water supply, the arrival of textbooks for use in city schools, the imposition of a curfew, the examination of mailbags discovered in the Japanese embassy, and the interrogation of the chief technical officer of Telefunken, the large German communications enterprise. No subject was considered too trivial for attention. One intelligence summary conscientiously noted the number of movie theaters open for business in the former Reich capital.[19]

Beleaguered by staff shortages, poor morale, and uneven professionalism, the American intelligence bases in German were often hard-pressed to cover even such "soft" targets as cinemas and road conditions. In general, collection efforts lacked focus and energy. All too often the collectors pursued only the information that was easiest to collect, and the resulting intelligence was often trivial and of purely local interest. The bases in Bremen, Heidelberg, and Kassel were frequently criticized by mission headquarters in Wiesbaden for their avoidance of clandestine operations and secret informants, their reliance on overt sources such as personal observation, casual conversations with Germans, and local gossip, and their failure to cover important targets. Some bases produced little intelligence at all. In Berlin, collection activities had to compete with black market speculations for the attention of officers. Munich Base proved completely inadequate, largely because the new commander (the first commander had been arrested for black market profiteering) and his deputy were too busy working their cover jobs of press officers for the local military command.[20]

Intelligence coverage would have been even shallower if Wiesbaden had not been able to draw upon the resources of its sister stations in other European capitals. The early collection programs of the German mission were supplemented by reports from other OSS stations, which routinely forwarded to Wiesbaden any intelligence they happened upon that related to German affairs. The station in Bern, for example, had developed several networks composed largely of Catholic priests in Switzerland, Germany, and Austria. From these sources Bern collected and transmitted to Wiesbaden information on political and social conditions in the heavily Catholic southern and western regions of Germany.[21]

In the summer and early fall of 1945, OSS Germany focused mainly on the American zone and ran relatively few operations beyond the zonal boundaries. When intelligence managers in Wiesbaden did look outward, they were as likely to focus on British and French activities as Russian. Targets in the French occupation zone were particularly attractive, but they proved surprisingly elusive. Initially, Heidelberg Base (which seems to have been especially lethargic) was responsible for monitoring the French zone. American authorities correctly suspected Paris of harboring annexationist ambitions, exploiting German economic and industrial resources, and pursuing any number of political intrigues in its zone, but the Americans needed evidence to confirm their suspicions. At the end of August, intelligence coverage of the French zone remained very poor, a deficiency that did not exactly enhance the stature of the beleaguered Office of Strategic Services in Washington. The OSS station in Paris contributed items on French policy toward Germany, but not enough to satisfy American policy makers in Washington and Germany. Despairing of its lackadaisical crew in Heidelberg, in the late autumn Wiesbaden shifted responsibility for the French zone to NORFOLK, the small OSS collection unit attached to the U.S. Seventh Army in Bavaria. The reorganization improved the quantity but not the quality of reporting. NORFOLK's principal source inside the French zone, an allegedly well-placed informant code-named "Marcel," filed dozens of reports, all of which were judged "highly unreliable" by headquarters. Bereft of trustworthy information, American authorities remained distracted by the specter of French intrigue throughout the first year of the occupation. In January 1946 the American military government was still badgering the Strategic Services Unit to develop more clandestine networks in the French zone, and as late as June of that year SSU's headquarters in Washington reminded its German mission that various agencies were demanding more information on France's zone.[22] Coverage of the British zone was far better. Relying primarily on overt observation and exchanges with British administrators, OSS/SSU representatives generated useful information on a range of topics, particularly economic conditions, the revival of trade unions, and leftist political activity. In October the German mission characterized its activities in British-occupied areas as among its most productive.[23]

Operations in the Russian zone were slower to develop. In the months immediately following the German surrender, American occupation authorities knew very little about conditions and developments in the area controlled by the Red Army. Frankly acknowledging that "we have very little precise evidence from which to assess Russian policy towards the part of Germany which they occupy," an intelligence appraisal completed in early July 1945 urged immediate and maximum efforts to improve intelligence collection from the Russian zone.[24] The task, however, was easier to identify than to complete.

The lack of information concerning Russian-occupied Germany was an element of a larger problem: the lack of effective intelligence coverage of the Soviet Union and Soviet political, military, and economic activities in Europe and elsewhere. Several particular issues, however, constrained Russian operations in Germany, where the U.S. occupation zone shared a border with the Soviet zone. Many officers on the scene initially viewed the Russians with little trepidation and even less urgency. When, in June, presidential envoy Harry Hopkins stopped in Frankfurt on his return from consultations with Stalin in Moscow, he imbued American occupation authorities with confidence in Soviet cooperation and left his listeners with the impression that Washington expected few problems with the Soviet Union over Germany. Initially, neither Robert Murphy, the State Department's senior representative in Germany, nor General Lucius Clay, the military governor, ranked the Soviet Union among the problems facing American occupation authorities.

In July the Joint Intelligence Committee of the Supreme Headquarters Allied Expeditionary Force (SHAEF) affirmed this attitude. While acknowledging that American and British military authorities lacked information concerning conditions in the Russian zone, the committee assured its intelligence customers that "there is nothing peculiarly sinister about Russia's policy in her zone."[25]

The first mission directive for OSS Germany, issued by Washington headquarters in August 1945, identified twenty intelligence targets but made no reference to the Soviet Union or Soviet activities, emphasizing instead the surveillance of *Germans* to ensure compliance with the military and political terms of the occupation.[26] That same month, a staff memorandum suggesting the need for increased attention to the Russian occupation zone received a lukewarm reception from senior officers in the OSS mission. Some of these officers expressed concern that an "overemphasis" on Soviet activities would divert attention and scarce resources from other, more pressing intelligence assignments, such as coverage of social and economic affairs in the American zone. Furthermore, there was "terrible opposition" among senior occupation authorities, particularly the military governor, General Lucius Clay, to clandestine activities that would irritate and alarm a notoriously suspicious and irascible ally. The risk was unnecessary as well as imprudent if, as many of these authorities initially believed, sufficient information about conditions and developments in the Soviet zone would soon be available from open sources, thereby reducing the need for espionage. Such optimism was evident in an OSS memorandum of August 1945 that reviewed intelligence requirements in the Russian zone and concluded, "The category of overtly obtainable information will undoubtedly be gradually extended during the next several months, and the number of SI [secret intelligence] targets will accordingly contract."[27]

Complacency with regard to Soviet activities in their occupation zone might seem, in retrospect, shortsighted, but in the summer of 1945 such a posture was organizationally functional for OSS Germany. Struggling to establish itself in a climate of resource shortages, poor morale, and mission uncertainty, the unit was hard-pressed to collect *any* intelligence at all and would have found early operations against the Soviet Union and Soviet-occupied territory simply beyond its limited capabilities. None of the OSS subbases scattered across the American zone, each with its particular targets, was specifically charged with monitoring the Russians and their area. Berlin Base, surrounded by Russian-occupied territory would have been the vanguard of any espionage attack against the Soviet zone, but in the months immediately following VE Day the base was effectively sidelined by staff problems, and what operations it did mount were limited to the American section of the city and focused primarily on the pursuit of fugitive members of the Nazi regime and its security services.[28]

Of course, when intelligence managers considered possible targets in the months following VE Day, their eyes inevitably turned eastward, especially as the anticipated increase in open source coverage of that area did not occur. Gradually, a few officers in Wiesbaden, notably the energetic chief of secret intelligence Frank Wisner, fresh from the OSS mission in Soviet-occupied Romania, and the chief of the steering division, Harry Rositzke, began to urge more attention to Russian affairs. Still, it was late August 1945 before intelligence authorities in Germany developed a detailed questionnaire concerning the Russian zone, and the steering division, responsible for directing and evaluating collection programs, began to issue briefs devoted to areas east of the Elbe River. For the steering division the priority subjects were the organization and activities of the Soviet police and intelligence services, the goals and membership of emerging political parties and formations in the Russian zone, and the degree of Russian infiltration and control of such political groups. Secondary topics included such items as the organization of the Soviet military government, the recruitment of Germans into local administrations, policies regarding freedom of assembly and freedom of the press, and limitations on civil liberties.[29] In short, American intelligence managers in Wiesbaden were interested in determining how the Russians were dealing with the same problems that preoccupied occupation authorities in the western zones.

Looking East

Frank Wisner, reacting perhaps to his contentious encounters with the Russians in Romania, led the effort to redirect and focus American intelligence programs in Germany.[30] In the absence of specific directives or guidance from Washington, Wisner seized the initiative and, on 11 September 1945, informed Washington of his intention to pursue "maximal" coverage of the political, economic, social, and military situation in the Russian zone as a first priority. Secondarily, Wiesbaden would collect information on communist and leftist political activities in the American, British, and French zones. Political and economic conditions in the British and French zones would be the third priority, while "significant" political activities in the American occupation area were relegated to fourth place. Under Wisner's approach, coverage of public attitudes, the revival of commerce, trade union activity, educational and ecclesiastical institutions, and similar local news items concerning the American zone that had hitherto been the bread and butter of OSS Germany would be excluded entirely from collection efforts.[31]

Wisner intended to set American intelligence on a new course, but his ambitious agenda did not immediately translate into an extensive and systematic program of clandestine operations into the Soviet zone. In the early fall of 1945 there was little support for such an agenda in Washington, where the dislocations of demobilization and the transition from OSS to SSU monopolized the attention of intelligence managers. Wisner lobbied strenuously for his plan, even returning to Washington to press his views, but he could not convince his bosses. When headquarters denied a request for a piddling sum to purchase bicycles to improve the ability of agents to move around the Soviet sector of Berlin, Wisner could no longer contain his frustration. Concluding that American intelligence had little interest in developing Soviet operations, he resigned from the service.[32] Clearly, many officials did not share Wisner's agenda, and these people included many of his principal customers. For all their increasing interest in the territories east of the Elbe, American occupation authorities remained preoccupied with the immediate problems of administering their zone. To address these problems, the authorities required information concerning fugitive Nazis, public opinion, and local economic and social conditions in the cities and countryside, the very subjects Wisner proposed to eschew in order to focus upon Russian targets. Since the various civilian offices and military commands and staffs active in the American zone, including United States Forces, European Theater (USFET), the United States Group, Control Council, and the Office of the Political Adviser, relied heavily upon OSS/SSU for intelligence, the chief of secret intelligence and his collection teams could not simply abandon local targets without abandoning (and alienating) their principal customers. The obligation was reinforced by the fact that OSS/SSU was technically subordinate to the military occupation authority and depended upon that authority for cover and authority to operate, as well as billets, supplies, and transportation. Throughout the remainder of 1945, even as interest in the Russian zone gradually increased, the surveillance of events and conditions in the American zone would continue to consume significant intelligence resources and attention. In November, for example, news items on the Russian zone reaching the military government's Office of Intelligence, such as a report on agricultural conditions in eastern Germany, were still outnumbered by items of mainly local or historical interest, such as a report on the wartime German container industry, a survey of living conditions in Darmstadt (U.S. zone), and the interrogation of a German propaganda officer attached to SS units during the war. Apparently, American occupation authorities were not as eager to redirect their intelligence resources toward the east as Frank Wisner. As late as March 1946 SSU Germany would still be arguing for a focus on Russian-occupied areas and trying to convince their local customers that

"Amzon [American zone] units must be turned away from preoccupation with purely local events."[33]

Early operations against the Soviet zone and other Russian targets were necessarily modest since a collection infrastructure had to be constructed from scratch in areas that effectively were unexplored territories for American intelligence. By September 1945 intelligence requirements guides for the Russian zone had been circulated by the steering division at Wiesbaden headquarters, but, perhaps to dampen any expectations of immediate results, the division chief cautioned his superiors that operations directed against eastern Germany were at the same preliminary, that is, poor, stages of organization and preparation that had characterized the early, rather ineffectual efforts of OSS Germany in the U.S. zone immediately following VE Day.[34] At first there was little that the intelligence bases in the American zone could do to engage the new requirements, especially since some bases, such as the units in Munich and Heidelberg, had hardly been able to marshal the energy and competence to engage the old requirements. Additionally, many of the sources so far developed by OSS were poorly situated by geography and personal position to observe Russian targets. Until new sources in the Russian zone could be developed, operations would have to focus on organizations and movements that might serve as instruments of Soviet influence and that had the additional advantage of being relatively accessible to curious outsiders. In particular, the bases were directed to increase surveillance of communist and leftist political groups that were emerging from a decade or more of persecution and clandestine existence. The organization, leadership, popular appeal, and political programs of the German Communist Party and the Social Democratic Party were of special interest, particularly following the announcement in Berlin in December that the two parties in the Russian zone had established a working agreement that presaged unification into a single political movement. Coverage of leftist political activity, especially in the areas around Bremen and Mannheim, improved significantly in the fall of 1945, although such coverage had to compete for attention and resources with coverage of nascent right-wing movements, which were still of interest to American authorities.

From the start it was clear that Berlin Base would play the most significant role in operations directed against the Russian zone. When, in September, Richard Helms arrived in the former Reich capital to assume direction of clandestine intelligence, he carried explicit orders from Frank Wisner to expand coverage of the Soviet sector.[35] Under Helms and (more systematically) his successor, Peter Sichel, the base's intelligence office slowly rebuilt the professionalism, integrity, and sense of purpose that had earlier been compromised by indiscipline and corruption among some of the staff. Revitalized, the office gradually began to develop operations into Russian-occupied territory. At first these operations were limited to "tourist missions," forays into and occasionally beyond the Soviet sector of Berlin by base officers or, more commonly, German informants who would keep their eyes and ears open as they moved about the city ostensibly on personal business. Such missions were facilitated by the fact that movement across sector boundaries was generally unimpeded by police and border controls. Interviews with refugees and returning prisoners of war arriving in the American sector from points east provided additional information. By October Berlin SI was forwarding to Wiesbaden a steady stream of reports on such topics as rationing, prices, black market activities, public attitudes, and living conditions in the eastern precincts of the former German capital and the state of agriculture, industry, and transportation in Russian-occupied districts immediately beyond Berlin.[36]

While useful and, perhaps, a harbinger of riches to come, the early reporting on Russian activity and conditions in the Soviet zone did not produce an immediate information windfall for the German mission. Several factors combined to limit the quantity and quality of the intelligence product. Personnel shortages and uncertainties regarding the future of the service continued to plague SSU and its bases in Germany. When it opened for business in the summer of 1945 OSS Germany had a staff of almost 700, but that total had been relentlessly whittled down by demobilization and attrition. By the new year the entire SSU mission counted 190 personnel, of which only 50 were assigned to secret intelligence operations. Berlin Operations Base (BOB) had a staff of 27 including clerks and drivers, hardly half the number deemed necessary to perform its responsibilities. BOB's SI section, which carried the brunt of SSU's early operations against Eastern targets, had only 6 officers, including its chief, none of whom could read or speak Russian. The personnel situation was sufficiently serious that in late October Wiesbaden temporarily suspended all plans for future operations.[37] Sources were also a problem. In the autumn of 1945 the bases relied excessively on casual contacts and occasional informants, some of whom were interviewed only once before they disappeared into the local population. Wiesbaden headquarters pushed its secret intelligence units to develop chains of dependable informants inside Russian-occupied territory, but it would take time to identify and recruit such sources, test their reliability, and construct clandestine networks. Until then, Wiesbaden had to take its sources where and when it could find them. The frequently mediocre quality of the information resulting from these early operations made a poor impression on intelligence customers in the American military government and undermined their confidence in SSU's capabilities.[38]

Coverage of the Soviet zone was also limited by targeting decisions. Just as Berlin Base began to shift attention toward the Soviet sector of the German capital and other areas of Russian-occupied Germany, it embarked on an ambitious project to penetrate Poland. Although OSS/SSU had a small, clandestine X-2 unit attached to the U.S. embassy in Warsaw, there were no SI personnel inside Poland. By early fall 1945, the Steering Division in Wiesbaden had identified certain intelligence requirements for Poland, and Berlin Base was the natural choice to satisfy such requirements, both because of its geographic position and because its SI section included a Polish-émigré officer, Lieutenant Walter Wusza, who during the war had been involved in an abortive OSS program to drop Polish agents behind German lines and who, therefore, possessed the language skills and personal experience necessary to direct operations into his homeland. Poland, while nominally independent, was occupied by the Red Army and directed by leaders responsive to direction from Moscow, so Polish operations would be a useful component of any larger plan to expand intelligence coverage of the Soviet Union and areas under its control or influence. Additionally, the Moscow-backed government in Warsaw, actively supported by Soviet army and police units, was struggling to suppress an armed, anticommunist resistance movement that sought the overthrow of the regime. While not unreasonable, the decision to attack Polish targets had, however, the effect of distracting Berlin Base's attention and dispersing its scarce collection resources when both attention and resources might have been concentrated on developing and exploiting networks in Russian-occupied Germany.[39]

Berlin Base's early Russian operations were also constrained by an emphasis on industrial, agricultural, and economic information at the expense of political and military intelligence. Of course the former categories of information were never unimportant, and there were always customers for such products. BOB rather quickly established effective coverage of the railway system in the Soviet zone and by September 1945 was monitoring Moscow's takeover of this system. In addition to providing an opportunity to track the shipment of dismantled factories and other German research and manufacturing assets to the Soviet Union, an issue that would persistently complicate four-power reparations discussions, this coverage often provided actionable intelligence for American policy makers. For example, the negotiating position of the American delegation to a four-power commission on the future of the German railroads was strengthened by intelligence provided by the SSU mission concerning the number of track lines in the Russian zone that had been changed to Russian gauge. On another occasion in the fall of 1945, when the State Department was seeking details concerning the Soviet Union's plans for land reform in its zone, SSU was able to provide copies of the guidelines approved by Moscow for the use of its local representatives.[40]

SSU's greatest success in its coverage of economic developments in the Soviet zone came with its recruitment of Leo Skrzypczynski, the director of the German Central Administration for Industry, a bureau concerned with economic planning and reconstruction in Russian-occupied Germany. A partner in a prewar telecommunications company, Skrzypczynski, perhaps through the influence of his wife, an active communist, had become involved in the Russian espionage network directed in wartime Berlin by Arvid Harnack, a senior official in the Reich Ministry of Economics. When, in 1943, the Germans rolled up the "Harnack Ring," Skrzypczynski escaped execution, the fate of most of the members of the network, but he was sent to the Oranienburg concentration camp, where he eventually became a camp clerk and worked quietly to improve the lot of incarcerated communists. After VE Day he took a post in the Brandenburg provincial administration, where his work, coupled with his wartime record, so impressed the Russians that he was selected to run the newly created Central Administration for Industry.

Initially Skrzypczynski believed that the Russians had the best interests of Germany at heart and that they would work scrupulously to build a prosperous, democratic, and antifascist society. By April 1946, however, he had become increasingly disturbed by Soviet behavior that seemed destructive of the very society he hoped to build. As a senior executive in the administration of the Soviet zone, Skrzypczynski had occasional contacts with American journalists and military government officials, and at some point in the spring of 1946 he began to pass to SSU information gleaned from his thrice-weekly department meetings with Russian occupation administrators. This intelligence provided American intelligence an excellent window on industrial and economic conditions and policies inside the Soviet zone.[41]

Political and military intelligence, however, was more highly prized. It was also scarcer, largely because it was harder to find and, when found, better protected. News concerning the dismantling of a German factory or the opening of a railway line might be picked up by casual observers walking past an industrial site or along a railway viaduct, but Moscow's plans concerning independent labor unions or the eventual reunification of Germany or the deployment schedules and combat readiness of Red Army units could not be discerned by a stroll past the gates of the Soviet Military Administration compound in Karlshorst.[42] Access to important political and military information required penetration agents and the very clandestine networks that were in such short supply in the autumn of 1945, and this is why Wiesbaden so insistently pushed its bases to recruit long-term secret sources. Mission headquarters was often frustrated when throughout the autumn of 1945 Berlin Base could not provide in sufficient quantity reliable information on political affairs and military dispositions in the Russian zone.[43]

Despite its limitations, OSS/SSU outpaced in capabilities and performance the other intelligence organizations operating in Germany in the months immediately following Germany's surrender. No other local American agency, civilian or military, was running agent networks or attempting clandestine coverage of Russian-controlled areas. Army and navy intelligence were slow in shifting their attention to the east. Admittedly, some of the earliest reliable intelligence on the Russian zone resulted from the observations of a United States Navy inspection team that briefly visited Baltic ports in August 1945. Not surprisingly, the naval inspectors had a sharp eye for military subjects, noting, among other things, that there was an operational airfield at Pillau capable of handling large transports, that the Schichau Shipbuilding works at Danzig were in good shape although the surrounding city was completely destroyed, and that hundreds of barges loaded with German heavy machinery had gathered at Swinemünde as a preliminary to sailing east to Russia.[44] The visit, conducted under Russian auspices, was, however, an overt mission and a unique opportunity. Generally, however, in these early months of peace American military intelligence in Germany paid little attention to its Soviet neighbors; indeed, one veteran of U.S. Army intelligence in Germany, who returned to the United States in late November 1945, recalled that during his time in the country none of his unit's activities were directed against the Soviet Union.[45] Lacking the directives, the resources, the experience, and the appetite to mount clandestine collection operations into Soviet-controlled territories, the various military intelligence organizations represented in Germany (G-2, CIC, ONI) largely limited their activity to German matters: pursuing fugitive Nazis, debriefing prisoners of war and refugees in various interrogation centers, and locating administrative and technical documents from surviving German archives and record caches. The Counterintelligence Corps, for example, did not launch its first collection operations into the Soviet zone until 1948.[46] Many of these activities proved useful, especially in such areas as denazification, war crimes prosecutions, and the exploitation of German research and technology, and some, such as the retrieval of Luftwaffe photo archives of aerial reconnaissance coverage of the Soviet Union, would later prove a boon to American intelligence, but in the first months of peace these activities provided only modest assistance to American decision makers seeking to observe, let alone understand, current conditions and developments to the east.

Foreign liaison, normally a useful supplement to American collection programs, added relatively little to American perspectives on Germany in the summer and autumn of 1945. The most important liaison connections were those with the British services, but while prepared to share information on Italy, Spain, Scandinavia, and Yugoslavia, SIS was relatively silent on German topics. As late as November American intelligence managers in Wiesbaden complained that London was still withholding information on Germany. British reticence may explain why, despite growing interest in the Soviet zone, Wiesbaden continued through the fall to run operations in the British area of occupation. Liaison exchanges with the Belgian, Danish, Dutch, French, Norwegian, and Swedish intelligence services provided occasional items on German affairs. Danish intelligence, for example, shared reports on relations between the German Communist Party and the German Social Democratic Party. In the first months of peace, however, the smaller European services were concerned more with reconstituting themselves in the postwar world and extending the dragnet for war criminals and Nazi collaborators than with developments in the defeated Reich.[47]

Communications intelligence, a rich source of information during the war, apparently contributed little to the sketchy picture of Russian activities and intentions in Germany available to policy makers in Berlin, Wiesbaden, and Washington, although a definitive conclusion must await the declassification of postwar decryption records. As we have seen (chapter 2) all high-grade Soviet diplomatic ciphers and most military ciphers successfully resisted every effort to penetrate their secrets well into 1946, so in the first months of peace neither American nor British cryptanalysts had direct access to the communications channels through which Moscow directed the activities of its military and political proconsuls in Germany. The situation may have improved in the spring of 1946 as American and British code breakers began to exploit successes against Soviet military ciphers in the CAVIAR, COLERIDGE, and LONGFELLOW programs. The results of these efforts remain shrouded in secrecy, but CAVIAR did reveal efforts by Soviet signals intelligence in Germany to identify American and British military radio stations and intercept their transmissions, confirmation (if any was needed) that the Russians considered their wartime partners legitimate intelligence targets.[48] A small-scale effort by the U.S. Army to use former Wehrmacht radio intercept operators to monitor local radio circuits in the Soviet zone showed promise when initiated in October 1945, but the program did not really move into significant production until 1946.[49]

Surveillance of the diplomatic communications of other countries, such as France, Spain, Switzerland, and Turkey, provided little perspective on political and economic affairs in Germany. In the seven months between 1 October 1945 and 30 April 1946 the Diplomatic Summaries, the daily communications intelligence report that circulated at the highest levels of American government, contained scarcely a half-dozen references to Germany, and all but one of these concerned *French* activities, particularly France's efforts to place the Ruhr under an international administration. Only one item, a

French message reported in the summary of 17 April 1946, referred to Soviet intentions in Germany by noting that Moscow intended to strip Germany of machines and goods in order to reconstruct Russia's devastated economy and suggesting that the Russians preferred to work through the German Communist Party while marginalizing the Social Democratic Party (the other party of the left).[50] In the spring of 1946 these observations could hardly have been considered news in Washington, because SSU had been reporting the same information for months.

In the fall of 1945 the small window on Soviet-occupied Germany provided by the Office of Strategic Services (and, subsequently, the Strategic Services Unit) was the principal vantage point for American occupation authorities trying to observe developments east of the Elbe and for their superiors in Washington. The Office of the Military Governor (OMGUS), the central authority in the American zone and Wiesbaden's principal customer, relied heavily upon OSS/SSU for its intelligence. OMGUS had its own intelligence section under Brigadier General Bryan Conrad that compiled and distributed weekly intelligence summaries, but this office had no independent collection or operational capabilities since all its personnel worked in offices in performance of routine administrative and liaison tasks. A report from Wiesbaden to SSU headquarters in Washington in December 1945 noted, "It should not be forgotten that almost everyone in OMGUS is bound to a desk and has neither the facilities, the authority, nor the transportation to go out and produce information on his own. . . . It is a fair statement to say that if SSU in Germany were withdrawn in toto, General Conrad would be out of business in the sense that he would have no way of securing information outside of the American zone."[51] The same was true for the military's field commands, particularly United States Forces European Theater (USFET), which had replaced the Supreme Headquarters Allied Expeditionary Forces (SHAEF) as the overall authority for American military units in Europe.[52]

Civilian authorities in Germany also depended on the reports disseminated by Wiesbaden. State Department representatives assigned to the Office of Political Affairs (OPA), for example, had few independent means for collecting information from the Russian zone. Well into the summer of 1945 OPA had representatives only in Frankfurt and Berlin, and these officers were hard-pressed to provide the State Department information regarding political, economic, and social conditions in areas under American control. Initially, coverage of the British, French, and Russian zones was practically nonexistent. Only in late August did OPA extend its presence by opening offices in Heidelberg and Munich. Coverage of the other zones, however, remained weak, and efforts by Ambassador Murphy to establish listening posts in the form of American consulates in the British, French, and Soviet zones were stymied by Russian obstructionism.[53] For information on the non-American zones Ambassador Robert Murphy relied on SSU reporting, which, for example, contributed as much as 90 percent of the political news from the Russian zone reported by the ambassador in his dispatches to the State Department. Reflecting on the diplomats' reliance on his organization, one senior SSU officer smugly noted, "Without SSU they would have scant information on which to base their reports, particularly on the non-American zones."[54] This dependence persisted well into 1946. Addressing a conference of SSU European station chiefs in Heidelberg in July 1946, a State Department representative admitted, "We have no agents working in the field in Germany. . . . We have to depend on you."[55] While Wiesbaden may have occasionally exaggerated its contributions to the American intelligence picture—in November 1945, for example, General Conrad's office received more intelligence items from the army's various POW and refugee interrogation centers than from SSU offices—it could legitimately claim to be a significant source of information on the eastern areas and the only source with clandestine access to that information.[56]

Steadily that access expanded. Berlin Base, established in the wooded district of Dahlem in a once-elegant three-story villa that had been the personal headquarters of Field Marshall Wilhelm Keitel, was the sharp point of the attack. Under the dynamic leadership of Peter Sichel the base's SI section aggressively probed the Russian-occupied territories, sending agents first into the Soviet sector of the former capital and then east and north into the farther reaches of the Soviet zone. By November 1945 Sichel had twenty-six agents reporting, sixteen operating in the various sectors of Berlin, five working the territory beyond the capital, and five observing targets in Poland. These sources were Germans or Poles—no Russians had yet been recruited—who worked in return for food packages and, less frequently, small cash payments. In the absence of formal boundary controls they moved freely about Berlin and the Soviet zone, ostensibly on professional trips or private business, noting general conditions; observing industrial, transportation, and military facilities; and conversing with subsources who might be family members, professional associates, or social contacts.[57]

Initially, these "tourist missions" (known more formally at Wiesbaden headquarters as "tactical line crossings") generated a rather narrow range of information: mainly observations on social and economic conditions in the eastern areas, much of it little better than rumor and gossip. Gradually, however, the number of sources increased and their experience deepened. The steering section at mission headquarters began more systematically to issue collection guidelines that specified the types of information desired, and SI field officers tasked their sources with specific questions. Coverage expanded in scope and improved in quality. By the end of 1945, for example, Berlin Base was sending Wiesbaden headquarters a steady stream of intelligence on industrial conditions in the eastern areas that accurately tracked Moscow's efforts to dismantle German factories and research institutes and ship them to the Soviet Union, efforts that directly challenged the American policy of maintaining peaceful German industries for the economic reconstruction of the country.

Stalin's National Front Strategy

The early operations into Russian-occupied territory provided scant coverage of political events and Moscow's attitudes concerning the creation of post-Nazi administrative institutions, the development of political parties, and the organization of elections. The Russians marched into Germany determined to smash the remnants of Nazism, remove any future threat of a militarily resurgent Germany, establish a stable administrative structure that would maintain order and resuscitate social and economic activity, and extract reparations in sufficient quantities to recover some of the costs of the war and subsidize the reconstruction of their devastated homeland. In pursuit of these goals certain priorities, such as $10 billion in reparations, acquisition of German scientific and technical resources, and comprehensive denazification, were more clearly articulated than others, such as the precise political arrangements that would replace the discredited administrative personnel and political institutions of the Hitler regime.

The three-power European Advisory Commission, established by the Moscow Conference of 1943, had proposed an "Allied Control Council" to coordinate the administration of occupied Germany. The proposal had been ratified by Allied leaders at the Yalta Conference (4–11 February 1945), but when the Germans surrendered the council had not yet been established nor had the Allies settled on specific guidelines for the revival of political activity in postwar Germany. Such matters awaited the next Big Three conference, scheduled to open at Potsdam in late July. In anticipation of formal decisions at Potsdam, allied representatives had institutionalized the concept of a control council, with a subordinate joint authority for Berlin, in agreements worked out in early June. Until the proposed control council took shape and began, through practice, to define the scope and nature of its authority, each occupying power would assume sole responsibility for administering its zone.

Like their Western allies, Moscow established a military government in its zone, the Soviet Military Administration for Germany (SMA) based in the Berlin suburb of Karlshorst under the command of Marshal Georgi Zhukov. In practice, the exercise of day-to-day authority devolved onto local Red

Army commandants and their political officers in the various zonal commands, while some occupation units, particularly the various detachments of the intelligence and security services and the removal squads dispatched to dismantle German factories, were entirely outside SMA command channels.[58] From the start, Red Army commanders were directed to employ in local administrations politically reliable, antifascist Germans. In this task they were assisted by cadres of the German Communist Party (KPD), whose leaders, having found wartime refuge in Moscow, returned to their homeland in the wake of the conquering Russian army. Reflecting the priorities of the military administration, these cadres focused on maintaining order and establishing an effective administration that would attract the support of all classes of Germans.

In this task, pragmatism, at least initially, often trumped ideology, and KPD leaders (again reflecting broader Soviet policy) did not hesitate to criticize and marginalize radical leftists who saw in the Russian occupation the opportunity to establish a "Red Germany" through the socialization of property, the suppression of the bourgeoisie, and the transfer of all power to workers' soviets. In the eyes of KPD leaders, such as Anton Ackermann and Walther Ulbricht, these "sectarians," who in some localities set about renaming streets and squares after revolutionary heroes and draping public buildings with red banners and revolutionary slogans, merely undermined order and sowed fear and revulsion among the middle and professional classes, whose support was critical for the resuscitation of normal economic and social life.[59] Of course party interests and ideology were never completely ignored. While at first KPD leaders generally sought to ensure that various social groups were represented in local administrative offices and that technical positions were filled by experts (so long as they were not seriously tainted by Nazi affiliations), they were also careful to ensure that key administrative posts, particularly in the police, education, and personnel offices, were reserved for communists.[60]

Moscow's initial approach to the role of German political movements in postwar administration did not foresee explicit and exclusive support for the communists. In keeping with his vision of "revolution by degrees" that he had also urged on the communist parties of Poland and Romania, Stalin recalled KPD leaders to Moscow in June 1945 to advise them to transform their party into a mass political movement that would join other antifascist parties in a national front to pursue the "completion of the bourgeois democratic revolution." Convinced that radical policies would frighten centrist political groups and alienate the Western powers, the Soviet leader believed that the German communists should abandon any notion of immediately imposing a workers' state upon their country in favor of a short-term policy of pursuing socialism through coalition politics and parliamentary democracy. Stalin, of course, assumed that in this process the KPD would assume a guiding, not to say dominant, role, with other political parties in subordinate roles. Communists would rule, but the system would possess enough of the appearances of a parliamentary democracy to satisfy Washington, London, and Paris.[61] Eventually, the KPD-led coalition model might be extended into the other occupation zones, providing the communists a pathway to power across the entire country.

In compliance with these directives, the KPD leaders returned to Berlin, where Ulbricht informed a meeting of party cadres that their organization would oppose "in the present circumstances" any effort to impose a "Soviet system" on Germany. Instead, the party would extend the hand of cooperation to all antifascist groups, including bourgeois parties, but especially to the Social Democratic Party (SPD), a leftist party and former political enemy that the KPD now castigated itself for rejecting as a partner in the prewar anti-Nazi struggle. This posture was publicly endorsed on 11 June 1945, one day after the Soviet military authority issued a directive permitting the establishment of antifascist political parties, when the KPD announced a postwar program that called for a broad collaborative effort to stamp out fascism, improve living conditions, and establish parliamentary democracy. While calling for the expropriation of the property of "Nazi bosses and war criminals," the liquidation of "the great estates of the Junkers, counts, and princes," and the subordination of utilities to local government authority, the party program contained no reference to socialism or communism. Other embryonic political movements, surprised by the early Soviet decision to allow political parties, rushed to launch their own organizations and programs. On 15 June the SPD proclaimed a party platform that in its explicit call for major social and economic reforms, including the nationalization of banks, insurance companies, utilities, and mineral resources, was significantly more radical than the program of the KPD. On 26 June the Christian Democratic Union (CDU) announced itself, followed nine days later by the Liberal Democratic Party (LDP). Not surprisingly, these middle-class parties expressed a commitment to private property, although both were prepared to accept nationalization of certain large industrial enterprises and agricultural estates.[62]

Before the end of the war, the Office of Strategic Services had no clear picture of Moscow's intentions concerning the political organization of occupied Germany, and OSS reporting represented mixed views on the subject. Some field reports, particularly those emanating from Allen Dulles's office in Switzerland in 1944–1945, tended to focus on the anticipated role of the Committee for Free Germany, an organization founded in Moscow in July

1943 by German communist émigrés and captured German army officers. Dulles's reports, which resonated among the more anticommunist officers at Washington headquarters, consistently exaggerated the strength of Free Germany, its appeal to Germans living within the Reich, and its centrality in Moscow's plans for a post-Hitler bolshevized Germany. In fact, the committee pursued primarily propaganda activities aimed at undermining the morale of German troops on the eastern front, limited efforts that showed few results. At the very time that Dulles was alerting Washington to the supposed threat of Free Germany, the movement was receding in both utility and importance in Moscow.[63]

Other reports, based on a broader range of sources, were less alarmist in tone and more prescient in substance, downplaying the role of Free Germany and anticipating that while Moscow would ruthlessly purge Nazis and their sympathizers from positions of political and economic influence, requisition railroads and utilities, and extract billions of dollars in reparations for war damages, its political plans were not yet fixed and would most likely evolve in the direction of a politically unified Germany governed, depending on circumstances, by either a communist regime aligned with the Soviet Union or a neutralist noncommunist administration with pro-Soviet and socialist characteristics. In a summary evaluation of Russian policy prepared for President Roosevelt in the summer of 1944, William Donovan anticipated that Stalin would ruthlessly eradicate all vestiges of Nazism and militarism in Germany and promote and support those German elements most friendly to the Soviet Union. According to Donovan, however, the Soviet dictator would pursue the latter initiative "very cautiously," and the OSS chief assured the president that "Stalin does not entertain any idea of Germany turning Communistic. He is, however, believed to favor the development of a Popular Front which would offer Russia greater liberty of movement."[64]

In the weeks following the Nazi surrender the scattered indications available to American intelligence regarding Moscow's German policy did not seriously challenge Donovan's earlier prognostications. The appearance of political parties and the announcement of their programs were, of course, publicized in the press. Struggling to establish itself in the American zone, the OSS mission in Germany had no secret sources that could provide privileged insight into the behavior and intentions of the Soviet Military Administration toward the emerging political movements. The available information was often impressionistic and drawn from a limited range of mainly open sources in the American occupied areas. While acknowledging that information from the Soviet zone was sparse, an appreciation by SHAEF's Joint Intelligence Committee in early June speculated that the Russians were treating Germans well, but concluded that it was too early to assess Moscow's plans for the defeated people. Throughout the summer OSS Wiesbaden reported evidence that the Communist Party in the American zone was eager to cooperate with the military government and all anti-Nazi groups to rebuild the country and that the KPD believed that economic rehabilitation should take priority over partisan politics. Communist Party publications collected by American intelligence officers reiterated the themes of political unity and common purpose. A summary of available intelligence on political affairs in the Soviet zone submitted to Washington by Allen Dulles in mid-September noted, "While the Russians have shown special favors toward the Communist leaders and have tended to give them preference, they have also encouraged general political activity and are permitting other Parties some freedom of action."[65] Since Dulles, from his wartime lair in Switzerland, had been the source of often alarmist reports concerning communist plans to control postwar Germany, his moderate stance in the early fall of 1945 suggests that both he and his service were trying to be open-minded about Soviet intentions.

Even as Dulles penned his report for Washington, political affairs in the Soviet zone were shifting in an ominous direction. In the fall of 1945 relations between the KPD and its putative partners in the popular front program began to deteriorate in suspicion and acrimony. The KPD and the Red Army's political officers at Karlshorst had assumed that, while welcoming other parties into a popular front, the Communist Party would be the dominant partner and determine the direction of the common program. Indeed, it is unlikely that Moscow would have pushed Ackermann, Ulbricht, and other party leaders toward a short-term program of interparty collaboration, moderate reform, and a commitment to parliamentary democracy unless it anticipated the primacy of the KPD. Unfortunately for Russian plans, the German communists failed to establish such primacy. The other parties, particularly the Social Democrats, exhibited an unexpected organizational vitality. Given a choice of organizations, a majority of Germans turned away from the communists, who were frequently seen as stooges for the Soviets and associated by implication with the rape, plunder, and ruthlessness that were the most hateful consequences of the Russian occupation. As their membership grew (in August 1945 the SPD alone had 225,000 more members than the KPD), the noncommunist parties were less inclined to submit to communist direction, while the communists found it more difficult to justify their claim to the leading role in any partnership. The KPD further alienated its partners by the rather high-handed behavior of certain communists who arrogantly claimed the most important administrative offices and the most comfortable living conditions in the Russian zone.[66]

The Russians and their KPD clients increasingly saw independent and active parties as a threat to their influence; after all, there was no place in the national front strategy for a national front led by noncommunist parties. The Social Democrats were the most dangerous threat because of their popular appeal, their organizational strength, and the anti-Soviet line adopted by SPD leaders in the western zones, particularly Kurt Schumacher, an articulate and outspoken personality in the British zone who was rapidly extending his influence over party cadres. Certain events in that first fall and winter of peace seemed to confirm these fears. In early October an SPD conference in Hannover repudiated the policy of cooperation with the KPD. Although the conference did not bind the party in the Russian zone, the statement was hardly a boost for the popular front program. On 9 November the SPD in the Soviet zone refused to join the KPD in a commemoration of Germany's abortive Red Revolution of 1918 and instead convened its own meeting on 11 November at which party leader Otto Grotewohl publicly questioned aspects of Soviet occupation policy. Soon thereafter, the KPD polled fewer votes than the SPD in elections for factory councils. Even more alarming, especially from the perspective of Soviet headquarters in Karlshorst, was the poor showing of communist parties in autumn elections in Hungary and Austria. In the Austrian case the communist party polled less than 6 percent of the vote. It was easy to conclude that, if forced to stand alone in free elections, the communists would never be more than a minority party.[67]

To ensure the dominance of the KDP, the Soviet authorities adopted a two-part strategy. Karlshorst abandoned its nominal posture of benevolent neutrality toward party affairs and threw its resources behind the KPD. The other parties in the Soviet zone soon began to feel the effects of the policy, which, depending on circumstances and locale, ranged from tiresome harassment to outright persecution. Soviet authorities were suddenly less inclined to issue the necessary permits for party gatherings. Party editors could no longer easily obtain paper to print their newspapers and pamphlets. When they did publish they found it increasingly difficult to escape the interference of Soviet censors. Noncommunist employees of local administrations, particularly police officers, were threatened or dismissed. SPD, CDU, and LDP leaders were summoned before Soviet district officers and berated for their allegedly uncooperative attitudes. SMA authorities relentlessly pressured the noncommunist parties to select leaders more sympathetic to Soviet occupation policies, at one point successfully compelling the Christian Democrats to remove two prominent members of their executive committee, Andreas Hermes and Walther Schreiber, for their allegedly uncooperative attitudes.

The second strand of the emerging Soviet strategy was to neutralize the SPD by securing its merger with the KPD. The poor showing of communist candidates in Austria and Hungary suggested to SMA political officers that the German party was unlikely to win any elections on its own.

A combination with the socialists would allow the KPD to benefit from the organizational strength and membership of its competitor while providing an opportunity to influence, if not control, its direction. Following the reestablishment of their party in the summer, some socialists had been inclined to forge closer links with the communists, but by the fall these inclinations had waned as SPD leaders, aware of their growing strength and alienated by high-handed communist tactics, perceived little advantage in combining with the KPD. By December 1945, however, the socialists were subject to increasing pressure from Soviet occupation authorities to commit to unification with the communists. Succumbing to this pressure, which included harassment of party members and impairment of party activities, SPD leaders agreed to meet their KPD counterparts in the so-called Conference of Sixty (thirty representatives from each party) on 20–21 December 1945. The socialists used the forum as an opportunity to complain about unequal treatment by occupation authorities, assert that unification should involve party elements from all zones of Germany, and express concern that party unification restricted to the Soviet zone might contribute to the prospect of a divided Germany. Having expressed such reservations and received in response only vague assurances that their concerns were misplaced or would disappear with unification, the SPD leaders then accepted a KPD-drafted resolution that affirmed the need for a unified working class in the creation of a democratic Germany, declared that "the deepening and broadening" of KPD-SPD collaboration was only the "prelude to the realization of the political and organizational fusion" of the two parties, and provided for a bipartisan study group to determine the structure and program of the new unified party.[68]

The SPD leadership may have considered the resolution, which included no specific timetable for unification and was silent about the issue of interzonal party relations, as merely a statement of intentions that anticipated merger at some point in the distant future, but the KPD leaders (and their Russian sponsors in Moscow and Karlshorst) considered the statement the go-ahead for immediate unification. The campaign of pressure and intimidation directed at anti-unification elements within the SPD accelerated, and uncooperative party members were arrested on trumped-up charges or threatened with the loss of their jobs in local administrations or party organizations. In contrast those SPD members who favored unification (not an insignificant number) or were undecided were the objects of assurances and blandishments. The mixture of carrots and sticks, plus more than a little pragmatism on the part of SPD officials, who just wanted to be left in peace, eventually diminished the party leadership's opposition to merger. On 11 February 1946 the SPD executive committee accepted unification, a decision subsequently endorsed by the chairmen of the party's provincial organizations. At a congress in Berlin on 21–22 April 1946 the SPD and KPD formally combined into a single organization, the Socialist Unity Party (SED). Despite claims to the contrary, the Soviet occupation authorities from the very start were closely involved in the direction of the new party's affairs.[69]

American intelligence had followed the partisan contest in the Soviet zone with increasing attention. Even at its low point in the summer of 1945 OSS had tried to follow the activities of the German Communist Party in the American zone, and by the end of the summer the service had reported on the early phase of the party's national front strategy. As we have seen, OSS field stations had provided relatively little political reporting from Russian-occupied Germany in the months immediately following the Nazi surrender, and even when, in the fall of 1945, the stations began to turn their eyes eastward, their glance was more likely to fall on economic or industrial targets. Gradually, political coverage expanded, although in November the steering group at Wiesbaden headquarters was still complaining that Berlin Base was focusing too much on economic information at the expense of political intelligence.[70] Wiesbaden's complaint was probably less a criticism of BOB's collection programs than an expression of increasing interest in Soviet zone politics on the part of SSU's customers. By October the clandestine operators were well aware that the national front embraced so hopefully by the KPD, SPD, CDU, and LPD in the early summer was cracking. By November the intelligence summaries distributed to American occupation authorities by the Office of the Military Governor, which relied significantly on SSU reporting, regularly featured items detailing SMA and KPD pressure on the socialists to merge with the communists.[71]

SSU Germany developed an excellent view of party conflicts in the Soviet zone. In the American and British zones, field stations cultivated contacts among Social Democratic and Christian Democratic leaders, such as the SPD's Kurt Schumacher, who were in regular communication with party colleagues in the east. The SPD had particularly good lines of information out of the Russian zone; indeed, the party's Ostbüro (Eastern Office), with which SSU was quick to establish relations, was effectively a private intelligence service for Eastern affairs. Even more useful were connections with party personalities in the Russian-occupied area. Although SSU had no well-placed informants inside the eastern KPD, the other parties in the Russian zone were penetrated at the highest levels. For example, Jakob Kaiser, the respected Catholic trade unionist who replaced Andreas Hermes as head of the Christian Democratic Union in the Soviet zone when Hermes was forced from his position by the Russians in November 1945, was a confidential source for SSU's Berlin Base. Kaiser was probably the source for

Berlin Base's reports on Russian efforts to intimidate the CDU in the fall and winter of 1945, including a particularly unpleasant meeting between Marshal Zhukov and CDU leaders on 12 December 1945 in which the commander of the Soviet Military Administration berated his German visitors for their uncooperative attitude. Other contacts were indirect. Fritz Kolbe, the anti-Nazi German diplomat who had been OSS's most valuable source inside the Third Reich, continued his relationship with American intelligence after the war and, using his contacts in the eastern SPD and CDU, became an excellent source on Russian and KPD efforts to subordinate the noncommunist political parties.[72]

Improved liaison with British intelligence provided additional perspectives on political developments inside the Soviet zone and the German Communist Party. By the spring of 1946 SIS, now more confident about the institutional future and stability of its American partner, was increasingly inclined to share information from its sources in the eastern zone. The British service, for example, passed to its American cousins information concerning the KPD conference that convened during Easter week in 1946. SIS sources reported that the party's central committee was dissatisfied with the pace of recruitment of new members in the western zones. To accelerate recruitment the central committee promulgated new directives, including the recruitment of former Nazis (if this could be done without public exposure and embarrassment), increased efforts to undermine and divide noncommunist trade unions, and better propaganda. The propaganda effort would emphasize the fundamental difference between the occupying powers in the West and the occupying power in the East by attributing to Britain and the United States a desire to keep Germany weak and divided and by praising the Soviet Union as the only champion of the workers and a new Germany. Lastly, the central committee issued instructions for the continued penetration of the police in the western zones, emphasizing that communist police officers must keep their true loyalties secret and avoid all connections with party personnel and offices.[73]

Largely through the efforts of Berlin Base, the Strategic Services Unit was able to keep its customers in Washington well informed concerning party politics in the Soviet zone and the Russian-sponsored efforts to merge the communist and socialist parties. In Washington the relevant intelligence reports were disseminated to the State Department as well as the War Department's Military Intelligence Division and the navy's Office of Naval Intelligence. By early 1946 the State Department in particular was very interested in the party merger issue, and from Germany Ambassador Murphy reported frequently on the subject. Gradually, the Office of the Political Adviser had developed its own contacts in Social Democratic and Christian Democratic circles, but these contacts were exclusively overt, and the diplomats still relied heavily upon SSU for secret political intelligence from the Soviet zone.[74] Pressure and intimidation remained the themes of the intelligence reporting reaching Washington. On 22 January 1946, for example, SSU submitted a report that the SPD leadership was split on the question of merger, that party elements opposed to unification felt intimidated by Russian occupation authorities, and that some opponents had received death threats. Within a week, SSU circulated to its customers a detailed report on Soviet intimidation of the Christian Democratic Union in the state of Saxony. By this time the service was also reporting details of the meeting of the Conference of Sixty and the subsequent debates over party unification in the central committee of the SPD, which were conducted in the intimidating presence of Soviet army officers. Informants inside the central committee reported that delegates from local SPD organizations opposed the Soviet-sponsored unification project but hid their opposition out of fear of reprisals. Reports in March included news that some sources inside the SPD were speaking of the "open terror" directed against the party by Russian occupation authorities and KPD functionaries and that CDU officials in Saxony had been taken from their homes at night by Soviet military police and interrogated at the offices of the local Red Army commandant about their political views. After the formal KPD-SPD merger into the Socialist Unity Party in April, American intelligence continued to report Soviet-sponsored intimidation of SPD members who demonstrated insufficient enthusiasm for the new party and the inability of the communists to capitalize on the merger to increase their popularity or legitimacy in the eyes of German citizens.[75]

The increasingly overt and heavy-handed intervention into partisan politics by Soviet authorities was accompanied by a propaganda offensive across Germany that proclaimed the Soviet Union as the only friend and champion of the German people. In February 1946, for example, an informant in the Soviet zone supplied SSU with a copy of a paper prepared by the KPD leader Erich Honecker for the guidance of a new communist-led youth movement. In this paper Honecker stressed that the young people of Germany needed to learn that only the communists and the Soviet Union, not the Western powers, were sincere advocates of the cause of German unity.[76] About the same time, American intelligence began to notice an increasingly strident anti-American tone in communist propaganda. Flyers, posters, and pamphlets collected by SSU featured lurid anecdotes of outrages by American soldiers such as children allegedly run over by reckless American drivers or innocent citizens shot by American sentries. The alleged sexual predations of African American soldiers figured prominently in these accounts.[77] With the founding of the SED, the theme of the defense of German unity became increasingly associated in KPD propaganda with crude anti-Americanism. The message was clear: to oppose the United States was to defend Germany. Arguments that Washington policy makers knew from intelligence reports that the KPD was unpopular, that Soviet efforts to reverse that unpopularity were ineffective, and that Moscow was prepared to accept some degree of political pluralism, but subordinated this knowledge to a visceral anticommunism, thereby missing an opportunity to avoid the "sovietization" of eastern Germany, misread American intelligence reporting and misunderstand the nature of Moscow's foreign policy.[78] In keeping with Stalin's preference for united-front governments, Soviet policy envisioned a German administration "guided" by the personnel and programs of the German Communist Party. Other political groups might participate in that administration only to the extent that they recognized the primacy of the KPD and accepted its lead. They could participate as junior associates, but not equal partners. Occasionally, as circumstances required, the Soviet Military Administration might offer gestures of accommodation or compromise to the Social Democrats or the Christian Democrats, but these were tactical maneuvers to diffuse opposition or divert attention. A carrot-and-stick approach sought to induce the SD and the CDU to accept the subordinate status reserved for them in Moscow's plans. The Russians much preferred to co-opt the opposition rather than suppress it, but they were prepared to use suppression if necessary.

American intelligence officers in Germany understood the means and ends of Russian policy. While recognizing the weaknesses of the KPD and SED and conscientiously reporting communist measures of accommodation toward other political groups, intelligence reporting indicated that, despite their rhetorical support for a popular front and parliamentary democracy, neither the Soviet occupation authorities nor their clients in the German Communist Party were prepared to countenance any challenge to their primacy, and both were prepared to intimidate potential challengers into submission. The claim that American authorities knew that the communists in Germany were weak is true but insufficient as a description of what intelligence reporting revealed to policy makers. Perceptions of communist weakness were combined with a growing awareness that to compensate for that weakness and ensure communist control, Soviet authorities would not hesitate to adopt repressive measures. Not only did SSU's coverage suggest that the Soviets would pay only lip service to the goal of open and democratic institutions, it also fueled suspicions, already sparked by Soviet behavior in Bulgaria and Romania, that Moscow was intent on forcibly imposing communist regimes on territory occupied by the Red Army.

Although SSU headquarters praised Berlin Base's improving coverage of political developments in the Soviet zone, not every customer was pleased with the service. At first this intelligence did not sit well with some senior officers in the American occupation government, including General Lucius Clay, the military governor, and (at least initially) Robert Murphy, the political adviser to the military government and the senior State Department representative in Germany. In the early, ragtag days of the OSS mission in Germany, Clay in particular had developed a rather skeptical attitude toward the intelligence forwarded to his office by Allen Dulles, dismissing most of it as little more than rumor and gossip. He was also determined to work cooperatively with the Soviets to move a united, democratic Germany into the postwar world and was ill-disposed to accept intelligence that suggested his putative collaborators did not share his agenda and were prepared to use high-handed tactics to advance their own program in Germany. Peter Sichel, then BOB's chief of intelligence, later recalled, "Murphy . . . was not too starry-eyed. The starry-eyed man was General Clay who wanted badly to build a cooperative American-Russian system for administering Germany. He ultimately saw the light, but later than Murphy, and he was not pleased by my reporting."[79] At the time, Sichel was summoned to Wiesbaden to discuss his station's operations. The young intelligence chief—he had just turned 23—strongly defended his collection programs and their product, insisting that the actions of the Soviet occupation authorities could not be ignored simply because they made some Americans feel uncomfortable. Eventually Sichel convinced his supervisors to support his reporting, although Berlin's intelligence remained controversial among some of its customers. As late as March 1946, SSU Germany advised Washington of "high echelon conflict on political reporting," a circumlocution that suggested that some elements in the American zone were still having trouble coming to grips with the political intelligence emerging from eastern Germany.[80]

Tracking Soviet Military Capabilities

In early 1946, as its coverage of eastern zone political affairs moved into high gear, SSU Germany unexpectedly found itself distracted by new requirements. General Edwin Sibert, the chief of G-2 (intelligence) for United States Forces, European Theater, had become increasingly interested in the disposition of Soviet military forces in his area of responsibility. It was his job to keep an eye on the armed forces of the various European states, and he could not help but notice that his view toward the east was rather clouded. In fact the army knew very little about the identity, location, equipment, morale, and general capabilities of Russian units in Central and Eastern Europe, a deficiency that by early 1946 appeared increasingly serious.

Great Power relations were under increasing strain. For several months tension had been rising in the Near East as the Soviet Union attempted to secure political, economic, and territorial concessions from Iran and Turkey. Moscow's demands had been accompanied by reports of Soviet troop movements, particularly in the Balkans, and American and British intelligence reporting from the region raised the possibility that the Russians might resort to military action to secure their designs. These designs, in turn, posed a direct threat to Britain's imperial position in the Near East, a position that Washington considered a crucial bulwark to Soviet expansion in the region. Increasingly decision makers in Washington worried that Moscow, miscalculating London and Washington's stake in preserving the status quo in the Near East, might spark a general conflict involving the major powers by initiating military action against one of its smaller neighbors. These concerns regarding the possibility of war began to increase in the early spring of 1946 and peaked in August and September of that year.[81]

Given the unsettled international situation and the fear that the nightmare of American forces defending Europe against a Soviet attack was no longer purely hypothetical, General Sibert was suddenly desperate for information concerning the identity, size, location, readiness, and command structures of Red Army and Air Force units, information referred to by intelligence professionals as "order of battle" (OOB) intelligence. Unfortunately in early 1946 the U.S. Army in Europe lacked the intelligence collection capabilities to satisfy Sibert's requirements. The Pond, the army's small clandestine intelligence unit, seems not to have been very active in Germany at this time, at least not on the operational level required by Sibert. A summary report of Pond activities in the period 1946–1947 reveals a preponderance of reports on France and Turkey, but relatively few on the Soviet Union, and those few focused not on Soviet military affairs but on Moscow's economic penetration and political subversion in various European countries. In any event, in the first half of 1946 much of the Pond's information came not from clandestine operations but from liaison with foreign police and intelligence services.[82] With few clandestine sources of its own, G-2 relied primarily on the interrogation of refugees and prisoners of wars at various camps and transit centers in Germany and Austria and the examination of Nazi military records collected wherever they could be found. While useful, the information generated by such sources was usually dated or unreliable. G-2 needed spies. General Sibert didn't have any, but he knew where to find some.

A War Department directive in January 1946 had placed SSU Germany under the supervision of the European Theater G-2. General Sibert was, therefore, able to redirect the mission's growing clandestine capabilities away from political and economic reporting and toward Russian military targets.

As SSU expanded its operations in the Soviet zone in late 1945, the occasional item of military information had found its way into the stream of political and economic intelligence flowing into Wiesbaden headquarters, but military reporting had never been the priority. Now it was. Under pressure from G-2, the German intelligence stations, Berlin again in the forefront, rushed to expand their coverage of military targets in the Soviet zone, a program that eventually received the code name GRAIL. The result was "a whole slew of low level tourist missions" that produced "small mosaic stuff": a report that the Fourth Guards Infantry at Eisenstadt-Sopron was being mechanized; news that additional aircraft had arrived at the Red Air Force bases at Rangsdorf and Staaken; a description of the alleged chain of command of the Red Army's Central Group of Forces; information regarding training facilities at Zehrensdorf. By the spring of 1946, Russian order-of-battle reporting had become SSU's principal collection focus.[83]

The sources for this new focus were mainly former German army officers living in the American zone who were recruited in haste because they were available and because their wartime experience presumably schooled them to spot and describe the insignia and tabs on the collars and caps of Soviet troopers, the bumper markings on Red Army vehicles, the antennae on the roofs of buildings, the fuel tanks and revetments at bases and airfields, and the other minutiae that contributed to the growing mosaic of Soviet order of battle. Not a few of these former Wehrmacht officers had fought on the eastern front, and the opportunity to continue the battle against the Soviet enemy may have pushed them into the arms of American intelligence. Eventually, some of these early agents recruited relatives or associates who lived near army bases, airfields, or transit points in the Soviet zone, and gradually espionage chains evolved.

In addition to helping G-2 improve its picture of Soviet forces in Germany, the new emphasis on military targets revealed that, in flagrant violation of agreements reached at the Potsdam Conference that prohibited the manufacture of munitions, armaments, and "instruments of war" in Germany, the Russians were employing German factories to produce weapons for the Soviet military.[84] To be sure, none of the victorious allies had been reticent about exploiting the remains of the Nazi military-industrial complex. Even before Germany's surrender, American, British, French, and Russian intelligence teams, following close on the heels of Allied tank columns, scavenged in the ruins of the Third Reich for scientific and technical prizes. When, for example, in April 1945, U.S. Army units overran the V-2 rocket production complex at Nordhausen, a city in the designated Soviet occupation zone, a team stripped the underground facilities of every item that could be removed, including parts for 100 V-2 rockets, and shipped the loot to the United States before turning the city over to the Red Army. From Jena, another city in the future Soviet zone, teams searched the offices and workshops of Zeiss, the famous designer and manufacturer of optics, and removed archives and lenses.[85] Even after Germany's surrender, when the occupation zones were firmly established, U.S. teams occasionally slipped quietly into Soviet-controlled territory to recruit German specialists for postwar American research and development programs. In the summer of 1945 zonal boundaries were not yet well secured by fences and guards. At night, pairs of American intelligence officers, usually from the X-2 section of OSS, would drive unmarked civilian vehicles into the Soviet zone. They wore army uniforms stripped of insignia and unit patches and carried "Eisenhower passes," documents issued by American military headquarters that permitted the bearer unimpeded transit, at least in the western zones. It wasn't clear if the Russians would recognize these passes. If a team was stopped by a Russian patrol or control point (none ever were), the Americans depended, in the last resort, on their wits to get them safely through the encounter. The team would go to the last known address of the target, and if the scientist or technician was there, attempt to convince him of the advantages of returning with them to the American zone. If persuasion did not work, compulsion would. Though instructed to make the encounter as nonconfrontational as possible, the American teams were expected to return with their target whether the scientist was willing or not.[86]

Soviet exploitation of German military research and manufacturing was much more comprehensive than that of its wartime allies. Much of this activity violated interallied agreements on the disposition of German armaments. A Tripartite Naval Commission, for example, had agreed that the advancing allies would report the capture of all German naval vessels, including those still under construction, and that the American, British, and Russian navies would receive specified numbers of these vessels, including ten submarines each. Unallocated ships were to be destroyed. Among the submarines allocated to the Red Navy were four Type XXI U-boats, vessels more advanced than any in Allied service. In compliance with earlier agreements, Britain and the United States had destroyed all unallocated German submarines found in their occupation zones, including sixteen subs still under construction. The Soviets, however, had seized twelve uncompleted Type XXI boats beyond their allocation of four and had neither reported their seizure to the Tripartite Naval Commission nor destroyed the submarines, a violation of interallied agreements that American intelligence became aware of in the spring of 1946.[87]

Rather than snatching specialists, blueprints, and production samples as the Americans, British, and French had done, the Russians, in violation of the Potsdam agreements, set about reconstituting and reemploying facilities for both design and production. Leo Skrzypczynski, SSU's source at the top of the Soviet zone's Central Administration for Industry, reported that the Russians had elevated armaments production in their zone to a top priority. Throughout the spring and summer of 1946 confirming intelligence poured in from the expanding clandestine networks and from liaison partners, such as the Danish intelligence service: a report that the German telecommunications giant, Telefunken, was now manufacturing radios and radar for the Red Army and that the famed Zeiss optical company was producing range finders; news that the Schaeffer & Budenberg plant at Magdeburg was making tank parts for the Red Army, while the Borsig Works at Borsigwalde was constructing entire tanks; and reports of small arms and ammunition production in many locations. Coverage of the Soviet utilization of German aviation research and production was especially strong. In February 1946 SSU received information that the Junkers aircraft factory at Dessau, the Siebel factory in Halle, and the RAG plant in Berlin-Oberschoeneweide were developing jet fighters and accessories for jet-propelled aircraft for the Red Air Force. By April, aircraft manufacturing in the Soviet zone was so extensive that SSU reported shortages of aluminum.[88] There were also signs that the Soviets had taken over the German rocket program, rehabilitating the "V" weapons factory at Nordhausen as well as other sites connected to the design and production of missile components. SSU was well aware of the Soviet absorption of German rocket programs. By April 1946, the American service was reporting that V-2 rockets were in regular production at a factory in Sonderhausen under the supervision of the Red Army and that rockets were also manufactured "on a major scale" at Meyenburg. Facilities outside Berlin and elsewhere were developing and testing hulls and steering devices for the V-3 and V-4 generation of rockets.[89] In the context of rising international tension in the Middle East in the spring and summer of 1946, persistent evidence of Russia's intensive exploitation of the surviving German armaments industry could hardly have comforted American policy makers.

Not surprisingly, in some areas the information was vague. Definite production figures were not always available. The degree to which the Soviets were exploiting German synthetic fuel plants, for example, remained a mystery. By mid-April 1946, however, the intelligence from SSU was sufficient in quantity and quality to allow G-2 to conclude that "although the Soviets are actively engaged in dismantling many armament and other industrial installations in occupied Germany, certain other plants have been producing armament and equipment for the Red Army since September 1945."[90] The Strategic Services Unit's reports on Russian exploitation of German armaments factories circulated to the State Department, the War Department, and occupation authorities in the American zone. At the State Department the Division of Central European Affairs and the Division of German and Austrian Economic Affairs were special customers. These reports undoubtedly contributed to the decision to challenge Moscow's disregard for the Potsdam agreements. In April 1946, at a meeting of the Council of Foreign Ministers in Paris, and then again in May and June before the Allied Control Commission for Germany, American representatives called for an investigation of all aspects of German demilitarization, particularly the demilitarization of industry. The Soviets refused. Washington next resorted to publicity. In the summer of 1946 the American press featured "reliable reports" attributed to "American authorities" alleging Russia's misuse of German industry.[91]

In July the British, who had been sharing intelligence with the United States, raised the issue again at the Council of Foreign Ministers, where Foreign Secretary Ernest Bevin bluntly asserted, "I have received reports alleging that war material is being produced in the Soviet Zone of Germany." Soviet Foreign Minister Vyacheslav Molotov blandly denied the accusation. The British persisted. In August London indicated that it would insist on an investigation, a position later endorsed by Secretary of State James Byrnes.[92] In October, under increasing pressure from London and Washington, the Soviets agreed in the Allied Control Commission to a face-saving measure: inspections for illegal military formations and weapons production in *all* occupation zones. The inspections were scheduled for November, but Moscow stalled until January 1947. By then SSU knew from Leo Skrzypczynski, its source inside the Soviet zone's economic administration, that the Soviets were deeply concerned at having been caught out in a massive violation of the Potsdam accords. Believing that inspections could not be long delayed, they were considering a lawyerly expedient. Since the Potsdam agreements did not explicitly prohibit the manufacture of weapons in *Soviet* factories in Germany, the Russians would simply transfer ownership of much of the armaments industry to an industrial combine they would own.[93] In the end, Moscow settled on an even more desperate measure. Soviet security forces simply gathered up thousands of scientists, engineers, and technicians along with their families and belongings and relocated them to the Soviet Union. Equipment from the weapons factories and research centers was crated and shipped with the departing workers.[94]

Even after the mass relocation some illegal armaments work persisted in the Soviet zone. Production of guided bombs, for example, continued at a facility at Dessau until 1949. The Sauckel plant in Weimar continued to produce antitank guns, while the Shaeffer and Budenberg enterprise in Magdeburg maintained its production of armor plating and gun mounts for tanks. A mysterious "Zentral-werke Drei" in Sömmerda merely transferred its facilities to Sonderhausen, where it reestablished its rocket research. As late as the summer of 1947 American intelligence was reporting little diminution in the exploitation of war industries in the Soviet zone.[95]

Less detailed, but more alarming, than revelations of Moscow's exploitation of the German armaments industry were reports concerning German contributions to the Soviet atomic weapons program. Hiroshima and Nagasaki erased any doubts among American military leaders about the potential of atomic weapons and encouraged a belief that national security depended upon an Anglo-American monopoly of the new weapon. To secure this monopoly the U.S. War Department dispatched so-called ALSOS teams into the ruins of the Third Reich to determine the status of Nazi efforts to develop an atomic bomb and to collect what they could of the German atomic program for transfer to Britain and the United States. As part of this collection effort, ALSOS teams took into custody and moved to Britain several of Germany's leading physicists, including Werner Heisenberg, Walther Gerlach, and Max von Laue, and secured the high-grade uranium ore the Germans had acquired. Although the War Department's directives for ALSOS referred only to Germany's scientific programs, the teams were also part of an effort to delay Russia's development of an atomic bomb.[96]

The Russians, no less concerned than the Anglo-Americans to exploit Germany's nuclear weapons program, removed to the Soviet Union not only German scientists and technicians, but entire facilities. In Berlin the Russians dismantled the world-renowned Kaiser Wilhelm Institute for Physics, where Werner Heisenberg had worked, and shipped the entire facility—including the sinks and doorknobs—to the USSR. Other research institutes specializing in physical chemistry, electrochemistry, and physics were also transferred with their staffs to the Soviet Union. Lured by the promise of a comfortable standard of living and the opportunity to continue their research, prominent scientists, such as Gustav Hertz, a Nobel laureate, Manfred von Ardenne, Germany's foremost expert on cyclotrons, and Nikolaus Riehl, the senior scientist at the Auer Company, which had produced uranium metal for the Nazi nuclear program, also moved to the East.[97]

By the late summer of 1945 American intelligence had discerned the outlines of the Soviet effort, although some of the early information concerning the relocation of scientists came from Britain's Secret Intelligence Service.[98] By early 1946 SSU, depending on sources inside the Soviet zone and the surveillance of letters from the scientists to their families and friends in Germany, had definitely located German nuclear researchers and technicians at various sites in the USSR where the Russians were expanding or constructing research facilities. Though details concerning the progress of the Soviet nuclear weapons program remained elusive through 1946, the large-scale relocation of personnel and facilities was suggestive. Fueling concern were reports in early 1946 from clandestine sources in Czechoslovakia that the Russians were aggressively exploiting uranium deposits at Joachimsthal and recruiting mining engineers from that Czech town to develop uranium deposits in the Soviet republics of Kazakhstan and Uzbekistan. No less worrisome were the reports on Soviet activities that began to filter into SSU's German offices in the summer of 1946. In July, for example, there was information concerning increased activity at heavy water plants at Halle and Merseburg in the Soviet zone. In September SSU Germany received information confirming earlier reports that at the "radium spa" at Oberschlema the Russians had intensified efforts to extract pitchblende, a uranium-rich mineral, and that they had ordered the local labor exchange to draft all available men for this work. Another report indicated that the Soviets had begun research to determine if V-weapons (missiles) could be adapted to transport atomic bombs.[99]

For American policy makers intelligence reporting on the USSR's race to develop atomic bombs cast light on Moscow's approach to international control of nuclear weapons. On 14 June 1946, Bernard Baruch, the U.S. representative to the United Nations Atomic Energy Commission, had called for placing under international control all activities related to the production of atomic weapons. States would remain free to conduct research, under UN license and inspection, into peaceful applications of nuclear energy. Violators of these terms were subject to punishment, unshielded by the right of veto possessed by the great powers in the United Nations Security Council. On 19 June, the Soviet representative, Andrei Gromyko, presented Moscow's counterproposal, which called for an international agreement outlawing the production and stockpiling of atomic weapons and the destruction of all existing atomic bombs. The Russian proposal contained no provision for international inspection of nuclear facilities. Countries would pass purely national legislation providing for the punishment of their own citizens who might violate the agreement. Gromyko also spoke of an international committee to consider appropriate means for enforcement beyond self-enforcement but insisted on the great powers' right of veto in the committee as well as in the Security Council over any actions relating to atomic energy.[100]

The Soviet approach would require the destruction of the American nuclear arsenal while preventing any inspections or international controls that would constrain the USSR from developing its own arsenal. American officials, privy to SSU reporting on Russia's urgent effort to develop nuclear weapons, could only view Moscow's position as an effort to buy time for the Soviet effort while manipulating world opinion to Washington's disadvantage. This skeptical view of Moscow's intentions was confirmed by U.S.

intelligence in the fall of 1946 when a "penetration agent" who had proved "reliable and accurate in the past" attended, on October 26, a political indoctrination session in the Soviet zone of Germany for high-ranking officers of the Red Army. In a report that circulated at the highest levels of American government, the source related that a representative of the Central Committee of the Soviet Communist Party explained to the officers that the USSR was working energetically to develop atomic weapons. The United States, however, was continuing to manufacture atomic bombs and "A-bombers," a situation that, if allowed to continue, would only widen the American lead. To forestall this, Soviet diplomacy would push to include nuclear weapons in a comprehensive program of disarmament while blocking any effective system of international inspection. Simultaneously, a propaganda campaign would represent the USSR as a champion of peace. The United States, susceptible to the influence of public opinion, would be pushed "to disarm in line with an international agreement, including destruction of atomic bombs and discontinuance of further development." For its part, the Soviet Union, standing "firm in its refusal to agree to international inspection" would secretly continue to develop atomic weapons to its ultimate advantage.[101]

The new emphasis on Russian military targets had important consequences for American intelligence in Germany and elsewhere. For the Strategic Services Unit it finally confirmed the Soviet Union as the principal target. In the summer of 1945, Frank Wisner, then chief of SI at Wiesbaden headquarters, had proposed a major reallocation of resources toward the east. The growing interest in the Soviet zone affirmed Wisner's foresight, but through 1945 Russian affairs had to compete for Wiesbaden's scarce resources with any number of other targets. By early spring 1946, however, there was a growing consensus inside SSU that the Soviet Union and its occupation zone were the primary targets. In March, P branch, the headquarters section responsible for planning future collection programs, advised SI branch that the Soviet Union was now the top intelligence priority. In an aside that suggested that not all SI elements were committed to the new priority, P branch asserted that the focus on the Soviet Union "needs to be repeated again and again" and that SSU's collection efforts should be directed "with unequivocal emphasis" against this priority target. The word passed immediately to the field. Reflecting the new posture, SI Germany informed its local customers that it would no longer collect local political and economic information from within the U.S. zone for the use of American occupation administrators. For local information the administrators would have to rely on other agencies, such as the Counterintelligence Corps or the Information Control Division that monitored civilian mail and telecommunications in the American zone. SSU would be too busy with Russia.[102]

New Players

The Russian order-of-battle crisis in the spring of 1946 also broke SSU's monopoly on clandestine intelligence. In the rush to collect as much information on the Red Army, Air Force, and Navy as was possible in the shortest time possible, the American military decided that more hands would make better work. Additional hands might also do different work. For example, in both its OSS and SSU incarnations, the German mission had devoted very little attention to naval affairs. In the spring of 1946, however, as international tensions rose over developments in the Near East, the U.S. Navy flooded SSU with requests for information on the deployment of the Red Navy, technical details and photographs of its vessels, the location of its bases and shipbuilding facilities, and biographical details of its senior commanders. Suspecting, perhaps, that SSU already had too much on its agenda to devote immediate attention to naval requirements, or, more probably, reluctant to go cap in hand to another service for intelligence, the navy looked for opportunities to develop its own clandestine sources. By late 1946, for example, Captain William Graubert, the assistant chief of staff for intelligence on the staff of the commander of American naval forces Germany, had developed a network of informants in the Baltic directed primarily against Russian naval targets.[103]

For its part, the U.S. Army determined that it required additional clandestine capabilities beyond those offered by SSU. For all its success in collecting order-of-battle intelligence for the army, SSU had never shared G-2's single-minded obsession with the Red Army, an attitude that caused no little tension in its relations with General Sibert. Believing that its clientele extended beyond the U.S. Army and that its collection responsibilities were not limited to counting tanks and airplanes, SSU Germany (and Berlin Base in particular) chaffed under G-2's tasking and asserted the need to cover a broader range of targets, including political and economic affairs.[104] A new espionage service, devoted exclusively to military intelligence and directed against the Soviet zones of Germany and Austria, would be able to concentrate on the Red Army, the army's main intelligence interest, without chasing after items of political and economic news as did the spies in SSU. The army needed its own clandestine organization, but rather than building from scratch its own service, it decided to contract out the job.[105]

In late May 1945 a small group of German army officers had turned themselves in to an American CIC detachment in Bavaria. The senior officer, a General Reinhard Gehlen, several times asked to speak with high-level American officers, but his requests were ignored until the Germans reached the military detention and interrogation center at Wiesbaden. At this prison camp, Gehlen found a sympathetic listener in the person of Captain

John Broker, a German-speaking army intelligence officer and interrogator. Gehlen revealed to Broker that during the war he had commanded Fremde Heere Ost (FHO: Foreign Armies East) the German army's intelligence organization on the eastern front. He further informed his interrogator that senior personnel of his former command were in American custody and that before surrendering they had, at his direction, hidden several cases of intelligence files on the Soviet Union. Gehlen certainly expected his calculated confession to arouse the interest of his captors, and he was not disappointed. Captain Broker, one of the not insignificant number of army officers convinced that with the defeat of the Axis the Soviet Union remained as the principal threat to American security in the postwar world, convinced his superiors, including General Edwin Sibert, then G-2 of the Twelfth Army Group, to exploit the opportunity offered by their prisoner. Within a month the army had not only recovered Gehlen's files but had also located and collected in Wiesbaden all of the general's key personnel from FHO, including Hermann Baun, the officer who ran the Wehrmacht's clandestine networks (code-named "Walli I") on the eastern front.[106]

The army (or at least the small part of it that knew about Gehlen and his team) wasn't sure what to do with their prizes. In the summer of 1945, with the Big Three coalition still resilient and the shape and direction of peacetime American intelligence still uncertain, the peculiar skills represented by the FHO officers were not in great demand, and Captain Broker, Gehlen's earliest advocate, readily acknowledged that in many corners of the American government there was strong opposition to collecting intelligence on the Soviet Union. The army decided to put Gehlen on ice. In August the general, a few of his men, and all of his files were flown to the United States. Confined in rather spartan conditions at Fort Hunt, Virginia, the Germans (code-named BOLERO), who had expected to be welcomed as important collaborators, found themselves reduced to serving as fact checkers to a low-level army team writing a history of the war on the eastern front.

Back in Germany, Hermann Baun, who along with several other former FHO staffers had been removed from detention centers and established in a residential compound in Oberursel, a small community outside Frankfurt, had been trying to interest the army in several intelligence schemes, assuring his "hosts" that he could easily reconstitute his old networks and direct them again against Russian targets. In October 1945 General Sibert, now USFET G-2, asked OSS if it was interested in using Baun, but the clandestine service declined the offer. The following month Sibert tried again, and once more the service, now reconstituted as SSU, refused, dismissing out of hand Baun's "rather grandiose and vague suggestions." Like its predecessor agency, SSU knew very little about the army's growing relationship with

General Gehlen, and when it began to learn more its reserve only grew. It warned G-2 against relying on any of the Gehlen group and advised the army "to interrogate Baun at length and have nothing to do with his schemes for further intelligence activity." SSU's position was supported by a report from the Counterintelligence Corps that noted that during an extended debriefing by CIC interrogators Braun had acknowledged that none of his wartime operations against the Soviet Union had been successful and that the Russians had rolled up his agents as quickly as he sent them across the lines.[107]

The army ignored these warnings. It was not that military intelligence had a special predilection for German specialists, some of whom were seriously compromised by their Nazi past. G-2 was prepared to accept any available, experienced personnel who represented an opportunity to improve coverage of the Soviet military. In the early spring of 1946, for example, General Sibert was also interested in obtaining the services of a group of Polish operatives, then cooling their heels in Britain, that had been originally trained for wartime intelligence missions behind German lines.[108] As the demand for intelligence on the Red Army increased, G-2 simply decided that the Gehlen group, a collection of knowledgeable intelligence officers with recent experience against Russian targets, should not be wasted. In October 1945 the army had allowed Hermann Baun and a small team of German radio intercept operators at Oberursel to test their ability to monitor radio traffic in the Soviet zone. The Germans focused on the low-level tactical radio nets of Soviet forces in Germany, particularly those of the Red Air Force. Little of this routine traffic was important enough to be encrypted by the Russians (a fortuitous situation since the army prohibited their Germans from engaging in code breaking), but over time the radio chatter of Soviet pilots generated bits and pieces of information concerning the deployment, training, and readiness of Russian air units.[109]

Encouraged, perhaps, by the success of this modest radio intercept program, G-2 allowed Baun to develop his ideas for agent networks. From a new headquarters in a renovated hunting lodge in the mountains north of Frankfurt, Baun (whose group was designated KEYSTONE) moved quickly to recruit and deploy agents against Soviet targets. Desperate for intelligence on the Red Army, G-2 spurred their protégé to ever greater efforts. Baun responded by expanding radio monitoring, recruiting more agents (not a few of whom had been members of such notorious Nazi formations as the Gestapo and the Sicherheitsdienst, the intelligence service of the Nazi Party) and accelerating his collection efforts to meet the increasing demand. Baun's agent networks began producing their first reports in April 1946. In July 1946 the army transferred Gehlen and his small team from Fort Hunt to Germany with the intention of merging, under Gehlen's overall command, the analysts of BOLERO with the collectors of KEYSTONE. The combined operation, funded entirely by the U.S. Army, was designated RUSTY.[110]

By October 1946 RUSTY claimed to have more than 500 agents in the field. Initially, the focus was the Soviet zone of Germany, but by the autumn of 1946 Gehlen's networks had begun to probe Poland, the Balkans, and even the Soviet Union. The general never forgot that he had only one customer, the United States Army, and that his enterprise depended upon satisfying the needs of that customer. While the networks turned up occasional items on industrial activity, scientific research, and general social and economic conditions, the vast majority of reports concerned Red Army and Air Force order of battle. RUSTY was best at reporting the most basic level of OOB intelligence: the location and movements of Red Army elements ("twelve covered trucks, two military cars and a communications van are parked on the outskirts of Krankfeld"). It was much less successful, however, at moving to the next level of reporting: the identification of the units and their place in the command structure ("the 1st Signals Battalion of the 3rd Guards Division is now located at division headquarters outside Weimar"). It had no success at all in providing insight into Soviet military plans or intentions. Occasionally, Gehlen's organization found a gem, such as evidence of the Red Army's efforts to recruit former German Army officers or details on the production of V-4 rockets at a factory in the Soviet zone, but usually RUSTY's intelligence simply confirmed information already received from SSU or other sources. If G-2 had expected their Germans to provide an intelligence windfall, it was disappointed. There were no spectacular breakthroughs into hitherto denied intelligence territory. The best that a G-2 evaluation in September 1946 could say for RUSTY was that "It was about equal to SSU in reliability and quality of information, though usually somewhat later."[111]

Evidence of the army's disappointment might be found in G-2's persistent efforts to hand RUSTY over to someone else. Throughout 1946 SSU refused to adopt the Germans despite continued pleas from the army. This reluctance did not reflect any moral aversion to exploiting former members of the wartime German security and intelligence apparatus. Despite their public commitment to denazification and their compilation of "arrest on sight" lists of former Nazis, the wartime allies had an ambivalent attitude toward the postwar employment of former enemies. The ambivalence was especially strong in areas touching upon scientific research and development and the national security of the occupying powers and their respective zones. In the summer of 1945, for example, the Soviets began actively to recruit and relocate German scientists and technicians for service in Russian research establishments. The Soviet Military Administration in Germany, preoccupied with the need to ensure order in its area of responsibility, did not hesitate to employ in the new police units it was organizing former members of the Wehrmacht and the SS. For their part, Soviet intelligence and internal security services aggressively recruited former personnel of the German intelligence and security services, including members of the SS, for operations in both the eastern and western zones.[112]

In early postwar Germany the Office of Strategic Services and the Strategic Services Unit had generally avoided veterans of the SD, SS, and Gestapo, although they worked with former officers of the Abwehr, Germany's military intelligence service. At least in American eyes, the Abwehr was not as tainted by association with the Nazis regime, in part because certain military intelligence officers had been prominent in the anti-Nazi resistance. Still, SSU's problem with RUSTY was not that Gehlen was employing former Nazis. By the summer of 1946 the German mission (now relocated from Wiesbaden to Heidelberg) was influenced more by professional concerns. Gehlen steadfastly declined to reveal to his patrons the identities of his sources or the structure of his networks. Without such information, however, it was difficult for the Americans to assess the credibility of the information generated by these sources and networks. Additionally, without such information it was impossible for the Americans to check the background (and, thereby, the reliability and loyalty) of individual sources. Gehlen persistently refused to grant access to his personnel and operational records, and the Strategic Services Unit refused to have anything to do with Gehlen without such access.[113]

Of course there was more than a little condescension in SSU's posture. RUSTY was, after all, an upstart competitor for intelligence influence and attention. SSU thought little of Gehlen's organization, which it considered unprofessional and insecure, and less of its product, which it considered unreliable. Responding to a claim by General Withers Burress, General Sibert's successor as G-2 USFET who was trying to sell RUSTY to the Central Intelligence Group in the fall of 1946, that Gehlen's organization was "one of [the army's] most prolific and dependable sources," an SSU evaluation prepared for General Hoyt Vandenberg, the director of central intelligence, warned against allowing a U.S.-sponsored service to operate autonomously; criticized Gehlen's group for routinely "drawing broad conclusions from inadequate evidence"; and concluded that "there is no evidence whatsoever which indicates high-level penetration into any political or economic body in the Russian-occupied zone."[114]

The appearance of new organizational actors on the German espionage stage in 1946 may have retarded American clandestine collection programs more than they advanced them. In the absence of central oversight in both Washington and the field to identify priorities, assign collection tasks, coordinate operations, and assess product, the proliferation of collection programs threatened to disperse scarce resources, duplicate efforts, encourage bureaucratic competition, and complicate operational security. Two factors, in particular, seriously undermined the expanding American intelligence program in Germany as the battle lines of what would become the Cold War began to emerge.

In the summer of 1945 the Office of Strategic Services had been the only American agency conducting clandestine intelligence operations in Germany. A year later several American or American-sponsored agencies were engaged in such operations. Each of these agencies worked independently, recruiting its own sources, establishing its own networks, and assessing and distributing its own product. Of course in any given population, the number of individuals prepared by appetite, temperament, and personal position to work as spies is small. One might predict, therefore, that as the number of organizations seeking sources increases, the number of spies recruited by each organization would decline. Demand would soon outpace supply. In Germany in 1946, however, the supply of intelligence always seemed to increase to meet the demand. Not only did the various American services succeed in an increasingly crowded marketplace to develop productive and apparently exclusive sources, but these sources often had the uncanny ability to produce the very information required by the particular service. When the U.S. Navy needed information on the dispositions of the Soviet Baltic Fleet, rather remarkably sources were quickly found that could provide exactly that information. If SSU wanted to know what was going on inside the Karlshorst headquarters of the Soviet Military Administration, it would soon be approached by someone who just happened to have a cousin who worked in the Russian officers' mess. Occasionally these sources were real. Most of the time they were not.

In early postwar Germany espionage was big business; indeed, along with the black market, the purchase and sale of information was the only form of commerce that flourished amid the smoldering factories, smashed shops, and hungry populations of cities such as Berlin. Once it became clear that the Americans (and the British, French, and Russians) were willing to purchase information with cash, cigarettes, coffee, or canned food it was only a matter of time before entrepreneurs began producing products for the expanding market. Recalling a "veritable stream" of eager volunteers, one CIC veteran noted, "Almost everyone of them asserted that he had a network of agents in the Soviet Union and, for the right price of course, would place his network at our disposal."[115] Intelligence "mills" sprang up across Germany but particularly in Berlin, the spy capital of the country, where enterprising individuals fabricated "intelligence" from newspaper reports, street rumors, or (more commonly) their own fertile imaginations, created notional agents or, at times, entire networks, to provide a provenance for these tales, and sold the package to case officers who were unaware that the entire product was counterfeit. Among the American espionage organizations military intelligence proved the most gullible and SSU the least, although no agency escaped the swindles of the confidence tricksters.[116]

Kidnap City

More serious than the antics of the fabricators were the depredations of the Soviet intelligence and security services. These services had been operating across Berlin when the Western allies occupied their allotted sectors and the delineation of sector boundaries did not inhibit their forays. Initially the Russian services concentrated on locating and arresting individuals identified by Moscow as war criminals, and since the allies, in a joint directive of June 1945, had agreed to assist each other in the search for such fugitives and to allow the arrest on sight of any individual suspected of war crimes, the American military police and counterintelligence organizations generally turned a blind eye to the Russian activities. Both the Counterintelligence Corps and OSS's X-2 branch were too busy with their own manhunts for Nazis to bother much about Russian agents.

By the autumn of 1945, however, the activities of the Soviet services had taken on a more sinister aspect and had moved beyond Berlin to include operations in the American zone. In Berlin, Russian teams were snatching individuals off the streets with such frequency that the citizens took to calling their now rather squalid metropolis "Kidnap City." Many of the abductions occurred in American-controlled territory, and in several cases the Russians were reported as wearing American uniforms to escape notice.[117] Reports also suggested that the targets now included not just Nazi fugitives but also scientists and individuals known for their anticommunist attitudes. In October, for example, a former professor at the Kaiser Wilhelm Institute, Germany's principal center for research in physics and chemistry, who had begun working for the Americans was taken from his house in Frankfurt by an officer of the Soviet Liaison and Repatriation Mission working in the American zone. The scientist was not seen again. The threat to German scientists was so serious that by the spring of 1946 the Counterintelligence Corps had instituted "Operation Hell," a program to protect scientists in the American zone against Russian kidnappers.[118] Of course the Americans had not always allowed legal niceties to constrain their own pursuit of German scientists, but the Soviet actions seemed especially aggressive in their scope. Scientists were no longer the only targets. In one incident, for example, two German judges who were rumored to have offended the communists were seized in the American sector of Berlin and transported to Soviet-controlled territory by officers of the municipal police force, an organization known to be under the influence of the Soviet military administration. In the face of strong protests by the American, British, and French occupation authorities, the Russians agreed to investigate the disappearance, but neither information nor explanation was forthcoming. For their part, the Americans interpreted the incident as yet another indication that the Soviets were prepared to intimidate any Germans opposed to communist authority.[119]

By late 1945 Berlin Base was aware that the Russians were giving many of the abductees the opportunity to escape incarceration by agreeing to work for Soviet intelligence. These individuals, a number of whom had worked for the wartime German intelligence services, would then return to the American sector and seek employment with the occupation regime, particularly its intelligence components. The kidnappings were, therefore, as much a counterintelligence problem as a law enforcement issue. In its first months of operation BOB's X-2 (counterintelligence) section had devoted little attention to the threat of Soviet espionage operations. Well into the fall of 1945, X-2's operations, both in Berlin and the American zone, focused almost exclusively on the pursuit of fugitive Nazis and the infiltration of potential underground neo-Nazi movements. At the beginning of September, for example, X-2 Germany was running thirty-four operations, ten of which were inactive. Of the twenty-four active operations, all but one were concerned with the surveillance of former Nazis or neo-Nazi organizations.[120] By October, however, counterintelligence officers had begun to turn their attention to the activities of the Russian intelligence services operating in Berlin, particularly the NKVD (Narodnyy Komissariat Vnutrennikh Del).[121]

The first significant effort to investigate the Russian services involved the recruitment of a young, anti-Nazi Berliner who during the war had been transferred from his Wehrmacht unit to a labor battalion for spreading defeatist ideas among his fellow soldiers. Escaping to the east, the young soldier had been captured by the Russians and to avoid transport to the Soviet Union had agreed to collaborate with NKVD field units in the Red Army's advance toward Berlin. Released from Russian service after Germany's surrender, he resettled in the ruins of the German capital only to be recalled in July by his former masters, who now intended to use him to penetrate American intelligence in Berlin. Pretending to accede to this plan, the reluctant Russian agent contacted the U.S. Army's Counterintelligence Corps, which, too preoccupied with chasing Nazis to worry about Russians, promptly sent him to OSS. X-2 convinced their unexpected visitor to remain in play and work as a double agent for the Americans. Code-named MOCCASIN, the new source provided information concerning the organization and personnel of the NKVD in Berlin. X-2 also planned to use him as a channel for disinformation. This operation, however, was cut short when MOCCASIN had to be hospitalized with severe injuries after an attack by unknown assailants outside his home.[122] With their most promising source on the sidelines, Berlin X-2 had to be content, at least for the short term, with doubling a few low-level NKVD informants in the American zone, probing White Russian and Polish émigré circles to determine their relationship, if any, with Russian intelligence, and recruiting sources in the citywide black market to identify potential channels into the Soviet services, a program that was derailed when American military police, unaware of the plan, arrested and jailed X-2's black market contacts.[123]

As the extent of Russian intelligence operations into the American sector became increasingly apparent, X-2 dropped everything in order to address the threat from the east. In order to identify the Germans working for Moscow in the American sector of the city and develop a better picture of the organization, personnel, and methods of the Soviet services, Berlin X-2 relied on a program of double-agent operations. The most important began with Karl Krull (code-named ZIGZAG), a prewar prosecutor who had been drafted into the counterintelligence section of the Abwehr. Initially, Krull had been recruited by X-2 to locate former members of the Nazi intelligence and security services who had gone to ground in Berlin. Many of these individuals were on the Allies' automatic arrest lists, and some had been blackmailed into working for Soviet intelligence. Krull, who would later evade an NKVD kidnap squad, led his controllers to several of his former colleagues, including Hans Kemritz (code-named SAVOY), another attorney and former major in the Abwehr, who had reestablished a legal practice in the eastern section of the city. Kemritz had been captured by the Russians and after relentless interrogation had been released in October 1945 on the condition that he become an informant for the NKVD. The Abwehr veteran quickly became the linchpin in the Russian effort to recruit former German intelligence personnel and infiltrate them into American espionage programs. Holding out the promise of a business arrangement, he would lure former colleagues from his Abwehr days to his office in the Soviet sector, where they would be confronted by NKVD officers who would offer them the choice of collaboration or confinement as war criminals.[124]

Berlin X-2 doubled Kemritz and played him back against the Russians. SAVOY helped Berlin Base identify several Germans who had agreed to work for the NKVD, and at a time when American counterintelligence knew next to nothing about their opponents he became the base's principal source on the personnel, objectives, and tactics of the Russian services.[125] X-2 was particularly interested in a certain Captain Skurin, Kemritz's Soviet case officer, and through SAVOY American counterintelligence officers tried unsuccessfully several times to lure the Russian officer into the American sector of the city. By the fall of 1946 Skurin had become suspicious of his agent and had begun to question him about his contacts in the western sectors. By that time SAVOY, whose ultimate loyalties seem to have been somewhat conflicted, had aroused the suspicion of many others, including some in Berlin Base. To maintain his cover or, perhaps, to keep a foot in both camps, Kemritz had continued his recruiting work for Soviet counterintelligence, and his name was publicly connected with the disappearance of several German veterans who were last seen calling at his law offices. In late August 1946, even his American case officer admitted that "Savoy is about the most notorious agent of the MVD in Berlin." When BOB learned that Kemritz had mixed up his papers and turned over to Captain Skurin some reports intended for his American customers, X-2 evacuated their prize agent to the protection of the U.S. zone.[126]

SAVOY was not the only success registered by X-2 in early postwar Berlin. Beginning in 1946 the counterintelligence officers of Berlin Base conducted several important penetrations of the Berlin police, an organization largely reconstituted under Soviet supervision when the Red Army was in sole possession of the city and larded at senior levels with loyal German communists. The most important American penetration was Erich Zeitz, a senior official who was director of the administrative section responsible for police personnel, budget, and support services. A second early source was a police lieutenant who provided Berlin X-2 with the latest gossip circulating in the corridors and canteens at police headquarters. Another informant provided access to the teletype messages that passed between Berlin police headquarters and Soviet political and security officers at Karlshorst. By the spring of 1946 the reports of these agents had convinced SSU that the Russians thoroughly controlled the police forces in Berlin and other cities in their zone and used these agencies to advance their political purposes.[127]

These impressions were only confirmed when, in 1947, a period beyond the purview of this study, Berlin Base recruited its first important Soviet source. Captain Rebrov, a Red Army security and counterintelligence officer stationed at Karlshorst, first came to the attention of SSU when he toured the western zones as part of a four-power commission inspecting fire protection services. The American representative on the commission quietly suggested to BOB that Rebrov might respond to a low-key approach. Berlin X-2 decided to make the pitch through the Russian officer's German girlfriend, who also happened to work at Karlshorst and who was motivated by the dream of marrying her officer and escaping to a new life in the United States. Rebrov, who may have needed little convincing, succumbed to his girlfriend's importunities and agreed to spy for America. By then he was head of registry in the Karlshorst office of the Soviet Ministry of Internal Affairs. In this position Rebrov (soon promoted to major) was able to pass to SSU Berlin a large volume of documents on internal security matters and general political affairs in the Soviet zone; indeed his production was so large that it exceeded BOB's Russian-language-processing capabilities. His access became especially important in 1948 when the Russians launched the Berlin Blockade. His reporting indicated that while Moscow hoped to pressure the West by restricting access to Berlin, it had no intention of going to war over German issues.[128]

Despite these recruitments, the Strategic Services Unit often found itself struggling in a fog of ignorance with a clandestine opponent whose presence and shape were hard to fix. The penetrations in Berlin did not immediately provide X-2 a detailed and expansive view of Soviet clandestine activities across Germany, although by early 1946 some elements in American intelligence were convinced that those activities were extensive and included not only espionage but also covert political operations to undermine the authority of the Western occupation administrations, penetrate and undermine noncommunist political parties in the western zones, spread pro-Soviet propaganda, and support pro-Soviet organizations, all with the purpose of preparing the ground for a communist seizure of power. The suspicions of American counterintelligence officers were not allayed by occasional unguarded (or perhaps not) comments at social or official meetings by known Soviet intelligence officers who hid neither their hostility toward the West nor their pride in the capabilities of their service.[129]

By 1947 the concern for the machinations of Soviet intelligence had grown even stronger, but the picture remained murky. While it was certain that the Russian services were active in the western zones and that they utilized the Soviet Liaison and Repatriation Mission, the German Communist Party, and the remnants of the Free Germany Committee to cover and support their operations, details regarding such activity often eluded American officers, and their estimates of the strength and organizational structure of Soviet intelligence in Germany were little more than guesses. As late as April 1946 (before the recruitment of Rebrov) SSU wasn't even sure how many Soviet espionage services were actually operating inside Germany.[130] Occasionally, however, American intelligence would receive a dramatic reminder of the scope of the threat.

In the autumn of 1946, the Russian security services began rolling up SSU's espionage networks in the Soviet zone of Germany. Most of the chains had been created in the first half of 1946 in response to G-2's insistent demands for more Red Army and Air Force order-of-battle intelligence. In the rush to respond to the new requirements, operational security was sacrificed to operational expansion. SSU Germany, still seriously understaffed, found it difficult to oversee closely the expansion. Sources recruited subsources willy-nilly. New agents were not carefully vetted. Time-consuming trade-craft—infrequent meetings, carefully scouted travel routes, evasive proce-dures to avoid surveillance—was abandoned in favor of frequent and conve-nient meetings that only increased the exposure of the agents. Sources were allowed to know each other's identity, and, on at least one occasion, several agents were invited to celebrate their hard work at a large party where group photos were taken. At one time a single safe house, meant to provide a secure setting for a case officer to debrief, pay, and further task a single source, housed twenty-five agents at the same time. It was a prescription for disaster.

In a network where many of the members knew each other and some even knew individuals working in other networks, the arrest and interrogation of one source would set off a chain of arrests–denunciations–arrests that would reverberate across several networks. This is exactly what happened in the autumn of 1946, and it continued into early 1947. It was a perfect catastrophe. One after the other, SSU's eyes and ears in the eastern territories were lost as dozens of German agents were arrested and executed or condemned to years in Soviet labor camps. Fortunately, the loss, while serious, was not complete. Some networks survived, and several important sources providing political and economic intelligence, such as Leo Skrzypczynski, who were not links in larger chains, remained untouched, but the blow to order-of-battle intelli-gence was, at least in the short term, serious.[131]

The Russian counterintelligence offensive against American espionage networks in eastern Germany was a sign, if any was still needed, that the intelligence battle in Germany was well and truly engaged. The days in the summer of 1945 when most American intelligence officers viewed with com-placency and equanimity the Russian presence in Germany were now distant indeed. That attitude, though occasionally challenged by individual officers with previous experience of Soviet methods, generally persisted until the late fall of 1945, when the SSU mission in Germany began to observe and report Soviet attempts to intimidate independent political parties to accept the di-rection of the communist party. When combined with hard news of Russian mobilization of German war industries and distressing signs of aggressive Soviet intelligence operations against the American zone, intelligence report-ing from Germany would have raised questions in the minds of policy makers concerning Moscow's goodwill and intentions and challenged any lingering hopes that there was any community of interest between the United States and the Soviet Union in Germany. When policy makers placed the intelli-gence from Germany alongside reports from other areas, such as Austria and Eastern Europe, such concerns turned into real suspicions.

CHAPTER FOUR

Spies on the Danube: Austria

On 3 June 1945 a convoy of U.S. Army sedans, jeeps, and trucks, escorted front and rear by Red Army motorcyclists and staff cars, drove into Vienna on a ten-day reconnaissance tour. The military mission, the first Americans to reach the Austrian capital since the end of the war in Europe, received a formal welcome, complete with brass bands and official banquets, from senior Soviet officers whose armies had seized the city from its German defenders the previous April. Since then, the Soviets had solidified their control over areas occupied by their armed forces, a process characterized by the rapine and plunder that was invariably the fate of enemy territory occupied by the Red Army. To legitimize their occupation, facilitate the return of social and economic order, and curry favor with the defeated population, the Soviets had moved quickly and without consulting their allies to establish a provisional government under Karl Renner, a 75-year-old former state chancellor and president of the last democratically elected parliament in the prewar Austrian Republic. Based on a coalition of the prewar socialist, conservative, and communist parties (with the latter controlling the important interior and education ministries) the provisional government represented the same "national front" approach to organizing postwar administrations that the Soviets adopted in other countries occupied by the Red Army. Moscow anticipated that in Austria, as in those other countries, the communists would eventually dominate the coalition and create a communist and pro-Soviet nation amenable to Russian influence.[1] The United States thought well of Renner and his government, but regretted that it had been established without consultation. In a survey of Austrian affairs in June 1945 the State Department noted, "Whatever might be the regrettable nature of [the unilateral] Soviet action, it appears beyond serious doubt that, in terms of the men themselves and in terms of representation of political forces, the Renner Government is as good a coalition as could be devised at the present time."[2] Moscow recognized the Renner regime as the new government of Austria on 29 April. Dismayed by Moscow's unilateral actions, Washington and London declined to recognize the Renner government, a refusal that, combined with the failure of the Allies' European Advisory Commission to agree on control machinery and occupation zones for Austria and its capital, provided the Russians an excuse to delay American and British access to Vienna even after Germany's surrender.[3]

Commanded by General Lester Flory, the chief of the U.S. Army element responsible for planning the occupation of Austria, and charged with assessing conditions inside the city, the American mission's seventy-eight officers and men included specialists in civil engineering, public health, civil affairs, and transportation. The roster included a certain Lieutenant Colonel Charles Thayer, a quiet, self-effacing officer, who was listed as General Flory's interpreter. The name and duty assignment might well have raised eyebrows at Red Army headquarters, particularly in the offices occupied by Soviet intelligence, where some officers may have recalled that toward the end of the war a Lieutenant Colonel Charles Thayer had been a senior OSS representative in Yugoslavia. American intelligence had arrived in Vienna.

Only in retrospect does Charles Thayer's presence in the Austrian capital seem a harbinger of the future. Eventually, Vienna would come to rival Berlin as the "spy capital" of the Cold War and the principal arena in the covert war between East and West, but in the early summer of 1945 few American observers would have predicted that outcome. For most of the war Austria, which had been incorporated into the German Reich in the "Anschluss" of March 1938, had not been a priority for American intelligence. Early collection efforts had been limited to open sources and whatever tidbits OSS interviewers in New York, Washington, and London could glean from exiles, emigrants, businessmen, and journalists with recent experience of the country. In late 1943 the OSS stations in Bern and Istanbul had established links to the small anti-Nazi resistance inside Austria, and these connections stimulated plans for penetration missions that would support the resistance and collect intelligence. By early 1945, Secret Intelligence Central Europe (SICE), an element of the OSS detachment headquartered in Caserta, Italy, had begun to airdrop operatives into Austria with the mission of collecting tactical intelligence, particularly concerning the existence of an "Alpine Redoubt" into which diehard Nazi formations might retreat. These risky missions produced much adventure but little intelligence.[4]

After the collapse of the Third Reich, elements of the Office of Strategic Services accompanied units of Lieutenant General Mark Clark's Fifteenth Army Group as that formation moved from Italy into the area of Austria reserved for American occupation. OSS officers set up their headquarters in Salzburg, which also served as the administrative and logistical center for Fifteenth Army Group, soon to be reorganized as U.S. Forces Austria (USFA). Small intelligence outposts were established in Innsbruck, Klagenfurt, Linz, Zell am See, and, by late summer, Vienna. The onset of any military occupation tends to be rather chaotic, and the American experience in Austria was no exception as army commanders shifted units, searched for billets, bickered over areas of responsibility, and settled lines of authority.

Confusion was fueled by the fact that the Allies did not finalize the boundaries of their respective occupation zones and concentrate their troops in these zones until late July. As was true of other elements of the American military command, the intelligence units required time to settle into their new environment. OSS officers did not drive into Salzburg, leap from their Jeeps, and immediately begin recruiting legions of well-placed informants. In the weeks immediately following VE Day these officers, much like their OSS colleagues in Germany, were preoccupied less with intelligence operations than with various mundane housekeeping activities related to housing, feeding, and servicing a working intelligence service in a once hostile and now war-devastated territory. The OSS mission felt little sense of urgency and even less of threat; indeed, as late as September the tempo of work was sufficiently relaxed that one secret intelligence officer found sufficient leisure to enroll in a course of study at the University of Vienna.[5]

When, by midsummer, the OSS mission began focusing more on operational than organizational issues, the intelligence officers did not stray far from home. Again, the parallels with the experience in Germany are striking. Like its sister mission in Germany, OSS Austria was formally charged with supporting the work of American occupation authorities. At first the army wasn't sure it needed much support, and as late as July 1945 OSS managers in Washington were still trying to elicit from military authorities some sense of the types of intelligence the Army needed in Austria.[6] Eventually, these authorities and their representatives on the scene interpreted their mission directives in such a way as to require a focus primarily on the neutralization of surviving Nazi elements that might threaten the stability of the occupation and the security of American personnel and secondarily on the collection of information concerning public attitudes and political, economic, and social conditions inside the American zone. The result was an initial preoccupation with the Werwolfs and other real or imagined Nazi resistance groups. However alarming, the flurry of reports on resistance cells that OSS Austria forwarded to USFA commanders was usually submerged in a flood of the same mundane "suburban news items" that also dominated the early reporting of OSS Germany. The local focus of OSS Austria's activity in the summer of 1945 is apparent in the list of its collection priorities for August: the strength and intentions of emerging political groups, the reaction of Austrians to Allied occupation policies, the food situation, prospects for industrial revival, the collection of evidence for use in war crimes trials, and the exposure and suppression of clandestine Nazi resistance cells. In September, OSS headquarters in Salzburg still reported that denazification and the exposure of covert Nazi resistance networks topped its list of priorities, with public opinion and the local black market following in second and third place. Reports such as "The Bakery Industry in Vienna," "Food Situation in IX District of Vienna: The Housewife's Viewpoint," and "The Venereal Disease Problem in Vienna" typified the local news items that still dominated intelligence reporting through the late summer of 1945.[7]

Similar preoccupations—denazification, neutralization of diehard resistance movements, detention of war criminals and fugitive German intelligence and security personnel, and surveillance of social, economic, and political conditions inside the American zone—characterized the early operations of the other American intelligence organizations working in Austria.[8] The U.S. Army's Military Intelligence Service (MIS) deployed three small units inside the country, each of which contributed information to the intelligence staff (G-2) of United States Forces Austria. None of these units engaged in agent operations or clandestine collection. In Salzburg the Civilian Censorship Group monitored civilian postal, telephone, and telegraph communications to determine public sentiment toward the occupation and detect subversive activities. The United States Detailed Interrogation Center (USDIC) in Gmunden interrogated high-level prisoners of war and other individuals arrested or detained by occupation authorities for their alleged connections with the Nazi regime. Lastly, a documents center in Linz collected and analyzed as many records concerning wartime political, economic, industrial, and military affairs in Austria as it could get its hands on. The first priority for each MIS element was the collection of intelligence to support programs dedicated to the elimination of Nazism and German militarism. The second priority was intelligence to support the creation of a politically democratic Austrian government. Initially, "foreign" intelligence, in the sense of information concerning conditions and events beyond Austria, was not a central concern for army intelligence. Neither the Soviet Union nor the Soviet zone of Austria figured prominently in the operations of the Military Intelligence Service in the first months of the occupation. As late as October 1945 references to the Russians remained rare in the daily intelligence bulletin circulated by USFA's military intelligence staff.[9]

As with MIS, the first priority of the Counterintelligence Corps (CIC), the army's other intelligence organization in Austria, was denazification and the pursuit of war criminals. These tasks required the screening of displaced persons to weed out Nazi fugitives trying to escape arrest by blending into the sea of refugees that swept through Central Europe. This mission consumed the attention and resources of the Counterintelligence Corps almost to the exclusion of other assignments. As late as the spring of 1947, 90 percent of CIC's effort still focused on denazification. The second priority was coverage of Austrian domestic groups and organizations and key political personalities in order to detect subversion and to monitor public attitudes toward the occupation and various political, economic, and social issues. In practice this secondary task seems to have received little attention. In the first two years of peace, for example, CIC made almost no effort to collect personality data on leading figures of the Austrian communist party. When, in 1948, CIC decided to compile a complete card file on members of the party, it had to rely on information provided by the Austrian Interior Ministry. Not surprisingly, the Soviet Union did not at first figure prominently on the Counterintelligence Corp's agenda; indeed, CIC did not begin concentrating on Austrian communists and the Soviet intelligence services until the summer of 1947. Before then, when occasional intelligence items on the Soviet activities trickled into CIC offices, the material remained largely unprocessed because the organization lacked the resources to analyze and evaluate the information.[10]

Broadening Horizons

Intelligence coverage of areas outside the American occupation zone, particularly the Soviet zone and territories to the east, developed only slowly in the summer of 1945. In the case of OSS, the absence of clear directives from Washington concerning targets and priorities, an issue that bedeviled OSS/SSU stations throughout Europe in the early postwar period, discouraged an aggressive, expansive approach to early operations in Austria. Uncertainty regarding the long-term prospects for a peacetime clandestine service, prospects that were especially problematic after the dissolution of the Office of Strategic Services in October, also discouraged more extensive operations. Personnel shortages were an even greater constraint. OSS Austria was so weakened by the military transfers and demobilization measures that were gutting intelligence units across Europe that in August Charles Thayer, the chief of mission, actually had to appeal to Washington to keep his unit open. At the time, the Austrian mission employed about 200 personnel, but the roster was declining rapidly. An officer who served in the mission would later recall, "Only one thing counted at that time. The war was over. It was absolutely a first priority to get out of the army and find a wife, job or school."[11] As late as September the mission still had only one secret intelligence officer in Vienna, and a frustrated Thayer, who had been bluntly warned by the chief of the mission's intelligence section that for lack of staff he might have to terminate all operations, informed Washington that his command no longer had enough personnel to fulfill its intelligence assignment.

The warning fell on deaf ears. By November 1945 the outposts in Linz, Zell am See, and Innsbruck had been closed. Before the end of the year the mission's staff had declined to sixty, of whom twenty-five (including typists, translators, and drivers) worked in the secret intelligence section. Staff attrition would continue into the new year. Recalling that difficult period, a veteran of SSU Austria observed that the mission and its operations were devastated by the personnel crisis. By March 1946 the Strategic Services Unit had only seven officers in all of Austria working full time on positive intelligence collection. Inadequate staffing would continue to seriously compromise collection programs throughout the early postwar period.[12]

Despite the constraints on its activities, OSS Austria gradually extended its operations beyond the American zone of occupation. By the end of September OSS had recruited several well-placed informants in the neighboring French zone, including officials in various political groups, such as the socialists and the monarchists, and a British national living outside of Innsbruck who cultivated friendships with officers in the French occupation authority. These sources produced a steady flow of information on local political affairs, economic conditions, labor problems, reconstruction issues, and the state of Franco-Austrian relations. In the South Tyrol, a border region then part of Italy but long contested by the Austrians and Italians, several Austrian informants provided news concerning the propaganda and political intrigues of both sides.[13]

Coverage of the British zone (encompassing the districts of Styria and Carinthia and the Austrian border with Yugoslavia) proved a more delicate problem. Military tensions in this region were high because Josip Broz Tito, the leader of the communist anti-Nazi resistance movement that had claimed the leadership of postwar Yugoslavia, included Carinthia in his vision of a greater Yugoslavia. As the Third Reich collapsed, Tito's forces had occupied portions of the region, reaching Trieste, a regional capital, one day before the arrival of British Commonwealth forces. In February 1945 Tito had agreed that Trieste could serve, under a British-led military government, as a base for military operations into Austria, but with the collapse of German resistance the Yugoslavian leader reneged on the agreement and sought to exclude the British from the city. London, however, held firm. In June the two sides agreed on a temporary solution in which the Yugoslavs would administer the rural areas around Trieste while the British would control the city.[14] British-Yugoslav relations, however, remained embittered, with the British believing, with some justification, that Tito had not abandoned his ambition to absorb Carinthia.

At first, OSS Austria observed the situation from a distance. It refrained from aggressive penetration of the British zone, in part because it did not want to offend the British and thereby compromise bilateral relations, particularly the special and productive partnership that had (with occasional lapses) characterized Anglo-American intelligence collaboration since before Pearl Harbor, and in part because it trusted that London would pass to Washington through liaison channels sufficient information regarding political and military developments in the region. The Office of Strategic Services, however, could not entirely resist the temptation to have a look for itself. By September 1945 OSS was dispatching the occasional agent on "tourist missions" to Graz, Villach, Klagenfurt, and other towns in the British zone to supplement British coverage and to ensure that balanced reporting was being received on political and economic affairs. These sources confirmed that tensions remained high and that several British officials who had recently crossed the border into Yugoslavia had been jailed despite their proper credentials. Additional intelligence suggested that London was in no mood to compromise. OSS learned that the British army was solidifying its military position along the contested border, that British occupation authorities were initiating an anti-Tito propaganda campaign, and that Britain's Secret Intelligence Service (SIS) was deploying clandestine agents inside Yugoslavia. To improve its surveillance of Yugoslavian affairs, OSS established a small outpost in Trieste in the late summer of 1945. Situated at the northern end of the Adriatic Sea, the port city was a potential military flashpoint since its control was disputed not only by the British and Yugoslavs, but also by the Italians. Initially, the Trieste unit was seriously understaffed, and though OSS Austria saw in the outpost a potential for espionage operations into Yugoslavia using anti-Tito refugees or businessmen with commercial interests in both Italy and Yugoslavia, the unit's early activities were limited to maintaining liaison with the British and developing contacts with Italian police and intelligence organizations that were working actively against Yugoslavian interests.[15]

Coverage of the Soviet zone of occupation lagged behind coverage of the British and French zones. Aside from the occasional intelligence item, such as a report on 11 May 1945 that Soviet interest in German aircraft design had led the Russians to seize the records and the staff of an Austrian aeronautical institute, the early operational summaries of OSS Austria rarely mentioned Soviet targets. This was, in small part, a function of personnel shortages and limited access. Vienna, like Berlin a jointly occupied city in the heart of a Russian zone of occupation, should have been a valuable espionage beachhead for operations in the east. Four-power disagreements over the boundaries of the Allied sectors in the Austrian capital, however, delayed the arrival of permanent American, British, and French occupation elements, including intelligence personnel, until August. Once established, the OSS presence remained minuscule; at the end of September the secret intelligence side of OSS Vienna consisted of a single officer. Delayed access and insufficient staff, however, were not the principal constraints on operations into the Soviet zone. Vienna was, after all, not the only access point for Russian-controlled territory. The American and Soviet zones shared a border, and well into the fall of 1945, transit across this border remained relatively simple, not only for soldiers with military government travel permits, but also for German-speaking officers who might have wished to cross over clandestinely in civilian clothes. Once across the border travel in the Soviet zone was relatively uncontrolled.[16]

Given the permeability of the Soviet-American zonal boundary, it is difficult to avoid the conclusion that, in the summer and early fall of 1945, American espionage against the Soviet zone was constrained less by limited access and staff than by limited interest. As the American occupation established itself in Austria there was apparently little demand for information from the eastern portions of the country. In Washington the Office of Strategic Services, seeking guidance as to intelligence requirements, had to pester the military repeatedly before the Army finally acknowledged that it might be interested in a handful of Austrian topics, only one of which—information concerning the removal from the country of industrial and agricultural resources by the Russians—focused on the Soviet zone. Army commanders on the scene, moreover, had an even more narrow interest. The intelligence staff of United States Forces Austria made it quite clear to the local OSS mission that its interest in the Soviet zone was limited to information concerning the size and disposition of Red Army units, that is, the order-of-battle coverage of foreign armies that was the routine responsibility of military intelligence offices around the globe. For its part, the State Department did not provide OSS a short list of its intelligence requirements in Austria until mid-September, and Soviet matters did not figure prominently among the items. The department's interest in the Soviet zone focused on information concerning the food situation, although the diplomats in Washington also wanted to know if Moscow was directing communist propaganda in the occupied country.[17]

The limited intelligence interest in the Soviet zone and Russian activities in Austria is most evident in the operational field. In the summer of 1945, SI field officers did not believe that their mission included operations into the Russian-occupied portion of the country.[18] When the American survey party had visited Vienna in June, General Flory had explicitly forbidden Charles Thayer, the OSS representative in the party, to engage in any espionage against the Russians. A summary of OSS Austria's operations submitted to Washington headquarters in late August contains no reference to the Soviet Union or Soviet targets.[19] By September, OSS still had not launched any significant operations into the Soviet zone despite opportunities to do so. As in Germany, American intelligence in Austria developed close relations with socialists and other elements of the democratic Left. Socialist and trade union leaders, whom the Austrian mission cultivated by establishing in the American zone "Labor Houses" where party and union members could gather for meals and discussions, offered OSS the use of their contacts and clandestine courier links to collect political information from the Russian-occupied areas, but the intelligence officers did not rush to accept the offer. In September the OSS base in Linz informed Salzburg headquarters, almost as an afterthought, that the city offered excellent prospects for operations into the nearby Russian zone, "*if* reports on Russian occupational policies are desired" (emphasis added), phrasing that suggests that Salzburg had not yet expressed any such desire.[20]

Even if occupation authorities and Washington policy makers had been clamoring for more intelligence from the Soviet zone, the Office of Strategic Service's Austrian mission would still have been distracted from a clear focus on Russian targets by the promise of opportunities beyond Austria's borders. As we have seen, in the summer and fall of 1945 OSS (and later SSU) headquarters in Washington allowed its overseas missions to roam at the end of a long leash. In the case of Austria, the grip on the leash was not always firm; indeed, headquarters was so disengaged from the operations of its Austrian unit that as late as January 1946 it was not entirely sure how many officers were assigned to the mission. Free from close supervision and detailed direction, these missions were not components of an integrated intelligence collection program for the simple reason that Washington did not have an integrated collection program. Each mission, including the Austrian, was largely left to its own devices, with the result that collection efforts were usually a grab bag of disparate operations that reflected opportunity rather than plan, and diversity rather than focus. Alfred Ulmer, OSS Austria's first director of secret intelligence—and from January 1946 the chief of the entire Austrian station—was a man to seize opportunities and take chances.[21] As we shall see (chapter 5), by the early autumn of 1945, even as OSS Austria faced the reality of significant personnel reductions, Al Ulmer was investigating the prospects for operations, not only against Yugoslavia, but also Hungary, Poland, and even more distant targets, such as the Vatican. It is hard to avoid the impression that the understaffed and underresourced mission was stretching itself rather thinly by pursuing willy-nilly any operations that appeared on the intelligence horizon.

For all its limitations and distractions, the OSS (and, after October, SSU) mission remained the principal source of information—and the only source of *clandestine* information—concerning conditions and events inside Russian-occupied Austria throughout 1945. Other agencies of the American occupation were poorly equipped to reach into the eastern territories in search of political, economic, and military intelligence. At the end of the year the army's military intelligence organization in Austria still had no clandestine collection capability of any kind and no unit or element devoted to the Soviet Union or Soviet-occupied territories, simply because its mission directives, which focused on the suppression of Nazism, did not include those areas. To fill out the Russian section of its weekly intelligence summary, USFA's G-2 had to depend on information supplied by OSS/SSU.[22] At the same time the army's Counterintelligence Corps continued to concentrate its resources on denazification and made almost no effort to collect information on Austrian communist activity or the operations of foreign intelligence services such as the Soviet NKVD. When, in January 1946, SSU requested the Counterintelligence Corps's help in foiling a Soviet covert operation in Salzburg, CIC was hard-pressed to free even one operative from denazification tasks.[23]

For its part, the small State Department contingent attached to the occupation command was even more underresourced than its OSS counterpart. At the end of the summer of 1945 the contingent still numbered scarcely a dozen diplomats and clerks, and, except for a single staffer in Vienna, all personnel remained in Salzburg. Lacking clear directives from the State Department regarding mission and reporting priorities, the diplomats initially tended to focus on routine consular business. They readily acknowledged that they were poorly positioned to collect even overt information, let alone clandestine intelligence, and in the first several months of the occupation they relied upon OSS and then SSU for information concerning developments beyond Salzburg.[24]

Despite the lack of attention to Soviet-related targets in the early months of the occupation, intelligence coverage of Russian activities in Austria was never entirely absent. Relying largely on open sources, the Office of Strategic Services maintained a distant watch on Moscow's intentions and actions. In an early appraisal of the Soviet-inspired Renner regime, whose origins and composition caused some policy makers in London and Washington to suspect that Moscow intended to impose its control over Austria through the same kind of puppet governments that were emerging in Russian-occupied Bulgaria, Romania, and Poland, the Research and Analysis Branch at OSS headquarters in Washington suggested there was little cause for alarm. OSS assured its customers that Karl Renner was a moderate socialist who had always opposed the extreme left in Austrian politics and who could be counted on to resist manipulation and to collaborate with all political parties, not just the communists. In the first week of May 1945, before the OSS mission had entered Austria, Franz Neumann, a senior and respected analyst for Central European affairs, who (unbeknownst to his superiors in Washington) seems to have been a sometime contact for the NKVD, submitted a report in which he regretted Moscow's unilateralism in creating the Renner government, but suggested that no competent observer should have been surprised by the action. According to Neumann, who, despite his alleged connections to Soviet intelligence, presented an accurate and professional appraisal of the situation, much of which was borne out by subsequent events, the Soviet Union wanted to cast itself as the patron of Austrian independence, and Moscow's initiative was motivated, in part, by a realization that Allied discussions in the European Advisory Commission over the form of an Austrian government might well drag on for months. Furthermore, aside from the manner of its creation, there was little to criticize in the Renner government. "There is no reason to assume that the members of the cabinet are stooges of the USSR," Neumann noted. "[They] are unquestionably mature politicians with very definite political philosophies. They cannot be manipulated." Concluding that the Renner cabinet reflected fairly well the distribution of political forces inside the country and that it was probably "the best government that Austria ever had," the senior analyst recommended that if the United States wished to assert its influence over Austrian political arrangements it should work to reorganize rather than replace the Renner regime.[25]

It is difficult to determine if Franz Neumann's analysis influenced Washington policy makers, but it is interesting to note that the analyst's arguments were echoed in a subsequent position paper of the Department of State prepared more than a month later in anticipation of the "Big Three" Allied conference scheduled for the end of July in Potsdam, Germany, which President Harry Truman, Prime Minister Winston Churchill, and Premier Josef Stalin would attend. Evaluating the emergence of the Renner administration for the U.S. delegation to the conference, the State Department noted, "Whatever might be the regrettable nature of Soviet action, it appears beyond serious doubt that, in terms of the men themselves and in terms of representation of political forces, the Renner Government is as good a coalition as could be devised at the present time. It also appears that the distribution of offices among the three Austrian parties is not a serious misrepresentation of current political forces."[26]

The early appraisals of the OSS representatives in Austria concerning the Renner cabinet and Soviet intentions in Austria complemented the perceptions of the analysts in Washington. On 20 July 1945, OSS director William Donovan sent Secretary of State James Byrnes an overview of the Renner government and Soviet policy in Austria prepared by Charles Thayer, the chief of the OSS mission in Austria. Thayer had been attached to the U.S. embassy in Moscow during the 1930s, from which vantage point he witnessed the ruthless and bloody purges by which Stalin eliminated real and imagined political threats and solidified his control over the Soviet Union. The chief of OSS Austria had few illusions about the nature of the Soviet regime, and he was quick to recall the executions, labor camps, and secret police for junior officers who might have been excessively captivated by the images of "Uncle Joe" Stalin and the stalwart Russian ally so assiduously cultivated by wartime propaganda.[27] Still, Thayer was never viscerally anti-Soviet, and in the summer of 1945 he was prepared to give the Russians in Austria the benefit of the doubt. His report to Donovan anticipated no political or military threat from the communists, painting a picture of a Red Army more interested in stripping the country of all movable assets than in creating a Soviet satellite, a local communist party discredited by its association with a rapacious occupier, a citizenry disinclined to exchange one form of dictatorship for another, and a new civilian government so weak that it had yet to establish its authority even in the districts occupied by its Russian patrons. According to Thayer, the Soviets, aware of the opposition of the mass of people and the ineptitude and disrepute of the Austrian Communist Party, realized that they could impose a Moscow-controlled regime only by force—a step they had no intention of taking. Donovan's man in Austria assured his boss that "the Russian authorities have generally pursued a policy of non-interference in Austrian affairs" and suggested that Moscow was likely to continue that policy in the future.[28]

OSS Austria covered the Renner regime with whatever resources could be spared from its main priorities: denazification and surveillance of conditions inside the American zone. These resources were often modest. As late as September 1945 only one SI officer in Vienna was covering political affairs, but as the only SI operative working full time in that city that officer also had to report on economic, military, and social developments. Despite inadequate resources, the intelligence mission gradually established contacts with prominent political personalities in the capital and in cities in the American zone. By the end of 1945 SI Austria could boast that "the section has firm friends in all of the political parties, important labor unions, and semi-public societies," although it admitted that lack of personnel prevented complete exploitation of these contacts.[29] Contacts within Renner's cabinet and within the circle around the chancellor had been established early, and these informants proved a particularly rich and credible source of intelligence. In August, for example, Renner told an OSS source that the unsatisfactory condition of the Vienna police was the only problem that seriously troubled him. After occupying the city, the Russians had reorganized the police, mainly by introducing into the force two battalions of Austrian communists who had fought in Yugoslavia as part of Tito's partisan army. The new minister of the interior, the communist Franz Honner, had been instrumental in forming and leading these units, and as chief of the ministry responsible for the police, he subsequently shielded them from charges of indiscipline, brutality, and favoritism in the exercise of their police powers. According to the source, Renner expressed his hope that the Allies would quickly establish joint control over the police and substitute a professional force for the deputized partisans. On other occasions the chancellor privately assured OSS sources that the Soviets did not interfere with his administration and certainly did not exercise a veto over its decisions.[30]

In general, early political intelligence from Austria tended to confirm the appraisals of Washington analysts such as Franz Neumann that the Renner regime was not a stalking horse for Moscow and that Austria was not about to be taken over by communists. Some of this intelligence circulated at the highest levels of American government. In early July, for example, OSS sent the White House information from Adolf Schärf, a member of Renner's cabinet, who insisted that his government had no intention of becoming a tool of Moscow. That same month William Donovan forwarded to the White House a report explicitly denigrating alarmist accounts from Austrian Social Democratic sources that the communists, shaken by their poor showing in recent factory governance elections in which they attracted barely 10 percent of the workers' vote, were preparing a coup with the clandestine support of the Red Army. In late August, the OSS director sent the president a report detailing the views of the director of the Vienna political police, an official whose job required him to monitor political attitudes and developments. This official, a leading personality in the Austrian Communist Party who contemptuously dismissed the moderate Social Democratic and People's Party members of the Renner cabinet as reactionary "fossils," admitted to an OSS source that the communists had very little support within the country. Not only were the communists identified in the popular imagination with the rapine and plunder of the Red Army, but the party was also undermined by opportunists, including former Nazis, who posed as loyal communists in order to receive administrative positions from the Russian occupation authorities.[31]

No single event shocked American authorities into reassessing their attitudes concerning Moscow's intentions and goals in Austria, but in the autumn of 1945 intelligence reporting began to erode the initially sanguine perspective. American officials, for example, had long been aware that, as in Germany, the Red Army in Austria seemed intent upon stripping the land of anything that could be eaten, driven, or worn. At first these officials had been prepared to explain the looting as either the unfortunate excesses of a victorious army or "requisitioning" by an army known to live off the land. Similarly, intelligence reports that the Russians were—again, as in Germany—dismantling and removing to the Soviet Union Austrian factories, transportation equipment, and research facilities were initially seen as more or less legitimate confiscations of German-owned properties in lieu of reparations. Indeed, OSS was aware that the Russians were not the only power attracted by booty. Reports in the summer of 1945 also noted that the French were requisitioning horses, cloth, tin, and copper in their occupation zone.[32] By the fall, however, the rapacity of the Soviets seemed increasingly excessive, especially when removals extended to pre-Anschluss, non-German properties that were exempt from seizure under Allied agreements. At the end of August OSS explicitly alerted Washington that the Russians were seizing pre-Anschluss properties that should have been immune from confiscation. In one case American intelligence learned that the Soviets were stripping industrial assets, including high explosives, from factories owned by British interests. Later, SSU received reports that the Russians were behaving so egregiously that the normally passive population of the Soviet zone had begun actively to obstruct the removal program.[33]

Intelligence reports concerning Soviet efforts to secure control of oil wells and refineries in their occupation zone as well as shipping assets on the Danube River may well have impressed intelligence consumers in Washington as elements in a unilateral program to dominate the postwar Austrian economy in violation of Allied agreements that decisions effecting Austrian economic and political conditions should be arrived at jointly.[34] The attention of OSS customers may also have been attracted to reports (again, similar to those coming out of Germany) that the Russians were turning certain Austrian manufacturing plants to military production for the Red Army and that they were actively recruiting Austrian scientists for atomic research inside the Soviet Union.[35]

Political reporting in the fall of 1945 may also have contributed to a less sanguine attitude toward Moscow's intentions in the country. On 25 November Austrians went to the polls to elect their first postwar parliament. As in Germany and other countries occupied by the Red Army, Moscow preferred a national front approach to organizing new governments, and it assumed that the Communist Party would dominate a coalition of antifascist parties. Not for the first time, the Soviets overestimated the appeal of the local communists. The outcome of Austria's first postwar elections represented a serious setback for the Austrian Communist Party, which attracted only 5 percent of the vote, good for a mere 4 seats in the 165-seat parliament. In contrast, the moderate Peoples Party led by Leopold Figl captured 49.8 percent of the vote and 85 seats. The results allowed Figl to form a new cabinet in which the communists lost their hold on the important Interior and Education Ministries and were left only with the insignificant Ministry for Electrification. The November election impressed the Western powers, who abandoned their earlier misgivings about the independence of the Renner regime. On the other hand, the shock of the November elections soured Moscow on Renner. Arguing that "reactionary" forces were gaining ascendancy in the country, the Soviets now assumed a more hostile and obstructive attitude toward their one-time protégé.[36] In their zone Soviet occupation authorities tightened political controls, requiring, for example, that a Russian observer be present at any political meeting.

The Soviet Target

In Austria, as elsewhere in the early years of the Cold War, access to information on the inner workings of the Kremlin remained an unfulfilled ambition. Intelligence on the Soviet zone of occupation was to be had, but only at the expense of sharp lessons in the ruthless efficiency of the Soviet intelligence and security services. SI Austria did not begin systematically to launch operations against Soviet targets until the fall of 1945. These early missions focused on Red Army dispositions, perhaps reflecting directives from USFA's G-2 staff, which were filling out their order-of-battle charts. The first mission unfolded in late September when a German-speaking SI officer, posing as an Austrian communist resident in the British sector, crossed clandestinely into the Russian sector and developed contacts with several Red Army officers, including a political commissar. Noting that "with a good knowledge of Russian and two bottles of vodka you can get anything you want," this officer collected information on the location of Red Army units in and around the Austrian capital. This promising operation was abruptly terminated, however, when intelligence managers in Salzburg, increasingly uncertain about the future of their mission after the closure of the Office of Strategic Services on 1 October, hurriedly recalled their man to the safety of the American zone. Salzburg considered the mission a success, but it warned Washington that if headquarters decided to expand such operations the mission would require several months to establish the necessary cover and contacts, another suggestion that in the fall of 1945 offensive intelligence operations against the Soviets were still at the embryonic stage.[37]

Another source in the Soviet sector emerged about the same time, although this operation was the result more of fortuitous circumstance than of careful planning. One of the SSU officers had developed a romantic attachment to a young Austrian woman. As luck would have it, this woman had a sister who was similarly involved with a major in the Red Army. In return for the occasional bottle of brandy or whiskey, the sister passed on whatever bits and pieces of information she picked up during unguarded moments of pillow talk. Over the fall of 1945 this information included useful intelligence concerning Russian troop dispositions, particularly the replacement of front-line units by reserve formations.[38] Apparently the American officer was confident that the sisters were not playing a double game by passing information in both directions.

Some of the early operations relied on surrogates to penetrate the Soviet-controlled areas. Prisoner-of-war stockades and displaced-persons camps in the American zone were full of Russians, Armenians, Georgians, and other citizens of the Soviet Union, most of whom had ended up in Austria after surviving German prison camps. Some had joined the anti-Soviet "Vlasov Army" of Russian POWs organized by the Germans to fight against their homeland under the command of former Red Army General Andrei Vlasov. As of autumn 1945 OSS Austria had not systematically canvassed the camps for prospective agents, but not a few of the detainees, ostensibly anticommunist, fearful of repatriation to a suspicious and vengeful motherland, and certainly eager to secure their future well-being, were prepared to volunteer their services to the Americans, British, and French.

Project CROWN involved two such Russians code-named ANGEL and PRIEST by the Strategic Services Unit. Both claimed to be veterans of the Tsarist armies who fought with the Whites in the Russian Civil War and continued the struggle against the Bolsheviks by participating in White Russian resistance activities in the 1920s and 1930s. During the Second World War both collaborated with German intelligence in operations against the Soviet Union, activities that landed them in American custody in June 1945. During interrogation ANGEL claimed that before the war he had, on behalf of the White resistance, established agent and courier networks inside the Soviet Union and that he could resuscitate these networks for American intelligence. In October 1945 SSU Austria received from Washington permission to recruit the two Russians and exploit their alleged connections inside Russia. Code-named CROWN, the project produced a stream of reports on Soviet affairs, but rather quickly SSU began to have second thoughts. The case officers were especially troubled by ANGEL's reluctance to provide details concerning his networks. He claimed, rather improbably, to have around 300 agents inside the Soviet Union, but refused to reveal anything about their identities, locations, or activities. Concerns about their collaborators evolved into suspicion when Richard Kauder, a former Abwehr officer who had been ANGEL's case officer during the war and who now worked for American intelligence, told his SSU handlers that he believed that both Russians were double agents sent by the NKVD to penetrate Western intelligence services. Suspicion hardened into certainty in the spring of 1946 when phone taps recorded ANGEL and PRIEST discussing how easy it was to fool the naive Americans. SSU shut down CROWN, concluding that their two Russians had no networks inside the Soviet Union and that the two were at best fabricators and at worst Soviet disinformation agents.[39]

A second operation also had its genesis in the detention camps. By early October five Russian-speaking individuals in the camp at Bad Aibling, Bavaria, all of whom had fought the Soviet Union and expressed intense anti-Soviet passions, had come to the attention of SSU Austria. After preliminary interviews, three were considered worth recruitment, and in December they were transferred to a safe house outside Salzburg. By this time, the secret intelligence section of SSU Austria had taken to naming all operations conducted from Vienna after New York City department stores, while Salzburg-directed operations were named after New York nightclubs. The three new agents were collectively christened Project MACY.

At the last minute and after receiving initial briefings on the group's future work, one of the three developed cold feet and requested release from his commitment. Concerned that their erstwhile operative would deliberately or inadvertently betray the proposed operation, SSU Austria returned him under escort to an American POW camp in Germany with instructions that he should be detained in the camp for no less than six months and that upon his release he should be prohibited from leaving the American zone of Germany.[40]

The two remaining operatives were only slightly less problematic. In a autobiographical statement that his SSU case officer admitted was "definitely colored," Georgii Alexandrov recorded that he had been born into a bourgeois family in prerevolutionary St. Petersburg and educated in naval schools. In the First World War he survived the sinking of his destroyer, secured a transfer to the cavalry ("due to nervous fear of water"), and served in France as well as the eastern front. According to his autobiography, Alexandrov fought for the Whites in the Russian Civil War and returned to St. Petersburg (now Petrograd) after the conflict. Political persecution—he claimed his father died in prison and his brother was shot by the Cheka, the Bolshevik secret police—forced him to flee in 1923 first to Finland, then to Holland, then to Yugoslavia, where he studied at the "Russian Military Academy." Alexandrov acknowledged to his SSU interrogators that, driven by homesickness, he returned to the Soviet Union in 1929 using forged papers. Under this false identity he worked as an engineer in various power plants and served in the Red Army, rising to the rank of major. In 1936, fearful that several interviews with the police presaged exposure and arrest, Alexandrov again fled Russia, first for Romania, then to Yugoslavia. When the Germans occupied Yugoslavia in 1941 he was sent to Germany to work in the Todt Organization, the Nazi regime's engineering and construction conglomerate. He volunteered for the Vlasov Army, rose to command a regiment on the eastern front, and at the end of the war force-marched the remnants of his command west in order to surrender to the Americans.[41]

According to his testimony, Dimitri Moltshanov, a native of the North Caucasus, had a no less eventful life than his partner before connecting

with American intelligence. In his autobiographical statement, Moltshanov claimed to have fought in the Red Army during the Russian Civil War,
subsequently working briefly as a bookkeeper before rejoining the army in
1926. This second tour of military service allegedly included four years with
the NKVD, an assignment that ended abruptly when his father was shot as
a Trotskyist. After the German invasion of the Soviet Union Moltshanov
fought at the front as a regimental officer until his capture by the Germans
in September 1941. After some time in a POW camp, he offered his services
to the Wehrmacht, serving in several auxiliary units, and finally deserting
in early 1945 when ordered to report to the Vlasov Army. Evading arrest by
constantly moving about, he eventually surrendered to an American army
unit in early May.[42]

After contriving cover stories and documentation identifying Alexandrov
and Moltshanov as displaced Poles employed as translators by the U.S. Army,
SSU planned to establish the operatives in Vienna, from where they would
embark, sometimes in civilian clothes, sometimes in Red Army uniform, on
short excursions into the Russian-occupied regions of Austria. Pragmatic officers in Salzburg estimated that the MACY operatives could hope to evade
Russian counterintelligence for only a few months, but with luck, that would
be enough time for them to build up several chains of informants inside the
Soviet zone.[43]

Project MACY was delayed, however, first by the demobilization and return to the United States of the group's case officer in December, then by
difficulties in securing proper documentation in Vienna. There was also the
problem of their background stories, which included some rather curious episodes. Moltshanov, for example, claimed to have never joined the Communist Party, a story that some SSU officers found improbable given his alleged
service as a captain in the NKVD. Equally improbable was Alexandrov's
claim to have moved, apparently at will, in and out of the Soviet Union and
to have contrived a false identity and military record sufficiently convincing
to allow him to reach the rank of major in the Red Army. Alexandrov's story
of enrolling in the "Russian Military Academy" in Yugoslavia in 1926 also
struck a false note in the ears of some American officers who doubted that
any such institution existed at the time their agent claimed to have been a
student. These difficulties proved serious impediments to an operation that
originally held so much promise. As late as March 1946 SSU Austria had to
inform Washington that Project MACY "has as yet given no results" and
that the mission was thinking of occupying their two inactive agents with
Polish-language lessons.[44]

The paucity of productive sources inside the Soviet zone became an increasingly serious problem as 1945 drew to a close. For the U.S. Army, SSU's

principal customer, Soviet order of battle was increasingly a priority, and the intelligence service was hard-pressed to meet the demand. In the fall of 1945 the Russian order-of-battle charts in the offices of United States Forces Austria were largely blank. G-2 was so desperate for information on the Soviet military in Austria that a SSU officer was astounded by the excited reception of his report concerning the identification and location of a single Red Army unit, information he had acquired during a casual conversation with a hitchhiking Russian soldier he had picked up while driving through the Soviet sector of Vienna.[45] By November SSU's Vienna base had two officers (practically the entire strength of the small SI section) working exclusively on order-of-battle intelligence, but had been able definitely to identify and locate only two of the many Red Army divisions stationed in the country. By the end of the year performance had improved slightly; Vienna base had identified five additional divisions as well several regiments whose relationship to larger formations remained obscure. Lacking an espionage arm of its own, G-2 was unable to corroborate this intelligence, but the information was welcome by the army's order-of-battle specialists, who were desperate for any information. In December, for example, the air division was delighted to hear from SSU that a glider club had been organized at Eisenstadt in the Soviet zone, and positively ecstatic to learn that in the same area the Russians may have completed an airbase with underground facilities first begun by the Nazis.[46]

Despite these positive developments, collection programs directed against eastern targets faltered in early 1946. Coverage of Soviet military capabilities and dispositions remained especially problematic, and customers in Salzburg and Washington began to complain. In March 1946, for example, as international anxieties flared over Great Power tensions in the Balkans and Near East, USFA berated SSU for its inability to confirm or refute alarmist reports that Moscow had deployed 900 fighters and bombers to the Soviet zone of Austria. The following month SSU blotted its copybook again when SI Austria had to acknowledge a "most noticeable lack of success" in determining the dispositions and capabilities of the 400,000 Red Army troops reportedly present in Hungary.[47]

Lurking behind the mediocre performance were some familiar culprits. Operations continued to be plagued by too few staff spread across too many targets. Even as the army demanded more attention to Soviet military dispositions in eastern Austria, SSU continued to develop and expand operations against political, economic, and military targets in Bulgaria, Czechoslovakia, Hungary, Poland, and Yugoslavia. A mere handful of SI personnel were responsible for collection programs inside Austria and across central and southern Europe, a workload that would have taxed a station thrice the size of the Austrian mission. Since projects were minimally staffed, the departure for home leave, consultation, or demobilization of only a single officer could put an entire operation on indefinite hold. Items from the Austrian mission's report for December suggest the seriousness of the problem: "Serious losses in personnel . . . have caused a reduction in the number of reports from Salzburg"; "The absence of source SEAHAWK on leave from Trieste for the better part of December and the transfer of source WAUPACA to X-2 produced a pronounced slump in the work of [Trieste Intelligence] unit"; "The return to Washington on temporary duty of the chief of the Hungarian Section produced a decline in the quality and quantity of our coverage for December."[48] The officers who were available often lacked the experience or skills relevant to their assignments. As late as the spring of 1946, for example, as USFA was screaming for more Soviet order-of-battle intelligence, SSU Austria still had no Russian-speaking SI officers on its roster.[49]

Staffing problems were compounded by conflicting requirements from customers, a problem further aggravated by the inability of Washington headquarters to provide clear and consistent guidance concerning collection priorities. Like its sister mission in Germany, OSS Austria had originally been tasked with providing intelligence to assist the administration of the American zone of occupation. Occupation authorities expected OSS (and its successor, SSU) to be a news service that would keep them informed of local political, social, and economic conditions inside the American zone and, secondarily, the other Allied zones. In the fall of 1945 this original mission had to compete with growing demands from G-2 USFA for coverage of Red Army order of battle, a task that required a concentration on the Soviet zone alone. At the same time, SI officers effectively created a third mission requirement when they took the initiative to extend operations beyond Austria's borders. These requirements represented three collections arenas, each with distinctive targets and each with its own peculiarities concerning access, agent recruitment, trade craft, communications, and security. From the perspective of SI officers, for example, the identification of Soviet armor formations in eastern Austria posed a significantly different collection problem than a report on the labor market in American-controlled Linz, and as collection projects both differed substantially from an attempt to determine the degree of anticommunist sentiment in the Hungarian police. In short, not only did SSU have too many balls in the air, but the balls were significantly different in size and weight. By December 1945 SSU Austria was trying to transfer its responsibility for "general news coverage" to other elements of the occupation authority in order to better focus its scarce resources on critical foreign intelligence problems, but the transfer was retarded because other elements of the occupation authority were not positioned to assume the news coverage abandoned by SSU.[50]

In the first year of the occupation SSU achieved some notable intelligence successes—its penetration of the emerging Austrian government and reporting on internal Austrian politics was excellent—but surveillance of Soviet affairs was not one of them. Throughout 1946 SI Austria struggled in vain to establish effective coverage of the Soviet target. Not only did the poor results disappoint SSU's customers, but they also negatively affected future operations as SI officers grasped at straws to fill the intelligence void. Frustration, for example, may explain the eagerness with which the secret intelligence staff in the spring of 1946 seized on "Lister" and the alleged clandestine society of anti-Stalinist Red Army officers that would be the basis for Project PAREGORIC, apparently—pending the declassification of additional operational files—one of the worst fumbles in the experience of early postwar American intelligence (chapter 2). Desperate SI officers would come to rely on PAREGORIC for almost all of their intelligence concerning the Red Army; indeed as late as April 1947 SI Austria had only three sources on Soviet affairs other than the PAREGORIC chain. One, code-named JOY, was a Tass journalist who occasionally traveled abroad for the Soviet news service and who began working for American intelligence in early 1947. The second was a Russian army major who had been recruited by JOY. In the spring of 1947 both of these sources had been working for American intelligence for only a brief period, and their reliability remained uncertain. Red Army deserters who managed to cross into American-controlled territory represented the third source.[51]

Other American services were ill-prepared to take up the slack in SSU reporting. Despite the army's growing preoccupation with Soviet order of battle and its dissatisfaction with SSU's coverage of that target, the army's own Military Intelligence Service was late in developing a systematic intelligence program directed against Russian targets and an independent clandestine collection capability to implement such a program. Although coverage of Soviet activities was added to MIS Austria's formal mission directive in 1946, the military intelligence service did not get around to establishing "Special Sections" in Vienna, Salzburg, and Linz dedicated to eastern intelligence until November of that year. Of course bits and pieces of information from the east had always dribbled in from MIS censorship and prisoners of war (POW)/displaced persons (DP) interrogation programs, but the service had received little encouragement from either Washington or local headquarters to expand collection beyond order of battle. In the spring of 1946, for example, MIS began passing up the chain of command information concerning Soviet industry, but it received neither acknowledgment of its effort nor directives for further investigation until early 1947, almost a year after the original reports.[52]

In developing coverage of Soviet targets, army intelligence in Austria was constrained by many of the problems—demobilization of trained and experienced personnel, lack of clear directives from Washington, an early focus on denazification and local conditions and personalities—that plagued the early collection efforts of SSU. Its biggest problem, however, was the absence of a clandestine espionage capability. MIS was an intelligence service without spies. From the start it had been organized to pursue a relatively passive approach to intelligence; an approach that made MIS staffers gatherers rather than hunters. Information—monitored phone calls, DP and POW stories, and intercepted letters—poured into MIS offices, but in the early months of the occupation military intelligence officers did not recruit and run agents against the Soviet Union or any other power. The Pond, the army's clandestine service, seems to have been inactive in early postwar Austria.

As late as November 1946, MIS mission directives stipulated that intelligence from the east was to be acquired "through screening, interrogations and questioning of displaced personnel, repatriated Prisoners of War and escaped Prisoners of War from camps within Soviet-occupied countries and through questioning of any persons recently arrived from that area possessing such information."[53] Conspicuous by its absence was any reference to clandestine agent operations or operations of any type outside the American zone. Even interrogations of displaced people could prove difficult. The continued presence of the Soviet Repatriation Commission (SRC) in the U.S. zone seriously hampered the work of Special Section interrogators. Representatives of the SRC, many of them NKVD officers, had access to the refugee camps, and MIS had to take care that Russian personnel did not learn that Americans were seeking information concerning Soviet topics. Jewish refugees from the East, for example, were first questioned about war crimes committed by German police and military units in Nazi-occupied Russia, but then the interrogator would gradually shift the interview toward a discussion of factories, transport facilities, military camps, and general conditions where the displaced person might have lived or worked. In the first half of 1947 representatives of MIS's Special Sections used this technique in screening 1,570 individuals in the camps. Some 200 of these individuals provided positive intelligence on the Soviet Union or Soviet-occupied areas.[54]

Army intelligence did not improve its clandestine intelligence capabilities in Austria until 1947, when the Counterintelligence Corps shifted its focus from denazification to positive intelligence collection. Eventually, CIC would develop several collection programs, including PAPERCHASE, which recruited cleaning women at Soviet military headquarters to deliver the contents of office wastebaskets, and the aptly named CLAPTRAP, which relied on an Austrian medical specialist in venereal diseases to casually question the Red Army officers who represented the bulk of his practice. Project MONTGOMERY employed the services of Wilhelm Hoettl, a senior officer in the Sicherheitsdienst, the Nazi security and intelligence service, who recruited networks in Hungary from among his wartime associates and contacts, while Project MOUNT VERNON represented a network of informants covering the Soviet zone of Austria. The product of these operations, mainly Red Army order-of-battle intelligence, was not available in the immediate postwar period because most of these CIC networks did not come on line until late 1947 and some, such as MONTGOMERY and MOUNT VERNON, did not become fully operational until the summer and fall of 1948.[55]

Spy versus Spy

Project CAVIAR, the most audacious of the early espionage efforts in Austria against Soviet targets, actually began as a counterintelligence operation. In early August 1945 OSS Austria was approached by Chalva Odicharia, a fervent Georgian nationalist who had fled his homeland for France when the Bolsheviks finally dashed any hope that the Russian Revolution would bring independence to the people of the Caucasus. In exile Odicharia submerged into the murky, conspiratorial world of émigré politics where ephemeral anticommunist groups such as the "National Georgian Committee" or the "Georgian National Socialist Party" pursued the cause of Georgian nationalism, plotting against each other as much as against Moscow, competing for the patronage of foreign intelligence services, and facing provocation and penetration by the Soviet services. During the interwar period, Odicharia established connections with French, German, and Japanese intelligence, associations that carried him and his personal war against the Soviets as far afield as Lebanon and Iran. The German invasion of Russia found him in France, where he agreed to work with the "Georgian Liaison Staff" of anticommunist Georgian nationalists who collaborated with the Germans against their common enemies, Moscow and its communist minions in other countries. Under German supervision Odicharia recruited members of the Georgian colony in France for clandestine work against French communist resistance groups, an activity that continued until September 1944, when the Allied advance across France forced him and his Georgian associates to evacuate, first to Berlin and then, as the Third Reich collapsed, to Constance, Innsbruck, and finally Salzburg.[56]

Fearing postwar retribution from the French and the Soviets, the Georgians sought safety in the anonymity of a camp for Russian displaced persons, one of the refugee camps that grew up like mushrooms in the summer of 1945. In camp, Odicharia, now calling himself Alexander Tsagoeff, was recognized by two Georgians, who, after capture by the Germans on the eastern front, had joined the collaborationist Georgian Liaison Staff to conduct anti-Soviet propaganda. Now boasting the insignia of Red Army officers—a curiosity that seemed to confirm rumors that the two had secretly worked for Russian intelligence during their supposed collaboration with the Georgian Liaison Staff—the pair supervised the camp's inmates as representatives of the Soviet Repatriation Commission, an organization that provided cover for NKVD officers. Once recognized, Odicharia concluded that his survival depended on playing the role of a repentant renegade by convincing the Russians that he had abandoned his former beliefs and was prepared to do penance by offering his considerable clandestine experience to Moscow. Removed from the camp and subjected to extensive questioning during which his Soviet interrogators alternately abused him for his treacherous past and praised him for his resolution to make amends and return to the arms of Mother Russia, Odicharia eventually convinced Major Valentin Rumiantsev, a senior intelligence officer working under cover of the Soviet Repatriation Commission, that he was a potentially useful asset for intelligence and propaganda work, especially among anti-Soviet émigré groups.[57]

Soviet supervision of their prospective agent was surprisingly lax. While awaiting developments after his productive conversations with Major Rumiantsev, Odicharia used a certain Alexander Shingalaya, a shadowy fellow Georgian who was then working for an organization providing relief to anti-communist Yugoslavian refugees, to contact American intelligence. Perhaps to keep open his options, perhaps to strike another secret blow against his people's traditional enemy, Odicharia offered to work as a double agent for American intelligence. Without informing Washington of the approach, OSS Austria's X-2 section promptly accepted the Georgian's offer. Struggling like their colleagues in SI to define a role for themselves in the occupation regime, the small counterintelligence staff seized on an opportunity to extend its activity beyond the pursuit of war criminals and diehard Nazis and do some real CI work by monitoring the activities of Russian intelligence officers.

X-2 quickly concocted a rough operational plan. Odicharia would convince Major Rumiantsev to capitalize on his reputation as an anticommunist Georgian nationalist by allowing him to establish in Austria an ostensibly anti-Soviet émigré organization that would not only provide a cover for Odicharia's intelligence and propaganda operations against the Western powers but would also, by serving as a magnet for anticommunist émigrés and displaced persons, allow the Russians to penetrate and covertly control any anti-Soviet conspiracies by these émigrés. To facilitate and justify contact with his American case officer, Odicharia would also convince his Russian controller that he should establish contact with the American "police" in order to scout the potential for future penetration of the U.S. occupation administration by the Soviet services. X-2 Austria intended to use their new Georgian friends only for counterintelligence purposes, specifically, to identify Soviet intelligence officers and expose their operations. At no time was there any intention to support any nationalist activities aimed at liberating Georgia from Soviet control.[58]

From the start X-2 Austria was aware, at least in broad outline, that their new Georgian agent had a rather checkered past and that he had "to a certain extent collaborated with the GIS [German Intelligence Service], the [Ge]Stapo and the Wirtschaftspolizei in Paris along anti-Communist and anti-Soviet lines." Any uncertainty about the precise nature of that collaboration disappeared in early September 1945, within weeks of Odicharia's offer of services, when X-2 learned that a party of French police accompanied by an American CIC officer had arrived in Salzburg with arrest warrants for Odicharia and several of his Georgian associates on charges of being, respectively, the leader and members of the "Georgian Gestapo" in wartime France. To protect their new source from French vengeance, X-2 Austria provided the Georgians with false documents and hideouts in Salzburg. The counterintelligence officers seemed to believe that the implicit threat of denunciation to either the French or the Russians would make Odicharia a pliant accomplice. Once again, the field officers seemed to have acted without informing or consulting Washington.[59]

By mid-September Odicharia had renewed his conversations with Major Rumiantsev. Evincing an interest in the Georgian's proposal to create a notional anticommunist émigré organization and a concern to shield him and his associates from French search parties, the Russian intelligence officer convinced Odicharia to hide in a Russian DP camp. Rumiantsev assured Odicharia of his commitment to the proposed operation. He confirmed that he would run the operation personally and confided to the Georgian collaborator not only that he was on a special mission to coordinate all Soviet intelligence in Central Europe but also that he was a member of the Russian "Council of the Soviet People," an organ the NKVD officer likened to a council of ministers. The major also suggested that to make the operation more attractive to authorities in Moscow, who might question Odicharia's stature in anticommunist émigré circles, the Georgian and his colleagues should prepare personal histories that, if anything, exaggerated their wartime collaborationist activities against the Allies and the anti-Nazi communist resistance.[60]

News of Rumiantsev's growing confidence in Odicharia must have confirmed X-2 Austria in the wisdom of its decision to employ the Georgian,
a decision that seemed especially risky in view of the fact that by the first
week in October the counterintelligence (CI) officers had learned that not
only the French police but also the U.S. Army's Counterintelligence Corps
were actively pursuing the Georgian as a war criminal.[61] To protect their
man from the threat of arrest, X-2 had earlier prompted Odicharia to ask
Rumiantsev to remove him and his Georgian confederates to the Soviet zone.
The Russian intelligence officer acceded to Odicharia's request and proposed
that the Georgians lie low for a few weeks in Soviet-occupied territory before receiving new identities and reinfiltrating the American zone. The major
promised in the meantime to take Odicharia to Vienna and Paris to meet
Soviet intelligence officers with whom he would be working in the future.
On 2 October Odicharia, eleven of his men, and a couple of NKVD escort
officers departed the American zone for a camp at St. Valentin in the Soviet
zone. For weeks there was no word about their situation. In early November
X-2 Austria learned via a cutout that four Georgians had been executed at
St. Valentin. At the end of that month a man sent by X-2 to snoop around
the Soviet camp returned to report that camp guards recalled the arrival in
October of a group of Georgians who had been segregated under close guard
in an isolated barracks. The camp guards could not recall seeing any of these
Georgians for some time.[62] Chalva Odicharia had disappeared, and nothing
more was ever heard from him or his group.

The CI officers had fallen for a Soviet deception operation. Described
by his American opponents as "an ambitious officer, of keen intelligence, an
open mind, and great resourcefulness," Major Valentin Rumiantsev probably
had welcomed Chalva Odicharia's unexpected appearance in his office as a
providential opportunity to bring a notorious anticommunist troublemaker
to Soviet justice, neutralize a potentially troublesome group of Georgian
nationalists, and test the scope and nature of American counterintelligence
interest in Russian operations. Rumiantsev's ruse was facilitated in part by
missteps by the Georgians. Their agreement to compose accounts of their
wartime collaboration with the Nazis, thereby providing the equivalent of
voluntary confessions for a future trial, was a fatal mistake. For its part,
American counterintelligence blindly drove the operation forward without
once suspecting the sheer cliff that lay ahead. Inexperienced in the devious
ways of Soviet intelligence, persistent in its refusal to seek guidance and assistance from Washington, and surprisingly ignorant (or unimaginative) concerning Soviet administrative organs and practices—Odicharia's American
controllers, for example, found it perfectly plausible that an alleged member
of the Council of Ministers of the Union of Soviet Socialist Republics had

nothing better to do than lurk about Salzburg recruiting and running informants in postwar Austria—X-2 Austria was the perfect mark for Rumiantsev's confidence game.

Aside from providing a painful lesson in the skills and ruthlessness of Soviet espionage and security services, Project CAVIAR directly contributed nothing to the work of American intelligence in Austria, but a subsidiary operation unexpectedly paid substantial dividends. Sometime in the summer of 1945 Alexis Stachovitch, a strongly anticommunist Austrian citizen of Russian parentage who had served as a captain in the Wehrmacht, came to the attention of OSS Austria. X-2 hired Stachovitch, who was fluent in German, Russian, and English, to establish contacts in the various DP camps. Originally, the counterintelligence unit hoped that information culled by Stachovitch (code-named SYBILLE) from the various national groups living in these camps might provide an independent check on the activities of Chalva Odicharia and his Georgians. SYBILLE's industry and initiative, however, soon moved the operation to a different level. By October, Stachovitch had established several clandestine intelligence cells, each assigned a particular mission. For example, Cell #1, based at Camp Lehen, was responsible for the identification and surveillance of intelligence operatives working on behalf of the Soviet Repatriation Commission. Cell #2, one of two clandestine units working for Stachovitch inside Camp Parsch, surveyed recently arrived refugees for information concerning conditions in the Soviet zone and the Soviet-occupied countries of Eastern Europe.[63]

In its early form Project SYBILLE was principally a counterintelligence operation to monitor Soviet intelligence and propaganda activities particularly among émigrés and refugees. One of its earliest products was a report on the personnel and organization of the NKVD in the American zone that identified particular agents of the Russian service, traced the service's connections to the Soviet Repatriation Commission, and revealed some of its contacts inside various agencies of the military governments in the western zones. The fact that many of the identities and observations in this report paralleled an independent report of the American army officer attached as liaison to the SRC undoubtedly raised SYBILLE in the estimate of the Austrian mission. The SYBILLE chain also identified Soviet informants who were working inside the DP camps as interpreters or support staff and monitored efforts by Soviet agents to spread pro-Moscow propaganda in the camps. One of its most important successes was the exposure of a former employee of the SRC who continued undercover as a NKVD stay-behind agent when the commission staff was routinely rotated back to Russia. When identified by the SYBILLE network, this Russian source was working in U.S. Army headquarters in Salzburg.[64]

Under its energetic leader Project SYBILLE expanded so quickly that it was detached from the ill-fated Project CAVIAR and established as an independent operation. By December of 1945 Alexis Stachovitch was establishing chains across Austria and southern Germany, traveling unaccompanied, by motorcycle, with letters from SSU Austria introducing him to American intelligence officers and enjoining local military authorities to provide him with all necessary "motor pool, billeting and messing facilities."[65] As SYBILLE grew, its mission also expanded. Established as a counterintelligence effort, by late autumn the operation was generating significant positive intelligence for SSU Austria. The sources were usually refugees or Red Army deserters. Some of the intelligence items, particularly a sensational (though false) report in early October 1945, allegedly sourced secondhand to a Red Army general, that Stalin had survived an assassination attempt in late August, circulated within the State and War Departments.[66]

The bulk of SYBILLE's intelligence, while less breathtaking, was probably more useful. Reporting focused on the Red Army and security conditions in Soviet-occupied Eastern Europe, topics of particular concern to SSU's principal customer, the U.S. Army. SYBILLE sources, for example, confirmed reports flowing into other SSU stations in Europe in the fall of 1945 that Soviet occupation forces in Poland were heavily engaged against anti-Soviet partisans. Deserters and refugees brought information about the Red Army in Austria. Some of this information, such as news that Soviet troops had been withdrawn from Linz to the outskirts of Vienna, was classic order-of-battle intelligence. One source reported that war weariness was so pervasive and morale so low in Soviet army formations in Austria that desertions and even local mutinies were increasingly common and that, in response, political commissars were stressing the capitalist threat to the Russian homeland and the need to remain prepared and vigilant for the inevitable war against the United States and Britain. The same source noted that food supplies for the Red Army in Austria were so inadequate that the troops were forced to requisition or plunder, behavior that had so alienated the local population that attacks against Red Army personnel and property were not uncommon. Perhaps more alarming because they confirmed scattered reports from other sources in the summer of 1945 were SYBILLE reports in the fall that the Soviet military authorities in Austria were actively recruiting former German air force and SS personnel for service in the Red Army and Air Force.[67]

Project SYBILLE was a hybrid operation, a project that began with purely counterintelligence purposes and then expanded to include a positive intelligence mission. In the early postwar period X-2 Austria ran several such operations; indeed, counterintelligence, in most stations the poor cousin to the more glamorous espionage section, assumed an unusually prominent position in the Austrian mission. This status was, in part, the product of an energetic and aggressive CI staff, but it also reflected conditions peculiar to the clandestine environment of early postwar Austria. Much more so than in Germany and other countries of early postwar Europe, that environment was characterized by a war between services. The significant intelligence targets that came to dominate early intelligence priorities in Germany and require aggressive collection operations—for example, Soviet persecution of noncommunist political parties and the mobilization of surviving German war industries in support of the Soviet military machine—did not figure prominently on the early Austrian intelligence scene. While never entirely immune to the competition and suspicion that increasingly poisoned relations between East and West, Austria was, at least in the first year of peace, somewhat of a political sideshow to the main performances that were being played out in such places as Germany, Poland, and the Near East. Additionally, Austria (again unlike Germany) was more a staging ground than a hunting ground for positive intelligence operations. Almost from its establishment SI Austria was preoccupied with collection programs in *other* countries—Hungary, Poland, Yugoslavia—a focus that increasingly consumed scarce SI resources during the organizational retrenchments of 1945–1946 and largely relegated Salzburg and Vienna to support bases for "foreign" operations. This left the field inside Austria largely to X-2 and, rather later, the Army's Counterintelligence Corps.

As we have seen, X-2 was quicker off the operational mark than its SI counterparts, and it was also quicker to focus on the Soviet target. By the early fall of 1945, when SI section was still cobbling together its first operations against Soviet targets, the counterintelligence staff already had in hand two major anti-Soviet operations, CAVIAR and SYBILLE. In subsequent months the counterintelligence unit picked up the pace by launching a series of new and ambitious projects. Not all of these projects were aimed at the Soviet Union, but even operations directed against other targets often contained a Soviet component. Project SYRACUSE, another operation that combined CI and SI missions, recruited a prominent figure in Austrian financial circles who served as an economic advisor to the Renner cabinet to report on the new government and its personalities. Secondarily this individual was tasked with reporting any suspicious Russian activities, especially if such activities suggested the work of Soviet intelligence. RENARD was an operation aimed at the French intelligence service, which SSU rightly suspected of trying to recruit informants inside the American zone. The operation's principal agent was a former radio operator for the Abwehr whose postwar employment with a manufacturing firm in Vienna gave him an excuse to travel throughout the western zones. While ferreting out French intrigues, this operative was also to remain alert for evidence of Soviet espionage. The primary purpose of Project SYMPHONY was to penetrate the "Jewish Intelligence Service" by recruiting Yiddish-speaking agents inside the private organizations, such as the Rothschild Institute or the so-called Brichah (Escape), that were assisting death camp survivors and refugees hoping to reach Palestine, but X-2 also hoped to identify any agents infiltrated by Moscow into the immigration.[68]

The bulk of the operations controlled by X-2 Austria were directed explicitly against the Soviet intelligence services or the services of East European states, such as Bulgaria and Czechoslovakia. The extent of Soviet espionage against American targets, far exceeding the "routine" intelligence activity of other allies, such as France, was alarming and raised doubts about Soviet intentions in the minds of American intelligence officers. Especially worrisome was evidence that the intelligence services of countries occupied by the Red Army were acting as surrogates for Russian intelligence. Such surrogacy not only multiplied Soviet intelligence resources, but also raised questions concerning Moscow's influence over nominally independent governments and confirmed suspicions that the "popular front" regimes were, in fact, stooges for the Soviet Union.

As early as the fall of 1945, SSU's counterintelligence officers had received reports that NKVD officers held important posts in the Yugoslav intelligence service. By the spring of 1946 CI operations definitely confirmed reports filtering in to SSU headquarters from other sources that the East European services had become wholly owned subsidiaries of the NKVD.[69] Project MOONLIGHT, for example, began in the autumn of 1945 when two young Bulgarians appeared in Salzburg allegedly in search of a former acquaintance. The pair spent most of their time questioning anyone who would speak with them about the dispositions and equipment of U.S. Army units in Austria. X-2 monitored the two, and gradually the effort grew into an operation that targeted Bulgarian clandestine activities and personnel, including "a group of Bulgarian agents working for the NKVD" in Vienna, in order to monitor "NKVD-controlled Bulgarian intelligence activities in Austria."[70]

CHECKERS, a scheme to monitor the activities of the Czech intelligence service, was born in late 1945 when SSU's Austrian mission received a visit from a Czechoslovakia-born veteran of the German Army who was then living in Vienna as a student at the university. This individual (code-named DD603 by the Americans) reported that he had been approached by a fellow Czech who, though wearing civilian clothes, identified himself as Captain Bilek of the Czech army. Though a complete stranger, Bilek brought word that DD603's aged parents, who lived still in Czechoslovakia, were in good health but faced expulsion from their home as a result of government policies directed against the *Volkdeutsche*, Czech citizens of German heritage. The captain suggested that the elderly couple could escape this threat if their son agreed to spy for Czechoslovakia.[71]

X-2 convinced their Czech visitor to accept Bilek's offer, and under American supervision DD603 became over the next several months one of the most important double agents in early postwar Austria. The industrious Czech army captain had countless questions for his new source in Vienna. Could he obtain the names of former Wehrmacht officers now enrolled at the University of Vienna? Were there any new anti-Soviet organizations forming at the university or in the city? Was it true that the anticommunist remnants of the wartime Czech government-in-exile, now in opposition to the postwar government established in Soviet-occupied Czechoslovakia, were sending representatives to the Austrian capital? What did the identification cards carried by employees at American occupation headquarters look like? Could he obtain from friendly and always talkative American soldiers information concerning American Air Force units inside Austria? When, in response to the last assignment, his source volunteered that he knew about a Red Air Force base near Vienna, the Czech officer laughed and said of course he had no need for information concerning Russian bases. To facilitate his young source's work, Belik provided rudimentary training in trade craft and funds for travel in the American and British zones.[72]

For their part, American CI officers facilitated DD603's work by contriving convincing, though misleading, answers to Bilek's questions, which their double agent would then pass to his controller. The Czech captain was so pleased with the product provided by his source that he arranged for the man's parents to regularize their citizenship, thereby avoiding deportation from Czechoslovakia, and even went so far as to find the father a good job. By the summer of 1946 Captain Bilek was considering using his university student to develop networks inside the American zone. Everyone was happy, but none more so than X-2. CHECKERS allowed American counterintelligence to identify a Czech intelligence officer operating clandestinely inside of Austria, penetrate and control a hostile operation, and confound an opposing service through disinformation. From Bilek's questions and comments, SSU concluded that the Czech service was representing the interests of the NKVD. When, in the summer of 1946, Washington headquarters surveyed the counterintelligence scene across the globe and concluded, "Czechoslovak Intelligence Service activities in Austria have indicated that Czechoslovakia now considers herself to be inseparably linked with East and Soviet Russia, and is now concentrating on gathering intelligence on the Western Powers," it undoubtedly had Project CHECKERS in mind.[73]

The Soviets alarmed American counterintelligence not just by the extent of their operations, but also by the aggressiveness and ruthlessness of their methods. In the exercise of their presumed occupation rights the Red Army had frequently behaved recklessly. Military police and NKVD teams, often assisted by communist elements in the Austrian police, brazenly snatched Red Army deserters and Austrians suspected of anti-Soviet activities off the streets of Vienna in such numbers—more than 450 individuals in the period 1946–1948—that the Austrian capital came to vie with Berlin for the title of "Kidnap City."[74] Soviet authorities frequently interfered with communications between Vienna and the western occupation zones. All phone and telegraph connections used by American authorities were monitored. American trains carrying personnel and supplies to the U.S. sector of the capital were harassed and freight cars looted. On one occasion, the Russians stopped a train transporting the American occupation commander, General Mark Clark, and removed baggage belonging to members of his entourage. In January 1946 shots were exchanged and a Russian officer killed when U.S. Army military police resisted Red Army troops attempting to board an American train known as the "Mozart Express."[75]

As we have seen in the case of the Georgians involved in Project CAVIAR, the NKVD was prepared to deal ruthlessly with individuals suspected of anti-Soviet activities or connections with foreign intelligence services. The safety of SSU agents and their sources was constantly at risk from Russian special operations. Other foreign services, particularly the French, were known to be running operations against American targets, but the French and other services were not kidnapping or murdering American sources. The aggressiveness and ruthlessness of Soviet intelligence and counterintelligence operations in Austria, culminating in 1948 in the abduction and murder of an American official attached to the American Economic Cooperation Administration but possibly engaged in clandestine work for American intelligence, the kidnapping of four CIC informants, and physical assaults on American CIC agents, probably did more than anything to convince local American intelligence authorities that the Soviets were an immediate and dangerous threat. Such attacks also undermined collection efforts by scaring off sources and encouraging those who remained to demand compensation and protection commensurate with the danger.[76]

Most of the Soviet attacks in the war of intelligence services went unobserved and unrecorded in the back alleys of Vienna. Sources would disappear without explanation, and weeks or months later rumors or half stories would reach American ears that source X had been taken from her flat by three men in civilian clothes or that source Y had been executed in a Russian detention facility. Perhaps typical was the case of source SALOME, a young Pole working for the military intelligence service of the remnants of the wartime

Polish government-in-exile that remained in London in opposition to the Soviet-controlled regime in Warsaw. Moving between Britain, France, and Italy, SALOME shared with SSU officers in Austria information on Red Army order of battle. In late September 1946 she met her American case officer and handed over information concerning NKVD facilities and personnel in Austria and Red Army dispositions in Hungary. After that meeting, SALOME was never seen again. A handwritten note scrawled across the bottom of her last report curtly noted that she had been abducted by the Russians in Vienna.[77]

The Russian operation that particularly outraged American authorities began at two-thirty on a chill morning in late January 1946 when several men emerged from two black sedans that had pulled to a stop in front of a nondescript house on Salzburg's Nussdorferstrasse.[78] Three civilians and a uniformed American soldier wearing the insignia of the 250th Military Police Detachment of United States Forces, Austria, entered the building while the remaining men took up positions at the sides and rear of the structure. The party entered the apartment of Richard Kauder, a one-time Abwehr operative now working for the Strategic Services Unit. Erika Wahl, Kauder's companion, informed the intruders that the man they were seeking was out of town and she did not know when he would return. Without explanation the MP, who seemed to be in command, ordered a search of the house. Finding little of interest beyond a radio receiver and an American army cap (both of which they confiscated) the police party departed after instructing Wahl to tell Kauder upon his return that it would be best for him if he were to remain at home until they called again. At dawn, Wahl, who knew more about her companion's movements than she had let on, left the house and loitered on a nearby street corner, from which post she was able later that morning to intercept Kauder as he returned home. She told him of the visit and her fear that the men had come to kidnap him. Immediately Kauder and Wahl turned for advice and safety to their American case officer.

For Richard Kauder and Erika Wahl the sudden appearance of the police on their doorstep was the most dramatic in a series of suspicious encounters that had begun earlier that month with a visit by one Joseph Wiesinger, a mysterious individual who had first introduced himself as the representative of a refugee resettlement committee seeking housing for concentration camp survivors, but later revealed that he was actually an agent of the security section of the Austrian police. Over several visits Wiesinger closely questioned Kauder about his wartime work for the Abwehr and his current connections with American intelligence. When Kauder declined to satisfy his new acquaintance's curiosity, Wiesinger sheepishly acknowledged that he was not seeking the information as part of an official police inquiry but because he was hoping eventually to convince Kauder to invest in an enterprise to produce gasoline from peat and his questions were in the way of being a background investigation of a potential business partner. Kauder's doubts concerning his new friend were not assuaged by this unlikely story, and after one visit he had his driver follow Wiesinger after the police agent/entrepreneur left the Kauder residence. The chauffeur returned to report that his target had driven straight to the headquarters of the local Soviet military mission and had entered the building. The growing suspicion that Wiesinger was a Russian agent was further fueled when within hours of the police visit to the Kauder residence he contacted Erika Wahl to say that he had learned that the American military police were looking for her companion and that together they should go to him and warn him to hide.

Richard Kauder was no run-of-the-mill informant. During his wartime service with German intelligence he had, under the alias Richard Klatt, commanded a special unit, Air Intelligence Station Southeast, more commonly known as the "Klatt Bureau," which controlled the famous "Max South" network of sources inside the Soviet Union. Along with its counterpart, "Max North," Max South had provided the German military with most of its human intelligence on the Soviet Union. Although, at times, the Germans had second thoughts about Kauder, suspecting that he was, wittingly or not, spreading Russian disinformation, the sometime sporting goods and insurance salesman emerged from the war with his reputation as a spymaster intact if somewhat tarnished.[79] Captured by the U.S. Army at the end of the war, Kauder was not interrogated until June 1945, at which time he offered his services to American intelligence, burnishing his image by claiming (falsely) to have been arrested by the Gestapo for anti-Nazi activities.[80] X-2 Austria accepted the offer. At least initially, the counterintelligence staff was as much interested in the former Abwehr officer's knowledge of Nazi intelligence organizations and personalities as in his experience in running spies on the eastern front, but by the autumn of 1945 X-2 was directing their agent exclusively against communist targets. Now code-named SABER and established in Vienna as the owner of a transport firm, Richard Kauder became the principal agent in CACTUS, an umbrella project that encompassed several intelligence and counterintelligence operations extending into Bulgaria, Hungary, and Yugoslavia. In Project SWORD, for example, an anti-Tito physician in Belgrade collected political intelligence that she communicated to Kauder via the barges that plied the Danube River. FIGARO relied on anticommunist refugees to monitor and exploit the Yugoslavian monarchist organization in Austria, which claimed to control radio-equipped intelligence nets inside Yugoslavia. MOONLIGHT was an effort to penetrate the Bulgarian intelligence service by placing one of Kauder's informants close to two Bulgarians in the American zone who were suspected of spying for Sofia and (by extension) Moscow. ROBUST was an operation to exploit one of Kauder's wartime associates who now held a senior position in the Hungarian intelligence service.[81]

Clearly, Richard Kauder was the linchpin of SSU's counterintelligence operations in Austria, and his neutralization by the Soviets would have dealt a severe blow to American intelligence. Upon learning of Kauder's nocturnal visitors, X-2 checked with American military police headquarters and determined that no MPs had been dispatched to Nussdorferstrasse. This information combined with the reports of Joseph Wiesinger's suspicious behavior, convinced intelligence officers that Erika Wahl's fears concerning a kidnap attempt were correct. Anticipating another attempt that very evening, X-2 sent an armed party of officers and enlisted men to Kauder's residence. Three officers hid in one of the apartment's bedrooms while three others waited in a car down the street. In the early evening, Wiesinger phoned and, upon determining that Kauder was at home, suggested that they meet at the Hotel Bristol, a building some miles away. Kauder declined the invitation but suggested that Wiesinger call on him at home where he would be all evening. Within an hour a large black sedan bearing the license plates of the Soviet Repatriation Commission pulled up at the Kauder address. A uniformed American MP and two civilians entered the house. After opening the door to her unwelcome visitors, Erika Wahl walked calmly to the bedroom where her American protectors lay hidden and announced, "they are here." With pistols drawn, the Americans ran from the room and ordered the surprised visitors to raise their hands. Weapons were taken from the trio. One of the Americans immediately recognized the "MP" as Major Mihail Yankowski, an officer attached to the Soviet Repatriation Commission. He also recognized one of the "civilians" as a Red Army captain also attached to the SRC, an identification confirmed when the captain was found to be wearing a full Russian military uniform underneath his black overcoat. The third arrestee proved to be an official of the Austrian Communist Party. Meanwhile, the American party on the street ran to the sedan and arrested the driver, who, like the officer in the apartment, wore a Red Army uniform under a long civilian overcoat. They also arrested the second occupant of the vehicle, a Red Army lieutenant who hid his Russian uniform under the trench coat of a U.S. Army officer. Both Russians were armed. A third individual escaped down an alley in a hail of bullets from American guns.

The captives were taken to American intelligence headquarters, where they were booked, photographed (Major Yankowski in his MP uniform), and questioned. They remained largely silent, the others claiming that they knew nothing about Richard Kauder and the purposes of their mission and that they merely followed the orders of Major Yankowski. For his part, Yankowski insisted that he had organized the kidnapping on his own authority in order to capture a notorious former Nazi intelligence officer and that he had not acted on orders from the SRC. At one point he referred to Joseph Wiesinger as an informant for Soviet intelligence, a slip that led promptly to the arrest of the police officer/entrepreneur/Soviet agent. The interrogators did not have long with their subjects. The incident was the subject of an emergency meeting at USFA headquarters involving the deputy commander USFA and representatives of G-2, the judge advocate general, the political advisor, and the Strategic Services Unit. Arrangements were made to resolve the incident as quickly and quietly as possible. The attempted kidnapping was covered up (the culprits had been booked under German aliases), and on 25 January the Russians were transferred to the custody of Red Army officers.

Despite its expeditious resolution, the Kauder affair (known as the SHANGHAI Incident inside SSU) had a serious impact on American authorities in Austria. Following closely upon the shooting incident on the "Mozart Express," the attempted kidnapping had a particularly sobering effect on General Mark Clark, the American occupation commander, who was increasingly inclined to view the Soviets with suspicion. Suspicions were fueled when on 24 January—while Major Yankowski and his men were still in custody—Erika Wahl, Kauder's companion, escaped another abduction attempt by successfully fighting off a man who attempted to push her into a car as she walked with a friend along a Salzburg street.[82]

His cover obviously blown, SABER was of little further use to American intelligence. To protect their increasingly skittish agent, SSU moved Kauder to Camp King, the American interrogation facility at Oberursel, a small town near Frankfort-am-Main, Germany. Security was not the only motive behind the transfer to Oberursel. By early 1946 American intelligence, probably prodded by the British, wanted to talk with Kauder about his work for the Abwehr against the Soviet Union. During the war British code breakers had broken the cipher used by the Abwehr and, by intercepting the radio traffic between the Klatt Bureau in Sofia and its control station in Vienna, had been able to monitor the activities of Kauder's ostensible networks inside the Soviet Union. Eventually, the British came to suspect that Kauder was, wittingly or not, the channel for an elaborate Soviet deception that aimed to confuse and mislead the Germans.[83] Of course, if Kauder had been an instrument for Russian disinformation during the war, then the integrity of his postwar work for American intelligence, which supposedly drew upon his wartime connections and the remnants of the Klatt Bureau, became problematic. For several months Kauder and two of his wartime associates in the Klatt Bureau, Ira Longin (alias Ilya Lang), a Russian émigré, and General

Anton Turkul, a White Russian and professional anti-Bolshevik, were interviewed by American and British interrogators at Oberursel. At the end of the process—in the middle of which Kauder attempted suicide—the interrogators concluded that during the war Kauder had indeed been a conduit for Soviet disinformation and that, while never under direct Soviet control, he had begun to suspect the source of the intelligence pouring into his office from the Soviet Union but had swallowed his suspicions in order to maintain his position and reputation within the Abwehr. After the war Kauder nurtured the myth of the Klatt Bureau in order to secure a lucrative position with American intelligence.[84]

The investigation of Richard Kauder left some questions unanswered. For instance, was Kauder continuing to disseminate Soviet disinformation while working for SSU? If not, then was his product merely fabrication (a conclusion endorsed by his American interrogator) or did he truly develop some credible sources? If he was a channel for Soviet disinformation, then how does one explain Russian efforts to abduct him? Whatever the truth about Richard Kauder, there can be no doubt that the outcome of his interrogation was a heavy blow to American intelligence in Austria. As the controlling officer for Project CACTUS, Kauder had been a linchpin for several promising operations aimed at the Soviet Union, Bulgaria, Hungary, and Yugoslavia. Now CACTUS and its subsidiary operations (FIGARO, MOONLIGHT, ROBUST, SWORD) had to be considered compromised and their product tainted. Kauder himself survived the demise of his networks. Released from Camp King in mid-1947, he returned to Austria and continued for years to peddle his talents to any intelligence service gullible enough to purchase them.[85]

A recent student of American intelligence operations in early postwar Austria has argued that between 1945 and 1948 intelligence coverage of the Soviet Union varied little in content. According to this argument, American intelligence at the end of the period was reporting the same indicators of Soviet behavior (looting, rapine, kidnapping, etc.) that it had reported at the beginning of the period, with the difference that at the end intelligence authorities were explaining those indicators not as minor irritants or unfortunate lapses in discipline but as evidence of hostility and threat. What had changed, the argument goes, was not Soviet behavior, but Washington's decision to identify the Soviet Union as the principal political and military threat, a decision that led intelligence authorities in Austria to interpret Soviet behavior in a new, more suspicious light. Intelligence on the ground was, therefore, reinterpreted to complement perceptions in Washington.[86]

This interpretation misperceives the scope and nature of American intelligence in early postwar Austria. It ignores the fact that the perceptions of

American intelligence authorities in Austria, and by extension Washington, evolved over time in large part because intelligence coverage evolved. In the first months of the occupation, when coverage of the Soviet zone and Soviet affairs was practically nonexistent, and information from the east was scarce, it was easy (if not prudent) to dismiss reports of Soviet misbehavior as isolated or unfortunate episodes that reflected the confusion and adjustments natural to the end of any war. As intelligence coverage improved, however slowly, activities once dismissed as atypical or temporary were more readily seen to form a pattern of hostile and egregious behavior. American occupation authorities, for instance, might have viewed with regret but little alarm Soviet security officials' seizure of a handful of individuals in the western zones in the summer of 1945, but when by 1946–1947 the abductees numbered in the hundreds and included known anticommunists and individuals connected to the American occupation and its intelligence element, then even the most open-minded observers had to consider that this behavior was the rule rather than the exception.

Intelligence reporting from Austria was never static. Reporting in 1946 differed in volume and content from reporting in 1945. Counterintelligence coverage is a case in point. At first X-2 Austria did not have enough information concerning the operations and intentions of Soviet intelligence agencies to make a determination of friend or foe. By the fall of 1945 the counterintelligence officers were collecting evidence that the Russian agencies were aggressively attacking American targets. By early 1946 it was clear to these officers that the Russians were not only active, but also had mobilized the services of the regimes of Soviet-occupied Eastern Europe. As the information base expanded, the impression was one of growing hostility and threat. Intelligence officers in Austria did not need to be told by Washington that the Soviet Union was a danger. By early 1946 they already suspected this, and their impressions were based not on the spillover of fears developing in Washington, but on events in the field. In the diplomatic environment of early postwar Europe, Austria was another intelligence red flag.

CHAPTER FIVE

A Distant Arena: Eastern Europe

Eastern Europe is the region most closely associated with the origins of the Cold War. This prominence is not unwarranted, but it must be kept in perspective. The nations east of the Elbe had nothing like the economic and military potential of Germany, let alone of Western Europe as a whole. While the rapid and sometimes brutal Sovietization of Eastern Europe had a large and enduring effect on American public opinion, the intrinsic importance of the region in the estimate of American policy makers was slight, its fate being significant chiefly in relation to larger geopolitical issues, particularly what it revealed about the wellsprings of Soviet policy and the consequences likely to follow for the international system. The economic importance of the countries east of the Elbe was relatively modest. Their trade with the part of Europe of primary interest to the United States had been mainly in agricultural products. North and South America were more than able to replace what had come from Eastern Europe. Trade with the United States had always been slight, and the region did not beckon as promising areas for investment. It was, of course, Washington's policy to push for the development of international trade everywhere, but the specific reason for doing so in Eastern Europe was to dilute Soviet predominance.

The disillusionment in the United States at what befell most of Eastern Europe derived largely from a sense that the Kremlin had cynically violated wartime pledges not to interfere in the internal affairs of neighboring states. With the advantages of hindsight it now appears that Soviet policy was less cynical, if not necessarily less calculating and ambitious, than appearances might have suggested. When Stalin pledged free elections at the Yalta Conference in February 1945 he meant to keep his word, more or less. His fidelity, however, was predicated upon the expectation that the national front strategy would produce parliamentary regimes in which communist influence, while not exclusive, would be dominant and permanent. The enactment, under communist guidance, of social, agricultural, and economic reforms in countries where they were much needed would win the support of citizens and result in bourgeois democratic regimes responsive to Moscow but acceptable to the United States and Britain. In this way the wartime alliance might be preserved while the USSR recovered from the war and prepared for the day when inevitable economic crisis in the capitalist West created new opportunities to complete the Marxist-Leninist project in Europe.[1]

The national front strategy was well calculated to reconcile immediate Soviet priorities with the values and strategic interests of the Western democracies. Well before the end of the war, officials and opinion makers in the United States and Britain had become resigned to Soviet predominance in Eastern Europe exercised through treaties of mutual assistance and through parties of the left whose ranks were likely to swell as the war discredited the old political and social orders.[2] By the middle of the war American thinking was clear about the acceptable limits of Soviet hegemony in the region. An ad hoc group of senior diplomats empaneled to prepare for the Moscow Conference of 1943, for example, stated the matter succinctly: "some degree of Soviet supervision in foreign affairs" was acceptable, provided that the USSR's neighbors could "conduct their domestic affairs without interference."[3] There was, however, an irreducible minimum requirement for American tolerance of a Soviet sphere: domestic self-determination. States allied with the Soviet Union but not directly subject to it would not become instruments for aggression. An "open" sphere of influence might not introduce into postwar Europe the alliance rivalries that had more than once brought war to the continent.

The character of the regimes emerging in Eastern Europe was, therefore, a matter of great importance for the United States for reasons more pressing than the nominal ideals of the wartime Grand Alliance or the agitation of domestic ethnic groups. Diplomats and intelligence officers concerned with the lands east of the Elbe tried to answer many questions, but none was more basic than whether Soviet policy was trending, willfully or in response to the pressure of events, toward a destabilizing and ultimately dangerous domination of the region. By the end of the war suspicion of the Soviet Union was growing in the United States, and many Americans were inclined to answer the question pessimistically. Careful observers, however, were less certain. In September 1945, for example, the Office of Strategic Services' Research and Analysis Branch observed that while the Soviets would insist that communists participate in the governments of every country occupied by the Red Army, the final form and ultimate extent of Soviet influence in these countries remained uncertain.[4] The task of American intelligence was to end that uncertainty.

For all their early problems, the American intelligence units in Germany and Austria were privileged in relation to their sister elements in Eastern Europe. The Office of Strategic Services had entered the Reich in the wake of the U.S. Army and had established itself as a constituent element of occupational regimes that exercised administrative, legal, and military control over people and territory. This arrangement gave intelligence personnel an official status and allowed them to operate from secure facilities in a friendly and supportive environment where the instruments of political power, social control, and economic largesse were largely in the hands of Americans. Operations, especially in the Soviet occupation zones of Germany and Austria, were never entirely without risk, but at least the case officers did not reside in hostile territory and were not subject to constant surveillance and harassment. The situation in Eastern Europe was rather more problematic.

Except for an area around Pilsen in western Czechoslovakia, into which American troops had advanced in the last days of the war, Eastern Europe had been liberated by the Red Army. As victims of German militarism and active members of the anti-Nazi wartime coalition, Czechoslovakia and Poland reclaimed their sovereignty. In these countries there was no more need for occupation zones than there was in Belgium or Norway; the foreign troops were not occupiers but liberators who, in theory, would withdraw as soon as the reconstitution of the central government and logistical arrangements permitted. In Hungary, which had fought alongside Germany as a member of the Axis alliance, postwar authority resided in the Allied Control Commission, but the occupation (and effective control of local administration) was entirely in the hands of the Red Army. These conditions, particularly the absence of American military forces on the ground, meant that OSS personnel could not simply ride into Eastern Europe in jeeps at the rear of U.S. Army convoys, establish themselves in a corner of an American military compound, and operate with impunity under the authority of American proconsuls.

Poland

Initially, Poland posed the most serious problems for American intelligence. Although the United States contributed $10 million to the Polish government-in-exile in London for the support of the anti-Nazi underground, American espionage services eschewed operations in Poland during the war, and the Office of Strategic Services never established intelligence networks inside the country.[5] For information concerning Polish affairs and conditions inside the country OSS relied on liaison with Britain's Secret Intelligence Service and the Polish government-in-exile and the occasional item of information picked up by American espionage chains in Scandinavia and the Eastern Mediterranean.[6] By the summer of 1944, however, circumstances were forcing OSS to reconsider this policy of benign neglect.

With the successful invasion of Europe in June 1944 and the prospect of combat moving to the doorstep of Hitler's Germany, the Allies realized the need for significantly better intelligence from inside the Third Reich. Shortly after the Normandy landings, Major Joseph Dasher, the OSS liaison to the Polish government-in-exile, opened discussions in London with Polish military authorities with the intention of exploring prospects for more active intelligence collaboration, particularly in the form of joint operations into Germany. The Poles, who were eager to strengthen their connections with American clandestine agencies, needed little convincing, and the talks rather quickly produced agreement on a program to exploit for intelligence purposes the large number of Poles who were performing forced labor in German war industries. Under this plan, code-named EAGLE, the government-in-exile selected forty German-speaking Polish soldiers with working-class backgrounds and sent them to OSS for extensive training in communications, parachuting, and the tradecraft of espionage. After training, the Poles were to be parachuted into the Reich to develop networks among their fellow countrymen in German plants and factories. Originally, OSS anticipated that the EAGLE teams would be deployed in May 1945, but Hitler's Ardennes offensive in December 1944, which caught the Allies by surprise and fueled demands from American military planners for immediate intelligence from inside Germany on troop movements, supply dumps, and war plants, compelled intelligence authorities to advance the deployment date to March 1945. Eventually sixteen EAGLE teams were dropped into Germany, but most, if not all, were quickly rounded up by the Gestapo. Not one of the teams even managed to establish radio contact with its OSS controllers.[7]

With the onset of Project EAGLE OSS began to envision more aggressive operations. From using Poles to collect intelligence inside Germany it was only a short step to using Poles (or Americans) to collect intelligence inside Poland. In the summer of 1944 the absence of reliable and timely intelligence from within that war-torn country was increasingly apparent to American officials in Washington, London, and Moscow. Poland was now moving to the center of American diplomatic concerns as Russian forces advanced across the country. The central issue was whether the Soviets intended, their many assurances notwithstanding, to make a client state of their largest neighbor. The debate intensified with the Red Army's advance across the Curzon Line, the border between Poland and the Soviet Union established after the Russo-Polish War of 1919–1920, and Stalin's decision to establish in the city of Lublin the Polish Committee of National Liberation, a Moscow-sponsored group dominated by the communist Polish Workers Party (PPR), as the de facto administrative authority in the liberated areas. Since Britain and the United States (but not Russia) recognized the government-in-exile in London as the legitimate government of Poland, Russia's initiative on behalf of the Lublin Poles complicated Big Three relations by raising the prospect of opposing factions competing for control of the country, and it increased suspicions in London and Washington that Moscow was intent on unilaterally imposing upon the liberated nation a puppet regime that would exclude the London exiles and all but the most politically subservient noncommunist elements within Poland.[8] For its part, the United States refused to recognize the Lublin regime without clear evidence that it reflected the sentiments of the Polish people. The Soviets claimed that the Committee of National Liberation represented authentic democratic and popular forces, but decision makers in Washington were reluctant to accept this claim without substantial and independent evidence. The observations of American representatives on the ground would provide such evidence, but the Soviets opposed the introduction of official American and British observers into Polish areas liberated by the Red Army.[9]

The need for more direct and independent intelligence reporting was underlined by unconfirmed reports from the government-in-exile that PPR cadres, supported by Red Army and NKVD units, were arresting members of the London-affiliated underground Home Army and executing some of its officers, dismantling the clandestine military and administrative structures organized by the noncommunist resistance as a shadow government to the Nazi occupation regime, and establishing themselves as the sole legal authority in the liberated areas.[10] American intelligence was not inclined to accept such reports at face value. Elements in the Office of Strategic Services, particularly in the Research and Analysis Branch (RA), held the London Poles in low esteem. In the last year of the war RA reports repeatedly highlighted the reactionary political character of the government-in-exile, the reluctance of the prewar Polish government to cooperate in measures to restrain Germany, Poland's jackal-like feasting on the remains of Czechoslovakia after the Munich Agreements of 1938, its often brutal treatment of ethnic and religious minorities, and the general obtuseness of almost everyone charged with conducting the diplomacy of the exiled government.[11] Suspecting that reports from the London Poles might well reflect the political biases and ambitions of the strongly anticommunist and anti-Soviet exile government, General William Donovan, the director of OSS, advised the State Department that "only by having our own American sources will we be able to get reliable intelligence from that area." Desperate for objective information from inside Poland, the State Department agreed. In July 1944, Donovan initiated plans to parachute OSS teams into Poland—using aircraft of the London Poles— to collect intelligence and establish contact with the anti-Nazi resistance.[12]

Donovan's plans to infiltrate Poland proved abortive, although the reason for their demise remains obscure. Any program to air-drop clandestine teams into the areas of Poland liberated and occupied by the Red Army—the areas about which information was most needed—would have amounted to clandestine operations against the Soviets, and if exposed, would have seriously strained relations with Moscow. The participation of the London Poles in the operation would have been a certain provocation. That risk alone would have dampened enthusiasm for the program among intelligence and foreign policy authorities in Washington. A marginally less risky plan to infiltrate agents into the portion of Poland still controlled by Germany could more easily be rationalized, but the relentless advance of the Red Army made it unlikely that any German-occupied portion of the country would still be available by the time OSS had recruited and prepared its agents for deployment.

Whatever the reason for inaction, OSS failed to develop networks inside Poland, and at the end of the war Donovan still had no independent sources reporting from within the country. For information concerning political and economic conditions inside the country, which by April 1945 was completely occupied by Soviet forces, American intelligence continued to rely on liaison with the London Poles, reports from the U.S. embassy in Moscow, the observations of the few journalists who managed briefly to visit the country as guests of the Red Army, and accounts by the handful of refugees and escaped prisoners of war who could be debriefed by American and British representatives.

Not surprisingly, information originating with the government-in-exile described a country in the iron grip of the Red Army and Moscow's surrogates in the Lublin regime who were bent on suppressing noncommunist political institutions and sentiments in order to establish a Soviet puppet government against the will of the Polish people.[13] Though initially wary of such alarmist reports, American intelligence gradually began to accumulate evidence that confirmed the warnings from the London Poles. Communications intelligence, for example, revealed that independent observers shared the apprehensions of the government-in-exile. While American code breakers were unable to read any high-grade Russian diplomatic or leadership communications, coverage of other foreign diplomatic traffic occasionally provided insights into Polish affairs. French traffic was especially useful, since Paris was well represented not only in Moscow but also inside Poland, where a French diplomatic delegation was attached to the Polish Committee of National Liberation. Decrypted messages revealed that French diplomats believed that prospects for a truly independent, noncommunist Poland were dim. As early as January 1945 a message intercepted by American code breakers revealed that the French delegate in Lublin was convinced that the leadership of the Polish Committee of National Liberation was totally subservient to Moscow and that the regime was so unpopular that it could not sustain itself in power without the assistance of the Russians. Decrypted reports from the

French embassy in the Soviet Union that circulated to the White House and high-level officials in the State, War, and Navy Departments in Washington were equally stark. Throughout the spring of 1945 the embassy warned Paris that the Lublin Poles were totally under the control of Moscow and that the Russians, who would allow no outside interference in their plans to ensure a pro-Soviet Poland, would refuse to admit into any Polish government political cal elements who were not submissive to the Soviet Union.[14]

Journalists generally confirmed the impressions of the French diplomats. The first group of American correspondents to enter Poland—under the close supervision of the Soviet foreign ministry's press office—were interviewed by American diplomats upon their return to Moscow in late 1944. They reported that most Poles, though grateful to the Red Army for their liberation, were suspicious of Moscow's intentions, unenthusiastic about the Soviet-sponsored regime in Lublin, and loyal to the government-in-exile in London.[15] The Office of Strategic Services received a somewhat different appraisal from Richard Lauterbach, the Moscow correspondent of *Time* magazine, who reported that the Poles were resigned to becoming a Soviet sphere of influence and had no sympathy for anti-Soviet political initiatives. According to Lauterbach, who, unbeknownst to his OSS contacts, was a secret member of the American Communist Party and an individual of interest to Russian intelligence, the leaders of the Lublin administration were impressive patriots who had no intention of acting as puppets of Moscow.[16] This more sanguine appraisal (which may have reflected its source's communist sympathies) remained a distinctly minority view among Western journalists with experience of the country.

On balance, information culled from the testimony of Polish refugees and foreign visitors returning from the country tended to confirm the more alarmist claims of the London Poles. As early as November 1944, for example, the OSS station in Istanbul reported that such sources insisted that the sympathies of all groups inside Poland, with the possible exception of urban workers, were definitely with the London exile government and that these groups considered the Lublin regime nothing more than a creature of Moscow.[17] Subsequent intelligence reporting generally reiterated the theme of anti-Soviet sentiments and, less consistently, widespread support for the London exile government. By the end of the war, moreover, OSS reporting had begun to notice not merely resentment but active resistance against the Lublin Poles and their Soviet sponsors.

Some of the refugee reports were dramatic and seemed authoritative. In early May 1945 a former officer in "Berling's Army," the pro-Soviet Polish military force established by Moscow in 1943 and commanded initially by General Zygmunt Berling, reached Bucharest, where he was debriefed by

OSS officers. This officer, who admitted to participating in many of the actions he described, painted a picture of widespread terror directed by the security services of the Lublin regime, abetted by Soviet military and police units, against supporters of the London Poles and other "reactionaries" suspected of anticommunist sentiments. By the late spring of 1945, reportedly thousands had been arrested and any resistance brutally suppressed by the communists.[18] After VE Day, reports from POWs returning from camps in Poland, mainly French soldiers, but at least one American army sergeant, confirmed that hostility toward the Lublin regime was so intense that Poles were turning to active resistance and sabotage. In late June 1945 OSS sent the White House and the State Department a report from two of its officers who had just returned from a brief trip across Poland, during which they had conversed with a range of individuals including soldiers, office workers, and businessmen. These officers estimated that only about half of the Polish population supported their wartime leaders in London. Most of the remainder hoped for a new democratic government based upon a coalition of all political elements. Among both groups, however, there was widespread fear of the Soviet Union and distrust of the Polish National Committee now installed by the Russians in Warsaw. Opposition to Moscow and its surrogates, they reported, was increasingly taking the form of armed resistance by large, well-organized, and well-armed groups. Such reports must have been increasingly common for by mid-July OSS was estimating that more than 38,000 armed anticommunist partisans were active inside Poland.[19]

Though lacking networks and controlled sources inside the country, American intelligence was able to keep its customers in Washington well informed concerning the general state of political developments in Poland even if no great confidence could be placed in particular details. The reports of pervasive anticommunist sentiments, popular revulsion toward the Moscow-sponsored Committee of National Liberation, police repression of "reactionaries," and the growing armed resistance to such repression accurately described political conditions inside Poland in 1944–1945.[20] Such reports could only have fueled concerns in Washington regarding Moscow's intentions. At the Yalta Conference (4–11 February 1945) President Franklin Roosevelt, hoping to square the circle by securing a Polish government that was both authentically representative and friendly to the Soviet Union, had agreed to a formula calling for the reorganization of the Lublin administration into a "Provisional Government of National Unity" to include "democratic leaders from Poland itself and from Poles abroad." The Allied leaders agreed to leave decisions concerning the composition of the reorganized government to a commission composed of Vyacheslav Molotov, the Soviet foreign minister, and Averell Harriman and Clark Kerr, the American and British ambassadors in Moscow.[21]

Meeting in Moscow throughout the spring of 1945, the commission deadlocked over which Poles, Lublin or London, should be consulted regarding the composition of the National Unity government; whether that government should be entirely new or based upon the Lublin regime; which individual Poles should be invited to form the government; and whether the Lublinites should be able to veto invitations. By the end of March 1945 Moscow's diplomatic intransigence combined with particular acts, such as the arrest of prominent noncommunist Poles, some of whom Washington had hoped to include in the reorganized government, convinced American policy makers that the Soviets had no intention of honoring the spirit of the Yalta agreements and were intent on imposing a puppet regime in Poland. The decision to challenge the Soviet position, in part by opposing the inclusion of Poland in the upcoming San Francisco Conference to establish a postwar international organization until agreement on a provisional authority consistent with the Yalta agreements, may well have reflected the impact of reports reaching Washington from intelligence outposts on the periphery of Poland.[22]

The deadlock was broken in late May when Harry Hopkins, the late President Roosevelt's personal adviser, who had been sent to Moscow by the new president, Harry Truman, in late May 1945, hammered out an agreement with Stalin that provided for several prominent noncommunist Poles to be invited to the Soviet capital to join representatives of the Lublin regime in discussions looking toward the organization of the much-awaited National Unity government. These discussions quickly led to the formation of a government that included representatives of the Communist, Peasant, and Socialist parties. Although some American officials were disappointed that the communists retained control over a majority of portfolios in the new cabinet, including the crucial interior ministry that controlled the police, the new regime and its pledge to organize early elections sufficiently assuaged Washington's concerns regarding the implementation of the Yalta agreements. On 5 July 1945 the United States recognized the Government of National Unity in Warsaw and ended official relations with the government-in-exile in London.

Recognition, at least in the short run, removed an impediment to U.S.-Soviet understanding. More importantly, at least from an intelligence perspective, recognition allowed Washington to send professional observers into Poland. On 31 July 1945 three planes carrying Ambassador Arthur Bliss Lane, his staff, and their baggage arrived in Warsaw to open the U.S. embassy.[23] Few buildings survived in the ruins of the once-proud Polish capital, so the diplomatic mission established itself in the Hotel Polonia, a relatively undamaged structure that housed the diplomats of several governments. From a crowded suite of rooms that did double duty as offices and living quarters, Ambassador Lane and his staff worked to keep Washington abreast of conditions and developments in their host country. It proved an arduous task.

From the start the embassy was seriously constrained in its ability to collect and report information. The diplomats concluded rather quickly (and correctly) that their movements and activities were under surveillance by the NKVD and the Urzad Bezpieczenstwa (UB), the communist-controlled Polish secret police whose counterespionage branch actually maintained an office in the hotel.[24] The surveillance was often heavy-handed. Rooms frequently showed signs of having been searched. Hotel porters and waiters loitered outside doors and showed no embarrassment when caught eavesdropping. At one point the hotel suggested that Ambassador Lane employ the services of a young chambermaid who allegedly spoke only Polish. When the ambassador demurred, the management insisted. The hotel's insistence seemed suspicious, especially when it became evident that the woman knew nothing about the duties of a maid, although she assiduously collected papers from the embassy's trash baskets several times a day. Suspicions regarding the young woman's true employer were only fueled when the ambassador accidentally discovered that the supposedly monoglot maid actually understood both English and French.[25]

Surveillance extended to the embassy's communications. Initially the mission was not able to communicate directly with the State Department. All cables to and from Washington were routed through Moscow, and the cable facilities were entirely in the hands of Poles and Russians. The arrangements seriously compromised the embassy's ability to report frankly and in a timely manner. In Moscow Ambassador Lane's messages were delayed as long as forty days before being forwarded. Many messages never made it through at all. In the early fall of 1945 the State Department calculated that only 43 percent of the messages exchanged with its embassy in Warsaw were actually reaching their destination. In a warning to his superiors in Washington the American military attaché in Warsaw bluntly asserted, "The situation amounts to a blockade."[26] The problem was more than just delays. Like many other governments, including the United States, the Soviets routinely copied and scrutinized the enciphered diplomatic messages that passed through their radio and cable offices, so the Warsaw embassy had to hope that neither the Poles nor the Russians had broken the ciphers that protected its communications. Pouch communications were marginally more secure since the diplomatic bag traveled in the custody of an American courier, but the Poles allowed only one American plane to land at Warsaw each week. Infrequent air service combined with a scarcity of diplomatic couriers meant that pouches often were delayed for weeks.[27]

The American embassy in Warsaw was hard-pressed not only to transmit information but to collect it as well. Credible sources were difficult to find. In a pattern that would become all too familiar to American diplomats in postwar Eastern Europe, the communist-dominated government, now ensconced in makeshift ministries and offices across the city, had immediately embarked on a program to control information, stifle dissent, and intimidate real and potential political opponents as the national front strategy crumbled in the face of public hostility and armed resistance by anticommunist partisans. As a result of this repressive policy the diplomats were constrained in their ability to collect and report political information to the State Department. Contacts with officials of the new government were few. Diplomats routinely scrutinized the local press and radio for information on political, economic, and social conditions, but in the new Poland the newspapers were limited to publishing news items provided by the government's press office. Until October 1945, when the Polish Peasant Party received permission to publish a paper, noncommunist political groups had no press outlet, and even this concession was undermined when the Peasant Party along with Catholic organizations that were attempting to start newspapers found it difficult to obtain newsprint from government-controlled stockpiles.[28]

For intelligence concerning events and conditions in the country the embassy fell back on the personal observations of its officers, contacts with embassy visitors, and bits and pieces gleaned from conversations with foreign counterparts in the Warsaw diplomatic community. The value of the last was problematic, since every diplomatic mission, except the Russian, suffered from the same constraints on reporting as the American embassy. Polish visitors to the embassy proved a better source. Thousands of Poles called at the embassy in the hope of proving American citizenship and thereby acquiring an American passport or securing an American visa. Interviews with these applicants elicited useful information concerning political, economic, and social conditions across the country, including intelligence about communist persecution of Poles suspected of membership in the wartime Home Army or loyalty to the London government-in-exile.[29] Some visitors came to the embassy specifically to inform the Americans of events outside the capital. In September 1945, for example, representatives of the Catholic bishop of Przemysl told embassy officers that the Russians had begun to forcibly transfer members of the Polish Ukrainian minority to the Soviet Union.[30]

The personal observations and experiences of embassy personnel provided another perspective on Polish affairs. The seemingly endless convoys of Red

Army trucks and carts moving east through Warsaw with loads of machinery and other items seized in Germany and Poland were visible to everyone. Equally visible to embassy staffers were the street arrests conducted by UB agents. On one occasion Ambassador Lane personally observed someone being shot down on the street below his window in the Hotel Polonia.[31] American diplomats understood that much of this police activity was directed against political opponents of the regime, including some Poles whom the embassy believed to be American citizens. Conversations with Poles outside of the embassy brought news concerning political and social conditions in the capital and outlying areas. By the autumn of 1945, however, fruitful contacts were increasingly difficult to cultivate. Police surveillance made it hard for embassy officers to meet and develop sources in the community, especially since any Pole suspected of contacts with Americans was questioned by the police and placed under surveillance. Contacts beyond the capital were even scarcer. Initially, a shortage of automobiles limited the ability of American diplomats to visit the countryside, and once on the road travelers frequently encountered checkpoints and spot checks by police. Since travel beyond the capital was difficult, the diplomats' horizons did not extend much beyond Warsaw's suburbs. It was only in October of 1945 that Ambassador Lane, accompanied by his interpreter, Lieutenant William Tonesk, USN, and the naval attaché, Lieutenant Colonel Andrew Wylie, USMC, was able to leave Warsaw for visits to Krakow, Katowice, and Lodz. This brief tour, during which the travelers met Poles from many walks of life, confirmed earlier impressions of an unpopular regime whose authority depended upon censorship, pervasive police surveillance, and systematic repression of political dissidents.[32]

While OSS and SSU reported on Polish developments, these services did not greatly shape official perceptions of those affairs. There was little in intelligence reports that could not be found in diplomatic cables or the press. The United States still had few clandestine sources inside Poland to supplement the overt activities of its diplomats. The establishment of an American embassy in Warsaw provided an opportunity for the Office of Strategic Services to introduce intelligence personnel under diplomatic cover, but OSS and later SSU had struggled—perhaps because of staff shortages resulting from demobilization, perhaps from State Department reluctance to collaborate in espionage—to capitalize on the opportunity. D. Chadwick Braggiotti, an X-2 officer and former State Department official, had arrived in Warsaw with the embassy's advance party. He remained the only clandestine American intelligence officer resident in Poland until early 1946, when he was joined by Stephanie Czech, another counterintelligence officer. Because of State Department policy no SI (secret intelligence) specialists, as opposed to X-2 personnel, were assigned to the embassy in the period 1945–1946. While willing to welcome into its embassies X-2 representatives who could assist with vetting passport and visa applicants, the State Department refused to accept SI officers who would risk provoking the host government by conducting espionage. Inside the Hotel Polonia Braggiotti set up shop in the personal quarters of Ambassador Lane, since the ambassador's suite was considered marginally more secure than the other rooms allotted the Americans.[33]

The two counterintelligence officers worked diligently, but their efforts were hampered by the same impediments to collection and reporting that constrained the other embassy personnel. Necessary supplies were always scarce. For some time after their arrival, the OSS unit had no transport, and Braggiotti and Czech had to limit their activity to the neighborhoods surrounding the Hotel Polonia. Eventually, the SSU station in Paris shipped a Jeep and a sedan to Warsaw, but only the Jeep arrived, the sedan making it no further than Germany, where it was commandeered by the local SSU mission, which was experiencing its own transport problems. Supply proved a constant irritant. Essential items never reached Warsaw. Often it was the lack of little things, such as candy, soap, razors, and cigarettes that proved most detrimental to effective operations, since such barter items were used to secure goodwill and reward informants. Communications remained a problem that eluded solution. The X-2 team could not communicate directly with headquarters. Like all embassy communications, the team's messages initially had to pass through Moscow and Russian hands on their way to Washington. By the fall of 1945 Braggiotti had received from headquarters a radio to communicate directly with the X-2 office in Paris, but this connection proved a mixed blessing because Warsaw's encrypted messages were often unaccountably delayed in the French capital and just as frequently returned to Braggiotti by X-2 Paris with the notation "This code not held here."[34]

Cover proved equally problematic. Braggiotti and Czech posed as State Department officials, and their true affiliation was supposedly known only to Ambassador Lane and the embassy's number-two officer. Word of their intelligence connection, however, soon spread within the small embassy, and colleagues were often indiscreet. On one occasion, at a reception at the American embassy attended by Polish officials and Warsaw's entire diplomatic community, a foreign service colleague loudly enjoined Braggiotti to explain why it was necessary to hide his work for American intelligence. Such indiscretions were unlikely to escape the notice of Polish and Russian counterintelligence officers, who routinely monitored the quarters and activities of all American embassy personnel.[35]

Understaffed, underresourced, and under surveillance, the American intelligence outpost in Warsaw ran few, if any, operations. Their main effort was the compilation of a card file identifying various Poles of intelligence interest and listing their particulars. By the early spring of 1946 the file contained some 5,000 names. For information Braggiotti and Czech relied primarily on their personal observations as they moved about the Polish capital and on interviews with Poles who called at the embassy in search of passports or visas. The officers had some contact with the anticommunist underground, and their reports to Washington occasionally included material explicitly identified as originating with the resistance. These contacts, however, seem to have been limited in extent and results, since Braggiotti, in a report summarizing his office's experience prepared in the summer of 1946, felt compelled to advise Washington that closer and more systematic contacts with the resistance might generate useful intelligence on Soviet intelligence and security operations, advice that suggested that his own contacts had been neither close nor systematic.[36]

Unable to reinforce Braggiotti and Czech with qualified personnel and discouraged by "various technical problems" that poisoned the operational atmosphere in Poland, Washington closed the SSU office in the Warsaw embassy in March 1946 and transferred its records to the mission in Germany.[37] The modest capabilities and accomplishments of the Warsaw station—which, we must remind ourselves, was a counterintelligence team, not a positive intelligence collection unit—had already encouraged other stations in Europe to try their hand at penetrating the Polish target. As early as September 1945 the OSS mission in Germany was picking up from refugees and returning German POWs information on economic, military, and political conditions in Poland, particularly the resurgence of the Armja Krajowa, the anticommunist armed resistance, and the reorganization of the Polish Army under Russian direction. From Berlin Base, Lieutenant Walter Wusza, a native-born Pole who had immigrated to the United States before the war and worked for OSS on the EAGLE project, explored the possibility of cross-border operations. In the fall of 1945, Wusza made two clandestine visits to Poland during which he contacted former acquaintances. These initial contacts would subsequently evolve into the PHILLIPPA chain, a network of informants that allegedly extended to Warsaw, Poznan, Lodz, Gdansk, and Stettin, and included lawyers, military officers, and teachers. Supposedly, the most important source was the vice-minister for propaganda, whom American intelligence considered one of the dozen most influential members of the communist regime. Additional agents were infiltrated by means of the repatriation transports that returned to their homeland Poles who had spent the war in German captivity. Information was passed back to American controllers in Germany by couriers who worked on Polish coastal vessels sailing from Gdynia to Lubeck and Bremen.[38]

While Berlin Base was developing its networks inside Poland, other stations were also trying their luck. By January 1946, SSU France had acquired the services of four expatriate Poles who, unable to reconcile themselves to the new order in Warsaw, offered their services to the United States in return for the promise of American citizenship. To provide cover, SSU arranged for one of the four to be the European representative of an American museum while it pulled strings to secure surplus merchant vessels in order to establish the remaining three in the coastal and inland shipping business, excellent cover for moving people, material, and information across borders. Known as "Z Group," the Poles were highly valued by their American controllers in Paris for the intelligence they collected on Central and Eastern Europe, although details of that information are not available in the declassified record.[39]

The Austrian mission also got into the act. During the summer of 1945 it had developed contacts with couriers and intelligence officers of General Wladyslaw Anders's Second Polish Corps, an element of the armed forces controlled by the Polish government-in-exile during the war. After distinguishing itself in the Allied campaign in Italy, this formation was now performing occupation duties in that country while awaiting a determination of its postwar fate. General Anders and most of his men were strongly anticommunist, and the Second Corps served as a magnet for Polish refugees and former POWs who could not reconcile themselves to the postwar regime established under Moscow's tutelage in Warsaw. To collect information on home affairs and maintain contact with anticommunist resistance groups inside their country, the intelligence section of the Second Corps regularly dispatched clandestine couriers to Poland. While in transit across Austria, these operatives occasionally made contact with American intelligence officers who were well aware of the extreme anticommunist attitudes of General Anders and his military formation and so informed Washington. Initially the Americans cultivated these Polish links—known as Project BREGMA—for what they could reveal about Anders and his intentions, since the militant anticommunism of the Polish general and his command worried some American intelligence officers. In September 1945, William Donovan had passed to Secretary of State James Byrnes a memo stressing the dangers that the Polish Second Corps posed to American relations with the Soviet Union.[40] Although it was conceived as an operation to keep an eye on General Anders, BREGMA's controllers quickly recognized an opportunity to keep an eye on Poland by tapping into the information collected by the general's sources inside his homeland. In Washington, however, the reports originating with the intelligence section of Polish Second Corps were viewed with reserve by OSS analysts, who suspected that the anticommunist biases of the source tainted the information.[41] By September 1945, Lieutenant J. M. Rzonca, a Polish-speaking officer at OSS mission offices in Salzburg, began wondering if the Polish channels might offer an opportunity for American intelligence to develop independent sources inside Poland.

By December 1945 Lieutenant Rzonca's plans had evolved into two operations. Project GIMBEL (later renamed ASPIRIN) envisaged covert collaboration with the Jewish Joint Distribution Committee, a welfare organization with offices in Salzburg that worked to relocate survivors of the Jewish communities of Eastern Europe who appeared in postwar Austria as refugees. Processing at the Committee's reception centers included interviews that elicited personal and travel information from the new arrivals. Rzonca hoped to place American officers inside the reception centers in order to introduce into the interviews of Polish Jews questions regarding political and economic conditions in their homeland.[42]

Operation EL MOROCCO (later ARGYROL) was a more ambitious project. Aware from his connections with General Anders's intelligence operatives that there was an active anticommunist resistance inside Poland, Rzonca hoped to establish direct liaison with this underground movement in order to exploit their facilities for collecting intelligence. The big problem was how to make first contact. The clandestine lines established by the Second Corps intelligence bureau were available, but Rzonca preferred a channel independent of the fanatic anticommunist Poles in Italy. To implement EL MOROCCO, he recruited Zygmund Marchol, a Polish refugee in Austria who had already demonstrated his resilience and fortitude by surviving the Mauthausen death camp. Contemptuous of both the London and the Warsaw political factions, Marchol believed that his homeland's salvation depended upon close cooperation with the United States. "Courageous, intelligent, adroit and objective," the young and enthusiastic recruit seemed the perfect instrument for establishing a purely American connection with the underground.[43]

As a death camp survivor, Marchol was eligible for free repatriation to his homeland. Rzonca had his agent register for repatriation, and in late January 1946 Marchol departed Austria for Poland on a scheduled displaced persons train. Operational cover was easy since the young Pole actually was what he claimed to be: a displaced Pole and camp survivor returning to find his family and pick up the pieces of his life. Hidden among the shabby clothes selected by his American controllers as appropriate for a Polish refugee, Marchol carried US$100 and two bottles of American whiskey to pay or barter for assistance and information. To explain his possession of American items should they be discovered by Polish customs or police officers, Marchol also carried a document prepared by SSU Austria that purported to be a testimonial from a U.S. Army artillery unit then billeted in Germany, confirming his temporary employment as a housekeeper and recommending him to future employers. At the Polish border all returnees received identification credentials and a travel permit authorizing free rail travel to any destination in Poland. The plan was for Marchol to use this documentation to visit his family in Skorzysko-Kamienna. During the war the family had been active in the Armja Krajowa, and the agent expected to use their connections to establish contact with the underground. The mission was expected to last about five weeks, and Marchol would again rely on refugee cover to return to American-controlled territory, this time pretending to be a German or Austrian POW making his way home.[44]

The Polish operations of the American intelligence stations in Germany and Austria produced a trickle of low- to medium-grade information, but significant successes eluded the case officers. An assessment prepared in June 1946 after almost a year of operational effort observed that SSU had received fifty-seven reports concerning Poland, but only four had been judged worthy of dissemination to the service's customers in Washington. Intelligence coverage was so poor that Poland was placed in the same category as the Soviet Union. "Neither for Russia nor for Poland did coverage remotely approach adequacy," the assessment noted. "In both cases reporting was scattered, casual, and unsystematic."[45] Reports concerning the location of Red Army units inside the country, the prevalence of Russian officers in command positions in the reconstituted Polish Army, the unpopularity of the communist-dominated regime, and the persistence of armed resistance in the countryside were useful, but in the early postwar period American intelligence achieved no high-level penetration of the Polish-Russian administration comparable, say, to the successes in the Soviet zone of Germany. Initially, Lieutenant Wusza's PHILLIPPA chain promised such access, and Berlin Base praised the network's early product as "amazing." Rather quickly, however, the luster dimmed. While, perhaps, an imaginative and aggressive field operative, Lieutenant Wusza proved a very poor program manager. When, in the fall of 1946, Wusza was implicated in the black market scandals that afflicted American occupation forces in Germany and recalled to the United States under a cloud, his successors at Berlin Base, finding the PHILLIPPA files in disarray and discovering that Wusza had not bothered to document the operation, were hard-pressed to identify the sources and determine their credibility. By then the German mission was admitting to headquarters that Berlin Base's attempts to penetrate Poland had been a failure. Recalling those early Polish operations, a former senior officer at Berlin Base later acknowledged that many of Wusza's reputed sources turned out to be fabricators whose "intelligence" was worth little.[46] Another intelligence veteran, who supervised clandestine operations against Poland in the early years of the

Central Intelligence Agency, SSU's successor organization, observed that an operation of the scope claimed by Wusza—productive informants, including highly placed government officials, in four cities—would have occupied a prominent place in the documentary record and organizational memory of the CIA's Polish desk, but no such records or memories existed when he assumed direction of Polish operations. According to this veteran, the absence of such an operational footprint suggests that SSU eventually concluded that the PHILLIPPA network was disinformation either by fabricators or by UB/NKVD counterintelligence that penetrated the group and turned it against the Americans.[47]

While better managed, the operations out of Austria also produced no intelligence breakthroughs. Much of the effort focused on the slow process of identifying sources and building networks. By the late summer of 1946 Project BREGMA, the contacts with the intelligence bureau of General Anders's Second Corps in Italy, were complicated by plans to repatriate the Polish military personnel who wished to return to their homeland and to demobilize and resettle in Britain those who would not (or could not) return to a country controlled by the communists. At the initiative of James Angleton, the American intelligence representative in Rome who had developed productive relationships with Anders's intelligence staff, arrangements were put in hand to transfer to American control the most experienced Polish operatives and their networks in Eastern Europe, but nothing is known about the fruits, if any, of this plan.[48] For its part, Project ASPIRIN (formerly GIMBEL), the joint operation with the Jewish Joint Distribution Committee, had petered out. The Committee, whose cooperation with SSU seemed to have been purely notional, whisked the Jewish refugees through Salzburg too quickly to allow the Americans to identify and interview promising arrivals from Poland.[49]

The status of ARGYROL (formerly EL MOROCCO), SSU Austria's most daring operation into Poland, remained problematic. In April 1946 Zygmund Marchol had returned from his clandestine mission inside Poland, during which he had moved freely about the southwestern section of the country, Silesia, and the former Polish territories ceded to the Soviet Union. He had made contact with elements of the anticommunist underground and had established relations with individuals in all levels of Polish society.[50] These initial contacts, however, did not translate immediately into productive networks, and it is unlikely that much intelligence fruit was harvested in Marchol's newly sown fields before 1947.

Exchanges with friendly foreign services supplemented the modest results of agent operations run from Austria and Germany. Liaison with Britain's Secret Intelligence Service generated some information on Polish affairs. In

February 1946, for example, the SSU station in London received from SIS twenty-eight reports on Poland in the "Harbury" series, a reporting category composed of items compiled by the British from various sources, including overt press and radio material. Smaller services also contributed the occasional item. SSU cultivated close relations with the Danish Intelligence Service, which passed on information from its sources inside Poland. Danish networks, for example, confirmed the existence of widespread opposition to the Polish communists and their Soviet sponsors and provided information about the size and location of armed resistance groups.[51] The Danes aggressively attacked intelligence targets in Poland, and sometimes their plans proved too rich for American appetites. In 1946, for example, SSU declined to join its Danish counterpart in a joint operation (Project HORSES) that proposed to infiltrate Danish operatives into Poland under cover of the United Nations Relief and Rehabilitation Administration. Intelligence managers in Washington preferred not to compromise UN programs by utilizing them for intelligence purposes, and overseas stations were informed that it was the "definite policy" of SSU that philanthropic and international organizations would not be used "in any manner whatever for intelligence purposes."[52]

The prohibition apparently extended only to operations involving the direct use of American assets or resources, because SSU was happy to receive information from foreign services that ran unilateral operations under the cover of nongovernmental organizations. The Swedes, for example, shared information collected inside Poland by Swedish intelligence officers working under the cover of the Swedish Red Cross. With trained agents roaming the countryside the Swedes, like the Danes, had more "boots on the ground" than their American counterparts. The latter, struggling to find their boots, let alone put them on the ground, happily accepted whatever their Scandinavian friends might provide. In December 1945, for example, Swedish intelligence informed the SSU station in Stockholm that its observers in Poland were reporting deep antipathy toward the Russians and widespread opposition to the Warsaw regime. The reports also noted that the Russians had removed much of the surviving Polish industrial infrastructure, diverted UNRRA supplies for their own use, and confiscated a large portion of what coal Poland had. The Swedes also shared information concerning Soviet military developments in the country. In March 1946, for instance, they passed to SSU a report from one of their officers covertly embedded in a Red Cross detail supervising the repatriation of Dutch citizens caught or imprisoned in Poland during the war. This officer reported considerable increases in Red Army strength, particularly in harbor areas and the southwestern portions of the country, and the westward movement of heavy artillery and large transports. This information contradicted claims that the Soviets were reducing their military presence in Poland. Later, Swedish intelligence helpfully gave SSU maps and descriptions of the Polish road network.[53]

Communications intelligence added little to the Polish mosaic. During the war American cryptanalysts were unable to solve the high-grade ciphers used by the Polish government-in-exile to protect its most secret communications, but the code breakers had cracked two low-grade ciphers used by the London Poles for nonconfidential messages. After VE Day these ciphers, whose intelligence value had always been low, had been withdrawn by the Poles from service, closing even that modest comint window on the activities of the London Poles. Apparently the ciphers of the communist-dominated Warsaw regime proved even more resilient. As of the spring of 1946, none of Warsaw's high-grade diplomatic or military attaché ciphers were readable at Arlington Hall.[54] Occasionally, the diplomatic traffic of other powers provided a glimpse into Polish affairs. For example, a French diplomatic message decrypted in late October 1945 revealed that Warsaw had reversed an earlier decision to allow French representatives to investigate the condition of French industrial interests and investments in Poland. The decryption further revealed that Paris believed that the reversal came only after pressure on the Poles from Moscow, and that the action was part of a Russian plan to eliminate Western economic interests from areas under Soviet influence.[55] Such items, however, were rare; the daily summaries of intercepted diplomatic messages that circulated to foreign policy decision makers in Washington in the year following Germany's surrender contained hardly a handful of references to Poland.[56]

While underdeveloped and constrained by local circumstances, American intelligence reporting on Poland painted for policy makers in Washington a largely accurate picture of political, economic, and military conditions inside that country. Secret intelligence, however, did not determine Washington's perceptions of Polish affairs as much as it did in Germany. While the work of OSS and SSU certainly provided details that would not have been otherwise known, it on the whole added little of importance to what was available from State Department reporting and the world press. Its chief significance was to give policy makers in Washington confidence in the understanding of developments in Poland that they derived from other, more open, sources. The picture that emerged from all sources by early 1946 was of a country under the domination of the Soviet Union, which acted through a repressive and unrepresentative regime of local communists. The political situation belied the political premises of Moscow's national front strategy and the political hopes of Washington. Faced with widespread hostility to both itself and its Russian patrons, the Polish Communist Party was unable to govern without overt repression that gave the lie to the façade of "bourgeois democracy" through which Moscow had hoped to reconcile political control and social transformation with a continuation of a useful alliance with the United States and Great Britain. A similar picture would emerge, though perhaps not so quickly and clearly, when policy makers turned to Hungary.

Hungary

Unlike Poland, Hungary had cast its lot with the Axis powers, and Hungarian armies fought alongside their German allies on the eastern front. In the spring of 1943 Admiral Miklós Horthy, the wily "regent" and effective dictator of the country who had remained in power for twenty-three years in no small part because of his ability to discern future trends and navigate dangerous political shoals, extended secret feelers to the Allies in the hope of disengaging his country from Germany. Like most Hungarians, Horthy feared the Soviet Union and sought an accommodation that would allow Hungary to surrender and accept an Anglo-American occupation force and avoid an invasion by the Red Army. The regent's efforts were complicated not only by strategic realities that made an Anglo-American occupation of Hungary improbable, but by ambivalence among the Allies, who had little sympathy for the Hungarians, and by the risk of preemptive moves by Germany, which was aware of Horthy's intrigues, and its neo-Nazi supporters inside Hungary to block the country's defection. In one such move, German forces occupied the country in March 1944, and Berlin compelled the regent to appoint a pro-German cabinet, which would act under the watchful eye of a Reich plenipotentiary.[57]

Despite German oversight, Admiral Horthy continued to conspire with the Allies. In the summer of 1944 he swallowed his hatred and fear of the Soviet Union and dispatched secret emissaries to Moscow. Negotiations, during which the Russians consulted with the American and British ambassadors, resulted in an armistice agreement providing for Hungary to abandon the Axis and declare war on Germany. The announcement of the armistice would coincide with an anti-German coup in Budapest led by the regent and his supporters. The agreement proved abortive since the Germans moved more quickly and decisively, arresting Horthy and installing a puppet regime under Ferenc Szálasi, the leader of the fascist Arrow Cross movement. In response the Horthy mission in Moscow, encouraged by the Russians, joined with representatives of the Hungarian Communist Party (who, like so many European communist leaders, had found wartime refuge in the Russian capital) to form a provisional government under the supervision of the Russians. Following the popular front strategy favored at this time by Stalin, this government included representatives of the major prewar political parties: Communists, Smallholders, Social Democrats, and National Peasants. In December 1944 a provisional national assembly convened in Debrecen, a town in eastern Hungary that had been recently liberated by the Red Army. The government of "Free Hungary" promptly declared war on Germany, although the Szálasi regime remained in power in Budapest and some Hungarian army units carried on the war against the Soviet Union. With the fall of Budapest to the Red Army in February 1945 the remnants of the Szálasi government and the few troops still loyal to it evacuated westward with the retreating German army, with many finding themselves in Austria at war's end.[58]

During the war American intelligence had devoted little attention to Hungary. Most of the information gleaned by the Office of Strategic Services came from open sources and émigrés. OSS had attempted two clandestine operations against the country, but both ended badly. The first was a spin-off of the notorious CEREUS network run by the OSS station in Istanbul. In September 1943 a Hungarian known to work for the Germans as a double agent approached a CEREUS source with the news that the Hungarian General Staff wished to secretly establish contact with OSS. Aware of the Hungarian's dubious background, OSS Istanbul suspected a provocation, but decided to pursue the approach in the hope of securing some political and military information from inside Hungary. An OSS agent of Hungarian nationality was infiltrated into Budapest while a new military attaché, supposedly indoctrinated into the secret arrangement with American intelligence, arrived at the Hungarian embassy in Turkey to serve as the point of contact with the OSS station. The American intelligence officers should have trusted their initial suspicions. Although details are lacking, it is apparent that the "liaison" was a successful attempt by Hungarian and German intelligence to penetrate OSS operations in Turkey, especially the activities of the CEREUS chain.[59]

An operation run by the OSS station in Bern proved no more successful. In the first six months of 1943 the Horthy regime sent emissaries to Switzerland to contact OSS and open a secret channel for discussing Hungary's withdrawal from the war. Seeing an opportunity to test Hungarian good faith and develop a new intelligence source, the Bern station convinced the Hungarians to receive in Budapest a clandestine American team and provide them with intelligence which they would forward, via radio, to Bern. Code-named SPARROW, the operation experienced various delays, and it was only in March 1944 that a three-man OSS team parachuted into Hungary, where they were met and sheltered by Hungarian army officers. Unfortunately, within two days of the team's arrival and before they could transmit a single intelligence report, the German Army occupied the country and the Americans became Wehrmacht prisoners. Though interrogated by the Gestapo, who knew the whole story from the confessions of Hungarian staff officers, the OSS officers survived the war.[60]

Despite these disappointments, William Donovan did not abandon plans to establish an American intelligence presence in Hungary. In the fall of 1944, the secret intelligence section at OSS Mediterranean headquarters in Italy began to assemble a "Budapest Intelligence Unit" under the command of Major Abram Flues. Although at the time the pro-German administration of Ferenc Szálasi remained ensconced in the Hungarian capital, OSS wanted to be prepared should political or military developments force the sudden removal or flight of the fascists. When, in August, King Michael of Romania overthrew the pro-German dictator, Marshal Ion Antonescu, and brought his country over to the Allies, OSS had been able to overtly place a team in Bucharest ostensibly to oversee the repatriation of American airmen from POW camps and assess the impact of Allied bombing on the Ploesti oil fields, but also to report on political conditions and determine Soviet intentions toward the country now occupied by the Red Army. If events developed in a similar way in Hungary, OSS wanted to be prepared to have a forty-member team in the Hungarian capital within twenty-four hours.[61]

Unlike its counterpart in Bucharest, the Budapest "city team" did not include the Soviets among its prospective intelligence targets. The team intended to enter Budapest openly and limit its activities to overt operations. Its first priority was to seize any military records that the retreating Germans and their Hungarian puppets might leave behind. Secondarily, the team would survey the impact of the Allied bombing campaign, obtain from representatives of Hungarian industry estimates of German military resources and additional targeting intelligence for Allied air forces, report on conditions within Hungary, and secure militarily useful information concerning Germany and Japan.[62]

Although the Budapest Unit was packed and ready to deploy, the fall of the Hungarian capital in February 1945 did not herald the arrival of American intelligence. Soviet authorities, who claimed predominant authority by virtue of the Red Army's occupation of the country, blocked the deployment of the OSS team. Although Russian attitudes toward cooperation with Allied intelligence services shifted with the fortunes of war and Moscow sometimes allowed overt representatives of such services to establish themselves in Russian-controlled territory, such as Romania, the Soviets could never abandon the suspicion that all foreign intelligence services, whether Allied or not, were by definition hostile services and threats to the interests of the Soviet

Union. In the autumn of 1944, for example, the Soviets expelled from Russian-occupied Bulgaria an overt OSS team that had been repatriating American airmen from POW camps and trying (with little success due to Soviet restrictions) to collect information related to German order of battle, political and economic conditions inside Bulgaria, and war crimes investigations.[63]

Although William Donovan tried to assuage Soviet concerns by reducing the proposed OSS team from forty-eight men to twelve, the Russians would not compromise, although they did allow Major Richard Kuhn, a physician from the medical intelligence section of OSS and a member of the OSS mission in Romania, to briefly visit parts of the country, ostensibly to collect blood samples from German POWs to determine if they had been exposed to influenza or biological warfare agents. Major Kuhn returned to Bucharest with his samples and observations about conditions inside Russian-occupied Hungary, including the military situation around Budapest.[64] Donovan's efforts to get his people into Hungary were further undercut by the obstructive attitude of American representatives on the scene. Major General William Key, the American representative on the Allied Control Commission (ACC) that would supervise Hungary until the final peace settlement, refused to have any OSS officers on his staff. Anxious to foster amicable relations on the Control Commission, General Key hoped to avoid any possible irritant in U.S.-Soviet relations, and the Russians, who had quickly expelled from Sofia the small OSS city team that General Donovan had dispatched to Soviet-occupied Bulgaria, had recently made it clear that OSS units irritated them. In the end, Key would prove almost as great an obstacle to OSS ambitions as the Soviets. The State Department's representative in Hungary, H. F. Arthur Schoenfeld, also declined to adopt Donovan's operatives. Though harboring no particular objection to an OSS presence inside Hungary, Schoenfeld believed the question fell under General Key's purview since the Office of Strategic Services was technically in the military chain of command.[65] Eventually, the U.S. Joint Chiefs of Staff settled the matter. In late April 1945, with the Budapest City Team still languishing in their camp in Italy, the JCS issued an order ending further efforts to introduce American intelligence personnel into Russian-controlled territory except where such efforts were essential to the United States in its prosecution of the war. A follow-up directive specifically applied the prohibition to Hungary.[66]

With the demise of the Budapest City Team, Hungary moved to the margins of American intelligence activity, a shift abetted after VE Day by uncertainty within OSS concerning postwar intelligence resources and priorities in Europe. A cable to the senior OSS representative in Austria soon after the surrender of Germany revealed the more conservative posture: "The whole question of penetration to the east and southeast of Austria is a very thorny and delicate one and is subject to a lot of high policy considerations which are still far from clarified." Reflecting, perhaps, a concern that intelligence operations not rush ahead of official policy toward the countries of the region, the warning added, "It is true that we are very much interested in information from that eastern region, but we cannot possibly take an overt interest in it."[67] As late as August 1945, Washington headquarters was sending directives to the field explicitly prohibiting clandestine operations into Hungary.[68]

In September 1945 the Joint Chiefs lifted the prohibition on offensive operations into Hungary. OSS Austria promptly sent one of its officers on a brief undercover visit to Budapest to scout the intelligence terrain. Prospects seemed so promising that Al Ulmer, chief of the secret intelligence (SI) section in the Austrian mission, enthused, "Hungarian pastures are now wide open to OSS."[69] His enthusiasm, however, was not contagious. Fearing that espionage operations would compromise his position with the Soviets, General Key, the senior American representative in Hungary by virtue of his position as chief of the U.S. delegation to the Allied Control Commission, continued to resist all efforts to establish an American intelligence outpost inside the country. At one point he dismissed from the American delegation two naval officers when he discovered that they had been tasked by the Office of Naval Intelligence with collecting information concerning the Russians.[70] Aside from occasional items concerning the location and appearance of Red Army units sighted by staffers traveling about the countryside, Key's personnel made no efforts to collect intelligence; indeed, when the delegation prepared for Washington a report on Hungarian efforts to fulfill the armistice agreements, it had to rely on information provided by the Russians.[71] Since the ACC delegation represented the only effective cover for operations, the general's resistance amounted to a veto over any initiatives that OSS (and later SSU) might undertake.

General Key's intransigence meant that the burden of keeping Washington informed about Hungarian affairs fell upon the small American diplomatic mission in Budapest.[72] Recognizing the balance of forces that would prevail upon the ground at the end of the war, the State Department had concluded long before that any provisional government would have to be acceptable to Moscow. Still, the department's initial evaluation of the administration that emerged under Soviet auspices in Debrecen had been rather positive. In December 1944 H. Freeman Matthews, the director of the Office of European Affairs, assured Edward Stettinius, the newly appointed secretary of state, that the leadership included "responsible personalities" who formed "a well-balanced group representing the significant pro–Allied political forces in Hungary." The provisional government was certainly not another Lublin Committee preparing to march into the capital in the baggage of the Red Army and rely on Soviet bayonets to impose its illegitimate authority on a recalcitrant population.[73] It would not take long, however, for the initial optimism to fade.

The State Department hoped that any government in Budapest that was not hostile to the Soviet Union would be acceptable to Moscow. For Josef Stalin, however, an acceptable government meant not only a regime that was actively and reliably pro-Soviet, but one that would change the political and social structures that had made Hungary a bastion of reaction even in the days of the Austro-Hungarian Empire. The Russian dictator was not inclined to rely upon the vagaries of liberal democracy to produce such a regime. In Hungary, as in other states occupied by the Red Army, Stalin intended that the Communist Party should achieve political dominance by championing reform, especially sorely needed land reform, while maintaining, at least for a time, the semblance of pluralist democracy in the form of a national front government "guided" by the Communist Party. At least for a time the communists would eschew political monopoly and radical socialization in favor of liberal democracy and bourgeois reform. In a series of meetings in Moscow in September and October 1944, Hungarian communists had endorsed such a strategy as the most effective pathway to power.[74] In Hungary, as elsewhere, this effort would be greatly facilitated by the Red Army's complete control of the cities and countryside and Moscow's refusal to allow the American and British representatives on the Allied Control Commission anything more than a nominal voice in decisions affecting political and economic conditions inside the country.

The American diplomats in Budapest were relatively well positioned to report on high-level party politics because leaders of the noncommunist parties often confided their plans and concerns to Ambassador Schoenfeld in the hope of stimulating American political and financial support for their causes. The ambassador was also well-informed of deliberations inside the Hungarian cabinet because the cabinet secretary, István Balogh, was a frequent visitor to the embassy. Though embassy officers occasionally met senior members of the Hungarian Communist Party, including Matyas Rakosi, the English-speaking party secretary general who impressed Ambassador Schoenfeld as "forceful and highly intelligent," their coverage of the party was comparatively weak.[75]

Despite their initial hopes, the American diplomatic mission in Hungary rather quickly noticed that political affairs were moving in an undesirable direction. As early as March 1945, for example, the diplomats were reporting that, despite efforts by General Key to cultivate the Russians, Soviet behavior toward the Allied Control Commission in Hungary was falling into the same pattern of uncooperative unilateralism that characterized their posture toward the control commissions in Bulgaria and Romania.[76] Over the following months the mission accurately tracked the successful efforts of the communists—abetted and supported by the Soviets—to dominate the postwar coalition and the inability of the other parties to mount effective political resistance. In the expectation that the Communist Party would benefit from the earliest possible elections, the Soviet occupation authorities, in the summer of 1945, pressured the provisional government to organize a vote in October. Although Soviet representatives vehemently denied insisting on early elections, the embassy knew the truth because in mid-August István Balogh confidentially informed Ambassador Schoenfeld of the Soviet pressure and the decision by Prime Minister Bela Miklos to accede to the demands of the Russians and their Hungarian communist protégés. Shortly thereafter this information was confirmed by Bela Zsedenyi, the president of the Hungarian National Assembly, who appeared at the embassy to report that he and the prime minister had been summoned to Soviet headquarters and personally informed by Marshal Klimentii Voroshilov, the Russian proconsul in Hungary as chairman of the Allied Control Commission, that elections had to be held by the end of September. Shortly thereafter Balogh sent a trusted friend to tell the embassy that the Hungarian Communist Party was receiving large amounts of money, presumably from the Soviets, to prepare for the elections.[77] By September an embassy dispatch would note "the dictatorial drive of the Communist Party for full and unhampered control of Hungary," citing as evidence efforts by the party to remove "reactionary" individuals from the coalition cabinet and operations by the communist-controlled political police to intimidate opposition elements.[78]

With its access to noncommunist political leaders the embassy was able to monitor the steady political encroachments of the communists. In October 1945 the Smallholders Party beat the combined Communist–Social Democratic ticket in the Budapest municipal elections. Fearing that a political debacle awaited the communists in the national elections now scheduled for November if they went head-to-head against the Smallholders, Marshal Voroshilov urged the Smallholders' leader, Zoltán Tildy, to accept a common electoral list. The American embassy heard about the Soviet initiative directly from Tildy within hours of the meeting at Russian headquarters. On October 22, the day of an all-party conclave to consider a joint list and even before the resulting accord had been ratified by party executives, Tildy informed the embassy of an agreement by the Smallholders, Communists, Social Democrats, and National Peasant Party to form a coalition government irrespective of the outcome of the national elections.[79] As a result of this agreement, the communists eventually received a number of cabinet seats—including the crucial interior ministry, which controlled the police—

disproportionate to its small share of the national vote. Control of the police combined with the obtrusive and partisan occupation policies of the Red Army allowed the communists to browbeat the opposition parties, a process about which Ambassador Schoenfeld and his staff kept Washington well informed. The dismal cycle of communist demand and opposition submission culminated in June 1946 in the acquiescence of the (nominally) coalition government in a demand by the Soviet authorities to respond to trumped up "fascist terrorist acts" against the Red Army by dissolving various "fascist" organizations connected with the Catholic Church or noncommunist organizations and arresting their leaders. The Soviet-inspired directive further required the registration of all social organizations with the government, the arrest of certain Smallholder parliamentary deputies who had prominently opposed the communists, and the dismissal from the administration of certain officials who had proved unresponsive to communist direction.[80] Though the noncommunist coalition partners accepted some of the demands and prevaricated on others, the Soviet initiative and the government's response—texts of both of which were passed to the embassy by Balogh—effectively marked the point of no return in the demise of liberal democracy in Hungary. No one in Washington who had been reading the cables from the Budapest embassy would have been surprised.

In the immediate postwar period the overt reporting of the Budapest embassy probably provided Washington's best coverage of political developments inside Hungary. In contrast, the coverage provided by the intelligence services remained weak. In the face of General Key's opposition, hopes for clandestine intelligence operations inside Hungary languished, and intelligence managers in Washington relegated the country to the margins of operational planning. At the beginning of 1946 the Strategic Services Unit still had no officers inside Hungary, and as late as March the country did not rate a separate desk at SSU headquarters in Washington.[81] That same month, however, conditions took a slight turn for the better. On 29 March Captain Robinson Bellin, a SSU officer, arrived in Budapest to establish an intelligence office within the American ACC delegation. Bellin's acceptance by the delegation seems to have represented less a shift in General Key's visceral opposition to intelligence officers than a misunderstanding concerning the captain's real job description. For his part, the SSU representative also suffered from a misunderstanding. Bellin arrived in the Hungarian capital expecting to assume the cover assignment of security officer for the delegation, but discovered to his surprise and alarm that in its seventeen months of operation the delegation had never had a security officer and felt no particular need for one. Desperate to find "some kind of job which would pay for my rations and quarters [and] permit me to stay on at the mission," Bellin bombarded Key with memoranda pointing out the danger of foreign penetration of the delegation and offering to perform a security survey. The general grudgingly accepted the suggestions and appointed the importunate captain security officer for the delegation.[82] Ironically, what was meant to be a nominal job, office security, to provide cover for his espionage work became Bellin's actual job.

Working alone, unable to speak Hungarian, and denied clerical assistance by supercilious superiors who did little to hide their disdain for his work, Captain Bellin struggled to put in place security procedures for the American delegation while investigating the prospects for offensive intelligence operations, investigations that he kept secret from General Key and other members of the delegation. The security situation was a perfect disaster. No one in the delegation gave the least thought to security. Hungarians were hired as translators, drivers, and cleaners without vetting; officers received no security briefings; secret documents were left openly on desks in unguarded rooms; and no one had thought to sweep the offices electronically for hidden microphones. Bellin needed only a cursory survey to conclude that "the mission was insecure from every point of view and all classified material both incoming and outgoing as well as every activity of the mission was probably compromised." When the industrious captain identified a Hungarian employee as an informant for the Russians he could not get any of his superiors to take an interest in the matter. In despair Bellin considered requesting his own recall to the United States.[83]

Conditions improved slightly in the early summer of 1946 when Major General George Weems replaced General Key as U.S. representative to the Allied Control Commission. Weems exhibited more interest in security and intelligence matters, although he was put off by the "gruff and abrupt attitude" of his security officer. For his part, Bellin, an abrasive personality who seems to have irritated almost everyone with whom he came into contact, did little to endear himself to his new commander. When called on the carpet by Weems for threatening the Hungarian premier's chauffeur after the driver sideswiped an official American vehicle, the SSU officer angrily responded that the general's attitude was "incomprehensible and reprehensible." Fortunately for American intelligence, Bellin survived this encounter without disciplinary action for insubordination and, in time, developed with his new commander a relationship of mutual respect if not affection.[84]

With a more supportive commander, Bellin worked to improve offensive and defensive intelligence operations. He began to assemble files on Hungarians and Russians of intelligence interest and scouted out potential safe houses and mail drops. He tried (with mixed results) to place under his control Hungarian employees of the mission whom he suspected of being penetration agents for the Russians or the Hungarian police. When he discovered that several prominent members of the government received treatment for venereal diseases from the mission's dispensary, the energetic SSU officer saw an opportunity to play upon the victims' gratitude or embarrassment to secure information. Such steps represented a promising start, but no more. While laying the necessary groundwork for future operations and generating the occasional item of information, Bellin's initiatives could not be expected overnight to dramatically improve intelligence reporting from the American ACC mission.[85]

With the minuscule intelligence cell in Budapest constrained from conducting significant operations, the initiative passed by default to stations in other countries. As early as the summer of 1945 OSS Austria set up a small section to cover Hungary. Initially its efforts were modest. For information concerning political and economic conditions inside the country, the mission relied almost exclusively on contacts with returning POWS, individuals traveling on private or official business, and Germans and Hungarians who entered Austria as refugees.[86] When Washington lifted the prohibition on offensive operations into Hungary, Al Ulmer, the SI chief in the Austrian mission, had no officers or sources in place. Until the Vienna mission could recruit such sources and establish such networks, the bounty of the Hungarian "pastures" would remain unharvested. To jump-start his operations, Ulmer turned to a refugee Hungarian journalist whose fondest dream was to become an American citizen.

In prewar Hungary Szolt Aradi, a pious Catholic, had written for various Magyar journals and frequented the clerico-political circles associated with nonfascist conservative political movements. During the war he had served as press attaché in the Hungarian embassy to the Vatican. When, in October 1944, Germany overthrew the regent, Admiral Horthy, and installed Ferenc Szálasi, the leader of the fascist Arrow Cross movement, as chief of a puppet government, Aradi joined his ambassador, Baron Gabriel Apor, in refusing to acknowledge the legitimacy of the new government. Strongly anti-Nazi, Aradi became active in efforts to organize the expatriate Hungarian community in Italy against the Szálasi regime, efforts that brought him to the attention of American intelligence. By December 1944 he had been recruited by OSS and detailed to the Budapest City Team then awaiting an opportunity to enter Hungary. While awaiting deployment, Aradi worked on OSS plans to use Hungarian expatriate channels to penetrate Austria and Czechoslovakia and cultivated a wide range of contacts in the Vatican and Italian clerical circles.[87]

By VE Day the energetic journalist had so insinuated himself into the activities of SICE (Secret Intelligence Central Europe) that X-2, the OSS department responsible for security and counterintelligence, began to question whether a foreigner should have so much access to operational details. Not wanting to lose a valuable asset, SICE managers brushed aside these concerns. When, in the summer of 1945, OSS established itself in Austria, Aradi tagged along as a member of the team. By the end of the year he was listed on the roster of the Austrian mission, not as an informant or source, but as a senior intelligence officer—an exceptional sign of confidence since regulations prohibited the employment of foreign nationals on work concerning internal organization and operational plans.[88] Using Salzburg as a base, Aradi specialized in Hungarian and Vatican operations. Both of these targets—particularly the Vatican—were considered hard targets to penetrate, and Aradi was the only officer with the background, contacts, and language skills necessary for the task. When X-2 again raised concerns about placing the Hungarian in a position of authority ("this perennial subject"), Salzburg headquarters dismissed the complaints, noting wryly that "it has proved most difficult to penetrate Hungarian-Vatican lines with Indiana farm boys."[89]

At a time when American intelligence was casting about for secret sources inside Hungary, Szolt Aradi's Vatican connections provided a much-needed clandestine line into that Soviet-occupied country. The available documents contain only a handful of references to this sensitive operation, so only the broad outlines of the project are visible. In the late summer of 1945 OSS Austria recruited a papal representative who traveled between Budapest and the Vatican. The Austrian mission referred to this representative as a "nuncio," the ecclesiastical title designating a papal ambassador, and informed Washington that he was prepared to mobilize leading Catholic personalities and organizations to report on political and social conditions inside Hungary. Though reluctant to personally collect military intelligence, the priest arranged for two Hungarian Catholic youth groups to gather such sensitive information in return for secret American subsidies for the groups. Controlled by Aradi (code-named SARAZEN), the operation, known as the KLEIN-14th STREET Project, promised to develop networks across Hungary with lines extending into Poland and Romania.[90] The paucity of relevant documents makes it difficult to identify with certainty the "nuncio" and determine the scope of his operations on behalf of American intelligence, but the available signs point to a young, politically ambitious priest who was no stranger to the clandestine world.

No matter what he might have told his American contacts, Father Töhötöm Nagy of the Society of Jesus (Jesuits) was certainly not the pope's nuncio (ambassador) to Hungary. At the time of the KLEIN project, the Vatican had no diplomatic mission or representatives in that country. Along with the representatives of all the countries that had maintained diplomatic relations with the Nazi puppet regime of Szálasi, the last authentic nuncio,

Archbishop Angelo Rotta, and his staff had been expelled by the Allied Control Commission in April 1945. In the absence of a formal papal diplomatic mission in Budapest and with the legal status of the Hungarian embassy to the Holy See uncertain, the Vatican had to look around for an informal channel to maintain contact with the new regime and the Hungarian Church. Apparently, its eyes fell on Father Nagy.[91]

Before the war, Töhötöm Nagy had been one of the founders of the "National Federation of Hungarian Catholic Agrarian Youth." Better known by its Hungarian acronym KALOT and typical of the many Catholic organizations committed to conservative reform that sprang up in interwar Europe, this movement was nationalist, anticommunist, and not a little anti-Semitic. Dedicated to social justice for the Hungarian peasantry, KALOT quickly established itself in thousands of villages and hamlets, setting up "peoples' colleges" and printing presses to advance the cause of conservative Catholic reform. By the autumn of 1944, however, it was clear to Father Nagy and the other leaders of the movement that Germany would lose the war and that any group wishing to influence postwar Hungarian affairs would have to come to terms with the victors. In a later memoir, Nagy described how, in November 1944, he secretly crossed the battle lines and met with Red Army officers representing Marshal Klimentii Voroshilov, a close associate of Stalin and the future chairman of the Allied Control Commission for Hungary. The earnest young Jesuit, who looked to the creation of a Catholic reform party in the postwar environment, apparently hoped to work out a modus vivendi between the Russians and the Hungarian Catholic Church and develop political arrangements that would recognize independent political parties.[92]

In the spring of 1945 Father Nagy secretly traveled to Rome to inform the Vatican of conditions inside Hungary and his preliminary contacts with Soviet representatives. This would be the first of several clandestine trips between the Italian and Hungarian capitals in the course of which the enterprising Jesuit, acting as a secret and deniable conduit between the Vatican and the Hungarian bishops and the Soviet occupation authority, assumed various disguises, including that of a Finnish professor and a Rumanian pig merchant.[93] During his initial visit to the Eternal City Nagy apparently made contact with American intelligence, probably through Szolt Aradi, who certainly assumed control of the subsequent operation, for when he returned secretly to Hungary in September 1945 the OSS mission in Austria considered him an enrolled source code-named KLEIN. Father Nagy, who claimed that KALOT had a million members and was the only active anti-Soviet movement in Hungary, promised to mobilize the resources of his organization on behalf of American intelligence. He communicated with his American handlers by secret courier or during his clandestine visits to Austria and Italy.[94]

On one occasion the Jesuit returned to Hungary dressed as an American soldier in an American convoy. After one visit to the Vatican he was flown by SSU to Vienna and then driven by night in a SSU vehicle to the Austrian-Hungarian border for a clandestine crossing.[95] His early product seemed promising. In October 1945 Al Ulmer informed Washington that KLEIN had returned again from Hungary with information concerning the political situation inside the country, the existence of an anticommunist underground, and the activities of supporters of Otto von Hapsburg, the pretender to the Hungarian throne. KLEIN also provided a report from a Catholic bishop in Romania concerning conditions in that country. Ulmer added that his source had informants placed inside the Hungarian Communist Party and the "Hungarian-Soviet Association." In January 1946 the Austrian mission proudly claimed that KLEIN had produced the intelligence "headline of the month"—a report allegedly revealing Moscow's interest in fomenting communist revolutions in Central Europe.[96]

For all its apparent productivity, there may have been less to KLEIN than met the eye. The aforementioned dramatic headline of the month is a case in point. The report allegedly originated among young Catholics inside the Hungarian Communist Party. These sources reported the visit to Hungary of a special delegation of Hungarian communists long domiciled in Moscow who had traveled to Budapest to assess the prospects for armed revolution in their homeland. An assessment was crucial for Moscow's plans because "a successful communist uprising in Hungary would pave the way to similar operations in Rumania and other Balkan countries, and the situation in Poland would become more advantageous to the Russians." Apart from the fact that "uprisings" were demonstrably not a part of Soviet strategy at the time, the report contains one other indication that it was partisan disinformation: a self-serving reference to KALOT. The visiting communists were reportedly especially concerned to investigate "the liberal Jesuit organization which controls most of the progressively active Catholic movements in Hungary." The report, therefore, conveniently confirmed the image of KALOT that Father Nagy wanted his American handlers to accept. Perhaps suspicious of the report's authenticity, SSU analysts in Washington did not disseminate it among their customers.[97]

By the spring of 1946 references in the available documentation to the KLEIN project disappear. In cases such as this, caution is always in order. While the declassification of SSU's records is substantially complete, it is possible that the sudden absence of relevant operational records is a function of declassification decisions or the vagaries of archival procedures. It is more likely, however, that the end of documentation reflects the demise of the KLEIN network. By the end of May, if not earlier, Hungarian counterintelligence had learned of Father Nagy's clandestine missions and his connection with American intelligence. The Hungarians had an informant inside the SSU office in Vienna, an Austrian communist who worked in the motor pool and who, on at least one occasion, had driven the Jesuit to the Austrian-Hungarian border for a clandestine crossing.[98] Nagy's exposure would have seriously compromised the KLEIN project. By the spring SSU Austria was reporting that Hungarian coverage had been seriously impeded by much stricter border controls and closer scrutiny of travelers by Russian and Hungarian authorities. Under these conditions Nagy's chains may have found it harder to move their couriers. The operation may also have been hurt by the increasing police surveillance of noncommunist political groups such as KALOT. By the summer of 1946, KALOT and several other Catholic youth and workers associations, which allegedly formed the base of the KLEIN operation, effectively had been dismantled by the communist-dominated interior ministry. Still, given the reputed size of KALOT and the contacts of the Hungarian Catholic Church with Rome, the sudden and complete end of reports from the Jesuit organization well before the full imposition of totalitarian controls in Hungary suggests that Father Nagy's intelligence operation may have been largely notional, designed less to inform the Americans than to influence their attitudes toward the postwar regime in Budapest and the potential political role of Father Nagy. The "headline of the month," for example, has more than a whiff of disinformation. Perhaps KLEIN was another demonstration of Al Ulmer's credulous weakness for disinformation so clearly evidenced by the disastrous PAREGORIC operation (chapter 2). The Strategic Services Unit may have begun to suspect the integrity of KLEIN and decided to cut its losses.

The demise of the KLEIN network would have been a serious blow to American intelligence because in 1946 SSU had only one or two other networks active inside Hungary.[99] One was the Kovakö network, which was directed from Rome by two émigrés: Domokos Hadnagy and Janos Majoros, both former Hungarian air force officers who had been active in the anti-Nazi movement that sought in 1944 to remove Hungary from the war. The network collected information on the movements and activities of their fellow countrymen outside of Hungary as well as intelligence concerning conditions and developments inside the country. In addition to several Catholic priests, university students, and government functionaries, the group claimed several prominent sources, including General Gustav Henyey, a former senior officer in Hungarian military intelligence who had served briefly as foreign minister in the short-lived Lakatos government that had tried to quit the war; General Sandor Andras, a retired senior air force officer; Colonel Mihaly Nagy, one-time military attaché in Berlin; and Laszlo Solyom, police chief of

Budapest. The group also claimed to control the so-called Kopjas Group, an anticommunist organization of former Hungarian army officers resident in Austria that claimed to have several courier lines into Hungary.[100]

From the available documentation it is difficult to determine the success, if any, of the Kovakö operation, but its achievements were probably modest. It is even possible that the operation was yet another demonstration of SSU Austria's susceptibility to deception. Already in 1946 SSU headquarters advised its European stations to break contact with Miklos Csomos, a self-described anticommunist who was the operation's principal contact with Sandor Andras, Mihaly Nagy, and Laszlo Solyom. The State Department had alerted SSU that, despite his assertions, Csomos was in fact a communist. Furthermore, for all his claims of highly placed sources, Csomos provided very little useful intelligence. Perhaps some or all of his vaunted sources were purely notional or, even worse, perhaps one or more were double agents for the Hungarians. For example, Laszlo Solyom, the Budapest police official, claimed to be a member of the Smallholders Party, the main political opposition to the Communist Party, but in fact he was a secret communist who, as part of a larger strategy to infiltrate noncommunist political groups, registered with the Smallholders on the orders of his communist superiors.[101] Whatever the loyalties of its agents, the Kovakö network proved short-lived. By 1947 most of the Hungarian end of the chain had been rolled up by the Hungarian security service. Even earlier the Kopjas Group had fallen under the control of Hungarian counterintelligence, if it had not been a Hungarian disinformation operation from the start.[102]

From its clandestine sources inside the country, American intelligence developed a picture of Hungarian affairs that largely complemented the picture described by the diplomats in the Budapest embassy. Occasionally, the secret operators reported news that had escaped the notice of the diplomats, such as rumors that the Catholic clergy had played an important role in influencing voters against the communists in the Budapest municipal elections of 7 October 1945 or that 80–85 percent of senior officers in the secret police were communists.[103] More frequently, however, the clandestine sources added little to the information generated by the embassy. An alarmist SSU report from mid-October 1945 that the Soviets had armed 30,000 communists and social democrats in preparation for a coup added details to a similar—and equally inaccurate—report out of the embassy.[104] Similarly, an SSU report outlining disquiet in the Hungarian business community over increasing Soviet dominance of the local economy echoed embassy reporting on the same subject.[105] Echoes were also present in embassy and SSU coverage of successful communist efforts to intimidate and subordinate the Smallholders Party and other independent political movements by pressuring these groups to purge from their ranks "reactionaries," including sitting members of parliament.[106]

While struggling to develop its own networks, SSU was unaware that another American service had in place a functioning chain that was producing valuable political information. This chain was controlled from a small office in the American embassy in Budapest. For the typical American diplomat in Hungary overt observation of political personalities and developments was the bread and butter of professional routine. One embassy officer, however, was far from typical. Unbeknownst to his foreign service colleagues, James McCargar, the second secretary in charge of the embassy's political section, led a covert life as the representative in Budapest of the Special Service Branch, a War Department organization also known as "the Pond." Occasionally working under State Department cover, the Special Service Branch's representatives had their own funds and communications channels and generally performed their espionage work without reference to the local American ambassador, although the intelligence product went to the State Department via the Branch's Washington headquarters.[107]

Having grown up among Russians of the then large community of expatriates in San Francisco, James McCargar studied Russian at Stanford University before joining the State Department. After a brief stint at the Moscow embassy, he joined the navy, where he served as an intelligence officer. At some point after rejoining the State Department after the war he was recruited by the Pond. From inside the American embassy, McCargar ran a network that included a scion of a noble family who, as a member of the Smallholder parliamentary group, was well placed to provide information on the internal factions and intrigues of that important political party; a senior official in the Hungarian administration who provided transcripts of cabinet meetings; an executive in the national bank who supplied information concerning Soviet exploitation of the Hungarian economy and efforts by the communists to bring the nation's financial institutions under their control; a mid-level official in the Hungarian foreign ministry who contributed observations on diplomatic affairs, particularly activities of the Soviet diplomatic mission in Budapest; and a senior officer in the criminal police.[108]

Though relatively well placed to cover the Smallholders Party, the cabinet, and the economic impact of the Soviet occupation, McCargar's network remained rather narrow in its scope. The Pond's representative was well aware that, in the main, his informants came from the former ruling class and that their observations might well reflect a particular social and political slant. By the autumn of 1946 McCargar was working to expand his net to include better coverage of other political parties, particularly the communists, the labor movement, the armed forces, the political police, the Catholic Church, and the Soviet occupation authority. These efforts achieved little success and by the end of 1946 had been largely abandoned as McCargar had to worry more about protecting his existing sources as the communists began to extend their control over the government and the country. To discredit and intimidate their opponents, beginning in the summer of 1946 the communists discovered various "conspiracies" to overthrow the republic and return fascists to power, and their control of the political police allowed them to arrest opposition parliamentarians and activists, including Bela Kovacs, the secretary general of the Smallholders Party. Rather quickly the Pond's operations in Hungary were reduced to establishing and maintaining clandestine escape lines to move anticommunist politicians to Austria.[109]

Czechoslovakia

The situation of Czechoslovakia at the close of World War II differed from those of Poland and Hungary. The latter country had joined the Axis and participated in the invasion of the Soviet Union. Czechoslovakia and Poland, on the other hand, had been among Hitler's first victims, and their governments-in-exile had adhered to the cause of the United Nations and contributed to the fight against the Third Reich. There the resemblances between the two states ended. Poland's relations with the Soviet Union had been fraught, while those of Czechoslovakia had been to all appearances exemplary. The Czechs, moreover, seemed model democrats and responsible members of the international community, while Poland throughout the interwar years had at times inclined toward political reaction, anti-Semitism, and vaunting nationalism. During the last months of the war there had been continuous controversy over which of the rival Polish factions would take the lead in the formation of a postwar government. In the case of Czechoslovakia, however, there was no dispute. The principal Allied powers recognized the government-in-exile led by President Eduard Benes as the rightful successor to the democratically elected government overthrown by the Nazis, which Benes had also headed. Unlike the Poles, the Czechs were on the whole well-disposed toward the Soviet Union, the only power that had seemed willing to come to their aid during the Sudeten crisis of 1938, much in contrast to the performance of Britain and France. Benes's government remained close to the Soviets throughout the war, going so far as to sign a mutual assistance pact with Moscow in December 1943.

In the eyes of Western statesmen, Czechoslovakia's wartime status as both a democracy and the USSR's only formal ally in Eastern Europe made it a potential test of Soviet intentions. By the time the pact between Czechoslovakia and the Soviet Union had been concluded, Moscow's desire to create a sphere of influence in Eastern Europe and the Balkans had become increasingly evident to all. The Soviets' hostility to projects for regional confederations, such as the proposal floated by the Poles for a Polish-Czech confederation, sufficed to make their intentions clear. The British resisted the Soviet-Czech pact for as long as they could precisely because they saw in it the beginnings of an unwelcome Russian sphere in Eastern Europe. By the end of 1943 the Americans were rather more flexible. Washington regarded the several proposals for regional confederation that would place a potentially anti-Soviet bloc on Russia's western borders, as folly given Moscow's manifest opposition. At the Moscow Conference of October 1943, the American delegation had pointedly declined to support British Foreign Secretary Anthony Eden's opposition to the impending Czech-Soviet alliance.[110]

The promising Czech-Soviet relationship was probably the chief reason for the cautious but widely held view among American officials that a Soviet sphere of influence might not entail such a degree of domination that Eastern Europe would become a dangerously pliable instrument of Moscow's will. The sine qua non of domestic political self-determination defined the essential concerns of American diplomatic and intelligence reporting as war turned to peace, and, as more than one official observed, Czechoslovakia would be the "acid test" of whether the Soviets would exercise restraint in their dominance of the region.[111]

There appeared to be solid reasons for optimism concerning Czechoslovakia. The Soviet-Czech treaty included strict guarantees of noninterference in internal political affairs. In May 1944 these guarantees were reaffirmed in a civil affairs agreement intended to govern the period after the arrival of the advancing Red Army, an agreement considered completely satisfactory by American observers. The Czechs spoke well of the consideration that Soviet officials had shown them. Benes, in fact, was especially gratified by this attention, a feeling shared by the normally more skeptical Czech foreign minister, Jan Masaryk.[112] The Czechs were not alone in their optimism. Early in 1945 the State Department observed that Czechoslovakia's relations with the USSR were "excellent" and presented "no problems." The OSS representative working with the intelligence section of the Czech government-in-exile in London was equally sanguine in his appraisal of Czech-Soviet relations.[113]

Unfortunately, the liberation of Czechoslovakia in the spring of 1945 brought just the "problems" of which the State Department had earlier seen no trace. In April Benes, accompanied by the Soviet ambassador, Valerian Zorin, proceeded with the Red Army to the city of Košice. At the same time Moscow raised obstacles to the entry of American diplomats to Czechoslovakia, a stance that provoked resentment on the part of American officials. Only in late May did a small advance party of diplomats reach Prague. The other problem arose from the unexpectedly rapid advance of General George S. Patton's Third Army, which had advanced deep into Czechoslovakia and might even have taken Prague had the Supreme Allied Commander in the west, General Dwight D. Eisenhower, not diverted Patton to the destruction of the remaining enemy forces in southern Germany. Several of Patton's divisions, however, remained in Czechoslovakia, which thus ended the war with two Allied armies on its soil. Benes, together with most Czechs, wished to be rid of foreign armies, but he emphatically told the first American diplomats to reach Prague that he hoped the American forces would remain until a simultaneous withdrawal with the Soviets could be arranged. He did not need to add that he feared the consequences of a prolonged stay by the Red Army, especially as the Czech communists had made clear their desire that it remain. Also, the Soviet forces had rapidly worn out their welcome with what Alfred Klieforth, the leader of the State Department advance party in Prague, delicately referred to as its "general licentious conduct" and policy of living off a land that could ill afford the burden.[114]

On 10 May 1945, several days before the arrival of Klieforth's party, the Office of Strategic Services appeared in Prague, a move that had been planned at least since February 1945. The original intention was for a small OSS team to return to the Czech capital with František Moravec, the chief of intelligence for the Czech government-in-exile who had worked closely with OSS during the war. The sometime diplomat Charles Thayer was the first choice to lead the mission, but Thayer announced that he could not work with the ambassador-designate, Laurence Steinhardt.[115] In his place headquarters selected Major Charles Katek of OSS's Secret Intelligence Branch. Katek had been born to a Czech family that had moved to Chicago and prospered there without losing contact with its homeland. He had a native fluency in Czech and amplified his familial advantages by earning a doctorate in Czech history at Northwestern University in 1943. Entering OSS upon the completion of his degree, he was assigned to London as a liaison officer with the intelligence service of the Czech government-in-exile.[116]

Ambassador Steinhardt established guidelines for the OSS mission: the team should have only three or four members, preferably not attached to the embassy, and they should focus primarily on counterintelligence, the investigation of war crimes, and the identification of Nazi financial assets (Operation SAFEHAVEN). The Office of Strategic Services accepted the ambassador's conditions. Major Katek and his colleagues arrived in Prague ostensibly on detached service from the U.S. Third Army. Inasmuch as Katek had openly worked with Czech intelligence in London—he had publicly received a medal from the government-in-exile for his work—there was no denying his connection with espionage. Since he could not convincingly claim he was just a soldier temporarily attached to the U.S. mission in Prague, he frankly acknowledged that he had arrived in the Czech capital on a special mission— the investigation of war crimes, specifically the capture and execution by the Germans in 1944 of an OSS mission sent to assist the Slovak resistance— for which his intelligence background qualified him. Frank Wisner, a senior officer in the American service, acknowledged Katek's potentially awkward position: "We all recognize the fact that your cover is more a justification or pretext for your being in Czechoslovakia than a cover in the true sense of the word inasmuch as your own connection with our organization is so well known."[117]

Like other OSS posts in Europe in the first months of peace, OSS Prague, which administratively was an outpost of OSS Germany, received little guidance from headquarters as to the types of information Washington required. In May 1945 headquarters had sought the cooperation of various government departments in preparing a "Czechoslovakian Intelligence Guide," a list of topics and questions that the Prague station might investigate, but the response was modest. OSS could not provide specific collection requirements or targets to its field station because "the customers themselves are not able to tell us in greater detail just what it is they do not know." In the absence of guidelines from Washington, Charles Katek and his staff were directed to establish their own collection priorities and attack targets of opportunity.[118]

Katek established his station in an elegant mansion on Loretánské Square in the heart of old Prague, where his lavish receptions and dinner parties soon became a feature of the capital's social life. The guest lists were a veritable who's who of Czechoslovakia's social and political elites, including high government officials, journalists, and leaders of all the noncommunist political parties. Their host's position as the head of American intelligence in Czechoslovakia was an open secret and did not deter his guests from speaking openly about political developments in the country. Indeed, political information was a subject of conversation at Katek's soirees precisely because he was known to be America's spy. Hoping to advance their particular agendas by bringing those agendas to the attention of the United States, the guests at Loretánské Square *wanted* their host to report their conversations to Washington.

In the first summer of peace President Benes and his government were preoccupied with the issue of foreign troops—American and Russian—on Czech soil. The United States preferred to withdraw its forces as quickly as possible, but was reluctant to do so unilaterally for fear that the continued presence of the Red Army would intimidate the Czech government and facilitate Soviet dominance of the country. Benes, who had become more wary of his Soviet neighbor and the local communists since those heady days when all were united in the common cause of destroying the Third Reich, also worried about the insidious influence of a Soviet occupation force and confidentially expressed to American diplomats his appreciation for Washington's support for quick and simultaneous withdrawal of occupation troops. Among noncommunist politicians in Prague Washington's attitude toward occupation forces planted the notion that Washington was the best protector of Czechoslovakia against Soviet domination. This notion facilitated Katek's work by allowing him, through the mechanism of his social entertainments, to develop useful contacts among noncommunist political and social elites who were only too eager to keep Washington abreast of political developments.

Within six months of his arrival Charles Katek had developed an impressive list of sources, including a deputy prime minister who was also a member of the Slovak Democratic Party, the secretary of another deputy prime minister, the director of President Benes's private office, the chairman of the National Socialist Party, the general secretary of the Social Democratic Party, the general secretary of the Slovak Democratic Party, the chief of political intelligence in the Ministry of the Interior, a high official in the Ministry of Industry, and an air force colonel who had worked for the wartime Czech intelligence service. As the jewel in his intelligence crown Katek could claim a close relationship with President Benes himself.[119]

These sources provided a useful perspective on Czech politics and the prospects for Stalin's national front strategy. Largely as a consequence of Benes's pre-liberation agreement with the communists and their superior organization, Moscow's friends generally controlled the commanding heights of political power. They dominated the national front formed on 8 June 1945 and used their cabinet portfolios to colonize the most critical departments of state. This aggressive bid for power did not come as a total surprise to American intelligence. As early as May 1945 the Office of Strategic Services had advised the White House that the Communist Party, well organized and with a loyal membership and a clear program, had an advantage in the partisan struggles to organize the postwar Czech government.[120] The next month OSS's Research and Analysis Branch observed that "although it was to be expected that the Czechoslovak Provisional Government would be pro-Soviet, the dominant position held by the Communists in that government is particularly noteworthy."[121]

Once established in Prague, Major Katek's team soon began to provide details of the communists' single-minded pursuit of the levers of power. Intelligence reports identified communist efforts to claim a "guiding" position in Czech government, to bully political groups that resisted that claim, and to insinuate themselves into positions of control in the critical institutions of authority, particularly the military, the police, and the intelligence services. In July and August 1945, for example, Katek's sources reported that communists in the circle around the pro-Soviet minister of national defense, General Ludvik Svoboda, had established control over army administration and, with an eye toward purging the officer corps, had inaugurated investigations into the political reliability of noncommunist officers. Political considerations also influenced personnel policies in the paramilitary State Security Guard with reports that Communist Party membership was a requirement for entry into the unit. The leadership of the wartime intelligence service that had served the government-in-exile in London had been purged of noncommunist officers and its command entrusted to a loyal communist. From sources in the war ministry, Katek learned that the reorganized Czech intelligence service was responsive to Soviet direction. As early as July 1945 the service, on the orders of their Russian mentors, had begun to work on the order of battle of American forces in Germany. Within a year SSU had discovered that the Czechs were collaborating closely with Soviet intelligence on clandestine operations in Western Europe. General Svoboda had also agreed that Czechoslovakia would purchase military equipment only from the USSR, a decision which made the Czech army logistically dependent upon the Soviets.[122] In September 1945, a full month before it was adopted by the cabinet over Benes's objections, Katek obtained a copy of a communist-inspired decree calling for sweeping nationalization of industries. The following month his informants reported the failure of Soviet-Czech talks in Moscow in early October concerning the withdrawal of Red Army units from the country and curbs on the depredations of Russian soldiery against civilians. Shortly afterward Katek's office reported the adamant refusal of the communists during an all-night round of negotiations with other political parties to yield any of the cabinet portfolios they had acquired from Benes's pre-liberation agreement with them.[123]

In the first months of peace, Charles Katek and his small team of a half dozen assistants and clerks represented the primary American intelligence effort in Czechoslovakia. From the embassy the experienced military attaché, Lieutenant Colonel Aage Woldike, used his contacts in the Czech army to track the size of Soviet occupation forces in the country and, more importantly, to monitor Soviet seizure and exploitation of the important uranium mine and processing plant at the Czechoslovak town of Joachimsthal, an indicator of Moscow's pursuit of nuclear weapons.[124] Woldike, however, generally avoided political and economic reporting, topics he was pleased to leave to the OSS/SSU station. Lacking competition, Katek, consequently, monopolized political intelligence, a position that did not necessarily serve the interests of either American intelligence or its customers.

While useful, especially in providing detail or confirmation concerning information from other sources, Katek's reports did not add significantly to Washington's understanding of Czech affairs; indeed, they did not differ substantially from journalistic accounts or the routine reporting of the American embassy in Prague. This deficiency was apparent to Washington headquarters, which distributed relatively few of his reports to its customers in government departments. An early evaluation by the Reporting Board of intelligence from the Prague station praised the timeliness and style of the material but noted that a large percentage of the reports were superfluous since they conveyed information already available to anyone in Washington willing to listen to the nightly news broadcasts of Prague radio. The board dismissed the station's economic reporting as misinformed and lacking in detail.[125]

In the first year of peace Charles Katek's collection efforts suffered from three deficiencies. Perhaps the most serious was his failure to develop clandestine sources of information. As his superiors were aware, the Prague station chief scorned the use of secret informants, believing that what he needed to know he could learn directly from government ministers and members of parliament.[126] These exalted sources gathered at the frequent dinners and soirees Katek hosted at his well-appointed apartments on Loretánské Square. At these lavish entertainments, which seem to have been Katek's principal operational activity, politics was the main topic of conversation and indiscretion the main feature of every conversation as the guests enjoyed the food, liquor, and cigarettes liberally dispensed by their host. Cabinet ministers, parliamentarians, bureaucrats, and military officers openly discussed the events of the day and anticipated developments in the days to come. The information gleaned from these conversations by Katek and his assistants was little better than gossip, albeit well-informed gossip. Katek made no effort to seek out and recruit secret sources who might confirm or deny this gossip or address subjects that never came up over the postprandial cigars and brandy. In short, the Prague station chief did not seek out information, but rather waited for information to come to him, a practice that ensured that the resulting intelligence would reflect the agendas, interests, and biases of those who gathered around his piano to drink whiskey and sing popular songs. Eventually, the limitations of Katek's approach became apparent to his superiors, and in early 1947 the Prague station chief would be summoned to Frankfurt for consultations during which he was ordered to forsake cocktail parties and instead start building clandestine networks that might produce more reliable secret political and military intelligence.[127]

Major Katek's collection efforts were constrained not only by his operational reliance on parties but by his narrow guest lists. Lots of people were pleased to drink and dine chez Katek, but they were always the same people—or at least the same types of people. Attendance was heavily weighted in favor of the more conservative elements of Prague's political society, and few leftists lined up at the buffet or gathered around the piano. In August 1945 an early appraisal of the Prague station noted that Katek had developed good contacts with representatives of all political movements except the communists, a rather serious deficiency in a political intelligence program, given the prominent—not to say dominant—role of the Communist Party in Czechoslovak politics. Several months later, when the position of the Communist Party had become even more important, a senior SSU officer complained that Katek still relied upon his contacts with "middle of the road and right wing leaders."[128]

Katek's reports were necessarily shaped by his reliance upon contacts in the noncommunist political parties. In the first year of peace these parties tended to overestimate their popular appeal and underestimate the communists' popularity and single-minded pursuit of power, miscalculations that found their way into the reports of the Prague intelligence station and the dispatches of Ambassador Laurence Steinhardt, with whom Katek regularly shared his observations. Despite clear evidence that the communists and their allies were the strongest force in the cabinet and were actively infiltrating government departments, particularly those that controlled the army, police, and public information, noncommunist politicians remained sanguine concerning the prospects of democracy in their country, and consequently so did the SSU station and the American embassy. Over the summer of 1945, for example, Katek reported that, despite the machinations of the communists, noncommunist leaders were increasingly satisfied with the course of political events, believing that the communists were weakening and that any effort to force the country into a Soviet client state would be thwarted by the people and the democratic parties. These leaders were confident that the population would express its democratic spirit at any election and that when challenged the communists would back down.[129] This complacency, which might have been shaken if Charles Katek had made an effort to spend more time with left-wing politicians, led the intelligence station—and the embassy—to underestimate the strength of the communists. To the surprise of both, the communists captured 46.6 percent of the seats in local elections in February 1946, far outperforming all other parties, with the National Socialists running a distant second with a mere 14.5 percent.[130] Expectations were again dashed by the national elections to the constituent assembly in May. Both the intelligence station and the embassy predicted success for the moderate parties, but the communists again came in first, capturing 114 of the 300 seats, more than twice the number won by the National Socialists, who again came in second, with 55 seats.[131] In Washington, Katek's superiors put their fingers on the reason behind the Prague station's erroneous reporting. "The political scene," one evaluator concluded, had been "one-sidedly, hence, inaccurately, reported."[132]

The third factor that compromised the efforts of the Prague station was security. The station operated under the flimsiest cover. Initially, it was a "repatriation commission" ostensibly searching for missing American military personnel. Next, it operated for a time as a commission investigating war crimes. Both of these covers provided an excuse for station personnel to travel about the country and question people, although there is little evidence that anyone journeyed much beyond Prague's suburbs. In January 1946, after the communists orchestrated the purge or arrest of several "reactionaries," including the chief of political intelligence in the ministry of the interior, a pro-Western friend of Charles Katek, the station chief felt the need to protect his people with some sort of quasi-diplomatic cover and immunity. After discussions with Ambassador Steinhardt, the station was renamed, in March, the American Military Mission, with vague connections to the office of the military attaché in the embassy.[133] None of these changes fooled the Czech security services for a minute.

From the day of his arrival in Prague, Major Charles Katek was known to the Czech security service as the "head of the American espionage service in Czechoslovakia."[134] It could hardly have been otherwise given his wartime work as OSS liaison to the Czechoslovak government-in-exile. The security services knew, therefore, that wherever Katek was, no matter the sign on his door, there was the outpost of American intelligence. This knowledge was not limited to counterintelligence officers. The guests who visited Katek's mansion were well aware of his intelligence connection and assumed that their views would be reported to Washington; indeed this connection was the reason they patronized his soirees, although the food and drink ranked a close second among their motives. Unfortunately for the American major, the well-known connection also attracted the attention of elements who had little interest in publicizing their presence.

The Czech counterintelligence service (OBZ) had the station under surveillance from the first day it set up shop as the American repatriation commission. Station personnel were followed and their contacts noted. Katek's apartments, which doubled as his offices, were easily compromised. The first two floors of his building served as a Czech police post, which facilitated surveillance of the major's residence and his visitors. At night the gates to the building were locked and occupants and nocturnal visitors could access the building only by waking—and alerting—the concierge or by passing through the police offices, which were staffed around the clock. Such an arrangement was not conducive to clandestine activities, should Katek have engaged in such activities.[135]

Czech counterintelligence penetrated Katek's operation from top to bottom. Agents secretly entered the offices, which were unguarded, to photograph papers. Some of the guests who enjoyed the American major's lavish hospitality were informants for the security services, as were many, if not all, of the Czech staff employed on the premises. The cleaning lady, for example, regularly passed to OBZ the contents of office wastebaskets. The Czech's best informant, however, did not remove the trash; he produced it. Major Katek's Czech-born personal assistant and confident, Sergeant Kurt Taub, had been recruited before Pearl Harbor by Soviet intelligence, which facilitated his immigration to the United States. Taub joined OSS in 1943, but it is not clear if he assisted his Russian patrons at that time. After the war he joined Katek in opening the intelligence station in Prague, and the Soviets seemed to have activated him. Taub was a Soviet—and probably Czech—spy at the center of American intelligence in Czechoslovakia.[136]

By early 1946, the Strategic Services Unit seems to have developed doubts concerning Major Katek's situation in Prague because it moved to establish an alternate, more secret, station in the Czech capital. In February 1946 Spencer Taggart assumed the post of vice-consul in the embassy. Taggart, who had lived in Czechoslovakia as a Mormon missionary for three years before the war, had joined OSS in 1942 and continued into SSU after the war. Washington's new man in Prague was in every way the opposite of its old man. Abstemious, reserved, self-effacing, Taggart did not entertain even on a modest scale; indeed he avoided society and maintained a low profile in the diplomatic community. While Katek surrounded himself with a large staff in the Military Mission, the new vice-consul made do with a single assistant. Taggart's mission was to establish clandestine networks, an operational area completely neglected by Katek. Perhaps SSU headquarters hoped that the flamboyant and transparent chief of the Military Mission would attract all the attention of the local security services, leaving the vice-consul to quietly go about his espionage unnoticed. If so, then such hopes were dashed. Through their informants inside the American embassy and, perhaps, clandestine entries into the embassy to photograph documents, Czech counterintelligence soon uncovered the vice-consul's real work. If Taggart developed any clandestine sources by the end of 1946, they were almost certainly known to his watchers. In September of that year, the one-time missionary was summoned to Germany for consultations with his supervisors. After these interviews, Crosby Lewis, chief of station in Germany, concluded that "under present conditions [Taggart's] chances of effective operation are almost negligible" and recommended to Washington that their operative be recalled from Czechoslovakia.[137]

If the test of a clandestine intelligence service is its ability to produce from trustworthy informants a steady stream of timely, accurate, and useful information not readily available from other sources, then OSS and SSU performed poorly in Eastern Europe in the first year of peace. In Poland and Hungary the American services, constrained by shortages of personnel, severely limited resources, and actively hostile operational environments, struggled to develop reliable and productive clandestine networks. The available record, admittedly incomplete, suggests that relatively few networks emerged, and most, if not all, of these were largely imaginary constructs of fabricators or political opportunists or disinformation instruments under the control of local or Soviet counterintelligence services. Ironically, in Czechoslovakia, where the above-mentioned constraints were least present and, therefore, the prospects for espionage most promising, the failure to develop secret informants—at least before the arrival of Spencer Taggart—was not a function of conditions on the ground, but the result of a conscious decision by the station chief.

The absence of reliable clandestine informants meant that, unlike their counterparts in Germany and Austria, American operatives in Eastern Europe contributed relatively little to the flow of important information to Washington. It was not so much that intelligence reporting from the region was scanty, misinformed, or misleading, although it often was all those things; it was more that the reporting was not especially unique or insightful. Usually, the reports of the spies differed little from the reports of the diplomats in the American embassies in Warsaw, Budapest, and Prague. Sometimes this similarity was the result of common observation of conditions or circumstances that were obvious to any witness. In early 1946, for example, one did not require access to the secret minutes of the Polish cabinet or a whispered conversation with the personal secretary of the minister of war to understand that the Polish Communist Party, in close collaboration with the Soviets, was intent upon imposing an authoritarian, one-party state on the Polish people. Other times, the similarity between intelligence reporting and diplomatic reporting reflected a similarity in sources. Often the spies and the diplomats were talking to the same people, an overlap that was especially the case in Prague. The resulting echo chamber would have been less problematic if the sources, though common, were at least diverse. Unfortunately, American intelligence in the region—less so American diplomats, who at least had the professional requirement to interact officially with members of the host government—tended to cultivate contacts who represented a rather narrow range of political, economic, and social backgrounds. The result was that certain voices were overrepresented in reporting: opponents of the regime rather than supporters, the privileged rather than the disadvantaged, those who had something to lose rather than those who had something to gain from political and economic change, and those who needed Washington's support and intervention rather than those who didn't. Potentially, the limited range of sources might not only skew reporting, but also might make American intelligence an instrument of someone else's agenda. This danger, of course, was not unique to Eastern Europe.

CHAPTER SIX

The Nearer Shore: France and Italy

France

During the war no European target received more attention from the Office of Strategic Services than German-occupied France.[1] Although it came late to the French intelligence theater and often had to accept a secondary role while more experienced actors, such as Britain's Secret Intelligence Service and Special Operations Executive, monopolized the spotlight, OSS never ceased trying to expand its part and move closer to center stage. It put its first agent into metropolitan France (via a Free French submarine) in February 1943, a modest operational success that encouraged the Secret Intelligence (SI) Branch to seek other opportunities to penetrate the country. Throughout the war these efforts were constrained by a lack of experienced operatives, suitable transport, and necessary support facilities. These deficiencies compelled OSS to rely on its British, and to a lesser extent French, counterparts, who, not surprisingly, were not inclined to help the American service remedy its weaknesses.

Despite such obstacles, OSS scored some important successes against the French target. In 1943, for example, SI Spain, working with the Free French intelligence service, developed Project MEDUSA, a trans-Pyrenees program that by the spring of 1944 had evolved into the largest American clandestine intelligence operation in Europe, controlling more than a thousand informants in fifteen networks spread across southern France and reaching as far north as Paris.[2] On the other side of the country, SI Switzerland used French resistance channels to collect information concerning the disposition of German military forces and political and economic conditions inside France. Working on their own, SI officers in Bern developed additional useful sources, including an official in the Paris headquarters of the French national railways who, beginning in September 1943 and continuing for several months until his clandestine courier to Switzerland was captured by the Germans, provided important information on the condition of the metropolitan rail network, rail traffic, and the impact on the transportation net of Allied bombing and resistance sabotage.[3] Even SI London, which spent most of its energy and time fighting SIS and SOE for airplanes, radios, training slots, and missions, contributed to OVERLORD, the invasion of France in June 1944, by participating in the SUSSEX and PROUST projects (joint

American-British-French programs that infiltrated intelligence teams into France before D-Day to report on the strength and deployment of German army units) and in the JEDBURGH teams that parachuted into the country to support resistance operations.

By VE Day, the Office of Strategic Services had developed a cadre of seasoned managers, a network of proven contacts, and a body of operational experience upon which the service could base its future coverage of France. That future, however, remained uncertain. As the war wound down in Europe, OSS could not be sure what kind of postwar intelligence coverage, if any, Washington would desire. For that matter, OSS could not even be sure that it would continue in existence after the war. This uncertainty, which afflicted all OSS units, discouraged the officers concerned with France from making grand plans. Drastic budget and staff reductions could hardly be avoided. Hundreds of OSS personnel had been involved with French operations during the war, but by midsummer 1945 the SI section of the OSS station in Paris was down to thirty-three people, and senior officers were expecting a further decline to twenty. Long-term prospects were no brighter. A planning document that anticipated the status of the French station after the first year of peace, speculated that the SI staff would amount to no more than seventeen people, including secretaries, drivers, and maintenance personnel.[4] The loss of staff and the concomitant reduction in budget, problems experienced by all the OSS European stations after VE Day, seriously compromised the operational capabilities of the Paris office. In August 1945 the chief of SI France warned Washington that intelligence production had declined because a "radically reduced" budget and pressure from headquarters to reduce personnel required a contraction and, in some cases, a complete suspension of collection programs.[5]

Even if resources had remained plentiful, collection priorities would have posed a problem. In the last year of the war, SI collection efforts in Europe had focused primarily on tactical intelligence, such as enemy movements and order of battle, in immediate support of military operations. Broader strategic intelligence that addressed political and economic questions was relegated to a secondary position.[6] This hierarchy of priorities certainly applied to France, where for most of the war the principal intelligence question was not "what are the French up to?" but "what are the Germans up to in France?" With the end of the war American intelligence officers in France had to shift to the first question, a move that required not just a redirection of attention, but also a complete reorganization of operations. For example, networks that served perfectly well to cover the movement of German troops and equipment in Normandy or along the Rhone River Valley were ill-positioned to provide information about postwar industrial policy, the political prospects of the Radical Socialists, or French ambitions in Indochina. Indeed, French men and women who were more than happy to cooperate with American intelligence to defeat the hated *Boche* might cease cooperation after the war when the target became their own country.

Given the uncertainty surrounding the future status of the French mission and its resource levels, early postwar plans were necessarily vague. The first projection of peacetime collection objectives, circulated the day after the German surrender on 8 May 1945, contained a generic list of topics that might just as easily have applied to an intelligence station in Mexico, Portugal, or Siam: report political tendencies and developments; cover industrial activity and economic developments; monitor activities in the labor, educational, and religious sectors; report military developments and identify military installations.[7] By midsummer uncertainty regarding the institutional future of OSS had not lessened, so plans were only marginally more developed. In July Washington headquarters instructed SI France to focus on (1) developing a close liaison with the French foreign intelligence service, the Direction Générale des Etudes et Recherches (DGER), (2) supporting and directing the intelligence activities of the Basque émigré organization that had established itself abroad after the Spanish Civil War and continued clandestine operations against the regime of General Francisco Franco, (3) establishing contact with Central European and Balkan émigrés in Paris who might shed light on "the blacked out area of Central Europe," (4) assisting OSS Germany in Project SAFEHAVEN, an operation to trace the movement of laundered Nazi money and assets, (5) reporting political events in France, Belgium, and Holland, and (6) maintaining the connections into French labor and left-wing elements that had proved productive during the war.[8]

Staff reductions seriously compromised the pursuit of even these modest objectives, an effort further complicated by the fact that the OSS station in Paris, already hard-pressed to manage its own operational programs, also had for a time to supervise the activities of the small OSS offices in Brussels and Amsterdam. By the autumn of 1945 Philip Horton, the director of the station's secret intelligence section, had scaled back the operational plans formulated over the summer. In October the section's labor desk, which had developed very useful contacts in French trade union circles, closed, and ambitions to exploit labor connections were quietly set aside. The economic intelligence desk, which handled the SAFEHAVEN account, also closed. By January 1946, the "vast reduction" in personnel—the Paris station had by then only four officers collecting intelligence—required Horton to focus his scarce resources on three main collection programs.[9]

Two of these programs ran non-French sources against non-French targets. As we have seen (chapter 5), SI France controlled the "Z Project," an operation that relied on former intelligence officers of the wartime Polish government-in-exile to collect information from inside their now communist-controlled country. The second program also involved political exiles. Even before it recruited its Poles, SI France had been running a major operation that exploited the information networks of the Basque government-in-exile. During the Second Spanish Republic (1931–1939) the Basque provinces in northern Spain had acquired a degree of autonomy. At the onset of the Spanish Civil War, the government of the Basque Autonomous Region had raised an army to support the Republic against the Nationalists, but in 1937 the regional government had split over a decision to lay down arms and accept occupation by the forces of the Nationalist leader, General Francisco Franco. Some of the Basque loyalists then withdrew into Republican territory to continue the struggle. With Franco's victory, these diehards moved abroad, many to France, where there was an indigenous Basque population, particularly in the *département* of Pyrénées Atlantiques, but some as far as Mexico and the United States. Under the leadership of Jose Antonio Aguirre, the former president of the Basque Autonomous Region, these émigrés formed a government-in-exile to nurture Basque nationalism, maintain solidarity among the refugees, encourage resistance against the new regime in Madrid, and prepare for a return to the homeland.

The émigré Basques maintained clandestine links with supporters inside Spain. In 1943 the OSS organization in neutral Spain made contact with this underground, anti-Franco resistance. The political fallout should the Spanish security service discover that the Americans were talking with sworn enemies of the regime would have been great, but the operational benefits were too promising to dismiss. The Basques were reliably antifascist and anti-Nazi and they already had in place a clandestine network of informants, safe-houses, and communications lines, some of which extended across the Pyrenees into German-occupied Europe. Initially, OSS planned to use the Basques only as the basis for stay-behind networks that would conduct intelligence, sabotage, and resistance operations in the event of a German occupation of Spain.[10]

As the German threat to Spain receded, OSS relations with the Basques, now code-named AIREDALES, shifted in emphasis and target. The objective became intelligence collection, and the primary target became Spain. During the war the Office of Strategic Services had had a rocky experience in Spain. Intelligence collection operations had been undermined by poor relations between the local OSS station and the American embassy. Ambassador Carlton Hayes and his staff scorned the intelligence operatives as feckless, inexperienced adventurers, whose ill-conceived antics would, by poisoning relations with the Spanish government, play into the hands of pro-German elements in the regime. The concerns were not unfounded as not infrequently the spies exhibited poor judgment and a rather cavalier attitude toward operational security. On one occasion Donovan's organization shipped a container of pistols to its Madrid station. Apparently unaware of the diplomatic niceties, the logistics officers not only addressed the container to Ambassador Hayes personally, but also openly noted on the shipping manifest that the box contained pistols. On another occasion, when the Spanish counterintelligence service penetrated an OSS operation, three American officers who had been working undercover had to be hastily evacuated, but nothing could be done for their Spanish agents, who were either executed or imprisoned. After this episode, Spanish counterintelligence quietly made it known to OSS that while they might turn a blind eye toward discreet operations against purely German targets, they would not countenance operations against Spanish targets.[11]

Ambassador Hayes bombarded the State Department with protests concerning the behavior of OSS representatives, and he urged Washington either to shut down all OSS activities in Spain or to place operations under the control of the embassy. After two investigations by the Joint Chiefs of Staff, OSS agreed to scale back its activities in Spain, allow Ambassador Hayes to read the Madrid station's incoming and outgoing messages, and give the ambassador the right to approve all operations and veto the appointment of personnel deemed unqualified for service in Spain.[12] In view of this experience, advocates of a continued intelligence presence in the country after the war found few sympathizers. At a time when OSS was hard-pressed to maintain adequate intelligence missions in even those countries, such as Austria and Germany, where there was a consensus on the need for intelligence collection, the Spanish station simply could not be sustained. By the fall of 1945 all OSS personnel, except for a small X-2 contingent, had been withdrawn from the country.

After Washington pulled its intelligence officers out of Spain, the Basques moved from the periphery to the center of OSS operations. The AIREDALES had already demonstrated their intelligence value; on one occasion they passed to OSS a cipher used by the Spanish intelligence service. Shortly after the German capitulation, OSS France reminded Washington that the Basques were of "utmost importance" as a long-term source of information concerning France as well as Spain. Given the absence of an SI station in Spain, their clandestine lines into Spain offered a unique opportunity to monitor affairs in that country, if only from a distance. For their part, the Basques received from the Americans a monthly subsidy of $4,000, which, along with certain logistical support, helped them to maintain their clandestine organization and government-in-exile. SI France assumed responsibility for working with the Basques, and by the end of 1945 the AIREDALES had become one of Philip Horton's major operations, second only to liaison with the French secret services in significance and productivity. By the beginning of 1946 the Basques had become SSU's principal source of secret intelligence concerning Spain, having submitted to their American partners some 3,600 reports on conditions inside the country as well as occasional reports on other parts of the world where Basques resided. Horton considered the AIREDALES an enormous success, but Washington's appraisal, while positive, was more restrained. Intelligence managers understood that the Basque reports were colored by a political agenda and limited by their source's position on the periphery of Spanish politics. A review of the AIREDALE project prepared in February 1946 concluded that the Basques were a good source of information concerning ongoing Republican opposition to Franco, but they reported very little on the internal workings of the government, the decision-making circles around *El Caudillo*, and the non-republican (e.g., monarchist) opposition. Even so, one SSU office observed in May 1946, "It seems to us now that at least for a good while we will be wholly dependent on the Airdales for our Iberian coverage."[13]

SI France's third (and most active) collection program involved liaison with the French secret services. During the war OSS had developed connections with French intelligence, although the Americans were often befuddled by the byzantine and politically factionalized world of the French secret services and underwhelmed by the intelligence benefits of the connection. In the last month of the war an assessment of the liaison relationship concluded that the intelligence shared by DGER was "disappointing both as to quality and quantity," a deficiency the report attributed to institutional inefficiency and disorganization rather than any substantial withholding of information. The appraisal also noted that the French service was highly amateur in its approach to operations—at the time a rather condescending judgment from American officers whose own intelligence experience might still be measured in months. Despite these alleged deficiencies, the appraisal anticipated that after the war the DGER would evolve into an effective service whose reach would extend beyond Europe to encompass Africa, Southeast Asia, and other locales of the French colonial empire. The report recommended that OSS should seek to maintain close relations with its French counterpart.[14]

Dealing directly with DGER director André Dewavrin, SI France had negotiated a series of agreements covering liaison in three areas. The most sensitive was the exchange of information concerning the Soviet Union and Russian-occupied territories in Central and East Europe. Convinced that war between the western Allies and the Soviet Union was inevitable, Dewavrin had instigated this particular exchange in June 1945, and he insisted that the arrangement proceed outside of normal liaison channels and shelter behind the strictest secrecy.[15] The head of the DGER's Russian section, Commandant de Larney, personally passed the Russian material, code-named HAMPSHIRE/BARTON, to Lieutenant Colonel Michalowski, the head of the Central and East Europe desk in SI France. Other OSS officers in Paris were ignorant of the exchange, as were DGER officers who were in regular contact with American intelligence about other matters. In addition to transmitting to Washington the Russian material obtained from the French, the Paris station also forwarded the material to the OSS (later SSU) mission in the American zone of Germany for dissemination to General Lucius Clay, the military governor of the zone, his political advisor, Ambassador Robert Murphy, and General Edwin Sibert, the commander of U.S. Army intelligence in Europe. In return Lieutenant Colonel Michalowski selected items regarding the Soviets from among the intelligence reports received from SI Germany, retyped the information on plain paper that lacked both watermark and letterhead so as to obscure its origin, and passed this information to Commandant de Larney. DGER then circulated this intelligence within the French government as its own material without any indication of its true source.[16]

In their insistence on close security, the DGER officers may have been motivated by more than a concern that the Russians might discover the arrangement. After VE Day, the fragmented French intelligence community—the Interior Ministry alone had three different espionage services—was unsettled by personal and political feuds as prewar professionals, wartime *résistants*, communists, socialists, and Gaullists all fought for position, prerogative, and power. The French Communist Party, for example, denounced the DGER as the Direction Générale des Ennemis de la République, while strenuously seeking to infiltrate its own loyalists into the service. Within services factions formed and officers often distrusted the personal ambitions and political agendas of their colleagues. At one point relations between the socialist Henri Ribière, who replaced Dewavrin as director of the foreign intelligence service, renamed in January 1946 the Service de Documentation Extérieure et de Contre-espionnage (SDECE), and his second-in-command, the Gaullist Pierre Fourcaud, were so bad that they communicated with each other only by terse and nasty notes. At a meeting of chiefs of sections, Ribière was so angered by his deputy's manner that, cursing and brandishing his walking stick, he drove him from the room. For his part Fourcaud worked to undermine Ribière's authority and conspired with SDECE section chiefs to ensure that his boss did not see the most sensitive items of intelligence. Their mutual antagonism was so great and so public that when Ribière had a near-fatal automobile accident, rumor in professional circles held that Fourcaud had tampered with the brakes.[17]

In the Franco-American intelligence relationship the French were always the more enthusiastic partner, particularly eager to discuss joint operational initiatives against the Soviet target and expand cooperation into other fields. For their part, the Americans, while pleased to receive whatever the French offered, preferred a less active association.[18] This reserve may have reflected, in part, doubts concerning the security and stability of any relationship with a service so disrupted by corruption (underpaid officers sold intelligence to politicians while technicians marketed medical degrees, university diplomas, and birth certificates counterfeited in service labs) and political and personal feuds that questions about loyalties, authority, and control could not be answered with any confidence. Experience reinforced these doubts. When, in early 1946, the scandal-ridden Direction Générale des Etudes et Recherches, ridiculed by its rivals in the intelligence community as the Direction Générale des Escroqueries et Rapines (the Directorate General of Swindles and Plunder), was reorganized and renamed the Service de Documentation Extérieure et de Contre-espionnage, the French service practically ceased operations for a time as intelligence barons and their political sponsors jockeyed for power.[19]

The reserve may also have revealed doubts concerning the quality of the product obtained from the French service. Despite its aggressive posture toward the Soviet target, in 1945–1946 the DGER/SDECE was still struggling to extend its coverage to all of Europe; for example, stations in Bulgaria, Hungary, and Romania seemed to have been established only in early 1946. Well into that year, much of what French intelligence learned concerning affairs in the Soviet-occupied areas of Europe came not from clandestine networks, but from interviews with refugees and prisoners of war returning to Austria, France, and Germany from the East.[20] As the flow of returnees diminished with time, the productivity of this source would also diminish. The resulting intelligence, moreover, was probably little better than that already available to American intelligence. SI France, for example, initially had high expectations concerning the closely guarded HAMPSHIRE/BARTON material that derived primarily from French surveillance of Russian communications. Rather quickly, however, hope turned to disappointment. Much of this material consisted of low-grade Red Army and Air Force communications in the Russian occupation zones of Germany and Austria, which found a ready, if narrow, audience in American intelligence circles. General Edwin Sibert, the chief of U.S. Army intelligence in Europe, greatly appreciated French information on Red Army order of battle in Central and Eastern Europe. By the end of 1945 the strength and deployment of Soviet military forces in those regions had become Sibert's chief concern, and until American intelligence could get on top of that target he was grateful for any relevant information he could receive no matter what the source.[21] Being less desperate, SSU's secret intelligence officers were less impressed with the French comint. As early as July 1945, SI France had cautioned Washington headquarters that HAMP-SHIRE/BARTON should be treated with reserve. The warning proved prescient. In October 1945 headquarters informed its station in Paris that the judgment of intelligence analysts and consumers in Washington concerning the accuracy of the HAMPSHIRE/BARTON material was "quite unfavorable." SI France continued to forward the material to Washington and its sister office in Germany, but if information is the currency of the intelligence business, the French product had been significantly devalued.[22]

While there was plenty of information *from* the French, there was relatively little *about* the French. As a condition of cooperation, the DGER had required the OSS mission in Paris to forsake any intelligence operations directed against France, a prohibition that was explicitly affirmed in December 1945 by a directive from General John Magruder, the director of the Strategic Services Unit, to his chief of station in Paris.[23] Despite this prohibition, Philip Horton used his personal contacts in Paris to pick up bits and pieces of information concerning political and economic affairs. By the spring of 1946 Horton's quiet—and officially nonsanctioned—efforts had developed into a rather ragtag string of informants that included a monsignor at the papal embassy, an expatriate Polish nobleman who claimed to have worked for British intelligence in the interwar period, a couple of former *résistants*, and the usual anti-communist Russian and East European émigrés who inevitably showed up on the doorsteps of every foreign intelligence officer in Paris. At least three of Horton's sources were usefully placed. One individual, a member of the staff of *Force Ouvriere*, the weekly newspaper of the communist trade union, had close relations with leading personalities in the union. Another individual was the chief adviser to the police service of the French occupation authority in the Saar. Horton's best source, whose access to high government circles in Paris was so good that the SI office insisted that his reports receive only restricted circulation, was the assistant to the chair of the foreign affairs committee in the Constituent Assembly, the legislative body in the immediate postwar period, and a close friend of Gaston Deferre, a rising figure in the Socialist Party.[24] Such sources hardly represented deep and systematic coverage of French affairs, but the Paris station was constrained by its gentlemen's agreement with French intelligence and Washington's prohibition against launching operations against the French government. To ensure more adequate coverage of French affairs, other stations had to pick up the slack.

As we have seen, the OSS/SSU missions in Austria and Germany provided intelligence coverage of political and economic conditions inside the French occupation zones in those countries. The small station that remained in Italy after VE Day monitored French activities on both sides of the Franco-Italian border, especially in the Val d'Aosta region, where Paris harbored territorial ambitions and where clandestine DGER agents were working with separatist groups.[25] The main effort to penetrate France, however, fell to the station in Switzerland. During the war the OSS station in Switzerland, a neutral island in an Axis sea, had been the most important American intelligence outpost in Europe, running operations into Austria, France, Germany, and Italy, but with the coming of peace its future was uncertain. Intelligence managers in Washington, preoccupied by the demands of demobilization, might wonder if Switzerland was sufficiently central to American foreign policy concerns to justify a permanent intelligence station. The presence of OSS offices in Austria, France, Germany, and Italy reduced the need to observe these countries from a distance, further undermining the rationale for a postwar office in Switzerland. For the intelligence officers in Bern, Geneva, and Zurich the message was clear; if you want to keep the store open, you need to drum up some business.

Under the direction of its energetic and ambitious chief, Henry Hyde, the secret intelligence section of OSS/SSU Switzerland aggressively pursued targets of opportunity, taking all of Europe as their province. Hyde's motto might well have been "Any target, any source, anywhere," and he certainly cared nothing for jurisdictional lines. Though resented by intelligence officers in other European stations who did not appreciate the Swiss station poaching on "their" territory, this buccaneering approach was facilitated by the failure of Washington to provide Hyde with any guidance or direction. In November 1945, for example, SI Switzerland caustically reminded headquarters, "We are still without the indispensable directives which would permit us to concentrate on what is really significant and to avoid the gathering of material which is without importance or which is already known. . . . As things presently stand we have only our own common sense and necessarily limited knowledge of European developments to guide us to our targets."[26] His "common sense" soon led Hyde to targets across Europe.

Secret intelligence officers, working under diplomatic cover as embassy clerks in Bern or vice-consuls in Geneva, Lugano, and Zurich, had developed a remarkably diverse list of sources who generated an eclectic collection of information: SAFEHAVEN material from the prince of Liechtenstein; news concerning Spanish politics and the conservative opposition to General Franco from an individual in the entourage of the pretender to the Spanish throne, Don Juan de Borbon; information about financial affairs and right-wing groups in Italy from Italian monarchists; intelligence concerning political developments and social and economic conditions in Austria and Germany from informant chains based in Catholic monasteries. In addition to sources inside Switzerland, such as a member of the federal parliament's foreign affairs committee, by the spring of 1946 Henry Hyde was running espionage networks in Austria, Czechoslovakia, France, Hungary, Italy, Liechtenstein, the Vatican, and Yugoslavia.[27] Although the quality of these networks may have been uneven—one wonders just how much secret information was available to cloistered monks—their production was impressive, and the small Swiss unit was a collection powerhouse among the American intelligence stations in Europe.

As early as July 1945 Hyde, casting about for postwar work for his secret intelligence officers, had begun to identify French targets for potential exploitation, particularly the circles around General Charles de Gaulle, the leader of the Free French movement and the head of the provisional government established in Paris. Hyde's intelligence shopping list included the identity of the advisers upon whom de Gaulle relied; the degree to which the general personally influenced the direction of French foreign policy; and his political and diplomatic intentions, particularly with regard to postwar control of the Ruhr and the Saar, cooperation with the Communist Party of France, and the prosecution of Marshal Philippe Petain, Pierre Laval, and other leaders of the Vichy regime.[28]

The Swiss station's operations against France were significantly advanced in the fall of 1945 with the recruitment of source ICARUS.[29] The identity of this individual remains unknown, although he was sufficiently well placed to attend, at least occasionally, de Gaulle's conferences with his advisers. He also seems to have had access to the highest levels of the French administration. Developed through Henry Hyde's personal friendship with a DGER official (as a wartime OSS officer Hyde had liaised with Free French intelligence), the source may well have been a former or serving French intelligence officer who moved in the circle around de Gaulle, a possibility further suggested by the fact that ICARUS often included DGER/SDECE appreciations in his reports. Whatever his identity, ICARUS was the prize thoroughbred in Hyde's stable, producing a stream of insider reports on a broad range of subjects. A selection of ICARUS reports from the first four months of 1946 included such items as a description of the political loyalties of the population of the Saar, complaints about Henri Ribière's tenure as SDECE director, an appraisal of general economic conditions in France, projections concerning the outcome of legislative elections scheduled for the late spring of 1946, communist infiltration of the French police, and de Gaulle's conviction that war between Russia and the West was inevitable.[30]

While agents garnered information concerning French internal politics, communications intelligence provided the best window on French foreign policy. During the war the cryptanalysts at Arlington Hall, the former girls' school outside Washington that became the headquarters for the U.S. Army's code-breaking activities, had cracked several codes and ciphers used by the Vichy regime, but Free French cryptosystems had proven more resistant to attack. Only toward the end of 1944 were American code breakers able to break the high-grade systems that protected the most confidential messages of the Gaullists. Building upon these successes, Arlington accelerated its attack upon French communications, and the list of readable French codes and ciphers continued to grow. The attack did not end with the war. By early 1946 American intelligence was able to read every code and cipher used by the French foreign ministry and most of the systems used by the colonial ministry and the French army.[31]

The intelligence product of these code-breaking successes was significant; indeed between September 1945 and April 1946, French decrypts represented anywhere from 30 to 50 percent of the items included in the top secret "Diplomatic Summary," the daily compendium of communications intelligence that circulated among a handful of senior decision makers in Washington. By providing access to the confidential reports of French ambassadors, these decrypts supplemented the reporting of American diplomats in foreign capitals. They also provided insight into France's diplomatic activities and intentions on political and economic topics ranging from the expansion of French air service companies into South America to the competition between France and China for influence in Southeast Asia.[32]

Decrypts, unfortunately, shed no light on French domestic politics or on a subject of particular importance for American officials who concerned themselves with France: the Parti Communiste Français (PCF). With the collapse of Germany a reconstructed France would be the strongest continental power in Western Europe. If the PCF came to power, the consequences for the rest of the continent could hardly fail to be profound and, from Washington's perspective, disastrous. During the last year of the war OSS had warned the White House and the State Department repeatedly that the French communists had been empowered by their leading role in the resistance and by the admiration the French felt toward the Soviet Union for its preeminent contribution to Allied victory in Europe.[33] The leadership of the PCF, having been tutored in the national front strategy by Stalin himself, adopted a reassuringly democratic tone, but nonetheless there were grounds for concern. The immediate postwar period saw repeated warnings that the communists were colonizing critical ministries, creating cells in the army, and extending their influence in various regions of France.

American intelligence had no sources in the leadership circles of the French Communist Party. To compensate for this lack of direct access, OSS and SSU had to depend upon a variety of secondary sources, many of doubtful reliability. The most prolific were the anticommunist Russian émigrés. Before the war Paris had become the home of a large colony of White Russians who had fled their homeland after the Bolshevik Revolution. Consumed by fear and hatred of Bolshevism and all its works, intent upon convincing Western governments to embrace that fear and hatred, and desperate for financial patrons, the émigrés produced a stream of alarmist claims concerning the perfidious intrigues of Moscow and its minions in the Communist Party. As with all disinformation, this material was intended to capture the attention and influence the behavior of the reader while affirming the continued value and importance of the source in order to justify financial subsidies for that source. Invariably the émigré reports pointed to an imminent communist seizure of power in France: Soviet aircraft were dropping arms to communist partisans in the provinces, small groups of armed men from Central Europe were entering France through Belgium, communists were smuggling artillery into France from Switzerland, covert Soviet radio stations were broadcasting nightly throughout the country. Much of this information came from YORK/BINGLEY, a source that Philip Horton described as "an anti-Soviet Russian émigré group comprising members of both the old and the new Russian emigration." The Paris station maintained contact with this source only through a cutout, a certain Captain Bernard, whom Horton identifies as "a young French resistance member, extreme Rightist."[34] The reports from YORK/BINGLEY were unfailingly sensational. In January 1946, for example, that source reported that a hospital established outside Paris in the suburb of St. Germain-en-Laye by the Soviet Reparations Commission for France was in reality a secret Red Army base and that a Soviet aircraft on a clandestine mission to ferry arms to the PCF had crashed outside the town of Châlons-sur-Marne, an incident the French government allegedly decided to conceal. Reports of nighttime air drops of weapons to the PCF became rather a staple of early postwar intelligence reporting from France. Only in 1948 did a thorough investigation by the U.S. military attaché in Paris demonstrate conclusively that the reports were without foundation.[35]

Philip Horton was inclined to accept such reports uncritically, in particular assigning high value to the product from YORK/BINGLEY. Washington, however, did not share their station chief's confidence, although they did not always dismiss the information out of hand. In April 1946 YORK/BINGLEY reported that Polish planes were secretly ferrying weapons into Paris's Le Bourget airport in preparation for a communist insurrection. For their return flights the aircraft were loaded with shackled émigré Russian anticommunists kidnapped, apparently, off the streets of the French capital by Stalin's secret police. This scenario was, to say the least, rather unlikely and, not surprisingly, the news was received at SSU headquarters with skepticism. YORK/BINGLEY overreached again in May when the Paris station reported that "our tested and usually reliable anti-Soviet Russian émigré source" had reported indications that "The Soviets are preparing to occupy Western Europe, and particularly France, under one pretext or another, during the course of the summer." Headquarters, which may have begun to wonder about the judgment of its station chief in the French capital, refused to give the story any credence. "No dissemination. Tripe" reads the impatient assessment scrawled across the report by a desk officer in Washington.[36]

Despite Washington's skepticism toward the more alarmist reports emerging from its Paris station, headquarters was not beyond disseminating to its customers equally improbable news. The postwar period was still young, and the rules of the new international community were not yet clear. No one had a strong sense of what was to be expected from the USSR and its protégés in Western Europe, although experience and cultural disposition likely inclined many American and Western European officials to expect mischief from them. Some of the wildest reports about the Soviets and the communist parties, moreover, had a more general currency. They were the stuff not only of secret intelligence reports but of diplomatic cables, press accounts, and popular discussion. In the spring of 1946, for example, there was a flurry of reports concerning an imminent communist coup in France that would be supported by 50,000 Russian paratroopers who were gathering for the purpose in Czechoslovakia. The sources for this news were the suspect émigré organizations in Paris and Brussels. A certain Prince Bagration (code-named YORK/BRIDLINGTON), for example, actually presented SSU officers in Paris with what purported to be a directive from Moscow for the forcible Sovietization of France.[37] The impressionable Horton immediately shared the document with the American ambassador and military attaché in Paris and forwarded it to Washington, where it reached the State Department, G-2, ONI, and the FBI. Although leveler heads scoffed at the warnings—the British secret service dismissing the reports as fabrications by right-wing elements in France angling for American support and the intelligence section of United States Forces European Theater helpfully pointing out that there were not 50,000 paratroopers in the entire Soviet army—the reports were the subject of high-level meetings in Washington that gave General Joseph McNarney, USFET's commander, discretionary authority to move U.S. Army units into France to protect important supply depots.[38] There was, of course, no coup.

In late 1946 there was a new scare when Western capitals were abuzz with rumors that communist-led brigades of volunteers, patterned after those that had served in the Spanish Civil War, were poised to intervene in Spain and Greece in the cause of a communist revolution. These rumors, especially rife in France and Italy, became the subject of continent-wide intelligence reporting. Usually reliable sources, such as ICARUS and the AIREDALES, reported efforts by refugee Spanish Republicans to acquire large quantities of arms in preparation for a rebellion against Franco. Right-wing fabricators, such as YORK/BINGLEY, contrived ever more alarming stories in which small bands of impoverished exiles subsisting in refugee camps swelled into legions of thousands who stood ready not only to renew the civil war in Spain but to attack France with the aid of Soviet or, alternatively, Yugoslav paratroopers. From Italy SSU's representative, James Angleton, passed on reports from his sources in northern Italy that Italian volunteers were departing for Spain.[39] When, by the end of 1946, neither the much-anticipated international brigades nor the associated Spanish insurrection had appeared, the alarm passed, although excitement briefly returned in early 1947 when rumors spread of international brigades forming in Yugoslavia to assist a communist revolution in Greece. These brigades were also imaginary, but like the rumors of a communist coup in France the previous spring, they were the occasion for high-level meetings in Washington, where they appeared in White House working papers and State Department instructions to its embassies. In October 1947 the president of France, Vincent Auriol, noted in his diary "extremely grave information" from the Americans, who were "very concerned and following closely the reconstitution of the international brigades."[40]

Philip Horton's best source on the PCF, although given his enthusiasm for the anticommunist émigrés he may not have known it at the time, was code-named HAMPSHIRE/BRAMLEY-1. Born into a royalist family, this individual had pursued a career in industry and at the time of his connection with U.S. intelligence, the summer of 1945, was a director on the boards of several large businesses. He claimed to represent an informal association of prominent—though unnamed—industrialists, businessmen, scientists, and intellectuals who claimed the mantle of France's modern elite and disdained the regime of General Charles de Gaulle. This group sought for France close cooperation with the United States as the only alternative to Soviet dominance of Europe and hoped to provide information to balance the allegedly erroneous and distorted intelligence originating in official French sources. According to HAMPSHIRE/BRAMLEY-1, this information would include items resulting from his group's contacts among the leadership of the French Communist Party.[41] The promise of access to the inner circle of the PCF may have opened eyes in SSU offices, but it would also have raised eyebrows. Was it likely that representatives of France's financial and industrial elite would rub elbows with representatives of France's proletariat? Would the leaders of the PCF share confidential information with their class enemies?

At first glance there was little to distinguish HAMPSHIRE/BRAM-LEY-1 from the many con men, fabricators, and fantasists who created a veritable cottage industry of disinformation around the offices of intelligence services across Europe. In their effort to empty the pockets or influence the attitudes of their American contacts, these sources invariably claimed special and privileged access to the inner circles of whatever groups—communists, fascists, monarchists, anarchists—worried these contacts at the time. Surprisingly, HAMPSHIRE/BRAMLEY-1 appears to have been something else. He worked closely with a left-wing journalist, code-named HAMP-SHIRE/BRAMLEY-2, who had long experience as a political analyst and commentator in Paris. This journalist may have been the channel into the PCF. Whatever its organization, the HAMPSHIRE/BRAMLEY chain accurately described the PCF's commitment to pursuing power through a national front strategy and "bourgeois democracy." During a meeting in Moscow on 19 November 1944, Stalin had personally emphasized to Maurice Thorez, the leader of the PCF, the need to abandon confrontation in favor of conciliatory and moderate policies that would appeal to a broad swathe of French public opinion and make possible a coalition of left-wing forces, under communist guidance, that would come to power through elections. In March 1946 HAMPSHIRE/BRAMLEY passed to SSU France a report based on personal conversations with a member of the PCF's central committee. This communist leader revealed that though the party had grown less sanguine about its electoral prospects—in the multiparty elections for the Constituent Assembly the previous October the PCF had come in first with 26 percent of the vote—and more fearful of rightist reaction in the country, it remained committed to a parliamentary strategy of pursuing power in coalition with the socialists. Later that month the chain passed along comments Maurice Thorez made to a meeting of the party's central committee. Reportedly the communist leader had noted that neither the United States nor the USSR wanted a war and that a conflict was unlikely for the next five or six years. Thorez also told the central committee that the PCF would probably not acquire a dominant political position in France in the near future, since that position would require the party to lead a stable communist-socialist majority coalition, an unlikely outcome given the competitive multiparty system and the relative balance among the political left, center, and right.[42]

At a time when other sources, such as the Russian émigrés of the YORK/BINGLEY network, were predicting on a weekly basis imminent catastrophes from communist revolution to aerial invasion, HAMPSHIRE/BRAM-

LEY presented a less alarming picture of the communists and their intentions. If Philip Horton was inclined toward the alarmist perspective, the American ambassador in Paris, Jefferson Caffery, was not. The ambassador's dispatches to the State Department appear to have been influenced by the HAMPSHIRE/BRAMLEY reports, all of which SSU shared with the embassy. Throughout 1946 Caffery consistently assured Washington that the PCF would not resort to violence to seize power.[43] SSU France can likely claim some credit for the realism and moderation that distinguished the ambassador's reporting, even as it must bear a measure of responsibility for occasionally making the political situation in France appear more perilous than it was.

Italy

At the time of Germany's surrender, the Office of Strategic Services was well established on the Italian peninsula. From their earliest operations in support of the Allied invasion of Sicily in July 1943 to their role in securing the surrender of the last German and Italian fascist military units in northern Italy in April 1945, OSS elements, particularly secret intelligence (SI), special operations (SO), and morale operations (MO) units, participated actively in the Italian campaign. Their contributions covered the gamut of clandestine activity—neutralizing Axis garrisons on the Ventotene and Lipari Islands; infiltrating espionage teams behind enemy lines by plane, PT boat, or submarine; arming and training resistance groups in hostile territory; and catching the spies sent across the battle lines by the enemy intelligence services. The work of OSS Italy's secret intelligence section proved especially important. American ground commanders relied on SI for information concerning the enemy's order of battle and the movements and location of enemy units. For their part, air commanders were assisted in preparing their target folders and planning their air attacks by information collected by SI observers concerning road and rail networks, bridges, transportation hubs, and railway repair and production facilities.[44]

On 8 September 1943, the Italian government abandoned the Axis by announcing an armistice with the Allies. The previous July, King Vittorio Emanuele III had dismissed Benito Mussolini, the fascist leader of Italy since 1922, and appointed a career army officer, Marshal Pietro Badoglio, as prime minister. Mussolini had been arrested and confined. Upon learning of the armistice, German troops poured into Italy, freeing Mussolini and removing him to the north, and occupying Rome on September 10. The king, Marshal Badoglio, and senior government officials fled Rome for the Allied-controlled south, where they aligned Italy and its remaining military resources with the Allies against its erstwhile partner, Germany. When the Allies liberated Rome in early June 1944, the Committee of National Liberation (CLN), a coalition of antifascist political groups, seized the political initiative and formed a new national government under the well-known antifascist figure Ivanoe Bonomi. The new regime forced Badoglio from power and left open the question of the future of the monarchy.

Despite Italy's shift in loyalties, OSS continued to attack Italian as well as German intelligence targets as Allied forces fought their way up the peninsula. At the time of Germany's final surrender in May 1945, SI officers in Rome, Milan, and Palermo were directing dozens of informant chains against political, military, and economic targets. The highest levels of Italian government and society were penetrated. In Rome alone, the OSS claimed twenty-nine highly placed sources inside the administration of Prime Minister Bonomi and the six political parties that made up his coalition government. The informants included Bonomi himself, Count Carlo Sforza, a leading antifascist political figure who, after the armistice, returned from exile and assumed a position as minister without portfolio in Bonomi's cabinet, Benedetto Croce, a well-known philosopher who also served as minister without portfolio, Randolfo Pacciardi, the head of the Republican Party, Pietro Nenni, leader of the Socialists, Alcide De Gasperi, chief of the Vatican-backed Christian Democratic Party, and (perhaps most surprisingly) Palmiro Togliatti, the leader of the Communist Party, and two or three of his party associates. In the foreign ministry alone, American intelligence received information from the ministry's secretary general ("has been very cooperative and has acted exclusively with us on several highly secret and important matters") and several of his subordinates. Many of these sources may simply have volunteered information on occasion and may not have been under American control or direction, but some, De Gasperi for example, were actually on the OSS payroll, receiving monthly subsidies from their American handlers.[45] This broad penetration of governing circles continued throughout the early postwar period, probably reaching its height when, in December 1945, Alcide De Gasperi, a paid informant, became prime minister.

OSS elements in other parts of the country were no less industrious. Among these elements the Palermo Unit could claim seniority, having been in continuous operation since September 1943. After the armistice the unit's SI officers extended their operations from Sicily to the region of Reggio Calabria in the toe of the Italian peninsula. They developed excellent contacts inside local police agencies and the prefectures that were principally responsible for the administration of the provinces. The intelligence product included confidential documents covering political and economic affairs in southern Italy, including the activities of the Mafia and separatist organizations; reports from the police commissioners of the various provinces, who monitored political as well as criminal activity; and the monthly information bulletins of the general commanding the Carabinieri (military police) units in the region. A host of American military and civilian agencies in Sicily, particularly the State Department, the Office of War Information, the Office of Naval Intelligence, and the Counterintelligence Corps, relied on this intelligence to perform their tasks; for example, 75 percent of the reports forwarded to Washington by State Department representatives in Sicily after the liberation of that island were based on information provided by OSS Palermo.[46]

In the final days of the war, as German resistance faded and the remnants of the Italian Social Republic, a rump fascist government established by Mussolini under German auspices in the northern Italian town of Salo, collapsed in ignominy, an OSS team entered Milan and immediately began scouring the city and its hinterland for fugitive fascists and the archives of various ministries of the so-called Salo Republic that were said to be hidden in the area.[47] Under the energetic direction of Major Max Corvo, SI officers quickly recruited a chain of informants that covered political, economic, and industrial targets in and around Milan and monitored the activities of local partisan bands to determine their relative strengths, identify their political affiliations, and locate their weapons caches.[48]

The OSS detachment assigned to Turin did not reach the city until 15 May 1945, but by July it had established six intelligence networks that covered industrial and social conditions in Turin itself, agricultural problems in the nearby provinces of Alessandria and Asti, the activities of the strong communist resistance organization in Novara, and French political machinations and military dispositions in the Val d'Aosta and along the Franco-Italian border. To better cover the latter target, OSS Turin sent agents across the border to identify French army units deployed along the boundary. When, after the German surrender, press reports announced that French forces had withdrawn from Italian border valleys, Turin's agents correctly informed their headquarters that the French army had not left Italian territory and that French policy concerning the postwar status of the border regions, where Paris harbored annexationist ambitions, was not as conciliatory as the press suggested.[49]

With operational bases in the major Italian cities, informant chains covering every region from the Alps to the heel of the peninsula, and sources in the highest reaches of the government, no other country division in OSS was better positioned than SI Italy to face the intelligence challenges of the postwar period. These challenges promised to be both numerous and daunting.

Italian political, economic, and social institutions had to weather not just the transition from war to peace, but also the shift from the authoritarianism of fascism to some yet unformed but ideally more liberal regime. The dislocations caused by these changes threatened to fuel instability and unrest that, in turn, would require the attention of the Allied powers and complicate the reconstruction of the country. The political transition might prove especially rocky since it would raise questions concerning the future of the monarchy (compromised in the eyes of many Italians by its accommodation with Mussolini and his disastrous war policies), the status of former fascists, the nature of the postwar regime, and the inevitable competition for power among the various political groups, such as the communists and the socialists, which had been suppressed by the fascists only to reemerge after the liberation of Rome as major elements in the armed, antifascist resistance. Additionally, Italy's geographic position made it a good platform from which to observe the activities of the new and unpredictable regimes established across the Adriatic Sea in Yugoslavia and Albania by, respectively, Josip Broz Tito and Enver Hoxha and their communist partisans. Such a platform would be especially valuable given Tito's aggressive designs on the port of Trieste and the region of Venezia Giulia.

Proud of their accomplishments and convinced that Italy would remain a significant intelligence arena in the immediate postwar period, OSS officers were shocked when in late May 1945, without warning, Washington headquarters recalled from the field the chief of secret intelligence in Italy, Vincent Scamporino, and his director of operations, Max Corvo, and ordered SI officers in the country to curtail their operations in anticipation of terminating all intelligence activity, closing all SI facilities, and repatriating personnel by mid-July. The explanation from Washington was that headquarters wanted to eliminate wartime structures and operations in Italy prior to a reorganization that would eventually produce a new secret intelligence organization for the country. What headquarters did not say was that the demise of SI Italy had been provoked by an evaluation of the unit prepared in April by Robert Joyce, the senior officer for Rear Zone Intelligence in Europe. While acknowledging the wartime accomplishments of the unit, Joyce concluded that postwar intelligence requirements in Italy would differ significantly from those of wartime and that "the present personnel of Italian SI is not by background, education and training prepared to cope with entirely new problems of secret intelligence of a non-military nature." Joyce also noted that in an effort to ingratiate themselves with the victors, Italian officials at all levels of government were falling over themselves in the rush to provide information to the Americans. In such circumstances there was little need for clandestine intelligence since the press and overt American organizations, such as the State Department, could easily gather necessary information.[50] That same month, Joyce's report was the focus of attention at a meeting in Paris attended by senior OSS officials, including Whitney Shepardson, director of the Secret Intelligence Branch at Washington headquarters, and Allen Dulles, chief of the OSS station in Switzerland and the acknowledged dean of American intelligence on the continent. The meeting endorsed Joyce's position and recommended it to Washington, where it sparked the decision to reorganize OSS operations in Italy.

As they paid off their informants, prepared their final reports, and packed their bags, field officers, unaware of the earlier deliberations in Paris, concluded that the sudden demise of SI Italy was due to a combination of headquarters politics, bruised egos, and ethnic prejudice. In the Washington offices of OSS, Earl Brennan, chief of the Italian section, had developed among his fellow managers a reputation for abrasiveness and independence. A similar reputation afflicted his field officers, who not infrequently exhibited impatience with bureaucratic procedures and the chain of command, and who often launched operations over the objections of senior managers. This impatience was especially evident in the days after Germany's surrender when Allen Dulles, still basking in the glory of his role in Operation Sunrise, the capitulation of all German forces in Italy, and perhaps assuming that SI Italy would soon be a thing of the past, swaggered unannounced into the offices of the OSS team in Milan to sort out certain jurisdictional issues regarding the operations of OSS units in Italy and Switzerland. Irritated by his visitor's arrogant and patronizing attitude, Vincent Scamporino responded with some blunt and undiplomatic language. Dulles stomped from the meeting, muttering that he had never been so humiliated in his life. Such impolitic gestures did not endear SI Italy to anyone and probably fueled the whispers heard in headquarters corridors that, maybe, there were too many rough and hot-headed Italian-Americans in the unit and that some personnel changes might be appropriate.[51]

By midsummer 1945, SI Italy had ceased to exist, but not all OSS operations in the country were terminated. In late 1944 the X-2 regional headquarters in London had dispatched to Rome James Angleton, a 27-year-old officer whose natural talents in the arcane art of counterintelligence had propelled him through the ranks from corporal to lieutenant in six months. Angleton assumed command of the local X-2 office, a floundering unit that had lost the respect and cooperation of other American and Allied services because of poor management and inability to stay on top of the activities of enemy espionage organizations. Within weeks of his arrival, the energetic young lieutenant had revitalized morale in his new command, renewed contacts with sister services, and reinvigorated counterintelligence operations across the Italian peninsula.[52] Impressed by Angleton's success, reassured by his quiet, nonconfrontational professionalism, and, most importantly, reminded that the vetting and security tasks normally performed by X-2 units remained useful at a time when fugitive fascists and the potential resurgence of extreme right-wing groups continued to preoccupy American officials in Italy, OSS managers decided to retain a small X-2 office in the Eternal City even after the closure of SI operations.

In the immediate aftermath of Germany's surrender, X-2 Italy continued to emphasize its counterintelligence and security functions: chasing fugitive fascists, identifying former agents of the German intelligence services, sorting out the legitimate from the suspect among the Albanian, Belgian, Croatian, Dutch, French, Hungarian, Norwegian, Polish, Romanian, and Serb refugees and former POWs who now appeared in surprising numbers in Italian cities, and vetting Italians whose claims for visas, jobs, or financial compensation brought them to the attention of American authorities. In the fall of 1945, however, Angleton's unit began to diversify its operations beyond its formal assignment of counterintelligence and security.[53]

OSS managers could eliminate SI Italy, but they could not eliminate the need for Italian intelligence. American military and political authorities in country and in Washington still required information concerning political personalities and events in Italy but—as was the case in other countries of early postwar Europe—American organizations dedicated to the collection of such information, especially in its more clandestine forms, were not to be found on every *piazza* or *corso* in Rome. When it came to espionage the State Department would not even agree to try. The intelligence arms of the military services tended to focus on narrow order-of-battle issues and had very weak collection capabilities. The only military unit with field agents in Italy was the Army's Counterintelligence Corps (CIC), but in early postwar Italy this organization focused primarily on providing security services at ports and army bases, mopping up the remnants of the German intelligence service in Italy and apprehending war criminals who were hiding in the northern part of the country.[54] In the first year of peace clandestine collection of political, military and economic intelligence was not part of CIC Italy's job description. There remained, therefore, a real need for an organization to conduct offensive intelligence operations. Jim Angleton moved to satisfy that need.

As William Donovan's senior representative in Italy at a time when uncertainty about the future of OSS and the scope and nature of postwar American intelligence distracted senior managers in Washington and weakened their supervision of field operations, Angleton had substantial independence to define his unit's mission. This independence was further encouraged, by the autumn of 1945, by the departure from Italy of other OSS elements, such as SI, that might have jealously challenged any perceived encroachments on their turf by an aggressive X-2 unit. Left largely to his own devices and unchallenged by organizational competitors, Angleton moved into the vacuum created by the closure of SI Italy and began to collect positive intelligence.

Operating in Rome, as "Special Counterintelligence Unit Z" (SCI/Z), from a suite of rooms in a nondescript apartment block on the Via Sicilia, just around the corner from the American embassy on the Via Veneto, Angleton supervised five field offices, all in north Italy. A unit in Genoa was responsible for watching French activity in northern Italy, and to that end it controlled a subunit in San Remo that was particularly charged with monitoring illegal and clandestine activities along the Franco-Italian border. In cooperation with the Italian police the Genoa unit was also responsible for maintaining security in that important port and across the coastal region of Liguria. An office in Milan monitored political and economic developments in the financial capital of the country and directed the work of a subunit in Turin that was chiefly concerned with political activities of leftist groups in Italy's industrial heartland. The unit in Trieste had the most difficult assignment. That city and its hinterland were contested by Italy and Yugoslavia, and both countries considered the region a fertile field for clandestine political, propaganda, and paramilitary operations. Since the Yugoslav leader, Tito, had on more than one occasion proclaimed his intention to incorporate Trieste into a communist Yugoslavia, Angleton's men in Trieste were particularly concerned with monitoring Tito's military and intelligence services.[55]

Like other OSS/SSU units in postwar Europe, Special Counterintelligence Unit Z suffered from a shortage of personnel. At the end of the war, OSS Italy had been one of the largest divisions in William Donovan's secret army, but by the end of 1945 demobilization had reduced that force to a corporal's guard. As late as October 1945 the Italian station still deployed 42 officers, 116 enlisted personnel, and 39 civilians. By January 1946, however, Angleton's command, including the field offices in northern Italy, had shrunk to 13 officers, 9 enlisted personnel, and 14 civilians.[56] This truncated force was barely sufficient to handle the security and vetting side of its responsibilities. Once it added positive intelligence collection to its routine counterintelligence and security tasks, the force was completely inadequate. The wartime contacts and informant chains so diligently nurtured by OSS had been shut down when SI withdrew from the country, and it would take time and personnel to rebuild them. Angleton realized that, for the foreseeable future, reinforcement from the United States was unlikely. If SCI/Z was to succeed in its expanded mission, it would have to look for help in other places. Angleton decided to look close to home.

Because Italy had switched sides after the armistice of September 1943, the Italian armed services remained in existence, as did their respective espionage organizations, the army's Servizio Informazioni Militari (SIM) and the navy's Servizio Informazioni Segrete (SIS). These military resources had been deployed in support of operations against German forces in Italy. Four Italian army divisions—designated "combat groups"—saw action in the Allied push into northern Italy, while Italian naval vessels patrolled and engaged in convoy duties alongside Allied fleet units in the Mediterranean.[57] The Office of Strategic Services had moved quickly to establish connections with the military intelligence services as well as the Pubblica Sicurezza, the civilian police agency in the Interior Ministry. Collaboration with the naval service became particularly close. Within days of the armistice Italian naval intelligence had already agreed to provide OSS with fast motorboats to infiltrate American agents into German-occupied northern Italy.[58] Upon his arrival in Rome, Angleton set out to expand these liaison arrangements. In November 1944, for example, he was talking to Captain Carlo Resio, chief of intelligence in the SIS about using some of Resio's radio operators for clandestine missions behind German lines. About this time, Resio (codenamed SALTY by OSS) began sharing with Angleton the product from SIS espionage networks. The X-2 chief also used Pubblica Sicurezza files and investigators to identify fugitive fascists and German agents in Allied-controlled areas.[59] Carefully nurtured during the final months of the war, these liaison relations offered a partial solution to Angleton's postwar problems. The Americans could compensate for their lack of resources by piggybacking on the operations and agent networks of their Italian friends.

By early 1946 the Italian services had become "the most useful sources of information" for SCI/Z.[60] Angleton relied almost exclusively on his Italian partners in the Pubblica Sicurezza and the Carabinieri (military police) for the investigative and surveillance work so necessary for the security and vetting tasks that, well into 1946, represented the bulk of his unit's work. In the counterintelligence field he received from the Carabinieri and the military intelligence agencies information on the operations inside Italy of foreign intelligence services, particularly the NKVD, France's Service de Documentation Extérieure et de Contre-espionnage (SDECE), and Tito's Otsek Zascita Naroda (OZNA), as well as the clandestine activities of the political and information agencies of various émigré groups, such as the Albanians, Croats, and Georgians. Liaison, moreover, was not limited to security and counterintelligence matters; positive intelligence also poured into the offices on the Via Sicilia. The Italian services, particularly SIS, routinely shared with SCI/Z their periodic surveys of political conditions across Italy and the activities of various Italian political parties and organizations. Since their reach extended beyond their borders, particularly into the Balkans, the Italians also provided intelligence concerning such foreign topics as the order of battle of the Yugoslavian army, political and economic conditions inside Yugoslavia, political developments in Albania, and the naval dispositions of various Mediterranean powers. Clandestine Italian lines into Albania and Yugoslavia were especially valuable, since the wartime American intelligence missions that had been sent into those countries to observe and support the partisan resistance had been recalled at the end of the war.[61]

While valuing the connections to the Italian secret services, Angleton was too good an intelligence officer to rely primarily on sources whose interests and goals might diverge from those of the United States and its intelligence station in Italy. Alternative sources were necessary, not merely to expand collection but also to check the biases of his partners in the Italian services. Within the limits imposed by personnel shortages, SCI/Z's chief set out to develop an independent network of informants. His first effort was a disaster.

In the fall of 1944 SI Italy had accepted an offer of services from an individual purporting to be in touch with a source inside the Vatican who was prepared to sell to the Americans documents concerning papal affairs. SI code-named this source VESSEL. About the same time, James Angleton, freshly arrived in Rome and unaware of SI's arrangement, received a similar offer from an individual whom the X-2 officer code-named DUSTY.[62] From Washington's perspective the appearance of VESSEL/DUSTY was most opportune, coming at the very time that American intelligence was increasingly interested in the world behind the high walls of Vatican City. During the war more than thirty countries maintained diplomatic relations with the Vatican. Vatican City was too small to provide space for foreign diplomatic missions, so the embassies and legations were located elsewhere in the city of Rome. When Italy entered the war, the representatives of the Allied powers were forced to leave Italian territory and move into Vatican City, which was recognized as sovereign and neutral territory.

With the liberation of Rome in June 1944, Axis diplomats accredited to the Holy See had abandoned their embassies and residences in the city proper and moved into the neutral territory of Vatican City, occupying the same apartments that had just been vacated by the diplomatic representatives of Britain, Belgium, Poland, the United States, and other Allied governments, who were now free to move into larger accommodations in Rome. Allied intelligence authorities considered these Axis diplomats in the middle of the Eternal City a security threat that demanded vigilance. Additionally, many former officials in Mussolini's now discredited regime had sought refuge in monasteries and religious houses in Rome, and these fugitives required apprehension or at least surveillance, requirements that might be facilitated by confidential contacts inside the Vatican.

In the minds of American intelligence authorities VESSEL also was the key to a veritable Aladdin's cave of secrets. Like their counterparts in other countries these officers believed that the pope sat at the center of an intelligence web along whose strands flowed information from a worldwide network of bishops, priests, monks, nuns, and pious Catholic laypeople. At a conference of German intelligence and security officers in 1941 a speaker had warned his audience that "every Catholic is practically speaking an instrument of [the pope's] intelligence operation." Such views were commonplace in the secret services and foreign ministries of the world, including those of the United States. In 1939 the American ambassador in Rome had urged Washington to establish an embassy at the Vatican with the argument that "the Vatican would be a new source of political information of the highest importance." Officials in the State Department concurred. Ambassador Hugh Wilson, upon his return to Washington from the embassy in Berlin, asserted that the Holy Father had "the best information service in Europe," while Sumner Welles, the undersecretary of state, agreed that "the detailed and accurate knowledge of the Holy See of conditions in every part of the world, particularly in the countries of Europe, is proverbial."[63] Such views, while widespread, were without foundation. The "every priest a spy" trope was, perhaps, one of the most enduring myths associated with the Papacy. In reality, the pope was not the best-informed ruler in Europe, but one of the worst-informed; American intelligence officers, however, embracing the myth, believed that anyone who penetrated Vatican City would access a treasure trove of secrets, concerning not only the Papacy, but many other countries, including Germany and Japan.[64]

By the fall of 1944, Washington was also increasingly concerned about the Vatican's attitude toward the role of the Soviet Union and communist political parties in postwar Europe. The Papacy's suspicion of the "godless" regime in Moscow might complicate Great Power relations in the Catholic countries of postwar Europe, especially those, such as Poland and Hungary, that would find themselves in the shadow of a victorious and powerful Soviet Union. Additionally, a hostile attitude toward Russia on the part of the Vatican might reverberate in American domestic politics as American Catholics responded to the anticommunist cues of religious authorities in Rome. In the last year of the war Washington worked assiduously to convince the Vatican that Catholicism and Western Europe had nothing to fear from a powerful Soviet Union. The success of this effort depended, in part, on identifying the Vatican's specific concerns and anticipating its moves. Unfortunately, hard intelligence on the Vatican was a rare commodity.

For much of the war, Washington's best source on the Papacy had been Harold Tittmann, a State Department officer and assistant to Myron Taylor,

Franklin Roosevelt's personal representative to Pope Pius XII. Unlike his boss, who lived in the United States and made flying visits to the Vatican, Tittmann resided in Rome, but moved into the neutral territory of Vatican City when Italy declared war on the United States. An experienced and conscientious diplomat, Tittmann diligently kept Washington informed of events and personalities inside the papal enclave, but he avoided any suggestion of espionage from fear of embarrassing the pope and compromising U.S.-Vatican relations. On one occasion he actually refused to accept from an anti-Nazi officer in German military intelligence information concerning the dispositions of the German army.[65] Tittmann's refusal to act as a spy would have been less troublesome if someone else was available to step into the role, but for most of the war the United States had no spies inside the Vatican.

American intelligence had been tardy in establishing coverage of the Vatican, and its early efforts produced only modest results. In the fall of 1943 the code breakers in the U.S. Army's Signal Security Agency had opened an attack on the ciphers that protected the correspondence exchanged by the Vatican and its nuncios (ambassadors) in foreign capitals. Although they managed to break a cipher used by the Vatican for messages involving routine administrative and nonconfidential matters, they made no headway against the higher-grade cryptosystems that protected the more important and sensitive communications of papal diplomats. After several months of effort the code breakers simply gave up their attempt to crack the pope's ciphers.[66] Communications intelligence, America's most potent collection method against most countries, would not work against the Papacy, so other methods were required.

The efforts of the Office of Strategic Services were hardly more successful. Preoccupied by the need to support military operations against the Fascist regime, SI Italy initially had little time and few resources for the Vatican, which was militarily irrelevant. Political geography was also a problem. Until the fall of Rome in June 1944, Vatican City remained a small neutral island in a sea of fascists and Nazis, and American intelligence faced imposing problems in gaining access to papal territory and personnel. Even after the liberation of the Italian capital brought OSS detachments into the Eternal City and, figuratively, to the doorstep of the pope, American intelligence was slow to move against the Vatican. The first clandestine effort was PILGRIM'S PROGRESS, a project to exploit the ecclesiastical contacts of Father Felix Morlion, an anti-Nazi Dominican friar and journalist who, before the war, had directed the Brussels office of Pro Deo, an organization devoted to propagating specifically Catholic perspectives on political, economic, and social issues. Relocating to the United States after the German conquest of Belgium, Father Morlion established the Catholic International Press (CIP), a news service affiliated with Pro Deo. In the summer of 1944, he moved to Rome as CIP's resident correspondent, and he immediately began to cultivate a range of influential contacts in the ecclesiastical milieu of the Eternal City. These contacts provided material for the press dispatches he filed for CIP and for the special reports that found their way (along secure OSS lines) to intelligence offices in Washington. Unfortunately Morlion's rather verbose reports were judged largely useless by analysts. Reflecting their author's special interest in Catholic education and social action, the reports were fat with information regarding such topics as current trends in Catholic social theory, plans for the spiritual development of workers, and prospects for Catholic secondary education in a postwar Europe, but they were lean on factual and timely information concerning political developments inside the Vatican. At OSS headquarters, where analysts were much more interested in the Vatican's support for the Italian monarchy or the pope's attitude about a postwar international organization than a review of the nineteenth-century origins of the Catholic labor movement or prospects for government aid to parochial schools in postwar Belgium, not a few intelligence managers dismissed the earnest friar's reports as little more than clerical-conservative social propaganda. PILGRIM'S PROGRESS simply failed to provide the access to Vatican decision-making circles that Washington required.[67]

A second effort at espionage was only slightly more successful. In December of 1944 Martin Quigley, an OSS officer who had previously served in Ireland, arrived in the Eternal City ostensibly as the representative of American film companies interested in scouting postwar markets. Washington had sent Quigley to Rome to gather information from the Vatican but with the rather curious instruction to reveal his mission to papal officials should he conclude that such transparency would advance his mission. Since the agent immediately implemented this latter directive, his mission partook of more a quiet liaison channel than a clandestine operation, and the information he passed to the local OSS station via dead drops (he operated independently and had no contact with other OSS officers in Rome) consisted largely of items the Vatican wanted Washington to know.[68]

Given the mediocre results of previous efforts and the paucity of hard political intelligence from inside the Vatican, it is no wonder that OSS embraced the anonymous source who, in the form of the cutout VESSEL/DUSTY, appeared so fortuitously with an offer of secrets from the innermost circles of the papal administration. Soon the VESSEL/DUSTY channels began to bedazzle SI and X-2 officers with a stream of documents of a type about which intelligence collectors usually only dream: copies of top-secret telegrams exchanged by the Vatican secretariat of state and its nuncios abroad, including the papal representatives in Berlin and Tokyo; minutes of the pope's conferences with cardinals, bishops, and visiting dignitaries; and confidential memoranda from various departments of the Vatican administration. Beyond anyone's expectations, OSS had acquired a source at the very heart of an institution whose political acumen, access to information, and global reach were proverbial. Many of the VESSEL/DUSTY reports were deemed so important that they were forwarded to the White House for the particular attention of President Roosevelt. It all seemed too good to be true. It *was* too good to be true.

The VESSEL reports (as they came to be called) were the product of the fertile imagination and skillful pen of Virgilio Scattolini—journalist, pornographer, sometime film critic for the Vatican newspaper, *L'Osservatore Romano*, and the most brazen intelligence fabricator of the Second World War. As early as 1939 Scattolini began to sell to interested parties accounts of events and personalities inside Vatican City. The fact that he had no access to decision-making circles in the papal enclave proved to be no impediment. Working from the comfort of his apartment near the Spanish Steps in the heart of old Rome, Scattolini simply concocted stories based on a careful scrutiny of the pope's audience schedule as published in the Vatican newspaper, combined with a large measure of fanciful detail concerning the alleged content and results of such audiences. The artful fabricator did not stop with fictional meetings; soon he was creating diplomatic telegrams and departmental memoranda. Scattolini's lucrative business was interrupted by the Italian police in 1942, but after the liberation of Rome he returned to his old stand, and soon his unsuspecting customers included newspapers, banks, embassies, and the intelligence services of several countries.

The American side of Scattolini's edifice of lies and forgeries began to collapse in early 1945 when the State Department was astonished to read a VESSEL report forwarded from OSS Italy that described a meeting between Myron Taylor and the Japanese ambassador to the Vatican. No one in Washington had authorized such a meeting, and when asked for an explanation Taylor vehemently denied any contact with enemy diplomats. The affair caused OSS analysts to scrutinize the VESSEL reports, checking for inconsistencies and comparing details to reports from other sources. The more they looked, the more the analysts disliked what they saw. In February 1945 OSS headquarters warned its Italian station that the VESSEL material "has earmarks of being concocted by a not too clever manufacturer of sales information. As a result, for the time being we are withholding the dissemination of most of this material." Two weeks later Washington was even more emphatic: "Whereas some unimportant items of Vessel material may be based on factual knowledge of the source, the more important items are believed to be manufactured by the source out of whole cloth or are plants."[69]

In Italy, OSS officers, including James Angleton, were loath to admit that they had been taken by a con artist. In Washington some senior officers shared this reluctance, and for a short time OSS headquarters, desperate for any human intelligence from inside Japan, convinced itself that VESSEL reports dealing with that country, particularly documents purporting to be copies of the dispatches of the papal diplomatic representative in Tokyo, were more credible than reports dealing with other topics. In the face of accumulating evidence of Scattolini's deception, this fantasy could not be sustained. After a review of five months of VESSEL reports, the OSS section responsible for Japan submitted, in June 1945, a scathing report that described the material from Rome as confused, vague, and self-contradictory and concluded that VESSEL had produced "hardly a shred of positive intelligence" and that the source "would seem to be of almost no value to us."[70] After the VESSEL debacle, OSS, and later SSU, would conduct other operations against the Papacy including surreptitiously reading papal mail and recruiting informants inside Vatican City, and though Angleton participated in some of these programs, the Vatican was not a primary concern for SCI/Z in the immediate postwar period.[71]

Angleton was burned by Scattolini, but his embarrassment made him more cautious about accepting approaches from promising sources unless those sources could be checked and their information confirmed. From then on, the SCI/Z chief would look every gift horse in the mouth. The VESSEL affair proved a rare misstep in Angleton's efforts to develop a network of informants that would produce positive intelligence concerning political and military subjects. His first success came at the expense of his putative friends in Italian intelligence. While happy to accept the voluminous reports that flowed into his office on the Via Sicilia through liaison channels, Angleton retained a healthy skepticism concerning the intentions of the Italian services. The SCI/Z chief was aware that SIM and SIS had always been strongly monarchist and conservative in their political orientation, and he was convinced that such sentiments continued to pervade the services even after the collapse of fascism and the end of the war.[72] He believed that the accuracy of the political reports he routinely received after VE Day from his liaison partners was seriously compromised by the political biases of Italian intelligence officers who used these reports to advance a conservative, if not reactionary, political agenda. As early as the autumn of 1945 Angleton informed Washington that the Italian espionage and security services had purged those among their personnel who harbored sympathies for a liberal democratic republic and the organizations had developed close connections to extreme right-wing groups "which have determined the direction and the policy of the Italian intelligence organizations."[73] He warned his superiors that, as a product of their alliance with the extreme right, SIS and SIM were using every opportunity to foster the idea that the Soviet Union, working through its puppets in the Italian Communist Party (PCI), was intent upon undermining the political and social order in order to pave the way for the Bolshevization of Italy. By bombarding their American counterparts with alarmist reports of Red conspiracies and revolutionary activities, Italian intelligence, Angleton believed, hoped to scare Washington into adopting an anti-Soviet and anticommunist policy that would include the preservation of the Italian monarchy and support for conservative political organizations.[74]

Although later in his career with the Central Intelligence Agency James Angleton would become one of the most rigid of the cold warriors, in 1945–1946 he was neither reflexively anticommunist nor uncritical toward reports of Soviet skullduggery. He was aware of the political agenda of his liaison partners because he had clandestinely recruited informants inside the Italian services, who provided channels of information that functioned independently of formal liaison procedures. One such agent, code-named SAILOR, had been SIS's chief of station in Istanbul before being recalled to a senior position at naval intelligence headquarters in Rome. A republican sympathizer angered by the militant monarchism of his colleagues, SAILOR passed to Angleton material covering the full spectrum of his agency's operations, some of which material contradicted the information American intelligence was receiving through official liaison channels. He proved especially effective in keeping X-2 Rome apprised of his service's active support of monarchist elements who were working against the creation of a republic in Italy.[75]

Angleton's knowledge of the political goals of SIS and SIM probably explains the relative equanimity of American intelligence in the face of dramatic reports of communist conspiracies in the summer and fall of 1945. Varying in details but following a common theme, these reports, most of which originated in the Italian intelligence services, warned that the Italian Communist Party (PCI), directed by Moscow and abetted, depending on the report, by Albanian, French, Swiss, or Yugoslav comrades, was secretly receiving funds, stockpiling weapons, providing firearms training to cadres, establishing factory soviets, infiltrating the police and local administrations, and preparing propaganda with the aim of launching an armed revolution against the government in Rome and installing a Bolshevik regime subservient to the Soviet Union. The allegations were buttressed by reports of Red Army officers in mufti moving about northern Italy. These officers, whose presence was known to OSS, conducted propaganda operations aimed at two units of non-Russian subjects of the Soviet Union—mainly Turkomans— who had been recruited into the German army for antipartisan operations in Italy. Other Red Army officers served as advisers in the Garibaldi Brigade, a partisan formation that included Russian escapees from German POW and labor camps.[76]

In contrast to Philip Horton, his more excitable counterpart in Paris, Angleton treated such reports of communist conspiracies with skepticism. In passing the information to Washington, he often included a disclaimer that reminded the reader that the intelligence originated in rabidly anticommunist circles that had an interest in provoking American fear and suspicion of the PCI and the Soviet Union. At one point in the fall of 1945 he flatly dismissed the alarmist reports, noting that "at no time have the various items of intelligence (when submitted to the test) been proven to be other than consciously composed for the purposes of provocation."[77]

Despite the alarmist reporting of their Italian counterparts, senior American intelligence representatives in Italy refused to credit the threat of an imminent revolution. Drawing, perhaps, on their own sources inside leftist organizations, including the Communist Party, these representatives developed a more nuanced view of the ambitions and tactics of the communists. Though certain that the PCI received instructions and, as Angleton established, funds from Moscow, they believed that neither the local communists nor their Russian directors were committed, at least in the short term, to revolution, and that while the PCI would seize every opportunity to advance its political influence, it would eschew armed insurrection in favor of building and dominating a broad coalition of antifascist parties. This theme had begun to appear in OSS reporting as early as the fall of 1944. In November of that year, for example, SI Italy had noted that the new communist mayor of the important port city of Livorno had been informed personally by PCI chief Palmiro Togliatti that the party would continue to propagandize against capitalism and political reaction but would cooperate fully with the Allies and the Italian government, nurture good relations with the Catholic Church and the Christian Democratic Party that was closely connected to the Church, and attempt to cultivate the goodwill of the middle classes.[78]

OSS reporting maintained this moderate tone during the various "revolution scares" of 1945. While it conscientiously passed to Washington reports of arms caches, communist plots, and itinerant Soviet officers, it refused to be stampeded. In the spring, for example, SI Italy, noting reports that leftist parties in northern Italy opposed the government of prime minister Bonomi for relying on pro-fascist elements, assured its customers that these parties had no intention of revolting against that government after the war.[79]

By the summer, American intelligence outlets were explicitly dismissing the constant rumors of imminent revolution. An appreciation of the political situation in Italy that circulated in late August 1945 acknowledged that the long-term policy of the PCI was the creation of a communist state within the Soviet sphere of influence, but the report noted, "To achieve this [the PCI] is ready to wait a long time and meanwhile to cooperate with the Government in power." Concerning the "unsubstantiated rumors" that the communists were preparing an uprising, the report insisted that "there are no serious indications that the Communist Party intends or is capable of armed insurrection before the holding of elections," although the party would opportunistically exploit conditions of social unrest and political dissent to enhance its position.[80] An intelligence survey of the political scene in the autumn reached similar conclusions, reminding its readers that the many rumors of an insurrection have been fostered by political elements that hope to benefit from a climate of fear and uncertainty. The survey concluded that such rumors "have no foundation in fact."[81]

American intelligence officers in Italy may have been encouraged in their skeptical response to rumors of an imminent communist insurrection by reports from British intelligence that also denigrated the stories. For example, a British report, shared with OSS in the late summer of 1945, warned that right-wing elements were spreading rumors of communist preparations for revolution but that MI6 sources in the communist and socialist parties rejected these claims, noting that the Italian people, exhausted by the war, were psychologically ill-prepared for revolution, that the presence of American and British troops made a revolt madness, and that the PCI would, at least for the next few years, adopt a moderate course that eschewed violent attempts to overthrow the government.[82]

The American and British assessments were not far off the mark. Before the fall of Mussolini, the Communist Party of Italy had been a small, persecuted movement with a membership of only a few thousand. By the end of the war, the party had emerged as a significant political force with more than a million adherents. The dramatic growth was due, in part, to the party's now respectable history of opposition to fascism; its leading role in the antifascist partisan movement that resisted the German occupation of the country; and its association with the Soviet Union, whose heroic sacrifices during the war had elevated Stalin and the Red Army in the popular imagination. Party growth was also facilitated by a decision to loosen the requirements for membership, in particular by downplaying class and ideology in favor of a more general antifascist commitment on the part of applicants.[83]

Committed to the abolition of the monarchy, the communists initially withheld support from the post-armistice government headed by Marshal

Pietro Badoglio. In April 1944, however, the party suddenly dropped its insistence on the abdication of the king and offered its support to the government in Rome. The dramatic reversal was the result of a meeting in Moscow between Stalin and the leaders of the Italian and French communist parties, Palmiro Togliatti and Maurice Thorez, at which the Soviet dictator outlined the "national front" strategy he expected the parties to adopt in the immediate postwar period. For the Italians the first priority was to widen the party's base of support by proclaiming a policy of national unity and reaching out to form alliances with other political groups on the left. The short-term goal was a powerful left-wing coalition led by the PCI that would participate as a central element of the government. To facilitate this coalition building and convince parties to its right that it was a reliable partner, the party had to project an image of political moderation and support for parliamentary democracy. This required the party to abandon some of its more radical proposals, such as the immediate abolition of the monarchy, as well as some of its cherished tactics, particularly revolutionary agitation. Stalin made it very clear that the PCI had to avoid any suggestion of revolutionary action because such action would only strengthen the political right by scaring more moderate elements in the country, alarm London and Washington, and create an excuse for the western Allies to intervene in Italy against the communists much as Britain had done in Greece at the end of 1944.[84]

Since his party was subservient to Stalin's will, Togliatti hastened to dampen any revolutionary enthusiasm before it could flare into insurrection. Senior PCI leaders visited the Soviet embassy almost daily to discuss political developments and plan political tactics.[85] The PCI leadership was especially concerned to rein in overexuberant party members, especially from the wartime partisan formations, who saw the end of the war as an opportunity to exact revenge against class enemies and pursue expropriations and other instruments of class war.[86] Party formations were instructed in the new national front strategy, and party discipline was invoked to deter any deviation from the line set by Moscow. Not a few were frustrated by a policy that seemed to ignore a golden opportunity to seize power at a time when the conservative regime in Rome was struggling to establish its legitimacy and disassociate itself from the fascist past, while the communists had never been stronger or more popular. The frustration was shared by some Russian officials on the scene. In a rare (and potentially dangerous) expression of dissent from the official line, Aleksandr Bogomolov, the senior Soviet diplomatic representative in Italy, criticized Togliatti for failing to arouse the Italian masses behind a call for radical political and economic reform. In his dispatches to Moscow in the summer and early fall of 1944, Bogomolov condemned the PCI leadership as insufficiently revolutionary and warned that the party's moderation would only legitimize the established Italian government and play into the hands of the Americans and British.[87] When Bogomolov was transferred to the Soviet embassy in Paris, his replacement in Italy, Michail Kostylev, also recognized that the party line ran contrary to the expectations of many of its supporters. In one dispatch the ambassador observed that the Italian left "is ready for courageous revolutionary action. Only the moderating influence of its vanguard, the PCI can halt this rush of the masses towards premature insurrection."[88]

As was the case with communist parties in other countries, the PCI's conversion to parliamentary democracy was merely tactical. Despite its public call for postwar cooperation among all nonfascist political groups, the party privately maintained its belief in a Manichean world divided between two blocs: the capitalist, whose paladins were Britain and the United States, and the communist, whose defender was the Soviet Union. The differences between these blocs (and between their adherents) were so irreconcilable that war was inevitable some time in the not distant future. The PCI simply intended to use the instruments of parliamentary democracy to kill parliamentary democracy. In the meantime it would seek to increase its popular appeal, while using its position as a partner in the government to infiltrate communist loyalists into positions of authority in the various government ministries, from which posts they could influence the direction of policy and channel to Moscow intelligence about Italian foreign and domestic affairs. In the foreign ministry, for example, two undersecretaryships were allotted to the PCI as part of the power-sharing arrangement among the parties collaborating in the national government. The two communists selected for the posts put the interests of their party and its Soviet patron above the interests of their country. They routinely passed to the Soviet embassy in Rome information concerning foreign ministry personnel, the deliberations of senior officials, and the correspondence between the ministry and the Italian ambassador in Moscow. They also worked assiduously to secure the appointment to important embassies of Italian diplomats who were secret communists or fellow travelers.[89]

American intelligence accurately read the political situation in general and the policy of the Italian Communist Party in particular. Intelligence officers knew that the PCI was in direct and frequent contact with Soviet representatives in Italy. Reports from Rome consistently emphasized that the PCI would eschew insurrection in favor of a "united front" approach that included collaboration with other parties of the left, participation in the government, and acceptance of parliamentary politics. The reporting, however, explicitly and accurately recognized that this approach was simply a short-term strategy and that in the long term the PCI was committed to creating in Italy a communist state within the Russian sphere of influence.[90] This information may have contributed to the "considerable circumspection" that characterized American policy toward the PCI and the leftist partisans in 1945. Previous appraisals have suggested that Washington chose a relatively benign rather than hostile posture toward the communists from a desire to exploit their military capabilities in the last months of the war and a conviction that moderation was the best way to secure communist cooperation in restoring order and the authority of Rome after the war.[91] Reading the intelligence reports from Rome, policy makers in Washington, who hoped that a stable, friendly, parliamentary regime would emerge in the country without the necessity of open American intervention, may also have concluded that, at least in the short run, the PCI and its leftist allies were not an immediate threat to their vision of postwar Italy. Whether an opportunistic tactic or not, the national front strategy of the communists might provide a breathing spell during which the Italians could establish the foundations for a stable parliamentary democracy.

For all the scares and alarms, political developments and the threat of a communist insurrection were not the only topics to preoccupy American intelligence in Italy in the first months of peace. They were not even the most important. For SCI/Z counterintelligence and security were priorities, a focus befitting an organization that was originally deployed as an X-2 unit. The principal task remained the "almost incredible number of demands for screening" individuals, mainly but not exclusively Italians, who had come to the attention of the Allied occupation authorities or the Italian police. By November 1945, X-2 Italy had vetted some 31,000 individuals, a figure that led one wag in Angleton's office to calculate that if the present Roman birth rate remained constant, the unit would have screened the entire population of the Eternal City by 2025.[92] Even with the assistance of Italian police agencies whose officers did most of the investigative work, SCI/Z could barely stay on top of the job. Vetting and the associated task of locating fugitive fascist bigwigs and personalities wanted for war crimes, responsibilities the group on the Via Sicilia shared with the army's Counterintelligence Corps, would remain the principal preoccupations of Angleton's unit into 1946.

Counterintelligence operations also continued to reflect wartime preoccupations even after VE Day. As far as X-2 Italy was concerned the specter of fascism did not dissolve with the collapse of Mussolini's rump Republic of Salo and the capture and execution of *Il Duce* by partisans when he sought to escape into Switzerland. Angleton believed that fascism had simply gone to ground and that its adherents, many of whom returned to authority in Badoglio's government of "experts," might destabilize the already shaky provisional government in Rome. At the Via Sicilia the threat from the extreme right was taken as seriously as the threat from the extreme left. In SCI/Z's monthly report for October 1945, a time when wild rumors of leftist conspiracies remained current, the section on internal political subversion focused exclusively on right-wing groups. As late as January 1946, the "Subversive Movements" portion of the general security summary published by Allied headquarters in Italy discussed only the activities of right-wing and monarchist groups, and had nothing to report concerning possible leftist subversion.[93]

Until late 1945 both SCI/Z and CIC also devoted significant resources to extirpating the remnants of the German intelligence services that survived in Italy, either as individual agents gone to cover or as underground cells of a "stay-behind" network left to prepare for a Nazi/fascist revival. Although the stay-behind organization proved in the main illusory, the presence of individual German operatives did not, and well into 1946 American units continued to track down the occasional agent. In January of that year, more than seven months after the end of the war, a survey of counterintelligence activity in northwestern Italy by Angleton's Milan subunit recorded the arrest of German intelligence operatives as its principal achievement for the period.[94]

Gradually SCI/Z shifted its focus from the old wartime enemies to new counterintelligence targets. Although Angleton's unit kept an eye on the Soviet embassy in Rome, recording, for example, the arrival of new staff or the movement of Russian officials across the country, the available evidence does not suggest that the Soviets were the main counterintelligence focus in the months immediately following VE Day. Among the foreign intelligence services operating in Italy, the French and Yugoslavs received more attention. Through the SCI/Z office in Genoa, Angleton kept an eye on the activities of the Direction Générale des Etudes et Recherches (and its successor service, the Service de Documentation Extérieure et de Contre-espionnage) in Val d'Aosta and the alpine valleys that marked the border between France and Italy, noting that the French pursued the "saturation" tactic of passing across the border large numbers of agents (many of whom were formerly in the employ of the Nazi and Fascist intelligence services).[95]

Across the country, on another border, the Yugoslavs were even more active. Angleton considered the Yugoslav intelligence service (OZNA) a particularly ruthless organization that would go to any lengths to advance the purposes of the Tito regime. OZNA operated across Italy to identify and neutralize anti-Tito personalities and movements, but it was especially active in the disputed city of Trieste and the surrounding region of Venezia Giulia.[96] Beginning in the fall of 1945, SCI/Z closely monitored Yugoslav espionage and clandestine propaganda operations in the region. In October 1945, for instance, Angleton's officers determined that the Trieste office of the Yugoslav news agency Tanjug was a front for OZNA operations. The following month, in a report that focused primarily on OZNA's operations, SCI/Z informed Washington that Yugoslav operatives were establishing clandestine armed cells in Trieste. By early 1946 Angleton was forwarding to Washington information, much of which originated with Italian military intelligence, that the Yugoslavs were preparing for the eventuality that Trieste would remain part of Italy by arming local communists for an insurrection against the Italians and the Allied occupation forces.[97]

As we have seen, penetration of the Italian secret services was the highest counterintelligence priority for SCI/Z in the immediate postwar period. Successful infiltration of these services provided access to other targets. Sources in SIM and SIS revealed that these organizations were providing money and equipment to the various right-wing groups that were emerging among the thousands of émigré Albanians, Croats, Georgians, Hungarians, and Yugoslavs who had fled to or otherwise ended up in Italy, passing the days in refugee camps or the shabbier cafes of Rome and Milan, plotting their political return to their homelands. By the fall of 1945 Angleton had recruited his first contacts inside these groups and begun to monitor their activities.[98] This surveillance gave American intelligence a view into the intrigues of clandestine political organizations that might pose a threat to order and security inside Italy. It also provided a window onto the home countries of the émigrés, some of which were otherwise closed to American intelligence. In October, for example, the SCI/Z chief informed Washington that the communist regime of Enver Hoxha was consolidating its position in Albania by persecuting noncommunists. This persecution had spawned an armed resistance that was active in the central portions of the country. To preempt support for the resistance from Albanian exiles, Hoxha had dispatched to Italy a military mission whose covert task was to infiltrate exile circles and kidnap anti-regime refugees. Later, Angleton would cover Albanian exiles' formation of an anti-Hoxha resistance committee, political divisions within the exile community, and resistance plans to secure American and British support to overthrow the communists.[99]

Angleton wanted to know what the émigrés were up to, but he was leery of associating American intelligence with their ambitions and activities. The anti-Soviet Georgians and White Russians were especially suspect. In early 1946 Angleton informed Washington that the anti-Soviet exiles, some of whom had worked for Germany against their motherland, were entirely untrustworthy, and he warned against using them as anything more than sources of information regarding their previous work for various Axis intelligence services. Angleton was prepared to use the anticommunist émigrés to spy on Germans, but as late as the beginning of 1946 he exhibited little interest in using them to spy on the Soviets or the emerging communist regimes in Albania and Yugoslavia. The SCI/Z chief also believed that the security of the émigré organizations was so pitiful that operations were compromised almost before they could be implemented. Any intelligence service associated with these operations could expect only embarrassment. This belief was confirmed when he discovered that the Yugoslav intelligence service established in Italy ostensibly anti-Tito political committees as "fly traps" to attract and identify enemies of the Belgrade regime and ensnare and control any foreign intelligence service that hoped to exploit the émigrés for espionage and subversive purposes. Angleton, suspecting that organizations of the émigré Albanians, Croats, Georgians, and Hungarians were similarly penetrated, counseled against active association with such groups.[100]

While security and counterintelligence operations consumed the greater part of SCI/Z's time and resources in the first months of peace, Angleton was acutely conscious that his small unit was the only representative of OSS (and later SSU) in Italy. In the absence of any secret intelligence organization to run offensive operations, he did not believe that he could ignore opportunities to collect positive intelligence for Washington. Rather surprisingly, his superiors did not always appreciate his initiative. While Italy would by 1948 become a focus of clandestine operations by SSU's successor service, the Central Intelligence Agency, in the first year of peace it held no special attraction to intelligence managers preoccupied with other issues, including demobilization, reorganization, and institutional survival. While information concerning political developments inside Italy and the activities and plans of the Italian government was always welcome in Washington, senior officers at SSU headquarters did not believe that conditions called for special collection efforts that would require more money and personnel at a time when both were in short supply. The feeling was that after the recall of SI units from Italy and the suspension of in-country collection programs at the end of the war, the stations in Austria and Switzerland could fill the void and collect all the information that was necessary. In November 1945 headquarters considered and declined a suggestion to establish a secret intelligence station alongside Angleton's counterintelligence shop, and as late as the spring of 1946 the secret intelligence branch of SSU, responsible for directing all intelligence collection operations, still did not have an Italian desk at headquarters and SI branch was not conducting any offensive operations based in Italy.[101]

The passivity of headquarters was such that at one point in the spring of 1946 Angleton pointedly suggested to his bosses in Washington that it would be helpful if they would give him some idea of what sorts of intelligence they required. In the absence of any guidance, he began to seek out information concerning political and military affairs inside Italy and neighboring countries.[102] Of course the Italian services were only too eager to provide such information, but Angleton wanted independent sources that could serve as a check on the often biased reporting that came out of SIM and SIS. To this end the SCI/Z commander began the tedious process of rebuilding the networks that had fallen into disuse after the closure of SI Italy immediately after VE Day. Much of the evidence concerning this effort remains classified, but the available documentation suggests that Angleton scored some early successes. By the end of 1945, for example, SCI/Z had somehow gained access to the correspondence that passed between the Rome headquarters of the Socialist Party and its regional offices. In early 1946 the secretary general of the Italian treasury department provided Angleton a copy of the secret guidelines for Italian negotiators concerning Rome's proposals for the payment of war reparations. By the spring of that year Angleton had penetrated the office of the Italian prime minister and was securing photographic copies of important documents from the office's files.[103]

For all of Angleton's efforts to develop independent sources, liaison with the Italian services remained a crucial element of SCI/Z's positive intelligence collection program, especially as that program was directed against "foreign" targets. Yugoslavia was a case in point. Since the expulsion of the wartime OSS mission to Yugoslavia in May 1945, information about the newly established communist regime in Belgrade was scanty, a deficiency that was particularly distressing in view of Tito's aggressive designs on Trieste and the surrounding region of Venezia Giulia. The SSU station in Austria had established a small outpost in the contested city that worked to establish networks inside Yugoslavia. From Rome Angleton supplemented this effort by providing Washington with extensive reports on the disposition of Yugoslav military forces. All of this order-of-battle information as well as occasional items on economic and political conditions inside Yugoslavia came from Italian military intelligence.[104]

Italian intelligence may also have provided a window on the activities of the Soviet embassy in Rome. Assurance in this matter is elusive, in part because the available evidence is limited to two items and in part because these items originated with the Italian services, agencies whose veracity and motives were not always beyond question. In late January 1946, Angleton received from SIM two reports concerning the embassy. The first reported that the Russian military attaché displayed in his embassy office a large map of Turkey on which the Dardanelles and the Turkish districts of Kars and Ardahan were highlighted, with special attention to the defenses of the Turkish Straits. This fact, which must have originated with someone with access to the attaché's office, was interesting in view of the growing tensions between Moscow and Ankara over Russia's claims concerning access to the straits and control of the districts that had been ceded by Russia to Turkey after the First World War. These claims had attracted the attention of Washington, which opposed any expansion of Soviet influence in the area, and would lead to a serious war scare in the spring of 1946.[105] The second report purported to be a verbatim translation of an embassy cable to the foreign ministry in Moscow reporting various news items, including the arrival in Rome of two political commissars and the opposition of Pertini, the secretary general of the Italian Socialist Party, to any program leading to the party's fusion with the PCI.[106]

These reports are intriguing because if the information was authentic and if they are indicative of similar reports received from the Italians, then they represent a rare penetration of a Soviet embassy and the only such penetration evident in the records available for the period 1945–1947. The item concerning the embassy cable is especially intriguing since it suggests (1) the Italians were intercepting and decrypting Russian diplomatic traffic, or (2) they had a source inside the embassy cipher office, or (3) they had managed a clandestine entry into the embassy premises for the purposes of photographing documents, a scenario that might include a glimpse of the maps in the office of the military attaché.

The first explanation, while not impossible, is rather improbable given the acknowledged sophistication of Russian diplomatic ciphers, which had resisted during the war every attack by American, British, Finnish, French, Japanese, and Polish code breakers. The second scenario is more plausible, but still unlikely. Russian embassies were notorious among foreign espionage services for their tight security. Before the war, the Russians had employed only members of the Italian Communist Party for whatever local services (gardeners, housekeepers, butlers) were necessary. When Moscow reopened its embassy in 1944 it dispensed with the services of even loyal Italian communists in favor of using Russians in all embassy positions. If the Italian services had recruited one of these Russians it would have been another rare intelligence coup. Of course SIM or SIS might have had an informant among the PCI officials who regularly visited the embassy for consultations, although it is hard to see how such an informant would have had access to the military attaché's office or the embassy cable files.

A clandestine entry is the most attractive of the three explanations. Before the war SIM had specialized in such operations, developing a special team, the Sezione Prevelamento (Extraction Section), for nocturnal burglaries. This team had the run of embassies in Rome, with notable penetrations of the American, British, and French missions (to note only the more important targets). Some embassies were hit more than once. Weighing against acceptance of this scenario is the fact that before the war "Sezione P" had been unable to break into the Soviet embassy because security was too tight. It is unlikely that security was any less tight after the war. Also, it is not even certain that Sezione P continued in existence after the war. Its commander, the highly capable Major Manfredo Talamo, had been executed by the Germans in 1944 for his anti-Nazi sympathies. In the end the possibility of a penetration of the Russian embassy in Rome remains an intriguing possibility that cannot yet be confirmed.

More certain were Angleton's successes against other "foreign" targets. The Vatican remained an object of interest to American intelligence. Having been burned by his first attempt to penetrate the headquarters of the Catholic Church (the VESSEL debacle), Angleton seems to have abandoned clandestine operations in favor of direct (if only occasional) contacts with high papal officials. In December 1945, for example, he met with Monsignor Giovanni Montini, a senior official in the papal secretariat of state (who would go on to become Pope Paul VI), and learned that the Vatican, allegedly inflexible in its anticommunism, had secretly been making overtures to the Soviet Union and would continue to do so even though the first approaches had been rebuffed.[107] Angleton also worked out an arrangement with SSU's Vienna station that allowed him to piggyback on the close contacts developed inside the Vatican by Zsolt Aradi, a Hungarian national who was an officer of the Vienna station operating under the code name SARAZEN. Aradi's ecclesiastical contacts had proved especially useful in penetrating Hungary in the KLEIN-14th STREET Project (see chapter 5), and these contacts generated occasional items of information for the Rome station. In late 1945, for example, source "AE752" (almost certainly Töhötöm Nagy, a Jesuit priest and American agent who traveled clandestinely between Budapest and Rome as a confidential informant of the pope) reported to Angleton the substance of his conversations with Father Robert Leiber, a close confidant and collaborator of Pope Pius XII, concerning the Vatican's attitude toward the Soviet Union. Leiber told Angleton's source that the pope hoped to reach a modus vivendi with Moscow, and toward that end the Vatican would avoid, at least for the moment, an aggressively anti-Soviet policy. This information was confirmed by another ecclesiastical source (identified in the documents only as "AE754") to whom Leiber had mentioned that the Vatican shunned a crusade against communism and hoped to reach an accommodation with the Soviet Union.[108] Occasionally, all this activity around St. Peter's Square produced information about more distant lands. In early 1946, for instance, another Hungarian Jesuit, Father Joseph Janosi, appeared in Rome as an unofficial representative of the government in Budapest, charged with negotiating the resumption of diplomatic relations between Hungary and the Vatican. The envoy brought to his discussions with senior papal authorities a long report on economic conditions inside his homeland. Working through his ecclesiastical contacts, Angleton obtained a copy of the report and may have recruited Father Janosi as a source. To protect the Jesuit the SCI/Z chief asked Washington to classify the report in such a way as to restrict its circulation to only American officers.

By the summer of 1946, James Angleton had largely reestablished the position of American intelligence in the Italian peninsula that had been left in shambles after the closure of SI Italy at the end of the war. He had creatively expanded the reach of his understaffed and overworked unit by piggybacking on the broad backs of the Italian intelligence and police services, while cleverly avoiding becoming a creature of those services by penetrating their ranks with his own secret informants. Similar penetrations of the government, particularly the office of the prime minister, the ministries of finance and foreign affairs, and various political parties ensured broad coverage of Italian political affairs, while contacts with the Vatican provided a window on the policies and activities of this important international actor. Finally, liaison relations supplemented by coverage of émigré organizations and the occasional recruitment of foreign agents generated information concerning such targets as Albania, Hungary, and Yugoslavia. Given the small size of his unit and the minimal support of headquarters, Angleton's achievement was probably the equal of any American intelligence station in early postwar Europe.

CHAPTER SEVEN

Conclusion

In the historiography of American intelligence the twelve months follow-ing the end of the Second World are a lost time. The intelligence history of the war itself has been well studied, as has the early history of the Cen-tral Intelligence Agency after that agency's creation in September 1947, but the immediate postwar period makes hardly an appearance in the many books and articles devoted to American espionage. Figures from OSS and the early CIA—William "Wild Bill" Donovan, Allen Dulles, Frank Wisner, William Colby—attract the attention of biographers, while their services' programs—SUNRISE, GEORGE WOOD, Radio Free Europe, the JED-BURGHs, Congress for Cultural Freedom—are the subjects of monographs and doctoral dissertations. No one, however, has written the biography of John Magruder or William Quinn, the two army officers who, in succession, commanded the Strategic Services Unit, or of operatives such as Peter Si-chel, SSU's twenty-three-year-old chief of secret intelligence in Berlin, who fought on the first front of the intelligence wars of the Cold War, or Zsolt Aradi, the young Hungarian journalist turned spy handler who, after OSS and before CIA, ran agents across Central Europe and even into the Vatican. Students will search library shelves and Internet sites in vain for accounts of PAREGORIC, EL MOROCCO, ICARUS, the AIREDALES, and other examples of a clandestine effort of which no one is aware.

If writers pay any attention to the early postwar period at all, that atten-tion is narrowly, one might say selectively, focused. Some writers concentrate on a small number of activities or events with the intention of revealing that U.S. intelligence agencies and the government they served had started to fight the Cold War even before the hot war against the Axis powers was over and that to win that fight the services and their government eagerly em-braced any number of unsavory elements, including war criminals, fascists, and anti-Semites. More commonly the focus is the organizational turmoil and bureaucratic infighting that were the result of the closure of the Office of Strategic Services and the debate within the Truman administration over the requirements of a peacetime intelligence structure. This focus is often merely a prelude to explaining the origins of the CIA and the emergence of the "secret state."[1] Implicit in this focus is the suggestion that at this time intelligence was more a matter of domestic politics than international politics and that during the turmoil and debate espionage operations were temporarily suspended. One is left to wonder how the absence of secret intelligence affected the ability of foreign policy decision makers to make sense of the complicated world that remained after the guns fell silent.

As we have seen, American intelligence history was not interrupted at the end of the war. Washington's intelligence capabilities extended beyond the Office of Strategic Services, so the end of OSS did not mean the end of espionage. Other organizations, such as the Signal Security Agency or the Counterintelligence Corps (CIC), remained in existence and continued, on a reduced scale, their work. Even in the area of clandestine collection—the world of spies, double agents, purloined documents, and safe houses, an area practically monopolized by OSS—operations continued through the efforts of the Strategic Services Unit, a neglected stepchild of American intelligence history.

Admittedly, in the first year of peace U.S. agencies, particularly the Strategic Services Unit, were compelled to operate under conditions that seriously undermined their effectiveness. Demobilization, by releasing men and women from the military services, stripped the foreign intelligence agencies of most of their experienced personnel. Even civilian organizations, such as the Federal Bureau of Investigation, lost staff as wartime budgets and activities returned to peacetime levels. Fewer people and fewer dollars required the intelligence services to reduce significantly their operational tempo by shrinking and at times eliminating collection programs. For SSU, which was especially hard hit by the cutbacks, this meant the closure of secret intelligence (SI) stations in some countries (Italy, Portugal, and Spain), the elimination of desks (labor, war crimes, Nazi financial assets) in some of the stations that survived, and a reliance on one or two officers to run operations that previously occupied a half dozen or more personnel.

Uncertainty concerning postwar intelligence requirements and a decentralized intelligence community that lacked, even after the creation of the Central Intelligence Group in January 1946, a strong coordinating authority combined to discourage the identification of common collection priorities and the development of synchronized collection programs. Agencies identified targets and pursued operations without reference to the activities of other agencies. In the Strategic Services Unit, where insecurities concerning the very survival of the organization compounded the problem, headquarters initially was unable to provide guidance or direction to its foreign stations, which, at least until early 1946, were left, operationally, to fend for themselves. Rather than pursuing a systematic and coordinated collection program, these stations attacked a variety of targets selected on the basis more of opportunity than of careful plan. One has only to recall the tensions between

SSU Germany and the intelligence directorate of American Forces European Theater over the centrality of Red Army order-of-battle intelligence, or the different approaches toward the use of anticommunist émigrés exhibited by SSU chiefs of station in Paris and Rome, to understand that mission confusion and lack of coordination often led services—as well as elements within services—to pursue not only different operations but conflicting operations.

This diversity of purpose and direction makes it difficult to identify a central theme in early postwar intelligence. In particular it undermines assertions that U.S. intelligence—often in conjunction with its British counterparts—struck the first blows of the Cold War by preparing operations against the Soviet Union even before the war against the Axis had been won.[2] For support these claims rely primarily upon evidence that American military intelligence agencies were actively collecting intelligence on the Soviet Union before Germany's surrender, mainly by debriefing German POWs about their knowledge of Russian matters, and that this interest intensified over the summer and autumn of 1945. There are, however, several problems with this assertion and its evidence. Intelligence interest in a particular country may be, but is not necessarily, evidence of fear, hostility, or evil designs toward the target. If it was, then one could plausibly argue that the USSR struck the first blows of the Cold War when it recruited spy networks inside the U.S. government in the 1930s, a time when the United States probably did not have a clandestine espionage network anywhere in the world.[3]

During the war, the United States had embraced, in practice if not as a matter of formal policy, the concept of total intelligence, an approach that sought to collect information on all countries whether friend or foe—an approach, coincidentally, also adopted during the war by the Soviet Union. Of course practice always fell short of intentions, and total intelligence remained an elusive goal. Circumstance, particularly the exigencies of war and the availability of resources, prevented truly global coverage and compelled intelligence managers to make choices about priorities. Also some countries were more open and shared information more readily, and these countries required less attention from American secret services because there was less to be uncovered. The principle—total intelligence—remained, however. The United States would try, with varying degrees of effort, to learn as much as possible about the countries of the world, even those countries that posed no threat. American intelligence services consequently collected information, sometimes clandestinely, concerning the politics, finances, and military posture of countries as varied as Mexico, France, Portugal, Liberia, and the Vatican without any hostile motive and without anyone suggesting that Washington was secretly launching a "cold war" against these targets.

It is an exaggeration to assert that U.S. intelligence turned against the Soviet Union in the last months of war and first months of peace by aggressively searching out for their experience and knowledge Germans with experience of Russian affairs. The systematic exploitation of German intelligence and security officers, some with backgrounds in the Gestapo and SS and some demonstrably connected to war crimes, would later become a notorious feature of CIA and CIC operations against the Soviet Union, and it is tempting, perhaps, to read back from that experience to assume that similar practices were widespread in the immediate postwar period. The suspicions, fears, and operational climate of 1947 or 1948, however, were not those of 1945. It is more accurate, perhaps, to say that in the latter year U.S. intelligence exploited whatever Germans they encountered for whatever knowledge these individuals possessed about anything. Given the want of central direction, the absence of a common perception that the Soviet Union was the new enemy, and the opportunistic or fortuitous nature of the various encounters between Americans and Germans in the spring and summer of 1945, many of those encounters focused on Russian affairs, but many did not. As we have seen (chapter 2), when captured German radio intercept operators, in late May 1945, surprised their American captors by offering to take them to where they had buried the equipment they used to monitor Russian radio messages, U.S. communications intelligence personnel were thrilled to exploit their knowledge and equipment. On the other hand, twelve months later, when attitudes toward the Soviet Union had changed for the worse, a major review of the earlier interrogation of captured German code breakers acknowledged that "the main interest of the interrogation officers normally was centered on gaining intelligence concerning American and British communications." Interest in German experience with the ciphers of Russia, the review noted, was never more than of "secondary importance."[4] In the context of American exploitation of German communications intelligence personnel, it is interesting to note that in mid-August 1945, three months after Germany's surrender, when a German army officer in the Bad Aibling POW camp mentioned that several senior officers from the German army's main code-breaking unit were being held at a nearby camp, investigating American intelligence personnel discovered that these officers were nowhere to be found, having apparently been released after only cursory vetting by camp authorities.[5] This episode suggests that if there was a dragnet in the spring and summer of 1945 for German intelligence personnel familiar with Russian matters, it was somewhat porous.

In the transition from war to peace it was often the Germans, seeking patrons and employment, who sought out the Americans. As we have seen, General Reinhard Gehlen, the chief of German army intelligence on the eastern front and the "poster boy" for U.S.-Nazi collaboration against the Soviet

Union, made several unsuccessful attempts to interest his U.S. army captors in his experience before attracting the attention of Captain John Broker, who, in turn, struggled to convince his superiors in military intelligence of the value of the German general. Even after the army eventually accepted Gehlen's offer of services, it could not convince other elements of the American intelligence community to take their German general seriously. The Strategic Services Unit, in particular, wanted nothing to do with the erstwhile German intelligence chief. Again, this is hardly a picture of an intelligence community aggressively and systematically seeking out German experts for assistance in attacking the Soviet target.

It is also possible to make too much out of the claim that U.S. army interrogators in 1945 pressed German POWs and refugees returning from what had been the eastern theater of the European war for information concerning the Soviet Union and areas occupied by the Red Army. It would be remarkable if they didn't. Were they likely to ask about France, Canada, or Brazil? The obvious questions to ask someone arriving from the east in 1945 would be about the east: "Where are you coming from?" "What were conditions like there?" "Were the railways operating?" "What was the state of the roads?" "Were the towns much damaged?" "Were bandits or guerillas active in the area?" It would have been senseless for an American army interrogator in Germany to ask a German POW with recent experience in Belorussia or the Ukraine about monarchist resistance groups in Tuscany, the food situation in Milan, and support for fascism among the peasantry in Lombardy, although military interrogators in Italy probably asked such questions of *their* German captives or displaced persons without historians later suggesting such inquiries reflected hostility toward Italy and anticipated a "cold war" against that country.

Even if every U.S. army interrogator in every POW camp and refugee reception center in Europe asked about nothing but the Soviet Union, it would be premature to conclude that American intelligence was preparing for trouble with the USSR. The absence of central direction and coordination in the American intelligence community encouraged individual components of that community to go their own way without committing other components. The code breakers at the Signal Security Agency, for example, established, for their own reasons, a Russian desk in February 1943, but SSU's secret intelligence branch still had no Russian desk as late as March 1946. The code breakers had been actively attacking Moscow's ciphers for more than two years before SSU launched its first tentative operations into the Soviet zones of Austria and Germany. The army's military intelligence division may have fixated early on the Soviet Union—the evidence is mixed—but the army's Counterintelligence Corps spent the first year of peace in Europe mainly chasing not Russians, but Germans—Nazi war criminals and the remnants of German intelligence networks. A fragmented intelligence community produced a fragmented approach to targeting and collection.

Despite the occasional and opportunistic foray into Soviet intelligence collection, such as the STELLA POLARIS affair, neither SSU nor its predecessor, the Office of Strategic Services, considered the USSR an intelligence priority in the first months of peace. In neither Germany nor Austria, the OSS/SSU missions most directly facing the Russians, were secret intelligence officers directed against Soviet targets during this early period. Berlin Base, deep in the Soviet occupation zone, didn't even have a Russian speaker among its SI officers. As for the small stations eventually established in Budapest, Prague, and Warsaw, these units initially were expected to produce information on their host countries, although by the late fall of 1945 it was increasingly difficult to distinguish collecting intelligence on Czech, Hungarian, and Polish affairs from collecting intelligence on Soviet affairs. Since OSS and SSU represented almost the entirety of American clandestine espionage capabilities, the absence of an early Russian focus is further evidence that the United States had not begun a covert war against Moscow even before the ink was dry on the German surrender protocols. Even when SSU began to turn its attention toward the USSR in the autumn of 1945, it did so slowly, with headquarters making the Soviet Union an intelligence priority for all stations only in March 1946.

In the twelve months of its official existence (1 October 1945–19 October 1946) the Strategic Services Unit's efforts against the Soviet target were constrained by several factors: the need to build informant networks from scratch in a region of the world where U.S. intelligence had very little experience; a tendency, especially in Eastern Europe, to rely upon sources from a narrow spectrum of society; a struggle to distinguish reliable sources from those, such as the anticommunist émigré groups, consciously advancing through disinformation a political agenda that eagerly anticipated conflict between Washington and Moscow; and the opposition of the Soviet Union's alert and ruthless security services and their apprentices in the services of countries occupied by the Red Army. Frequently the Strategic Services Unit was unable to overcome these obstacles, with the result that the information it collected was often sparse or unreliable or no different from the information available from open sources or State Department reporting. This condition was especially apparent in the mediocre performance of the intelligence stations in Eastern Europe. To its credit, SSU headquarters was aware of the deficiencies in its clandestine collection programs, particularly those directed against the Soviet Union, as were the more astute station chiefs such as James Angleton in Rome and Peter Sichel in Berlin, and by the fall of 1946 was working to alleviate them.[6]

How well, then, did the U.S. intelligence community perform the task of informing American policy makers about the activities and intentions of the Soviet Union in the immediate postwar period? If the standard for judging the performance of espionage services is the degree to which they can provide timely and accurate information that is relevant to the needs of decision makers and not available from other sources, then the community, particularly the Strategic Services Unit and the code breakers in the army and navy communications intelligence agencies, performed fairly well. Without human sources in the Soviet Union and without breaks into the ciphers that protected the high-level communications of Russian political and military leaders, the community could not deliver much reliable information of a strategic character, but the American services did provide sufficient information to allow policy makers to answer with some confidence three questions central to an appraisal of Moscow's capabilities and possible intentions in the early postwar period:

1. How quickly could the Soviet Union reconstruct from the losses of the war and how much would that reconstruction depend upon economic assistance from the United States?
2. How large and capable a military establishment did the Soviets intend to maintain in the postwar world?
3. Would Moscow use communist parties as surrogates to extend its influence beyond its borders and ensure domination of its neighbors?

As we have seen (chapter 2) the Office of Strategic Services' Research and Analysis Branch had answered the first question even before the end of the war. In a comprehensive analysis that circulated at the highest levels of the White House, the State Department, and the Joint Chiefs of Staff, in the fall of 1944 OSS economists, working entirely from open sources, demonstrated that despite the devastating human and material losses of the German invasion the Soviet Union would probably be able to reconstruct its economy to prewar levels within a few years of the end of the conflict, much sooner than observers might have predicted. More importantly for decision makers considering the future direction of U.S.-Soviet relations, the analysts further concluded that Russia would be able to rebuild itself without economic assistance from the United States or other outside patrons. Whatever the nature of postwar relations, Washington should not expect to influence Moscow with the promise of credits or other economic aid. According to OSS, the economic card would not significantly improve Washington's hand at the diplomatic table.

The military card was also problematic. Postwar demobilization drastically reduced the size of the American armed forces. In 1944 the army deployed 89 divisions, but by the summer of 1946 only 16 divisions remained. By that summer the 213 combat air groups available in 1945 had declined to 63 groups, only 11 of which were fully operational. The number of combat ships available in the navy had shrunk from a wartime high of 1,166 to 353 ships after a year of peace.[7] Britain, Australia, Canada, France, and other partners in the wartime alliance against the Axis also demobilized their armed forces in a process that was largely transparent to American journalists, diplomats, military attachés, and liaison officers. The demobilization plans of the Soviet Union, however, were not nearly so transparent, a condition that may explain, in part, the U.S. army's obsession with Red Army and Air Force order-of-battle intelligence. In 1945 the Red Army fielded the equivalent of 520 divisions and had more than 11 million men and women under arms. If, after Japan's surrender, Moscow declined to reduce these numbers significantly, then its alliance partners, to say nothing of its small neighbors, might legitimately worry about its intentions.[8]

By the fall of 1945, the army's Military Intelligence Division had instituted the "Soviet Military Roundup," a weekly newsletter covering the identification, location, and movements of Red Army units inside Russia and in areas occupied by Russian military forces. For its information the Roundup relied upon open sources, such as the *New York Times* and the Associated Press, as well as confidential reports from OSS (later SSU), military attachés, and American military officers attached to the Allied Control Commissions in Hungary, Bulgaria, and Romania.[9] The newsletter was not alarmist; indeed, it often seems to have gone out of its way to place a benign interpretation upon the reports from the field. When, for example, in early October 1945 Turkish intelligence reported through liaison channels the presence of twelve Red Army divisions in northern Iran and eighteen in the Caucasus, the Roundup, which listed only ten divisions in the entire region, reminded its readers that the Turks always exaggerated Soviet military strength, particularly along the Soviet-Turkish border in the Caucasus. The newsletter also pointed out that during the war the Trans-Caucasus region had been used by the Red Army as a training and recuperation area, suggesting that even if there were more divisions present than MID reported, these units were not likely to be first-line, combat-ready formations. The following month, when the Turks reported significant Red Army troop movements into Bulgaria, the newsletter noted that the alarmist reports may have been motivated by self-interest in that Turkish-Soviet relations were tense over Moscow's desire for readjustments in their common border, and Ankara may have hoped to portray the

Soviets as resorting to blackmail or force. The Roundup suggested that if new Russian troops were entering Bulgaria they were probably not reinforcements but replacements for demobilized soldiers who were returning home.[10]

While casting an appropriately critical eye on dubious reports of Russian troop concentrations and readily acknowledging that between VE Day and 1 November 1945 Moscow had reduced its army by twenty-seven divisions and 1.7 million men and women, military intelligence was hard-pressed to explain why the Red Army still maintained in peacetime five times the number of divisions (477) that the U.S. army had at the height of the war. More troubling was the discovery that the number of Russian troops in Austria, Germany, and Poland was actually greater than American military intelligence initially believed. In September 1945, for example, military intelligence officers estimated that Moscow had 600,000 troops in Germany, 100,000 in Austria, and 300,000 in Poland, but by November of that year the numbers for those countries had been revised upward to 1.2 million, 230,000, and 500,000 respectively. Whether the higher numbers were the result of now more accurate or earlier less accurate counting of static force levels or evidence of the arrival of additional reinforcements, the new totals would have worried the generals and their civilian masters in the U.S. War Department. Why would Moscow, almost six months after the Nazi surrender, continue to deploy seventy divisions in Germany alone, a number almost as large as the number of divisions in the entire U.S. army at the time of the Normandy invasion?[11]

Red Army troop levels in Europe appeared even more troubling when set beside reports that the Soviet Union was salvaging and reconstituting the German armaments industry in its occupation zone. This behavior was an explicit violation of the agreement reached at the Potsdam Conference (16 July–1 August 1945) that in the defeated and occupied Reich "the maintenance and production of all aircraft and arms, ammunition and implements of war shall be prevented."[12] Moscow's exploitation of German war industry was a particular feature of SSU clandestine reporting in the spring of 1946, and this coverage gained additional detail and credibility with the recruitment of SSU's prize agent in the Soviet occupation zone, Leo Skrzypczynski, the head of the Central Administration for Industry. Credible intelligence about the remilitarization of German industry—as well as intelligence on the deployments and readiness of Russian troops—might also have come from the breaks into Soviet communications by such cryptanalytic programs as CAVIAR and COLERIDGE. If the numbers on the U.S. Army's Soviet order-of-battle charts were "soft" or subject to interpretation, the intelligence on military production was solid. In such areas as aircraft and rocketry design and manufacturing, tank production, and optics, the Soviet Union was refurbishing and using German facilities to reequip and modernize its armed forces. Even without the additional evidence that Russia was rushing to develop atomic weapons, evidence that was increasing in the first half of 1946, the news from Germany would have set off alarms. American military observers might reasonably conclude that instead of downsizing its military capabilities after the war Moscow was upgrading them, and those observers might reasonably have asked, "For what purpose?"

Some in Washington may have discerned the answer to that question in the political intelligence reports from Europe. By the end of the war many American foreign policy makers were resigned to a Soviet sphere of influence in Eastern Europe. They hoped, however, that influence would be limited to foreign policy and military affairs and that the countries of the region, all of which hosted large numbers of Russian troops, would be free to conduct their domestic affairs without undue reference to Moscow. An important test of Moscow's intentions would be the degree to which it would use its military and police resources to privilege local communist parties in the competition to form postwar governments. Intelligence reporting revealed that Moscow had flunked the test. As we have seen, SSU was not reflexively anti-Soviet or anticommunist and in many (certainly not all) cases its political coverage was insightful, cautious, and nuanced. As early as the autumn of 1945, James Angleton at SCI/Z in Rome had discerned and reported the broad outlines of Stalin's "national front" strategy and the secret intelligence officers at SSU Germany were quick to follow. In his reporting, Angleton, who at the time was worried more by the threat to postwar Italian political stability and democracy from a reactionary right than from a revolutionary left, assured Washington that, at least in the short run, the Italian communist party (Partito Comunista Italiano, PCI)—and by implication, other communist parties in Western Europe—would eschew armed revolution in favor of participation in parliamentary politics. The SCI/Z chief was well aware that the PCI was responsive to Moscow's direction, but unlike Philip Horton, his more excitable colleague in Paris, Angleton believed that direction would favor moderation, and he correctly dismissed alarmist reports of impending insurrection as provocations by right-wing groups hoping to sow trouble between Washington and Moscow.

Intelligence from the Russian zone of Germany and Eastern Europe showed a different face of Stalin's national front strategy. In these regions, unlike Italy, occupation by the Red Army gave Moscow important levers of influence, and reliable reports suggested that the Russians were prepared to use those levers to ensure the dominance of the communist parties. Where evidence, such as the results of elections, indicated that communist dominance of a national front coalition could not be taken for granted, the Soviets would use the available instruments of power, including press controls and communist-dominated police and security services, to isolate, intimidate, or incarcerate noncommunist political elements who declined to acknowledge the leading role of the communists. By early 1946, these developments were a regular feature of SSU reporting from Germany, and they offered a counterpoint to Angleton's dispatches. The general picture that emerged was one of stark contrasts. Where local communist parties could not rely for support on the presence of Soviet proconsuls and the Red Army, they would pursue tactical accommodation with other political forces in a program of shared power. Where they could rely on immediate Soviet support, however, the communists would use that support to ensure, through intimidation if necessary, their dominance of any national front coalition. They would parlay that dominance into control of the centers of power—army, police, information, education—and then exercise that control to deepen and solidify further their hold on power, a hold they had no intention of releasing. By the summer of 1946 the intelligence signs and portents from Germany and Eastern Europe—when placed alongside such events as Stalin's "election speech" of February 1946, George Kennan's "long telegram," and Moscow's attempts to intimidate Iran and Turkey in early 1946—may have encouraged policy makers in Washington to see the Soviet Union as an expansionist power, intent on controlling, not just influencing, a yet to be determined number of client states, using national communist parties or, in certain circumstances, those still numerous divisions of the Red Army as instruments of intimidation, capture, and control.

Of course, to conclude simply that American policy makers must have rationally and deliberately responded to the available intelligence from Europe is to confuse the mere existence of intelligence with its influence. Before intelligence can influence policies, relevant information must be available to the policy makers. In 1945–1946 the circulation—that is, the availability—of secret intelligence within the U.S. government was constrained primarily by security considerations and secondarily by subject matter. In order to secure the content of an intelligence report and protect the identity, indeed the very existence, of the source of that information, intelligence services were inclined to limit distribution to circles of policy makers that expanded or contracted according to the sensitivity of the information and the nature of the subject matter. A member of one information circle might not be a member of other information circles, which meant that diplomats in the State Department and presidential assistants in the White House might not receive the same intelligence as generals in the War Department, a little-studied phenomenon that was already complicating the intelligence process during the Second World War.[13]

Because of the decentralized nature of the U.S. intelligence community, each service distributed its own product and decided who should see it. The Army Security Agency's "Diplomatic Summary," the daily compendium of decrypted foreign diplomatic communications, was so secret—circulating to the president and a dozen or so senior military and diplomatic authorities— that even other intelligence services, such as the Strategic Services Unit, could not see it. The army's weekly top-secret "Soviet Military Roundup" was published in only eleven copies and circulated only inside the War Department.[14] The military intelligence service apparently decided that other government departments, such as State and Treasury, had no professional interest in the Roundup's subject matter and therefore no need to know about it. It is unlikely that other departments were even aware of the existence of the Roundup, although its content, in condensed form, may have been included in other, more general, intelligence appreciations that the War Department shared with outsiders. Liaison with Britain's Secret Intelligence Service (SIS) brought SSU a bounty of high-level intelligence, but General Magruder, the chief of SSU, did not at first circulate that information within the U.S. government after SIS asked him not to because the intelligence—or more likely the source(s)—was so precious. Apparently, some intelligence is too good to show anyone. Of course, intelligence hoarded and not pushed out to the people who can use it is intelligence wasted, as Secretary of War Robert Patterson sharply reminded Magruder when he learned of SSU's secret cache and ordered him to release it.[15]

Actually, the Strategic Services Unit was one of the most liberal of the services in its distribution policies. SSU's reports circulated not only to departments in Washington, but also to American diplomatic, intelligence, and military missions abroad. Of course not every intelligence report went to every customer. In Washington, the Military Intelligence Division and the Office of Naval Intelligence received copies of almost every report, while civilian departments, such as State and Treasury, received only those reports deemed relevant to their work. In all cases SSU decided what was relevant, but the clandestine service seems to have been generous. In May 1946, for example, SSU sent 899 intelligence reports to the State Department, only 16 fewer than it sent to the Office of Naval Intelligence; indeed, in certain areas, such as East European affairs, the clandestine service considered State its chief customer.[16] Within the State Department SSU reports circulated among senior and mid-level officers down to the level of the geographic divisions and desks. Most of the reports were sent to Assistant Secretary for Administrative Affairs Julius Holmes, who would then distribute them to interested offices in the department, but occasionally SSU would send intelligence directly to the regional desks, such as the Division of Central European Affairs.[17] In European capitals SSU offices shared the fruits of their collection efforts with the local U.S. embassies or diplomatic delegations. In the fall of 1945, for example, the SSU station in London, the recipient of reports from other SSU units in Europe and also from the British intelligence service, routinely shared its information not only with the local American embassy but also with the U.S. delegation to the Council of Foreign Ministers, then meeting in the British capital.[18] Such contributions were appreciated by the diplomats whose own information sources were narrower. In Washington, for example, the State Department's chief of research for Europe and Africa acknowledged that SSU reporting, while uneven in geographic coverage, was of "considerable value," particularly because the clandestine operators sought out informants unavailable to the diplomats.[19] In Prague Ambassador Laurence Steinhardt was effusive in his appreciation. "I always read every single one of your reports," the ambassador assured an SSU representative. "The information is exceedingly useful to me."[20] Addressing a conference of SSU European station chiefs, a senior American diplomat readily acknowledged, "We have to depend on you." The State Department further kept its embassies in the intelligence loop by incorporating SSU reports, in paraphrase rather than verbatim, in the "Situation Reports" sent out periodically by State to all American diplomatic missions. In the spring of 1946, Charles Thayer, who before the war had served at the embassy in Moscow before embarking on an intelligence career that included organizing the OSS mission in Austria after the war, arranged to transmit to the Moscow embassy verbatim copies of any reports on the Soviet Union obtained by SSU Austria. The embassy was delighted, explaining that "it is difficult to obtain any information as to Soviet activities of this nature from within the Soviet Union, and we must depend largely upon reports emanating from the periphery."[21]

It is curious that while SSU reports were flying off to any number of customers, none landed at the White House. There is no mention of the president in any of the documents detailing SSU distribution practices. Although William Donovan during his command of OSS routinely sent memos on various intelligence subjects to President Franklin Roosevelt and continued the procedure when Harry Truman assumed the office, John Magruder apparently allowed the practice to lapse when, after the demise of OSS and the departure of Donovan, he assumed command of the remnants of the clandestine service. During the debates over the shape of postwar intelligence, Magruder probably preferred to keep a low profile when it came to dealing with the president who had abolished the Office of Strategic Services. Until the appearance of the Central Intelligence Group's "Daily Summary" in February 1946, a compilation that relied mainly upon SSU reporting, intelligence from the clandestine service probably reached the president indirectly—and perhaps without attribution—through his principal foreign policy adviser, Secretary of State James Byrnes.

The intelligence collected by the Strategic Services Unit was certainly ubiquitous in policy-making circles—probably no American intelligence agency served as many customers on such a broad range of subjects—but ubiquity is not the same as influence. Intelligence reports may cover a policy maker's desk, yet have little influence on that individual. They may not even attract that individual's serious attention. During the war President Franklin Roosevelt did not study the communications intelligence decrypts that his code breakers sent to the White House, preferring instead to have his naval aide read the reports aloud to him each morning while he was shaving.[22] This rather insouciant attitude may explain why Roosevelt never came to appreciate the enormous decision-making resource represented by the communications intelligence accomplishments of the code breakers, arguably the greatest achievement in American intelligence history. In November 1943, at a time when the cryptanalysts had almost total coverage of Tokyo's diplomatic communications and increasing access to its military communications, the president actually lamented to the secretaries of war and navy that Washington had "practically nothing" in terms of information from Japan.[23] This is the complaint of someone who is not paying attention to intelligence.

Something as simple as the format in which the intelligence is presented to decision makers may undermine its impact. Aside from the daily Diplomatic Summary, which contained only communications intelligence, in the immediate postwar period there was no dissemination instrument that compiled information from all sources in one document, for the benefit of the president and his principal advisers. The practice was for various agencies to distribute their recent intelligence in a series of memos. The stream of intelligence memos, some dealing with only a single topic, which flooded the Oval Office caused President Truman to throw up his hands in frustration and confusion, a reaction that led directly to the creation of the Daily Summary in early 1946. While a vast improvement over the uncoordinated memo traffic it replaced, the new format alone did not ensure that policy makers would pay more attention to intelligence. Secretary of War Robert Patterson was an avid consumer of the Daily Summary, while Secretary of the Navy James Forrestal found it only mildly interesting and General George C. Marshall, army chief of staff and James Byrnes's successor as secretary of state, didn't bother to read it at all, believing it merely duplicated information he received from other sources.[24]

The causal relationship between intelligence and decision is often the most elusive element in intelligence history. Intelligence is only one of any number of factors—personal ambition, bureaucratic and partisan politics, previous experience with a government or national leader, decision-making style, race, education, economic status, religion, ethnicity, gender—that might influence a foreign policy maker, and it is very difficult to determine the relative influence of any one of these factors. We cannot say with certainty that secret intelligence directly prompted a particular decision or more generally influenced the course of American foreign policy in the immediate postwar period, but then we cannot say with certainty that other possible factors, such as gender or religion, did either. What we can say is that in this period the United States maintained active clandestine intelligence programs; that after a slow start these intelligence programs produced for policy makers a picture of the Soviet Union's behavior and capabilities that was largely accurate in general if not always in detail; that the picture revealed a Soviet Union that was deceptive, untrustworthy, hostile, and belligerent; and that this picture was circulated in a timely fashion to those officials responsible for making American foreign and military policy. In short, we can say enough about American espionage in the early postwar era to suggest that it may deserve a more prominent place not only in the history of American intelligence, but the history of the origins of the Cold War.

Notes

Chapter 1. On the Precipice of Peace

1. Though now somewhat dated, the best survey of American intelligence history remains Christopher Andrew, *For the President's Eyes Only: Secret Intelligence and the American Presidency from Washington to Bush* (New York: Harper Collins, 1995).

2. For judicious views of American intelligence in the interwar period, see Thomas C. Mahnken, *Uncovering Ways of War: U.S. Intelligence and Foreign Military Innovation, 1918–1941* (Ithaca, NY: Cornell University Press, 2002), and Robert G. Angevine, "Gentlemen Do Read Each Other's Mail: American Intelligence in the Interwar Era," *Intelligence and National Security* 7, no. 2 (April 1992): 1–29.

3. Mahnken, *Uncovering Ways of War*, 26; David Alvarez, *Secret Messages: Codebreaking and American Diplomacy, 1930–1945* (Lawrence: University Press of Kansas, 2000), 51; Bruce W. Bidwell, *History of the Military Intelligence Division, Department of the Army General Staff: 1775–1941* (Frederick, MD: University Publications of America, 1986), 434.

4. Quoted in Andrew, *For the President's Eyes Only*, 92.

5. Quotations from Jeffery M. Dorwart, *Conflict of Duty: The U.S. Navy's Intelligence Dilemma, 1919–1945* (Annapolis, MD: Naval Institute Press, 1983), 50.

6. Quoted in Andrew, *For the President's Eyes Only*, 92.

7. Bidwell, *History of the Military Intelligence Division*, 434.

8. Wyman H. Packard, *A Century of U.S. Naval Intelligence* (Washington, DC: Department of the Navy, 1996), 68, 70–71. For a rare foray into clandestine intelligence by the navy, see Dennis Noble, "A U.S. Naval Intelligence Mission to China in the 1930s," *Studies in Intelligence* 50, no. 2 (2006), unclassified electronic edition, no pagination. This article may be accessed on the "Library–CSI Publications" page of the CIA website, www.cia.gov.

9. Dorwart, *Conflict of Duty*, 132; Bidwell, *History of the Military Intelligence Division*, 386–387.

10. G. Gregg Webb, "The FBI and Foreign Intelligence: New Insights into J. Edgar Hoover's Role," *Studies in Intelligence* 48, no. 1 (2004): 47–48.

11. Ibid., 49.

12. [Michael Warner], "COI Came First," in *The Office of Strategic Services: America's First Intelligence Agency* (Langley, VA: Central Intelligence Agency, 2000), 3. This publication may be accessed on the "Library–Publications" page of the CIA website, www.cia.gov.

13. Thomas Troy, *Donovan and the CIA: A History of the Establishment of the*

Central Intelligence Agency (Frederick, MD: University Publications of America, 1981), 84–86, 105.

14. Bradley F. Smith, *The Shadow Warriors: O.S.S. and the Origins of the CIA* (New York: Basic Books, 1983), 92.

15. Ibid., 125.

16. Data on OSS personnel levels can be found in Memorandum for Rear Admiral Sidney W. Souers, 22 March 1946, National Archives and Records Administration, College Park, Maryland, Record Group (RG) 226 (Records of the Office of Strategic Services), Entry 210, box 309. Unless otherwise specified, all unpublished documents cited in this work are located at the National Archives facility in College Park. A comprehensive history of OSS based on the full range of the organization's records (which have been, with very few exceptions, declassified) remains to be written. The best overview, though written before the full release of the operational records, is Smith, *The Shadow Warriors*.

17. Dorwart, *Conflict of Duty*, 207.

18. Even today little is known about the operations of the Special Service Branch. For a path-breaking study, see Mark Stout, "The Pond: Running Agents for State, War, and the CIA," *Studies in Intelligence* 48, no. 3 (2004), unclassified electronic edition, no pagination. This article may be accessed on the "Library–CSI Publications" page of the CIA website, www.cia.gov.

19. For the expansion of American communications intelligence programs, see Alvarez, *Secret Messages*, passim.

20. Douglas Waller, *Wild Bill Donovan: The Spymaster Who Created the OSS and Modern American Espionage* (New York: Free Press, 2011), 305–306; Troy, *Donovan and the CIA*, 227–228.

21. Waller, *Wild Bill Donovan*, 306.

22. Ibid., 308–309; Troy, *Donovan and the CIA*, 256, 280–281.

23. Waller, *Wild Bill Donovan*, 335–337. For the controversy surrounding the so-called Lisbon Affair, see David Alvarez, "Tempest in an Embassy Trash Can," *World War II* 22, no. 9 (January–February 2008): 55–59.

24. Donald C. Stone to Harold Smith, "Termination of the Office of Strategic Services and the Transfer of its Activities to the State and War Departments," 27 August 1945, *Foreign Relations of the United States, 1945–1950: Emergence of the Intelligence Establishment* (Washington, DC: United States Government Printing Office, 1996), 22–23. Hereinafter, this collection of documents will be referred to as *FRUS: Emergence of the Intelligence Establishment*.

25. Michael Warner, "Salvage and Liquidation: The Creation of the Central Intelligence Group," *Studies in Intelligence* 39, no. 5 (1996) no pagination, https://www.cia.gov/library/center-for-the-study-of-intelligence/kent-csi/vol39no5/html/v39i5a13p.htm.

26. Ibid.; Memorandum for Brigadier General John Magruder, 27 September 1945, RG 226, M1642, reel 113, frames 142–143. Hereinafter, citations to this microfilm collection will note reel/frames.

27. Emperor Hirohito announced the unconditional surrender of all Japanese

forces on 14 August 1945, but Japanese and Allied representatives did not actually sign the surrender protocols until 2 September.

28. Memorandum for the President from Robert Patterson, 22 October 1945, RG 226, M1642, 113/528–531.

29. Matthew M. Aid, e-mail message to David Alvarez, 12 September 2007; Matthew M. Aid, "The National Security Agency and the Cold War," in *Secrets of Signals Intelligence during the Cold War and Beyond*, ed. Matthew M. Aid and Cees Wiebes (London: Frank Cass, 2001): 32; Minutes of the Postwar Planning Board, 7 August 1945, RG 457 (Records of the National Security Agency), Historic Cryptologic Collection, Box 1364.

30. Summary of War Diary, July 1946, RG 38 (Records of the Chief of Naval Operations), CNSG Library, box 111, 5750/160. The authors are indebted to Ralph Erskine for calling their attention to this source.

31. Milton Katz, to William Quinn, 30 November 1945, RG 226, M1642, 113/50.

32. Director of the Strategic Services Unit to the Assistant Secretary of War, 25 October 1945, *FRUS: Emergence of the Intelligence Establishment*, 243–245; "Exhibit One: Present and Contemplated Future Deployment of SSU," n.d., RG 226, Entry 210, box 142.

33. William W. Quinn, *Buffalo Bill Remembers: Truth and Courage* (Fowlerville, MI: Wilderness Adventure Books, 1991), 240.

34. Philip Horton to Whitney Shepardson, 6 August 1945, RG 226, Entry 215, box 2; "Report from Chief of OSS Austria," 24 August 1945, RG 226, M1642, 3/635–636; "Operational Status Report," 24 September 1945, RG 226, Entry 215, box 8; "Summary of SSU Activities During January 1946," [n.d.], RG 226, Entry 210, box 191; John Magruder to the Assistant Secretary of War, 25 October 1945, RG 226, Entry 210, box 142.

35. "Interview with Mr. Gilpatric of Staff Division II," 3 March 1946, RG 226, Entry 190, microfilm reel 1.

36. Letter from President Truman to Secretary of State Byrnes, 20 September 1945, *FRUS: Emergence of the Intelligence Establishment*, 46–47.

37. Memorandum from the Director of the Bureau of the Budget to President Truman, 31 October 1945, ibid., 89–90.

38. "Founding of the National Intelligence Structure: Introduction," *Foreign Relations of the United States, 1945–1950: Emergence of the Intelligence Establishment*, www.state.gov/1997-2001-NOPDFS//about_state/history/intel/intro.html, no pagination.

39. Memorandum from the Joint Chiefs of Staff to Secretary of War Stimson and Secretary of the Navy Forrestal, 19 September 1945, *FRUS: Emergence of the Intelligence Establishment*, 40–44.

40. Letter from Secretary of State Byrnes, Acting Secretary of War Royall, and Secretary of the Navy Forrestal to President Truman, 7 January 1946, ibid., 166–169.

41. Presidential Directive on Coordination of Foreign Intelligence Activities, 22 January 1946, ibid., 178–179; Warner, "Salvage and Liquidation," no pagination.

42. Memorandum by the Director of the Strategic Services Unit, 14 February 1946, *FRUS: Emergence of the Intelligence Establishment*, 253–254.

43. Central Intelligence Group Directive No. 1, 19 February 1946, ibid., 255–256.

44. Michael Warner, "Prolonged Suspense: The Fortier Board and the Transformation of the Office of Strategic Services," *Journal of Intelligence History* 2 (Summer 2002): 69–72.

45. "Fact Finding Board Minutes of Meetings, 20 February–6 March 1946: Secret Intelligence," RG 226, Entry 210, box 329: 10. At its peak, the wartime SI section in OSS had slightly fewer than 2,000 staffers.

46. "Fact Finding Board Minutes of Meetings, 20 February–6 March 1946: SSU Organization," RG 226, Entry 210, box 329: 5.

47. Ibid., 6; "Fact Finding Board Minutes of Meetings, 20 February–6 March 1946: Secret Intelligence," RG 226, Entry 210, box 329: 11–15 (quote on 15).

48. Chief SI Switzerland to Chief SI Washington, 15 November 1945, RG 226, Entry 210, box 191; "Report of SSU/France for October 1945," 30 November 1945, RG 226, Entry 210, box 208.

49. "Fact Finding Board Minutes of Meetings, 20 February–6 March 1946: SSU Organization," RG 226, Entry 210, box 329: 6, 14.

50. Woodrow Kuhns, ed., *Assessing the Soviet Threat: The Early Cold War Years* (Langley, VA: Central Intelligence Agency, 1997), 4–5.

51. Ibid., 4, 7.

52. "Individual Surveys of SSU Branches," RG 226, Entry 210, box 329; "Current Status Report of the European Division and Cairo," 28 February 1946, RG 226, Entry 210, box 435.

53. "Interview with Mr. Gilpatric of Staff Division II," 3 March 1946, RG 226, Entry 190, microfilm roll 1.

54. Minutes of Meetings, Fact Finding Board [Fortier Committee], 20 February–6 March, 1946: "Secret Intelligence," RG 226, Entry 210, box 329: 7.

55. Homer Hall to Stephen Penrose, 28 June 1946, RG 226, Entry 210, box 182.

56. "Distribution and Dissemination of SSU/SI Material, 1 January–31 May 1946," RG 226, Entry 210, box 182.

57. Lester Houck to Laurence Houston, 27 June 1946, RG 226, Entry 210, box 182.

58. The authors are indebted to Mark Stout, the leading authority on the Pond, for information concerning the relationship between the State Department and the Special Service Branch.

59. Lieutenant General Hoyt Vandenberg to Dean Acheson, 22 August 1946, RG 226, Entry 210, box 273; Robert Joyce to Stephen Penrose, 4 October 1946, ibid.

60. Vienna to Washington, 19 March 1946, RG 226, Entry 210, box 470.

61. Colonel William Quinn to all stations, 16 October 1946, RG 226, Entry 210, box 520.

62. Minutes of Meetings, Fact Finding Board [Fortier Committee], 20 February–6 March, 1946: "Secret Intelligence," RG 226, Entry 210, box 329: 10.

63. "Fact Finding Board Minutes of Meetings, 20 February–6 March 1946: Background," RG 226, Entry 210, box 329: 7.

64. John Magruder to S. Leroy Irwin, 15 January 1946, in Michael Warner, ed.,

The CIA under Harry Truman (Washington, DC: Central Intelligence Agency, 1994), 23.

65. Crosby Lewis to General Magruder, 20 February 1946, RG 226, M1642/73.

66. Philip Horton to Whitney Shepardson, 16 August 1945, RG 226, Entry 215, box 2; Edgar Valk to Whitney Shepardson, [no day] January 1946, RG 226, Entry 215, box 8.

67. "Report for SSU Mission to Great Britain, 1–28 February 1946," 5 March 1946, RG 226, Entry 210, box 208; "Current Status and Activities of SI London," 28 February 1946, RG 226, Entry 210, box 435.

68. "Covering Report for SSU Mission to Great Britain, 1–31 March 1946," 8 April 1946, RG 226, Entry 210, box 208.

69. Warner, "Prolonged Suspense," 74.

70. William Quinn to SSU Shanghai, Bangkok, and Kuala Lumpur, 17 June 1946, RG 226, Entry 210, box 379.

71. "Functions of the Office of Special Operations," 25 October 1946, RG 226, Agency Selected Documents from the Office of the Director of Central Intelligence, box 4.

72. William Quinn to Chiefs of Mission, 5 September 1946, RG 226, Entry 210, box 480; William Quinn to SSU stations, 13 September 1946, RG 226, Entry 210, box 239.

Chapter 2. A Mystery in an Enigma

1. Joint Intelligence Staff, "Soviet Postwar Foreign Policy-General" (Enclosure D to Joint Intelligence Staff 80/20, "Capabilities and Intentions of the U.S.S.R. in the Post-War Period," 2 January 1946), National Archives and Records Administration, College Park, Maryland, Record Group (RG) 218 (Records of the Joint Chiefs of Staff), Geographic File 1946-1947, box 153, CCS 092, USSR (3-27-45), Sec. 4.

2. Quentin Reynolds, *The Curtain Rises* (New York: Random House, 1944), 43, 53.

3. W. Averell Harriman to the Secretary of State, 20 February 1944, *Foreign Relations of the United States, 1944*. Vol. 4: *Europe* (Washington, DC: Government Printing Office, 1966), 944–945.

4. John Morton Blum, ed., *From the Morgenthau Diaries: Years of War* (Boston: Houghton Mifflin, 1967), 305.

5. *New York Times*, 7 July 1944, 9.

6. Research and Analysis Branch, OSS, Report 2060, "Russian Reconstruction and Postwar Foreign Trade Developments," 9 September 1944, RG 59 (Records of the Department of State), Central Decimal File, 861.50/9-944.

7. Charles Bohlen to Dean Acheson, 19 October 1944, RG 59, F.W. 103.918/10-1944; F. F. Lincoln to Dean Acheson and Emilio Collado, 9 November 1944, RG 59, F.W. 103.918/11-1944.

8. S. Sherwood, "Memorandum for the President," 18 January 1945, Papers of James F. Brynes, Clemson University Library, folder 632.

9. Thomas G. Paterson, *Soviet-American Confrontation: Postwar Reconstruction and the Origins of the Cold War* (Baltimore: Johns Hopkins University Press, 1973), 37–43, 46–54. By the summer of 1945 it was also increasingly apparent that Congress was unlikely to approve significant credits for the Soviet Union.

10. Bradley F. Smith, *Sharing Secrets with Stalin: How the Allies Traded Intelligence, 1941–1945* (Lawrence: University Press of Kansas, 1996), 33–34.

11. Bradley F. Smith, *The Shadow Warriors: OSS and the Origins of the CIA* (New York: Basic Books, 1983), 212–213. As U.S. consul general in Moscow in 1918, Dewitt Clinton Poole had run clandestine operations to undermine the newly established Bolshevik regime.

12. "Joseph A. Michela [Class of] 1928" [Obituary], apps.westpointaog.org/Memorials/Article/8346.

13. Smith, *The Shadow Warriors*, 215.

14. Betty Abrahamsen Dessants, "Ambivalent Allies: OSS' USSR Division, the State Department, and the Bureaucracy of Intelligence Analysis, 1941–1945," *Intelligence and National Security* 11, no. 4 (October 1996): 729–731.

15. Smith, *Sharing Secrets with Stalin*, 169. Fearing that an official NKVD contingent in Washington would facilitate Soviet espionage against the United States, J. Edgar Hoover, the director of the FBI, and senior military officers convinced President Roosevelt to reject Donovan's proposal for an exchange of intelligence missions.

16. Ibid., 117, 130, 153, 175.

17. Ibid., 112; Richard Aldrich, *The Hidden Hand: Britain, America and Cold War Secret Intelligence* (London: John Murray, 2001), 36.

18. Smith, *Sharing Secrets with Stalin*, 160.

19. Ibid., 238–239, 247.

20. Ibid., 156, 160.

21. Ibid.

22. Matthew M. Aid, "Stella Polaris and the Secret Code Battle in Postwar Europe," *Intelligence and National Security* 17, no. 3 (Autumn 2002): 24–25.

23. Alfred McCormack to Generals Bratton and Lee, 12 February 1942, RG 457 (Records of the National Security Agency), Historic Cryptologic Collection (HCC), box 1305, Special Branch, G-2, Military Intelligence Division.

24. "Expansion of the Signal Intelligence Service," [April 1942], RG 457, HCC, box 1296; Colonel Carter Clarke to Alfred McCormack, 6 May 1942, RG 457, HCC, box 1305, Special Branch, G-2, Military Intelligence Division.

25. In June 1942 the Signal Intelligence Service was renamed the Signal Intelligence Division. In the next year the organization would be renamed the Signal Security Division, the Signal Security Service, and finally the Signal Security Agency. Since the three agency names between SIS and SSA had only brief lifespans and since the name Signal Security Agency survived from early 1943 through the end of the war, Signal Security Agency will be used in the text as the successor to the Signal Intelligence Service.

26. For Arlington Hall's work on Vatican codes and ciphers, see David Alvarez,

Secret Messages: Codebreaking and American Diplomacy, 1939–1945 (Lawrence: University Press of Kansas, 2000), 177–179.

27. Ibid., 176, 178, 187, 188. The foreign ministries and military services of most governments employed several cryptosystems of varying degrees of complexity. So-called low-grade cryptosystems were used for relatively unimportant communications, such as routine administrative matters, while high-grade systems were reserved for the protection of more sensitive messages.

28. "SSA. Cryptanalytic Branch Annual Report, FY 1944," RG 457, HCC, box 1115.

29. For American interest in Soviet codes and ciphers before 1943, see Alvarez, *Secret Messages*, 193–203.

30. Robert Louis Benson and Cecil James Phillips, *History of Venona* (Fort George Meade, MD: National Security Agency. 1995), 8, 13. The authors are indebted to Lou Benson for arranging the declassification of portions of this multivolume in-house history of the so-called Venona project.

31. Robert Louis Benson and Michael Warner, eds., *Venona: Soviet Espionage and the American Response, 1939–1957* (Washington, DC: National Security Agency and Central Intelligence Agency, 1996), xiii; See also John Earl Haynes and Harvey Klehr, Venona: *Decoding Soviet Espionage in America* (New Haven, CT: Yale University Press, 1999), 8.

32. Alvarez, *Secret Messages*, 206.

33. Ibid., 206–207.

34. For success against South American systems in 1942, see ibid., 168–169.

35. There was only one possible exception to this rule: Great Britain. For a discussion of Arlington Hall's policy toward British communications, see ibid., 188–190.

36. Matthew M. Aid, "The Anglo-American Signals Intelligence Effort against Russia, 1945–1950," paper delivered at the annual meeting of the Society for Historians of American Foreign Relations, 6 June 2003, Washington, DC, 3, 12; B Branch Inquiry Committee, no. 3, "Cryptanalytic Effort Underway in the SSA, 1943," RG 457, HCC, box 948.

37. Benson and Phillips, *Venona*, 20–21; Entry for August 15, 1943, Naval Communications Activity, Naval Communications Station, Washington, DC, "Russian Language Section History, 1943–1948," [n.d.], document released to the authors under the provisions of the Freedom of Information Act. Personnel numbers include only individuals working in the cryptanalytic offices and not those working at far-flung radio intercept stations.

38. Entry for "September 1944," Naval Communications Activity, "Russian Language Section History, 1943–1948"; Benson and Phillips, *Venona*, 22. Cecil Phillips, who at the time was a cryptanalyst in Arlington Hall's Russian section, categorically stated that "no diplomatic or trade message was translated or published before September 1945." Phillips recalled that by mid-1944 the code groups representing numbers in the so-called Trade (i.e., commercial and Lend-Lease) messages had been solved, so that parts of Trade messages, mainly numerical tables in purchase

orders and invoices, were readable. Cecil Phillips, e-mail message to David Alvarez, 18 February 1998.

39. Aid, "Stella Polaris and the Secret Code Battle in Postwar Europe," 28.

40. David Alvarez, "Tempest in an Embassy Teapot," *World War II* 22, no. 9 (January–February 2008): 55–59.

41. Quoted in Aid, "Stella Polaris and the Secret Code Battle in Postwar Europe," 29.

42. OSS Stockholm to OSS Washington, 29 October 1944, RG 226 (Records of the Office of Strategic Services), Entry 216, box 1.

43. R. Taylor Cole to Colonel Edward Buxton, [1 November 1944], RG 226, Entry 210, box 362.

44. OSS Washington to OSS Stockholm, 3 November 1944, RG 226, Entry 210, box 362.

45. Wilho Tikander to William Donovan, 11 December 1944, RG 226, Entry 210, box 362.

46. Aid, "Stella Polaris and the Secret Code Battle in Postwar Europe," 34–35. The Russians were told that OSS had run across the cryptologic materials in the course of an unrelated operation and had taken possession of the materials in order to prevent them from falling into the hands of the Germans.

47. Smith, *The Shadow Warriors*, 352–354; Aid, "Stella Polaris and the Secret Code Battle in Postwar Europe," 34 (quote).

48. Benson and Phillips, *Venona*, 53.

49. Ibid., n43; Cecil Phillips, e-mail message to David Alvarez, 15 March 1998.

50. Aid, "Stella Polaris and the Secret Code Battle in Postwar Europe," 55. Cecil Phillips, who not only co-authored the official history of the early "Russian Problem" at Arlington Hall but also served in the Russian Section in 1945–1946, recalled that STELLA POLARIS materials did not reach Arlington Hall until 1946. For an internal history of OP-20-G's Russian section, see Naval Communications Activity, "Russian Language Section (July 1943–January 1948)," document released to the authors under the provisions of the Freedom of Information Act.

51. Benson and Phillips, *Venona*, 58–59 and n57.

52. Ibid., 51.

53. Aid, "Stella Polaris and the Secret Code Battle in Postwar Europe," 47. By the summer of 1945 some of the STELLA POLARIS group had returned to Finland, while others had entered Swedish service.

54. Aid, "The Anglo-American Signals Intelligence Effort against Russia, 1945–1950," 10.

55. Alvarez, *Secret Messages*, 222–224; Benson and Phillips, *Venona*, 59.

56. Quoted in Randy Rezabek, "The Russian Fish with Caviar," *Cryptologia* 38, no. 1 (January 2014): 62.

57. Aid, "The Anglo-American Signals Intelligence Effort against Russia, 1945–1950," 19.

58. Quoted in ibid., 21.

59. Ibid.

60. Matthew Aid, *The Secret Sentry: The Untold History of the National Security Agency* (New York: Bloomsbury Press, 2009), 14–15; David Alvarez, "Behind Venona: American Signals Intelligence in the Early Cold War," *Intelligence and National Security* 14, no. 2 (Summer 1999): 180–181.

61. Aid, *The Secret Sentry*, 16.

62. David Alvarez, "Tying to Make the MAGIC Last: American Diplomatic Codebreaking in the Early Cold War," *Diplomatic History* 31, no. 5 (November 2007): 875.

63. Aid, "The Anglo-American Signals Intelligence Effort against Russia, 1945–1950," 15.

64. Staff totals are drawn from Naval Communications Activity, "Russian Language Section History, July 1943–January 1948."

65. G4-A, "Summary of War Diary," May and June 1946. The authors are indebted to Ralph Erskine for providing copies of these diaries.

66. N51 to N5, Memorandum, subject: "Report on Status of Projects," 7 August [1946]. The authors are indebted to Ralph Erskine for providing a copy of this document.

67. Naval Communications Activity, "Russian Language Section History": Chronology; Benson and Phillips, *Venona*, 67n1. The authors are indebted to Matthew Aid for information concerning the TANAGER reports.

68. The exception was the X-2 (counterintelligence) office of OSS, which had carefully controlled access to British communications intelligence regarding the activities of the German intelligence services.

69. For the limitations of postwar diplomatic code breaking, see Alvarez, "Trying to Make the MAGIC Last," passim. For the complications surrounding the wartime distribution of communications intelligence, see Alvarez, *Secret Messages*, 237–241.

70. "Interview with Mr. Gilpatric of Staff Division II, 3 March 1946," [Fortier Committee Hearings], RG 226, Entry 190, reel 1; John Magruder to the Assistant Secretary of War, 1 October 1945, RG 226, M1643, reel 113: William Hood, telephone interview with David Alvarez, 10 December 2004.

71. Harry Rositzke, *The KGB: The Eyes of Russia* (New York: Doubleday & Co., 1981), 2.

72. [Beurt SerVas], "Open Memorandum: Personal Opinion re Intelligence Penetration of Russia," 18 March 1946, RG 226, M1642, 57/712–15.

73. Quoted in John Lewis Gaddis, *The United States and the Origins of the Cold War, 1941–1947* (New York: Columbia University Press, 1972), 300.

74. Melvyn P. Leffler, *A Preponderance of Power: National Security, the Truman Administration, and the Cold War* (Stanford, CA: Stanford University Press, 1992), 108.

75. Ibid., 109.

76. Bruce R. Kuniholm, *The Origins of the Cold War in the Near East: Great Power Conflict and Diplomacy in Iran, Turkey, and Greece* (Princeton, NJ: Princeton University Press, 1980), 317–318.

77. William Maddox to Chief SI, 25 March 1946, subject: "Priority Intelligence Targets," RG 226, Entry 210, box 432.

78. Ibid.

79. Harry Rositzke to S. B. L. Penrose, 11 July 1946, subject: "Current Status of the Procurement of Intelligence on the USSR by SSU and Major Foreign Secret Intelligence Services," RG 226, Entry 210, box 329.

80. Ibid.

81. Seventh Army Interrogation Center, "Notes on Soviet Naval Intelligence Agencies and the Soviet Merchant Marine," 13 September 1945, RG 319, Entry 1041, "Formerly Top Secret Intelligence Documents, 1943–59," box 20.

82. Kevin C. Ruffner, "Project SYMPHONY: U.S. Intelligence and the Jewish *Brichah* in Postwar Austria," *Studies in Intelligence* 51, no. 1 (2007): 43.

83. Lt. Col. James Collins to Asst. C of S, G-2 USFET, 5 June 1946, subject: Interrogation of Red Army Personnel Apprehended in the U.S. Zone, RG 319, CIC Collection, IRR Case Files: Impersonal Files, box 39.

84. Harry Rositzke to S. B. L. Penrose, 11 July 1946, subject: "Current Status of the Procurement of Intelligence on the USSR by SSU and Major Foreign Secret Intelligence Services," RG 226, Entry 210, box 329.

85. Aid, "Stella Polaris and the Secret Code Battle in Postwar Europe," 52–53.

86. Ibid., 57–59.

87. Ibid., 59.

88. Alfred Ulmer to Richard Helms, 3 May 1946, RG 226, Entry 215, box 8; Crosby Lewis to SSU Washington, 4 October 1946, RG 226, Entry 210, box 480.

89. Vienna to War Department (SSU), 18 March 1946, RG 226, Entry 210, box 469; Vienna to War Department (SSU), 30 March 1946, RG 226, Entry 210, box 470.

90. Alfred Ulmer to Colonel William Quinn, 22 April 1946, RG 226, Entry 190, Director's Office, reel 73.

91. Harry Rositzke to S. B. L. Penrose, 11 July 1946, subject: "Current Status of the Procurement of Intelligence on the USSR by SSU and Major Foreign Secret Intelligence Services," RG 226, Entry 210, box 329.

92. Crosby Lewis to SSU Vienna and Washington, 26 September 1946, RG 226, Entry 210, box 480; Crosby Lewis to SSU Washington, 30 September 1946, ibid.

93. Christopher Andrew and Vasili Mitrokhin, *The Sword and the Shield: The Mitrokhin Archive and the Secret History of the KGB* (New York: Basic Books, 1999), 34–35.

94. Christopher Andrew and Oleg Gordievsky, *KGB: The Inside Story of Its Foreign Operations from Lenin to Gorbachev* (New York: Harper Collins, 1990) 387–388.

95. Philip Horton to Frank Wisner, 29 June 1945, RG 226, Entry 108B, box 17.

96. Philip Horton to SI Branch, Washington, 18 August 1945, RG 226, Entry 215, box 2.

97. Philip Horton to Whitney Shepardson, 6 August 1945, RG 226, Entry 215, box 2.

98. Lester Houck to Philip Horton, 15 October 1945, RG 226, Entry 210, box 512; Harry Rositzke to S. B. L. Penrose, 11 July 1946, subject: "Current Status of the

Procurement of Intelligence on the USSR by SSU and Major Foreign Secret Intelligence Services," RG 226, Entry 210, box 329.

99. Philip Horton to Whitney Shepardson, 16 August 1945, RG 226, Entry 215, box 2.

100. The relationship between SLC and SIS remains obscure. The former may have specialized in information resulting from liaison with foreign services, particularly the French, while the latter collected more widely through British networks around the world.

101. Alton Childs to S. B. L. Penrose, 22 April 1946, RG 226, Entry 210, box 435.

102. Aldrich, *The Hidden Hand*, 83.

103. "Current Status and Activities of SI, London," 28 February 1946, RG 226, Entry 210, box 435.

104. Ibid.; "Covering Report for SSU Mission to Great Britain, 1–31 March 1946," 8 April 1946, RG 226, Entry 210, box 208.

105. Harry Rositzke to S. B. L. Penrose, 11 July 1946, subject: "Current Status of the Procurement of Intelligence on the USSR by SSU and Major Foreign Secret Intelligence Services," RG 226, Entry 210, box 329.

106. "Report for SSU Mission to Great Britain," 1–28 February 1946, RG 226, Entry 210, box 208.

107. General John Magruder to General Clayton Bissell, 7 December 1945, RG 226, M1642, 29/1122.

108. Robert Patterson to General John Magruder, 18 December 1945, RG 226, M11642, 29/1128.

109. General John Magruder to General Clayton Bissell, 19 December 1945, RG 226, M1642, 29/1129; Alton Childs to S. B. L. Penrose, 22 April 1946, RG 226, Entry 210, box 435.

110. William Maddux to Robert Joyce, 18 November 1944, RG 226, Entry 210, box 148.

111. Peer Henrik Hansen, *Second to None: U.S. Intelligence Activities in Northern Europe, 1943–1946* (Dordrecht: Republic of Letters, 2011), 180.

112. "Taylor" to OSS, Washington, 10 July 1945, RG 226, Entry 210, box 480; "Taylor" to OSS, Washington, 1 August 1945, RG 226, Entry 210, box 379.

113. Crosby Lewis to General John Magruder, 20 February 1946, RG 226, M1642, 73/1316–1317; Hansen, *Second to None*, 179.

114. Hansen, *Second to None*, 158, 170–171; Crosby Lewis to General John Magruder, 20 February 1946, RG 226, M1642, 73/1316–1317. The Russians withdrew from Bornholm in April 1946.

115. Harry Rositzke to S. B. L. Penrose, 11 July 1946, subject: "Current Status of the Procurement of Intelligence on the USSR by SSU and Major Foreign Secret Intelligence Services," RG 226, Entry 210, box 329.

116. Memorandum by Henry Sutton, 26 June 1946, subject: Project Aladdin, RG 226, Entry 210, box 324.

117. Kevin C. Ruffner, "Draft Working Paper. Chapter 5: Long Experience in

the Anti-Soviet Game," 5, Central Intelligence Agency, Library: Electronic Reading Room, www.foia.cia.gov/document/519697e8993294098d50c29a.

118. Quoted in ibid., 6.

119. Gordon Stewart to Whitney Shepardson and S. B. J. Penrose, 20 February 1946, RG 226, Entry 214, box 4.

120. "Project for Ukrainia," 10 May 1946, RG 226, Entry 210, box 187. Though the author of this report is not identified, it was almost certainly Zsolt Aradi, an OSS/SSU officer who specialized in Vatican matters. Bishop von Preysing may have opposed Father Gehrmann's return to Berlin because he knew that the priest had been an informant for Germany's Weimar Republic during the 1920s, providing information from inside the Vatican embassy in Berlin. David Alvarez, *Spies in the Vatican: Espionage and Intrigue from Napoleon to the Holocaust* (Lawrence: University Press of Kansas, 2002), 162.

121. "Vatican Contacts," 4 June 1946, Central Intelligence Agency, Library: Electronic Reading Room, www.foia.cia.gov/document/51966ecb993294098d50ac84.

122. "Project for Ukrainia," 10 May 1946, RG 226, Entry 21, box 187. The Ukrainian Greek Catholic Church is a self-governing community within the Roman Catholic Church. They acknowledge the primacy of the pope, but their liturgies reflect practices in the Eastern Orthodox Church.

123. Ibid.

124. Acting Chief, PBM, to SSU Mission, Austria, 5 August 1946, RG 226, Entry 108C, box 21.

125. "U.S. Objectives with Respect to the USSR to Counter Soviet Threats to U.S. Security," NSC 20/4, 23 November 1948, articulated a policy of supporting the national aspirations of separatist movements inside the Soviet Union. The Central Intelligence Agency would become the instrument of that support.

126. SSU Bern to SSU Washington, 12 July 1946, RG 226, Entry 210, box 482; "Background on Ukrainian Movement," Central Intelligence Agency, Library: Electronic Reading Room, www.foia.cia.gov/document/519a6b2b993294098d5119fb. The date of the latter document is obscured, but internal evidence puts it no earlier than June 1946.

127. Quoted in Kevin C. Ruffner, "Cold War Allies: The Origins of CIA's Relationship with Ukrainian Nationalists," Central Intelligence Agency, Library: Electronic Reading Room, www.foia.cia.gov/documents/519697e8993294098d50c281.

128. Ibid., 27, 29.

129. Quoted in Ruffner, "Draft Working Paper," 13.

130. Quoted in ibid., 15–16.

131. Quoted in ibid., 25.

132. Ibid., 26, 33.

Chapter 3. Signs and Portents: Germany

1. Richard Helms (with William Hood), *A Look over My Shoulder: A Life in the Central Intelligence Agency* (New York: Random House, 2003), 53, 56.

2. Lucas Delattre, *A Spy at the Heart of the Third Reich: The Extraordinary Story of Fritz Kolbe, America's Most Important Spy in World War II* (New York: Atlantic Monthly Press, 2005).

3. For a survey of OSS operations inside Germany, see Christof Mauch, *The Shadow War against Hitler: The Covert Operations of America's Secret Intelligence Service*, trans. Jeremiah Riemer (New York: Columbia University Press, 1999), chapter 6.

4. "Monthly Report of Steering Division, SI/Germany," 2 August 1945, National Archives and Records Administration, College Park, Maryland, Record Group (RG) 226 (Records of the Office of Strategic Services), Entry 214, box 4.

5. Gary Trogdon, "A Decade of Catching Spies: The United States Army's Counterintelligence Corps, 1943–1953." Ph.D. diss., University of Nebraska, 2001, 128, 131–133.

6. William Suhling to John Magruder, 12 October 1945, RG 226, M1642, reel 73, frame 1154 (hereinafter reel/frames).

7. Ibid. For problems of morale and discipline among American occupation forces, see John Willoughby, *Remaking the Conquering Heroes: The Social and Geopolitical Impact of the Post-War American Occupation of Germany* (New York: Palgrave, 2001), 16–26.

8. Quoted in Burton Hersh, *The Old Boys: The American Elite and the Origins of the CIA* (New York: Charles Scribners, 1992), 160.

9. Kevin C. Ruffner, "You Are Never Going to Be Able to Run an Intelligence Unit: SSU Confronts the Black Market in Berlin," *Journal of Intelligence History* 2, no. 2 (Winter 2002): 3, 4.

10. Hersh, *The Old Boys*, 160.

11. Peter Sichel, letter to David Alvarez, 17 July 2002.

12. Historians have tended to denigrate claims of pro-Nazis resistance in early postwar Germany. Recent research establishes not only that such resistance was real and varied but also that it seriously engaged the attention of Allied intelligence and security authorities in every occupation zone. See, Perry Biddiscombe, *Werwolf! The History of the National Socialist Guerrilla Movement, 1944–1946* (Toronto: University of Toronto Press, 1998); Perry Biddiscombe, "Operation Selection Board: The Growth and Suppression of the Neo-Nazi 'Deutsche Revolution,' 1945–47," *Intelligence and National Security* 11, no. 1 (January 1996): 59–77; Richard J. Aldrich, *The Hidden Hand: Britain, America and Cold War Secret Intelligence* (London: John Murray, 2001), 182–183.

13. Ann Bray, John Finnegan, and James Gilbert, *In the Shadow of the Sphinx: A History of Army Counterintelligence* (Fort Belvoir, VA: Department of the Army, 2005), 88.

14. Trogdon, "A Decade of Catching Spies," 128–129; Earl Ziemke, *The U.S. Army in the Occupation of Germany, 1944–1946* (Washington, DC: Center of Military History, 1975), 272, 382–383; Frederick Taylor, *Exorcising Hitler: The Occupation and Denazification of Germany* (New York: Bloomsbury Press, 2011), 254–256, 277–279. Before the German surrender the Supreme Headquarters Allied Expeditionary Force, the authority controlling Allied forces in northern Europe, issued

directives requiring the automatic arrest of members of the Gestapo, the Sicherheitsdienst (SD), commissioned and noncommissioned officers of the SS, and Nazi
party officials down to the level of local group leaders.

15. Letters to David Alvarez, 31 July 2002 and 15 August 2002, from a former
X-2 officer who prefers to remain anonymous. On the residual concern about Axis
intelligence, see "OSS/X-2 Branch Monthly Report of Activities for August 1945,"
3 October 1945, RG 226, Entry 210, box 278.

16. Peter Sichel, letter to David Alvarez, 17 July 2002.

17. Ziemke, *The U.S. Army in the Occupation of Germany, 1944–1946*, 305.

18. "Monthly Report of Steering Division, SI/Germany," 2 August 1945, RG 226,
Entry 214, box 4.

19. Robert Murphy to the Secretary of State, 23 July 1945, RG 59 (Records of
the Department of State), State Department Decimal File. 740.00119 Control (Germany), box 3668; Office of the U.S. Political Adviser for Germany to the Secretary
of State, 31 July 1945, ibid.

20. Harry Rositzke to Frank Wisner, 5 September 1945, subject: "Monthly Report
of Steering Division," RG 226, Entry 214, box 4; Harry Rositzke to Frank Wisner, 4
October 1945, subject: "Monthly Report of Steering Division," RG 226, Entry 214,
box 4.

21. For a description of Bern's Catholic networks, see "789" to Lester Houck, 29
August 1945, subject: "Dossiers on Trent, Massingham and Attleboro," RG 226,
Entry 214, box 7.

22. Harry Rositzke to Frank Wisner, 5 September 1945, subject: "Monthly Report
of Steering Division," RG 226, Entry 214, box 4; Harry Rositzke to Frank Wisner,
5 November 1945, subject: "Monthly Report of Steering Division," RG 226, Entry
214, box 4; "Summary of SSU Activities During January 1946," RG 226, Entry 210,
box 191; Donald Greer to Lester Houck, 10 June 1946, subject: "Monthly Evaluation
Report," RG 226, Entry 210, box 4.

23. Harry Rositzke to Frank Wisner, 4 October 1945, subject: "Monthly Report of
Steering Division," RG 226, Entry 214, box 4; Operational Status Report, 24 September 1945, RG 226, Entry 215, box 8.

24. SHAEF Joint Intelligence Committee, Political Intelligence Report, 9 July
1945, RG 226, M1642, 10/1038–1042.

25. Robert Murphy, *Diplomat among Warriors* (New York: Doubleday and Company, 1964), 260, 283, 287; SHAEF Joint Intelligence Committee: Political Intelligence Report, 9 July 1945, RG 226, M1642, 10/1038–1042.

26. Office of Strategic Services, "Over-all and Special Programs for Strategic
Services Activities in Germany During the Occupation Period," 14 August 1945, RG
226, Entry 210, box 183.

27. "Intelligence Requirements on Russian Zone/Germany," 21 August 1945, RG
226, Entry 210, box 501; Kevin Ruffner, ed., *Forging an Intelligence Partnership: CIA
and the Origins of the BND, 1945–1949* (Langley, VA: Central Intelligence Agency,
1999), xv. For evidence that intelligence officers in Germany believed that the U.S.
military government feared that operations into the Russian Zone would poison re-

lations with Moscow, see David Murphy, Sergei Kondrashev, and George Bailey, *Battleground Berlin: CIA vs KGB in the Cold War* (New Haven, CT: Yale University Press, 1997), 8.

28. Murphy et al., *Battleground Berlin*, 11.

29. "Intelligence Requirements on Russian Zone/Germany," 21 August 1945, RG 226, Entry 210, box 501; Harry Rositzke to Frank Wisner, 5 September 1945, subject: "Monthly Report of Steering Division," RG 226, Entry 214, box 4.

30. For Frank Wisner's troubled experience in Romania, see Eduard Mark, "The OSS in Romania, 1944–45: An Intelligence Operation of the Early Cold War," *Intelligence and National Security* 9, no. 2 (April 1994): 320–344.

31. Frank Wisner to Whitney Shepardson and S. B. L. Penrose, 11 September 1945, subject: "Miscellaneous Operational Details," RG 226, Entry 108B, box 70.

32. Evan Thomas, *The Very Best Men: Four Who Dared: The Early Years of the CIA* (New York: Simon and Schuster, 1995), 23.

33. Hugh Cunningham to Chief of Mission, SSU/WD Mission to Germany, 13 March 1946, subject: "Progress Report," RG 226, Entry 215, box 8. For evidence that civilian and military occupation authorities depended heavily upon OSS/SSU for their intelligence, see Frank Wisner to Whitney Shepardson and S. B. L. Penrose, 11 September 1945, subject: "Miscellaneous Operational Details," RG 226, Entry 108B, box 70.

34. Harry Rositzke to Frank Wisner, 5 September 1945, subject: "Monthly Report of Steering Division," RG 226, Entry 214, box 4.

35. Ruffner, "You Are Never Going to Be Able to Run an Intelligence Unit," 8.

36. Ibid.; Harry Rositzke to Frank Wisner, 4 October 1945, subject: "Monthly Report of Steering Division," RG 226, Entry 214, box 4.

37. "Individual Surveys of SSU Branches," RG 226, Entry 210, box 329; Harry Rositzke to Frank Wisner, 5 November 1945, subject: "Monthly Report of Steering Division," RG 226, Entry 214, box 4; Donald Steury, ed., *On the Front Lines of the Cold War: Documents on the Intelligence War in Berlin, 1946–1961* (Langley, VA: Central Intelligence Agency, 1999), 16.

38. Steury, *On the Front Lines of the Cold War*, 19; For Wiesbaden's concern over the reliance on casual contacts and the lack of clandestine networks, see Harry Rositzke to Frank Wisner, 5 September 1945, subject: "Monthly Report of Steering Division," RG 226, Entry 214, box 4, and Harry Rositzke to Frank Wisner, 5 November 1945, subject: "Monthly Report of Steering Division," RG 226, Entry 214, box 4.

39. For evidence that Berlin Base later regretted its decision to pursue Polish operations at the expense of direct operations against Russian-occupied Germany, see Steury, *On the Front Lines of the Cold War*, 20.

40. Lt. Commander Richard Helms to General John Magruder, 18 December 1945, subject: "Relations of SSU with OMGUS," RG 226, Entry 92, box 622; Murphy et al., *Battleground Berlin*, 12.

41. For Skrzypczynski, see the biographical sketch appended to L-1724. "Economic Prospects of the Russian Zone and Russian Attitudes toward German Unity," 21 September 1946, RG 226, Entry 108A, box 23.

42. Harry Rositzke to Frank Wisner, 5 November 1945, subject: "Monthly Report of Steering Division," RG 226, Entry 214, box 4.

43. Ibid. This report notes that Berlin has produced several reports on the Red Army in Germany but these reports have been of limited value to U.S. Army intelligence.

44. For the report of the naval inspection team, see Naval Division, U.S. Group Control Commission, "Germany: General Observations on Ports in Russian Occupied Areas," 4 September 1945, RG 319 (Records of the Army Staff), G-2 "ID" File, box 1375.

45. Karl Abt, e-mail message to David Alvarez, 16 April 2005.

46. Bray et al., *In the Shadow of the Sphinx*, 94.

47. Harry Rositzke to Frank Wisner, 2 August 1945, subject: "Monthly Report of Steering Division, SI/Germany," RG 226, Entry 214, box 4; Harry Rositzke to Frank Wisner, 5 November 1945, subject: "Monthly Report of Steering Division," 5 November 1945, RG 226, Entry 214, box 4; Peer Henrik Hansen, *Second to None: U.S. Intelligence Activities in Northern Europe, 1943–1946* (Dordrecht: Republic of Letters, 2011), 201.

48. David Alvarez, *Secret Messages: Codebreaking and American Diplomacy, 1930–1945* (Lawrence: University Press of Kansas, 2000), 224.

49. Information from Matthew Aid.

50. "French Analyses of Russian and American Positions on Germany's Future," *Diplomatic Summary*, 17 April 1946. Document released to David Alvarez by the National Security Agency under the provisions of the Freedom of Information Act.

51. Richard Helms to General John Magruder, 18 December 1945, subject: "Relations of SSU with OMGUS," RG 226, Entry 92, box 622.

52. Frank Wisner to Whitney H. Shepardson and S. B. L. Penrose, 11 September 1945, subject: "Miscellaneous Operational Details," RG 226, Entry 108B, box 70.

53. Political Adviser for Germany to the Secretary of State, 24 July 1945, *Foreign Relations of the United States, 1945,* vol. 3: *European Advisory Commission, Austria, Germany* (Washington, DC:: Government Printing Office, 1968), 953; Political Adviser for Germany to the Secretary of State, 20 August 1945, ibid., 957; Political Adviser for Germany to the Secretary of State, 3 October 1945, ibid., 971.

54. Richard Helms to General John Magruder, 18 December 1945, subject: "Relations of SSU with OMGUS," RG 226, Entry 92, box 622 (quote); Frank Wisner to Whitney Shepardson and S. B. L. Penrose, 11 September 1945, subject: "Miscellaneous Operational Details," RG 226, Entry 108B, box 70. This evidence challenges the claim by Carolyn Eisenberg that in 1945 Ambassador Murphy and his office "had an immense range of contacts both inside and outside the Russian zone." The contacts were actually SSU's. Carolyn Eisenberg, *Drawing the Line: The American Decision to Divide Germany, 1944–1949* (Cambridge: Cambridge University Press, 1996), 196.

55. Crosby Lewis to Foreign Branch M (Washington), 29 August 1946, subject: "Transcript of Conference Held in Heidelberg, July 22 1946," RG 226, Entry 210, box 368.

56. For lists of intelligence reports received in the Office of the Director of Intelligence in November 1945, see Office of the Director of Intelligence, Intelligence Bulletins Nos. 21 (16 November 1945) and 23 (22 November 1945), RG 260 (Records of U.S. Occupation Headquarters, World War II), OMGUS: Records of the Executive Office, Weekly Intelligence Reports, 1945–1949, box 330.

57. Frank Wisner to Whitney Shepardson, S. B. L. Penrose and Howard Chapin, 17 November 1945, subject: "Report of SI Operations-Berlin," RG 226, Entry 190, Washington Director's Office, reel 74.

58. Norman Naimark, *The Russians in Germany: A History of the Soviet Zone of Occupation, 1945–1949* (Cambridge, MA: Belknap Press, 1995), 12, 25.

59. Ibid., 254–256.

60. Gregory Sandford, *From Hitler to Ulbricht: The Communist Reconstruction of East Germany, 1945–1946* (Princeton, NJ: Princeton University Press, 1983), 29.

61. Eduard Mark, "Revolution by Degrees: Stalin's National Front Strategy for Europe, 1941–1947," Working Paper 31, Cold War International History Project, February 2001, 36–37.

62. Henry Krisch, *German Politics under Soviet Occupation* (New York: Columbia University Press, 1974), 86; Sandford, *From Hitler to Ulbricht*, 48–52.

63. OSS Bern to OSS Washington, 26 January 1945, RG 226, Entry 160, box 1, and OSS Bern to OSS Washington, 5 February 1945, RG 226, Entry 190, Director's Office, reel 52; James Grafton Rogers to the Joint Chiefs of Staff, 6 August 1944, subject: "Manifesto to the German People by the Moscow National Committee of Free Germany," printed in Jürgen Heideking and Christof Mauch, eds., *American Intelligence and the German Resistance to Hitler* (New York: Westview, 1996), 52–55; Krisch, *German Politics under Soviet Occupation*, 49.

64. William Donovan to the Joint Chiefs of Staff, 17 November 1944, enclosing Research and Analysis Branch, "Russian Economic Policies in Germany in the Period of Military Occupation," RG 218, box 723, CCS 000.1 USSR, Sec. 1; William Donovan to President Franklin Roosevelt, 13 July 1944, subject: "Russian Policy Toward Germany," printed in Heideking and Mauch, *American Intelligence and the German Resistance to Hitler*, 225–229.

65. Heideking and Mauch, *American Intelligence and the German Resistance to Hitler*, 410–411; OSS Germany, Report L-159/L-312, 21 June 1945, RG 226, Entry 108, box 166; OSS Germany, Report L-319, 24 July 1945, RG 226, Entry 108, box 166; Allen Dulles to General William Donovan, 15 September 1945, RG 226, Entry 88, box 536.

66. Naimark, *The Russians in Germany*, 274–276.

67. Ibid.; Sandford, *From Hitler to Ulbricht*, 142–143.

68. Naimark, *The Russians in Germany*, 278; Krisch, *German Politics under Soviet Occupation*, 142–143.

69. Naimark, *The Russians in Germany*, 281–284.

70. Harry Rositzke to Frank Wisner, 5 November 1945, subject: Monthly Report of the Steering Division, RG 226, Entry 214, box 4.

71. Krisch, *German Politics under Soviet Occupation*, 146.

72. Murphy et al., *Battleground Berlin*, 12; Peter Sichel to Chadbourne Gilpatric, 26 April 1946, subject: "George Wood," RG 226, Entry 210, box 477; Peter Sichel, e-mail messages to David Alvarez, 3 June 2004 and 6 June 2004.

73. SAINT (London) to SAINT (Washington), 14 August 1946, subject: "Monthly Intelligence Review—Germany and Austria," 25 May 1946 to 25 June 1946, RG 226, Entry 210, box 368.

74. See, for example, Secretary of State to the Political Adviser for Germany, 13 March 1946, *Foreign Relations of the United States, 1946,* vol. 5: *The British Commonwealth; Western and Central Europe* (Washington, DC: U.S. Government Printing Office, 1969), 709, and Political Adviser for Germany to the Secretary of State, 29 March 1946, ibid., 714–715; Peter Sichel, e-mail message to David Alvarez, 24 September 2004.

75. SSU Germany, Original Report L-1149, 22 January 1946, RG 226, Entry 108A, box 21; SSU Dissemination Report A-64912, 28 January 1946, RG 226, Entry 108, box 169; SSU Germany, Original Report L-1354, 12 March 1946, RG 226, Entry 108A, box 21; SSU Dissemination Report A-65726, 7 March 1946, RG 226, Entry 108, box 169; SI Branch, SSU to James Riggleberger (Chief, Central European Affairs Division, State Department), 2 May 1946, RG 226, Entry 210, box 477.

76. SSU dissemination report A-66455, 26 March 1946, RG 226, Entry 108E, box 2.

77. SSU Germany, Original Report L-1350, 19 March 1946, RG 226, Entry 108A, box 21. Examples of leaflets and pamphlets can be found in RG 226, Entry 108B, box 74.

78. For such an argument, see Eisenberg, *Drawing the Line,* 224–225; 489.

79. Peter Sichel, e-mail message to David Alvarez, 24 September 2004.

80. Murphy et al., *Battleground Berlin*, 12: Crosby Lewis to SSUCC, 25 March 1946, RG 226, Entry 210, box 468; Peter Sichel, e-mail message to David Alvarez, 6 June 2004.

81. Eduard Mark, "The War Scare of 1946 and Its Consequences," *Diplomatic History* 21, no. 3 (July 1997): 388–389.

82. Much of the history of the Pond remains murky, so statements concerning its operations must be tentative. Still, if the organization was as active and effective as its chief, Colonel John Grombach, claimed, then the army would not have had to rely so much on SSU in this period. The summary report from the period April 1946–March 1947 lists the organization's "most important" sources. Five of the first six sources are foreign police or intelligence services. The seventh is "[an] organization in Berlin" that is tapping Russian phones. Such an organization appears nowhere else in the intelligence record of this period. It may have made its appearance in 1947. "Production Report, 1946–1947," RG 263, Entry P12, box 20. The authors are indebted to Mark Stout for providing a copy of this document.

83. Headquarters, SSU, Intelligence Brief No. 4, 12 July 1946, RG 226, Entry 210, box 329; Peter Sichel, e-mail message to David Alvarez, 17 February 2004. For samples of order-of-battle reports, see the collection in RG 226, Entry 210, box 477.

84. For the Potsdam decision on the German armaments industry, see *Foreign Relations of the United States: The Conference of Berlin,* vol. 2 (Washington, DC:

Government Printing Office, 1960), 1481. For the production of armaments in the Soviet Zone, see Naimark, *The Russians in Germany*, 214–220.

85. Naimark, *The Russians in Germany*, 214–215; Taylor, *Exorcising Hitler*, 258.

86. Letters from an OSS/SSU veteran who prefers to remain anonymous to David Alvarez, 15 August 2002 and 10 October 2002. This veteran participated in several of these clandestine missions.

87. Jeffrey G. Barlow, *From Hot War to Cold: The U.S. Navy and National Security Affairs, 1945–1955* (Stanford, CA: Stanford University Press, 2009), 162, 499n16.

88. SSU Germany, Original Report L-1310, 28 February 1946, RG 226, Entry 108A, box 21; SSU dissemination report A-67340, 23 April 1946, RG 226, Entry 153A, roll 1, frame 1163. The Danes provided information on Soviet efforts to refurbish and use German military installations and relocate to the Soviet Union technicians from the German aircraft industry. Hansen, *Second to None*, 195.

89. Mark, "The War Scare of 1946 and Its Consequences," 394–395; SSU Germany, Original Report L-1227, 23 February 1946, RG 226, Entry 108A, box 21; SSU Germany, Original Report L-1314, 8 March 1946, RG 226, Entry 108A, box 21; SSU Germany, Original Report L-1338, 26 March 1946, RG 226, Entry 108A, box 21; SSU Dissemination Report A-67016, 18 April 1946, RG 226, Entry 153A, roll 1, frame 0792; Donald Greer to Lester Houck, 10 June 1946, subject: "Monthly Evaluation Report," RG 226, Entry 210, box 411.

90. Assistant Chief of Staff, G-2, EUCOM, Special Intelligence Summary No. 15, 15 April 1946, RG 319, Publications File, 1946–1951, box 1145.

91. *New York Times*, 13 July 1946, 6; *Washington Post*, 25 July 1946, 1.

92. *New York Times*, 13 July 1946, 6; ibid., 23 August 1946, 6; ibid., 3 October 1946, 17.

93. Crosby Lewis to FBM, 25 September 1946, RG 226, Entry 216, box 2.

94. Naimark, *The Russians in Germany*, 220–226.

95. Lt. Colonel F. M. Potter to Economic Division, 14 January 1947, subject: "War Production—Soviet Zone," RG 260, OMGUS, Records of the Executive Office, Weekly Intelligence Reports, 1945–1949, box 330; Office of the Director of Intelligence, Headquarters European Command, Intelligence Summary No. 12, 21 July 1947, RG 338, box 2917.

96. Boris T. Pash, *The ALSOS Mission* (New York: Award House, 1969), 35, 216–217, 220–221, 239.

97. Naimark, *The Russians in Germany*, 208–213.

98. Frank Wisner to Whitney Shepardson, 1 October 1945, RG 226, Entry 210, box 431; Henry S. Lowenhaupt, "On the Soviet Nuclear Scent," *Studies in Intelligence*, 11 (Fall 1967): 13–14.

99. Lt. Colonel S. M. Skinner to Colonel W. R. Schuler, 30 January 1946, RG 226, Entry 210, box 431; "Notes on Soviet Atomic Research Efforts," 27 September 1946, RG 226, Entry 108A, box 23; "Ieuna-Werke at Halle and Merseburg," [late July 1946], RG 226, Entry 108A, box 23.

100. David Holloway, *Stalin and the Bomb: The Soviet Union and Atomic Energy, 1939–1956* (New Haven, CT: Yale University Press, 1994), 161–162.

101. General Mark Clark to the War Department, 8 November 1946, RG 319, Assistant Chief of Staff G-2, Top Secret Cables, 1942–1952, box 63.

102. William Maddox to Chief, SI, 25 March 1946, subject: "Priority Intelligence Targets," RG 226, Entry 210, box 432; Crosby Lewis to SSUCC, 25 March 1946, RG 226, Entry 210, box 468; Memorandum by Gordon Stewart (Chief, SI/Germany), 30 March 1946, subject: "SI Germany," RG 226, Entry 214, box 4. For all its intention to focus on the Soviet Union, SSU could not entirely escape the demands of its local customers. As late as the summer of 1946, the German mission was still covering political developments inside the American Zone.

103. War Department to SSU Vienna, 25 April 1946, RG 226, Entry 210, box 470; Jeffrey Barlow, e-mail message to David Alvarez, 11 July 2003.

104. Thomas Polgar, e-mail messages to David Alvarez, 16 & 17 June 2004.

105. Again, the Pond seems not to have served General Sibert's needs.

106. Timothy Naftali, "Reinhard Gehlen and the United States," in *U.S. Intelligence and the Nazis*, ed. Richard Breitman et al. (Washington, DC: National Archives Trust Fund Board, 2004), 379–380. Initially, Fremde Heer Ost was a research and analysis unit that processed and distributed intelligence collected on the eastern front by the agent networks, codenamed "Walli ," run by the Abwehr, the military intelligence service. When, in June 1944, the Abwehr was absorbed into the RSHA, "Walli" became part of FHO.

107. Ruffner, *Forging an Intelligence Partnership*, xv–xvii (quotes on xvi); Arnold Silver, "Questions, Questions, Questions: Memories of Oberursel," *Intelligence and National Security* 8, no. 2 (April 1993): 208.

108. Crosby Lewis to SSUCC, 21 March 1946, RG 226, Entry 216, box 1.

109. The authors are indebted to Matthew Aid for information concerning Baun's radio intercept unit.

110. Ruffner, *Forging an Intelligence Partnership*, xvii–xviii; Naftali, "Reinhard Gehlen and the United States," 382. Initially, Baun resisted his subordination to Gehlen, and the two struggled for control of the organization. By 1947 Baun had been moved aside to a position in strategic planning and Gehlen remained the uncontested leader of RUSTY.

111. Lt. Colonel J. L. Collins to Chief, Intelligence Branch, G-2 USFET, 24 September 1946, subject: Operation Rusty, published in Ruffner, "Forging an Intelligence Partnership," 124–126 (quote on 125).

112. Naimark, *The Russians in Germany*, 355–356, 379; Perry Biddiscombe, "The Problem with Glass Houses: The Soviet Recruitment and Deployment of SS Men as Spies and Saboteurs," *Intelligence and National Security* 15, no. 3 (Autumn 2000): 132–133. Only in June 1948 did the communist-controlled regime in East Germany purge from its police former members of the Nazi Party, but even then exemptions were allowed for former Nazis who were making important contributions to the work of the police.

113. Ruffner, *Forging an Intelligence Partnership*, xvi.

114. Ibid., xx. The Central Intelligence Agency, SSU's organizational successor, would eventually assume responsibility for the Gehlen organization in 1949. Still un-

der Reinhard Gehlen's command, that organization would become the Bundesnach-richtensdienst, the first intelligence service of the Federal Republic of Germany.

115. Silver, "Questions, Questions, Questions," 209.

116. Army intelligence would often take over sources or networks that SSU had determined were intelligence mills. Peter Sichel, letter to David Alvarez, 17 July 2002; Peter Sichel, e-mail message to David Alvarez, 22 June 2004.

117. "Soviet Apprehension of German Nationals, U.S. Zone," RG 319, CIC Collection, IRR, Case Files: Impersonal Files, box 22. The number of kidnappings varies with the source. In January 1946 CIC reported that 38 individuals had been seized in the American sector of the city since the preceding August. A later report recorded 1,871 kidnappings in the period 1945–1947. Arthur L. Smith, *Kidnap City: Cold War Berlin* (Westport, CT: Greenwood Press, 2002), 12, 15n33.

118. "Soviet Recruitment of German Scientists," RG 319, CIC Collection, IRR, Case Files: Impersonal Files, box 31.

119. Office of the Assistant Chief of Staff, G-2, USFET, "Special Intelligence Summary, No. 12," 28 January 1946, RG 319, Publications File, 1946–1951, Box 1145; Lucius D. Clay, *Decision in Germany* (Westport, CT: Greenwood Press, 1970 reprint), 133–134.

120. X-2, Germany, "Progress Report on X-2 Penetration Cases Run in the American Occupied Zone in Germany, August 1945," 1 September 1945, RG 226, Entry 213, box 3.

121. During the war the Soviet intelligence and security services underwent several reorganizations with attendant changes in name. In 1945–1946 American intelligence assumed, incorrectly, that the NKVD represented the entirety of Moscow's foreign intelligence and counterintelligence capabilities. For convenience and consistency, this study will follow the same practice.

122. Richard Cutler, *Counterspy: Memoirs of a Counterintelligence Officer in World War II and the Cold War* (Washington, DC: Brassey's, 2004), 89–90. In his memoir Richard Cutler, Berlin X-2 chief in the fall of 1945, recalls that MOCCASIN's attackers were Russian and suggests that the NKVD tried to murder the double agent. By the spring of 1946 SSU had developed reservations concerning MOCCASIN's reliability.

123. Richard Cutler to Crosby Lewis and Sidney Lennington, 9 November 1945, RG 226, Entry 213, box 1.

124. Cutler, *Counterspy*, 90–91.

125. Kemritz's importance depended less upon the quantity and quality of his reports than on the fact that X-2 had so few alternative sources in direct contact with the NKVD. Knowing almost nothing about the Soviet services, American counterintelligence valued *any* information, no matter how limited. Richard Cutler, the chief of Berlin X-2 in the early stages of the SAVOY operation, estimated that Kemritz contributed as much as 90% of what X-2 knew about Russian intelligence operations in Berlin in 1945–1946. This was, however, 90% of a relatively small whole. Thomas Polgar, who inherited SAVOY when he succeeded Cutler as Berlin X-2 chief, recalled, "Starting from zero, we got some information but nothing of

great importance." Richard Cutler, e-mail message to David Alvarez, 9 April 2004; Thomas Polgar, letter to David Alvarez, 31 May 2004.

126. Murphy et al., *Battleground Berlin*, 408–409. For additional information on ZIGZAG and SAVOY the authors are indebted to Richard Cutler and Thomas Polgar, who, in succession, directed Berlin X-2 in 1945–1946.

127. Thomas Polgar, letter to David Alvarez, 31 May 2004; Thomas Polgar, e-mail to David Alvarez, 5 June 2004. SAINT to SAINT, DB1, 3 May 1946, subject: "Russian Agents in Austria," RG 226, Entry 214, box 1. On Soviet relations with the German police, see Naimark, *The Russians in Germany*, chapter 7.

128. Thomas Polgar, e-mail message to David Alvarez, 16 June 2004. Rebrov was exfiltrated from the Soviet zone in 1948 and resettled in the United States.

129. Assistant Chief of Staff, G-2, USFET, "Special Intelligence Summary," No. 12 (28 January 1946), RG 319, Publications File, 1946–1951, box 1145; Assistant Chief of Staff, G-2, USFET, "Special Intelligence Summary," No. 31 (26 February 1947), RG 319, Publications File, 1946–1951, box 1147.

130. SAINT to SAINT Amzon (for Berlin), 26 April 1946, subject: "Identification of RIS Services in Berlin Area," RG 226, Entry 108B, box 20.

131. Murphy et al., *Battleground Berlin*, 16–18.

Chapter 4. Spies on the Danube: Austria

1. Wolfgang Mueller, "Stalin and Austria: New Evidence on Soviet Policy in a Secondary Theatre of the Cold War, 1938–53/55," *Cold War History* 6, no. 1 (February 2006): 66–67.

2. "Recognition of an Austrian Government Satisfactory to Allied Governments," 23 June 1945, *Foreign Relations of the United States, 1945: The Conference of Berlin (Potsdam)* (Washington: Government Printing Office, 1960), 1:334–335.

3. William B. Bader, *Austria between East and West, 1945–1955* (Stanford, CA: Stanford University Press, 1966), 22–23; Audrey Kurth Cronin, *Great Power Politics and the Struggle over Austria, 1945–1955* (Ithaca, NY: Cornell University Press, 1986), 25–30.

4. James Jay Carafano, *Waltzing into the Cold War: The Struggle for Occupied Austria* (College Station: Texas A&M University Press, 2002), 34–35; Siegfried Beer, "Target Central Europe: American Intelligence Efforts Regarding Nazi and Early Postwar Austria," Working Paper 97-1, Center for Austrian Studies, University of Minnesota, 3–4. For a description of a wartime intelligence mission, see Gerald Schwab, *OSS Agents in Hitler's Heartland: Destination Innsbruck* (New York: Praeger, 1996).

5. Hans Wynberg, e-mail message to David Alvarez, 22 December 2004. In the spring of 1945 OSS agent Hans Wynberg had parachuted into Austria as part of the GREENUP intelligence mission. After the German surrender he remained with OSS/SSU Austria as a SI officer until his discharge from the army in early 1946.

6. "971" to Charles Thayer, 31 July 1945, National Archives and Records Administration, College Park, Maryland, Record Group (RG) 226, Entry 108B, box 75.

7. "Report from Chief of OSS Austria," 24 August 1945, RG 226. M1642, reel 3, frames 635–636 (hereinafter reel/frames); "Operational Status Report, SICE, September 1945," 24 September 1945, RG 226, Entry 215, box 8. For local news items in September, see the reports collected in RG 226, Entry 108, box 168.

8. See the series of weekly intelligence summaries in RG 260 (Records of U.S. Occupation Forces), USFA, Historical File, box 6. The summary dated 18 August 1945, for example, focuses primarily on the alleged threat of Nazi underground, noting the recent discovery of a hidden cache of explosives and current intelligence that fugitive officers of the Sicherheitsdienst, the Nazi party intelligence service, were organizing and directing the resistance.

9. "History of G-2, USFA from Beginning to June 1947," 10, RG 260, USFA, Historical File, box 5. Daily intelligence bulletins can be found in RG 319 (Army Staff), G-2 "ID" Files, box 1372.

10. Gary Trogdon, "A Decade of Catching Spies: The United States Army's Counterintelligence Corps, 1943–1953," Ph.D. dissertation, University of Nebraska, 2001, 88–89, 95–98; "History of the G-2 Intelligence Section, July–September 1947," RG 260, USFA, "Historical File, box 5; "History of the Office of the Director of Intelligence, United States Forces in Austria, January–March 1948," RG 260, USFA, "Historical File," box 6.

11. Hans Wynberg, e-mail message to David Alvarez, 13 December 2004.

12. "Report from Chief of OSS Austria," 24 August 1945, RG 226, microfilm M1642, 3/635–636; Alfred Ulmer to Commanding Officer, OSS Austria, 2 October 1945, subject: "Progress Report for September 1945," RG 226, Entry 108B, box 76; "Operational Status Report, SICE, September 1945," 24 September 1945, RG 226, Entry 215, box 8; Beer, "Target Central Europe," 5, 7; William Hood, telephone conversation with David Alvarez, 10 December 2004 (quote).

13. "Operational Status Report, SICE, September 1945," 24 September 1945, RG 226, Entry 215, box 8.

14. Donald R. Whitnah and Edgar L. Erickson, *The American Occupation of Austria: Planning and Early Years* (Westport, CT: Greenwood Press, 1985), 55–56; Jonathan M. House, *A Military History of the Cold War, 1944–1962* (Norman: University of Oklahoma Press, 2012), 47.

15. "Operational Status Report, SICE, September 1945," 24 September 1945, RG 226, Entry 215, box 8.

16. Ibid.

17. "971" to Charles Thayer, 31 July 1945, RG 226, Entry 108B, box 75; Alfred Ulmer to Gerald Else, 21 September 1945, ibid.

18. Hans Wynberg, email message to David Alvarez, 13 December 2004.

19. "Report from Chief of OSS Austria," 24 August 1945, RG 226, M1642, 3/635–636.

20. "Operational Status Report, SICE, September 1945," 24 September 1945, RG 226, Entry 215, box 8.

21. David Strong to Commanding Officer, SSU Austria, 15 February 1946, RG 226, Entry 108B, box 75.

22. "History of G-2, USFA from Beginning to June 1947," 10; Hart Perry to Divisional Deputy, Europe, 7 August 1945, subject: "Relations with Foreign Service and Military Intelligence," RG 226, Entry 108B, box 76.

23. Harris Greene, "Cloak and Dagger in Salzburg," in *The Cold War: A Military History*, ed. Robert Cowley (New York: Random House, 2005), 16; "History of the G-2 Intelligence Section, July–September 1947," 2, RG 260, Historical File, box 5.

24. Carafano, *Waltzing into the Cold War*, 50; Hart Perry to Divisional Deputy, Europe, 7 August 1945, subject: "Relations with Foreign Service and Military Intelligence," RG 226, Entry 208B, box 76.

25. Günter Bischof, *Austria in the First Cold War, 1945–55: The Leverage of the Weak* (New York: St. Martin's Press, 1999), 46; Franz Neumann to Sherman Kent, 2 May 1945, RG 226, Entry 37, box 1.

During the war Franz Neumann seems to have been an occasional informant for Soviet intelligence, although he apparently lost his appetite for espionage toward the end and began to distance himself from his Soviet contacts. See, Allen Weinstein and Alexander Vassiliev, *The Haunted Wood: Soviet Espionage in America—The Stalin Era* (New York: Random House, 1999), 249–251, 254, 261.

26. "Recognition of an Austrian Government Satisfactory to All Allied Governments," 23 June 1945, *Foreign Relations of the United States, 1945: Conference of Berlin (Potsdam)*, 1:334–335.

27. Hans Wynberg, e-mail message to David Alvarez, 13 December 2004.

28. William Donovan to James Byrnes, 20 July 1945, enclosing undated copy of a memorandum by Lieutenant Colonel Charles Thayer, subject: "Observations on the Present Political Situation in Vienna," RG 226, M1642, 83/460–62.

29. Alfred Ulmer to Commanding Office, SSU/Austria, 2 January 1945, subject: "Progress Report, December 1945," RG 226, Entry 215, box 8.

30. Cronin, *Great Power Politics and the Struggle over Austria, 1945–1955*, 31; OSS, Original Report LS-402, 14 August 1945, subject: "Vienna Police Situation," RG 226, Entry 210, box 487. Renner seemed to have known or guessed that his interlocutor was an American agent since he specifically mentioned that he did not want his name mentioned as the source for this information from fear that it might complicate his relations with the Russians.

31. Carafano, *Waltzing into the Cold War*, 54; General John Magruder to the President, 7 July 1945, RG 226, M1642, 25/732–738; William Donovan to the President, 30 August 1945, RG 226, M1642, 57/548–556.

32. "French Requisitions," 3 August 1945, RG 319, G-2 ID Files, box 1350.

33. A-60605, "Information Concerning Russian Removal of Machinery," 31 August 1945, RG 226, Entry 108, box 168; #0205550, "Russian Evacuation of Austrian Repair Facilities," 10 September 1945, RG 319, G-2 ID Files, box 1345.

34. A-61410, "Russians Pressing for Control of Zistersdorf Oil Wells for Sixty Years," 20 September 1945, RG 226, Entry 108, box 168; LA-79, "Russian Seizure of Austrian Oil Fields," 8 October 1945, ibid.; LA-63, "Russian Relations with Donau Dampfschiffahrt Gesellschaft," 29 September 1945, ibid.

35. LA-74, "Russian Interest in Austrian Research Scientist on Atomic Energy,"

29 September 1945, ibid.; LA-566 (A-68840), "Plans for War Production," 3 June 1946, RG 226, Entry 108A, box 24.

36. Mueller, "Stalin and Austria," 68–69.

37. "Operational Status Report, SICE, September 1945," 24 September 1945, RG 226, Entry 215, box 8.

38. Hans Wynberg, e-mail messages to David Alvarez, 13 December 2004 and 22 December 2004.

39. To Commanding Officer, SSU Mission to Austria, 12 September 1946, subject: "CROWN Case," RG 226, Entry 210, box 368.

40. Robert Cunningham to Alfred Ulmer, 15 January 1946, subject: "Macy Project," RG 226, Entry 210, box 276.

41. Memorandum for Alfred Ulmer, 20 November 1945, subject: "Macy Project-Biographies," RG 226, Entry 210, box 276.

42. Ibid.

43. Memorandum by Gerhard Nellhaus, 2 October 1945, RG 226, Entry 210, box 276.

44. "For Macy File, Subject: Comments on Biographies," 23 November 1945, RG 226, Entry 210, box 276; "1098" to Commanding Officer, SSU Austria, 1 March 1946, subject: "Progress Report for February 1946," RG 226, Entry 215, box 8.

45. Hans Wynberg, e-mail message to David Alvarez, 22 December 2004.

46. Alfred Ulmer to Commanding Officer, SSU/Austria, 2 January 1946, subject: "Progress Report, December 1945," RG 226, Entry 215, box 8.

47. Vienna to War Department (SSU), 18 March 1946, RG 226, Entry 210, box 469; "1098" to Commanding Officer, SSU Austria, 1 April 1946, subject: "Progress Report for March 1946," RG 226, Entry 108B, box 76.

48. Alfred Ulmer to Commanding Officer, SSU/Austria, 2 January 1946, subject: "Progress Report, December 1945," RG 226, Entry 215, box 8.

49. Vienna to War Department (SSU), 18 March 1946, RG 226, Entry 210, box 469.

50. Alfred Ulmer to Commanding Officer, SSU/Austria, 2 January 1946, subject: "Progress Report," December 1945, RG 226, Entry 215, box 8.

51. "Informal Situation Report, Austrian Mission," 9 April 1947 RG 226, Entry 210, box 526.

52. "History of G-2, USFA, from Beginning to June 1947," 10, 20, RG 260, USFA, "Historical File," box 5; "History of the Office of the Director of Intelligence, United States Forces in Austria, January–March 1948," 10, RG 260, USFA, "Historical File," box 6.

53. "History of G-2, USFA, from Beginning to June 1947," 20.

54. Ibid.

55. James Milano and Patrick Brogan, *Soldiers, Spies, and the Rat Line* (Washington, DC: Brassey's, 1995), 110–112, 156. In his memoir former CIC officer James Milano recalls that his organization began anti-Soviet operations as early as the summer of 1945. Milano's account depends entirely upon his memory, and his testimony is clouded by a weak chronology that makes it difficult to place particular events and

operations in a particular time frame. The documentary evidence, including the previously classified staff histories of G-2 Austria, which were not intended for public consumption, does not support Milano's account of anti-Soviet operations in 1945.

For Projects MONTGOMERY and MOUNT VERNON, see the documentation in RG 263 (Records of the Central Intelligence Agency), CIA Subject Files, box 1, "Army/CIC Nets in Eastern Europe."

56. "Subject: Chalva ODICHARIA," 28 August 1945, RG 226, Entry 216, box 3. In the documents "Odicharia" is sometimes spelled "Odisharia."

57. Ibid.

58. "303" to "101," 31 August 1945, subject: "Project CAVIAR, Agent Alexander Nikolaevitch Tsagoeff, cover name OLGA, #3100 and his group," RG 226, Entry 216, box 3.

59. Ibid.; "Project CAVIAR: Progress Report #2," RG 226, Entry 216, box 3. A headquarters review of Project CAVIAR completed after the project's termination noted, "From the files presently available at the Austrian Desk it would appear that this operation was not brought to the attention of Headquarters until some time after it ended. There seems to have been nothing beyond local checks made on the principals—if this." "Review of Project CAVIAR," [n.d.], RG 226, Entry 216, box 3. This statement is curious in view of the fact that CAVIAR progress reports were marked for circulation to Washington.

60. "Project CAVIAR: Progress Report #5," 12 September 1945, RG 226, Entry 216, box 3, "CAVIAR: Basic Documents"; "Project CAVIAR: Progress Report #6," 15 September 1945, RG 226, Entry 216, box 3.

61. "Odicharia, Charles," 6 October 1945 [cover letter enclosing CIC report dated 24 July 1945], RG 226, Entry 216, box 3.

62. "Project CAVIAR: Progress Report #13," 5 November 1945, RG 226, Entry 216, box 3, "CAVIAR: Basic Documents"; "Project CAVIAR: Progress Report #14," RG 226, Entry 216, box 3.

63. To "101," subject: "Project CAVIAR: Sub-organization under agent SYBILLE," 1 October 1945, RG 226, Entry 216, box 3.

64. Major E. P. Barry to Commanding Officer, SSU Austria, subject: "Progress Report Covering the Period 1–30 April 1946," 30 April 1946, RG 226, Entry 215, box 8; "111" to "101," 2 October 1945, subject: "Project CAVIAR: NKVD agents and activities, and their relations with the Salzburg SRC and other foreign agencies and areas. Source: SYBILLE Cell #1," RG 226, Entry 216, box 3; SCI/A, "Project CAVIAR: NKVD Salzburg," 28 September 1945, RG 226, Entry 216, box 3; "111" to "101," 1 December 1945, subject: "Iljinskij" [sic], RG 226, Entry 216, box 3. The latter report on a Soviet agent who visited various DP camps allegedly on the orders of the American military government carries the handwritten notation by an SSU case officer, "Action should be taken to stalemate the activities of this man."

65. "111" to "101," 29 November 1945, subject: "Project SYBILLE: Expansion into Germany," RG 226, Entry 216, box 3; "To whom it may concern,"[signed Major E. P. Barry], 29 November 1945, RG 226, Entry 216, box 3.

66. "Project CAVIAR: Reported attempted assassination of Stalin," 5 October 1945, RG 226, Entry 216, box 3.

67. "Project CAVIAR: Conditions in Poland," 24 October 1945, RG 226, Entry 216, box 3; "Conditions in the Red Army and in the Soviet-occupied zone in Austria," 27 October 1945, RG 226, Entry 216, box 3; "111" to "101," 5 October 1945, subject: "Recruiting of German Army personnel by Soviet authorities," RG 226, Entry 216, box 3; "111" to "101," 1 December 1945, subject: "Recruiting of German Pilots by foreign powers" RG 226, Entry 216, box 3.

68. "Project Syracuse," 29 October 1945, RG 226, Entry 213, box 2; "Project Renard," 31 October 1945, RG 226, Entry 213, box 2; SAINT (Austria) to SAINT (Washington), 31 August 1946, subject: "[X-2] Station Activities, Month of August 1946," RG 226, Entry 210, box 368; Kevin Ruffner, "Project SYMPHONY: U.S. Intelligence and the Jewish *Brichah* in Postwar Austria," *Studies in Intelligence* 51, no. 1 (2007): 34.

69. For an early SYBILLE report that the Yugoslav intelligence service was controlled by Soviet NKVD officers and Yugoslavs trained inside the USSR, see, "111" to "101," 28 October 1945, subject: "OZNA in Slovenia," RG 226, Entry 216, box 3. For later reports that the Soviets were using the Yugoslav service for operations in Italy, see "X-2 Branch SSU, Counter-intelligence Summary," No. 8, Series II, 22 March 1946, RG 226, Entry 217, box 3. For a report from SSU Germany concerning Soviet infiltration of the Polish secret service, see "OSS Germany, Original Report L-1117," 4–7 January 1946, RG 226, Entry 108, box 167. For a report on Soviet influence over the secret services of Hungary and Romania, see "X-2 Branch SSU, Counter-intelligence Summary," No. 9, Series II, 22 April 1946, RG 226, Entry 217, box 3.

70. "Project MOONLIGHT Progress Report," 1 April 1946, RG 226, Entry 215, box 5; "Project CACTUS," 10 November 1945, RG 226, Entry 213, box 2.

71. Acting Chief, FBM, to Commanding Officer, SSU Austria, 5 September 1946, RG 226, Entry 210, box 368.

72. "CHECKERS Project: Progress Report, 27–28 June," and "CHECKERS Project: Progress Report, July 1946," These documents were released to the authors by the Central Intelligence Agency under the provisions of the Freedom of Information Act.

73. "SSU/X-2 Counter-Intelligence Summary," No. 11, Series II, 1 July 1946, RG 226, Entry 210, box 329.

74. Ralph W. Brown III, "Making the *Third Man* Look Pale: American-Soviet Conflict in Vienna during the Early Cold War in Austria, 1945–1950," *Journal of Slavic Military Studies* 14, no. 4 (December 2001): 93. For an intelligence report that certain Vienna police officials were collaborating with the NKVD, see Memorandum by Captain Peter Chambers, 26 September 1945, subject: "Austrian Personnel Employed by NKVD," RG 319, Entry 1041, box 19.

75. Brown, "Making the *Third Man* Look Pale," 85–86, 92–93.

76. Ibid., 96–98; "History of the Office of the Director of Intelligence, United

States Forces in Austria, January–March 1948," RG 260, USFA, "Historical File," box 6.

77. "SALOME Project: Progress Report, 14 June–14 August 1946," 5 September 1946. This document was released to the authors by the Central Intelligence Agency under the provisions of the Freedom of Information Act.

78. This account of the "Shanghai Incident" is drawn from a lengthy report by the Austrian mission, "Shanghai Incidènt (Project Cactus)," 5 March 1946, RG 226, Entry 215, box 5.

79. Kauder and the "Max South" networks remain controversial subjects in the espionage history of the Second World War. Most intelligence historians now accept that the Max South networks were largely imaginary. There is less consensus on whether Kauder was a fabricator or an instrument of Russian disinformation and whether, if the latter, he was a witting or unwitting instrument of Soviet intelligence. It is now clear that the "Max North" networks were completely under the control of Russian counterintelligence. For discussions of Kauder's wartime espionage, see Robert W. Stephan, *Stalin's Secret War: Soviet Counterintelligence against the Nazis, 1941–1945* (Lawrence: University Press of Kansas, 2004), chapter 6. See also, Nigel West and Oleg Tsarev, *The Crown Jewels: The British Secrets at the Heart of the KGB Archives* (London: Harper Collins, 1998), chapter 8, and David Kahn, *Hitler's Spies: German Military Intelligence in World War II* (New York: Macmillan, 1978), 312–317.

80. After the *Anschluss* of 1938 Kauder, whose mother was Jewish, fled from Austria to Hungary to escape anti-Jewish persecution. The following year he was arrested by the Hungarian police for lacking a residence permit and deported to Germany. He was briefly questioned by the Gestapo and then released. In December 1939 he was again arrested by the Gestapo, but was released when he agreed to work for the Abwehr. There is no evidence that Kauder ever participated in anti-Nazi activities.

81. "Project Cactus," 10 November 1945, RG 226, Entry 213, box 2.

82. DD102 to CO, SCI/A, 30 January 1946, subject: Report on the "SHANGHAI Incident," RG 226, Entry 215, box 5.

83. West and Tsarev, *The Crown Jewels*, 194.

84. Arnold Silver, "Questions, Questions, Questions: Memories of Oberursel," *Intelligence and National Security* 8, no. 2 (April 1993): 203–205.

85. In 1952 Kauder encountered one of his Camp King interrogators on a street in Salzburg and immediately tried to interest the American in a network that he "really" had inside the Soviet Union. As late as 1964 the CIA station in Austria informed its headquarters that it had received an approach from a certain Richard Kauder who claimed to have a chain of sources inside Russia. Ibid., 206.

86. Carafano, *Waltzing Into the Cold War*, 87–89, 91–92.

Chapter 5. A Distant Arena: Eastern Europe

1. For an elaboration of Stalin's national front strategy, see Eduard Mark, "Revolution by Degrees: Stalin's National Front Strategy for Europe, 1941–1947," Working Paper 31, Cold War International History Project, February 2001.

2. For expectations among American policymakers, see Eduard Mark, "American Policy toward Eastern Europe and the Origins of the Cold War, 1941–1946," *Journal of American History* 68 (September 1981): 313–336.

3. Policy Group, Document PG-14, "Soviet Attitudes on Regional Organizations in Eastern Europe," 23 September 1943, National Archives and Records Administration, College Park, Maryland, RG 59 (Records of the Department of State), Records of Harley A. Notter, box 119.

4. "Situation Report: USSR," 12 September 1945, National Archives Microfilm Publication M1221.

5. For the subsidy, see Secretary of State to the Ambassador in the Soviet Union, 18 July 1944, *Foreign Relations of the United States, 1944,* vol. 3: *The British Commonwealth and Europe* (Washington, DC: Government Printing Office, 1965), 1365.

6. For details on liaison between OSS and the intelligence service of the Polish government-in-exile, see Tessa Stirling, Daria Nałęcz and Tadeusz Dubicki, eds., *Intelligence Cooperation between Poland and Great Britain during World War II* (London: Valentine Mitchell, 2005), 350–353.

7. Patrick O'Donnell, *Operatives, Spies, and Saboteurs: The Unknown Story of the Men and Women of World War II's OSS* (New York: Free Press, 2004), 250–251.

8. After Germany invaded the Soviet Union, Moscow had recognized the Polish government-in-exile. In April 1943 the Germans announced the discovery of a mass grave in the Katyń forest near Smolensk. The grave contained the remains of thousands of Polish officers whom the Germans claimed were murdered by the NKVD. When the London Poles proposed an international commission to examine the site and investigate the German claims, Moscow broke diplomatic relations with the government-in-exile. In the West it was widely accepted that the Russians had massacred the Polish officers. In 1990, the fiftieth anniversary of the event, Moscow officially acknowledged that the NKVD had carried out the killings.

9. Memorandum by the Director of the Office of European Affairs to the Secretary of State, 20 July 1944, *Foreign Relations of the United States, 1944,* vol. 3: *The British Commonwealth and Europe,* 1296–1298. As late as May 1945 no official American and British observers had been permitted entry to Poland. Memorandum by the Appointed Ambassador to Poland to the Acting Secretary of State, 4 May 1945, *Foreign Relations of the United States, 1945,* vol. 5: *Europe* (Washington, DC: Government Printing Office, 1967), 279.

10. The Chargé to the Polish Government-in-exile to the Secretary of State, 18 January 1944, *Foreign Relations of the United States, 1944,* vol. 3: *The British Commonwealth and Europe,* 1356; Secretary of State to the Ambassador in the United Kingdom, 6 April 1944, ibid., 1359–1360; Memorandum by the Assistant Chief of the Division of Eastern European Affairs, 27 July 1944, ibid., 1369–1370.

11. For indications of RA's views on the London Poles, see RA Branch, "European

Political Report," 19 May 1944, RG 226 (Records of the Office of Strategic Services), Entry 19, RA reports, XL 1617; Samuel Sharp to William Langer, 18 March 1945, ibid., XL 7141; Sherman Kent to Roger Plaff, 8 January 1944, subject: "Activities of Polish Politicians Out of Poland," RG 226, Entry 37, box 2.

12. William Donovan to Cordell Hull, 29 July 1944, RG 226, Entry 180, Washington Director's Office, reel 82; Hugh Wilson to William Donovan, 28 August 1944, ibid.

13. William Donovan to Franklin Roosevelt, 5 October 1944, ibid.

14. Moscow (Garreau) to Paris, 16 January 1945, RG 38 (Records of the Chief of Naval Operations), "Translations of Intercepted Radio Traffic," box 2725; Magic Diplomatic Summaries for 18 March 1945 and 11 April 1945, RG 457 (Records of the National Security Agency), Historic Cryptographic Collection (HCC), box 16.

15. W. Averell Harriman to the Secretary of State, 30 August 1944, Library of Congress (Washington, DC), Manuscript Division, W. Averell Harriman Papers, box 173.

16. William Langer to William Donovan, 19 October 1944, subject: Report of Conversation of Lt. Samuel L. Sharp with Richard Lauterbach of *Life* Magazine, RG 226, Entry 1, box 2. For Lauterbach's secret communist affiliations see John Earl Haynes and Harvey Klehr, *Venona: Decoding Soviet Espionage in America* (New Haven, CT: Yale University Press, 1999), 237.

17. Report D-1889 (from Istanbul), 13 November 1944, RG 226, Entry 108, box 19A.

18. SAINT Bucharest to SAINT Washington, 2 May 1945, RG 226, Entry 108A, box 189. When Germany defeated Poland, remnants of the Polish Army were held in captivity inside the Soviet Union. After Germany attacked the Soviet Union, Moscow signed an agreement with the Polish government-in-exile providing for the release of these captives and the formation of Polish military units on Russian soil. These units were under the operational control of the Red Army but were commanded by General Wladyslaw Anders. Mutual suspicions and misunderstandings compounded by logistical problems delayed training and deployment of this force. In 1942 Anders and the bulk of his force transferred to British control in Persia, from where they went on to serve with distinction in North Africa and Italy. The Poles who remained in the Soviet Union were reorganized into a force under the command of General Zygmunt Berling and eventually participated in the Red Army's advance into Poland and Germany.

19. Harry Rositzke to Lester Houck, 20 June 1945. RG 226, Entry 180, reel 82; Allen Dulles to General William Donovan, 16 July 1945, subject: "General Situation Report No. 1," RG 226, Entry 108B, box 70; Harry Rositzke, interview by Eduard Mark and Vance Mitchell, 9 September 1992.

20. Recent scholarship, including studies based on newly available Polish and Russian sources, confirms the general accuracy of American intelligence reporting on internal Polish affairs in 1944–1945. See, for example, Marek Jan Chodakiewicz, *Between Nazis and Soviets: Occupation Politics in Poland, 1939–1947* (Lanham, MD: Lexington Books, 2004), 205–208; Rafal Wnuk, "Operations of the Communist Security Apparatus against Armed Resistance in Poland in [the] 1940s and 1950s," pa-

per prepared for the conference on "The Communist Security Apparatus in East Central Europe, 1945–1989," Warsaw, 16–18 June 2005.

21. "Fifth Plenary Meeting, 8 February 1945," *Foreign Relations of the United States, 1945: The Conferences at Malta and Yalta* (Washington, DC: Government Printing Office, 1955), 776–779, 815–816, 973; "United States Proposal Regarding the Polish Government," ibid., 815–816; Lynn Etheridge Davis, *The Cold War Begins: Soviet-American Conflict over Eastern Europe* (Princeton, NJ: Princeton University Press, 1974), 180–183. For details concerning the negotiations over Poland at Yalta, see Diane Shaver Clemens, *Yalta* (Oxford: Oxford University Press, 1970), chapter 5.

22. Davis, *The Cold War Begins*, 212–215.

23. Ambassador Lane had been preceded by a few days by Lieutenant William Tonesk, USN, an American-born officer of Polish descent who had attended the University of Kraków before the war. Lieutenant Tonesk had been attached to the embassy in Moscow as an aide to Ambassador Harriman and had been sent to Warsaw to prepare for the arrival of the American embassy delegation.

24. On communist domination of the intelligence and security forces, see Andrzej Paczkowski, "'The Leading Force': The Communist Party and the Security Apparatus in Poland, 1944–1956," paper prepared for the conference on "The Communist Security Apparatus in East Central Europe, 1945–1989," Warsaw, 16–18 June 2005.

25. D. Chadwick Braggiotti and Stephanie Czech, "Situation Report CH-Land," [June 1946], no pagination, copy in the possession of the authors; Arthur Bliss Lane, *I Saw Poland Betrayed: An American Ambassador Reports to the American People* (New York: Bobbs-Merrill Co., 1948), 22.

26. Colonel Walter Pashley to Chief, Military Intelligence Service, 26 August 1945, RG 319 (Records of the Army Staff), Entry 1041, box 17.

27. Braggiotti and Czech, "Situation Report CH-Land." No evidence has surfaced that Soviet intelligence was able to read high-grade American diplomatic ciphers in this period, but very little is known about Soviet code-breaking successes.

28. Lane, *I Saw Poland Betrayed*, 171–172, 181.

29. Ibid., 163.

30. The Ambassador in Poland to the Secretary of State, 11 September 1945, *Foreign Relations of the United States, 1945*, vol. 5: *Europe*, 371.

31. The Ambassador in Poland to the Secretary of State, 26 September 1945, ibid., 381.

32. Ambassador in Poland to the Secretary of State, 13 October 1945, ibid., 388; Lane, *I Saw Poland Betrayed*, 184–185.

33. Braggiotti and Czech, "Situation Report CH-Land."

34. Ibid.

35. Ibid.

36. Ibid.

37. The closure of the Warsaw unit is documented in "SSU Mission of Inspection, 5/7/46," RG 226, Entry 211, box 17.

38. Gordon Stewart to Richard Helms, 12 September 1946, RG 226, Entry 210, box 368; Peter Sichel to Gordon Stewart, 19 March 1946, RG 226, Entry 214, box 5.

39. Memorandum by Philip Horton, 1 July 1946, subject: Final Implementation of the Z Projects, RG 226, Entry 210, box 472.

40. William Donovan to James F. Byrnes, 17 September 1945, RG 226, M1642, reel 21, frames 792–793; Chief, SI Austria to Commanding Officer, SSU Austria, 1 March 1946, subject: Progress Report for February 1946, RG 226, Entry 215, box 8.

41. See, for example, the collection of field reports and the unenthusiastic assessment of them by headquarters staff in RG 226, Entry 210, box 511.

42. Alfred Ulmer to Commanding Officer, SSU Austria, subject: Progress Report, December 1945, RG 226, Entry 215, box 8.

43. Julor to Chief SI, Vienna, 10 December 1945, RG 226, Entry 210, box 187.

44. Ibid.

45. Donald Greer to Lester Houck, 10 June 1946, RG 226, Entry 210, box 477.

46. Gordon Stewart to Richard Helms, 13 September 1946, subject: "General Report on Intelligence Branch Activities," RG 226, Entry 210, box 368; Peter Sichel, e-mail message to David Alvarez, 16 February 2004; confidential information.

47. Tennent H. Bagley, letter to David Alvarez, 5 September 2007.

48. James Angleton to WASHA, 15 July 1946, RG 226, Entry 216, box 2; James Angleton to WASHA, 11 September 1946, RG 226, Entry 216, box 2.

49. Alfred Ulmer to Commanding Officer, SSU Austria, 1 March 1946, subject: Progress Report for February 1946, RG 226, Entry 215, box 8.

50. "1098" to the Commanding Officer, SSU Austria, 1 May 1946, subject: Progress Report for April 1946, RG 226, Entry 215, box 8.

51. Peer Henrik Hansen, *Second to None: U.S. Intelligence Activities in Northern Europe, 1943–1946* (Dordrecht: Republic of Letters, 2011), 184.

52. "Report for SSU Mission to Great Britain, 1–28 February 1946," 3 March 1946, RG 226, Entry 210, box 208; SAINT AMZON to SAINT Washington, 9 January 1946, subject: "X-2 Possibilities in Denmark," RG 226, Entry 213, box 2; Acting Chief, SPDS, to Acting Chief, FBL, 23 July 1946, subject: "Brief of Operations (Active and Pending) against Soviets," RG 226, Entry 210, box 329; William Quinn to all stations, 16 October 1946, RG 226, Entry 210, box 520.

53. Henry Hecksher to Captain E. O'Neal, 13 August 1946, subject: "Activities of Swedish Red Cross in Germany," RG 226, Entry 213, box 2; Hansen, *Second to None*, 186.

54. Army Security Agency, "List of Cryptanalytic Short Titles," 1 February 1946, RG 457, HCC, box 935.

55. Intelligence Summary—Red, #61, 25 October 1945, RG 457, HCC, box 192.

56. Statement based on a review of the Red Intelligence Summaries, which are available through December 1945, and the Magic Diplomatic Summaries, which are available through April 1946.

57. László Borhi, *Hungary in the Cold War, 1945–1956* (New York: Central European University Press, 2004), 20–21, 33.

58. Ibid., 35–36.

59. War Department (Strategic Services Unit History Project), *The Overseas Targets: War Report of the OSS* (New York: Walker, 1976), 270–271. CEREUS was

the code name of an intelligence chain based on several businessmen resident in Istanbul. These individuals claimed well-placed contacts across Central Europe. In 1943–1944 CEREUS produced hundreds of reports, most of which were later judged unreliable. OSS shut down the network in the summer of 1944 when it became apparent that it had been penetrated by the Germans.

60. Ibid., 276.

61. Howard Chapin to MEDTO Intelligence Officer, 15 October 1944, subject: "Semi-Monthly Report for Period 1–15 October 1944," RG 226, Entry 108B, box 32; Eduard Mark, "The OSS in Romania, 1944–45: An Intelligence Operation of the Early Cold War," *Intelligence and National Security* 9, no. 2 (April 1994): 321.

62. Howard Chapin to MEDTO Intelligence Officer, 15 October 1944, subject: "Semi-Monthly Report for Period 1–15 October 1944," RG 226, Entry 108B, box 32.

63. *The Overseas Targets: War Report of the OSS*, 333; Bradley Smith, *The Shadow Warriors: O.S.S. and the Origins of the CIA* (New York: Basic Books, 1983), 350–353.

64. Jonathan D. Clemente, "OSS Medical Intelligence in the Mediterranean Theater: A Brief History," *Journal of Intelligence History*, 2 (Summer 2002): 22–23. Jonathan Clemente, e-mail messages to David Alvarez, 6 March 2006 and 7 March 2006.

65. Robert Joyce to Commanding Officer, 2677th Regiment OSS (Prov.), 9 April 1945, RG 226, Entry 210, box 285.

66. Howard Chapin to Chief, SI, 1 May 1945, RG 226, Entry 99, box 25.

67. "971" to Charles Thayer, 18 July 1945, RG 226, Entry 108B, box 75.

68. Hart Perry to Commanding Officer, Detachment A, OSS Austria, 1 August 1945, subject: Progress Report for July 1945, RG 226, Entry 108B, box 76; G. F. Else to Charles Thayer, 20 August 1945, RG 226, Entry 108B, box 75.

69. Al Ulmer to Commanding Officer, OSS Austria, 2 October 1945, subject: Progress Report for September 1945, RG 226, Entry 108B, box 76.

70. Robinson Bellin to Colonel William Quinn, 25 July 1946, subject: Report on Mission in Hungary, RG 226, Entry 190, reel 47.

71. "Report by the Chief of the U.S. Military Representation on the Allied Control Commission for Hungary," 6 June 1945, *Foreign Relations of the United States, 1945*, vol. 4: *Europe* (Washington, DC: U.S. Government Printing Office, 1963), 823.

72. On 21 February 1945, a State Department party under Leslie Squires reached Debrecen, the temporary seat of the "Provisional National Government of Hungary." Ambassador H. F. Arthur Schoenfeld did not reach Budapest and assume direction of the diplomatic mission until 11 May 1945.

73. H. Freeman Matthews to Edward Stettinius, 28 December 1944, RG 59, Records of the Office of European Affairs, box 6.

74. Mark, "Revolution by Degrees," 22–23.

75. Schoenfeld to the Secretary of State, 17 August 1945, *Foreign Relations of the United States, 1945*, vol. 4: *Europe*, 849.

76. Kirk to the Secretary of State, 27 March 1945, ibid., 811–812.

77. Schoenfeld to the Secretary of State, 17 August, 1945, ibid., 851–852. Balogh carried the same information to General Key.

78. Squires to the Secretary of State, 15 September 1945, ibid., 869.

79. Schoenfeld to the Secretary of State, 17 October 1945 and 22 October 1945, ibid., 891–892, 897–898.

80. Schoenfeld to the Secretary of State, 10 July 1946, *Foreign Relations of the United States, 1946,* vol. 6: *Eastern Europe, the Soviet Union* (Washington, DC: U.S. Government Printing Office, 1969), 320–321.

81. "Individual Surveys of SSU Branches," [March 1946], RG 226, Entry 210, box 329.

82. Robinson Bellin to Colonel William Quinn, 25 July 1946, subject: Report on Mission in Hungary, RG 226, Entry 190, reel 47.

83. Ibid.

84. Ibid.

85. Ibid.

86. Hart Perry to Commanding Officer, Detachment A, OSS Austria, 1 August 1945, subject: Progress Report for July 1945, RG 226, Entry 108B, box 76; G. F. Else to Charles Thayer, 20 August 1945, RG 226, Entry 108B, box 75.

87. H. M. Chapin to Chief, SI, 17 December 1944, RG 226, Entry 210, box 386; A. G. Flues to Chief, SICE, 19 March 1945, RG 226, Entry 210, box 64.

88. For Aradi's position, see the roster of SSU Austria in RG 226, Entry 210, box 526. This document is undated but internal evidence suggests a date in late 1945.

89. Howard Chapin to Charles Thayer, 10 December 1945, RG 226, Entry 215, box 8.

90. "Operational Status Report SICE," 7 December 1945, ibid. At the end of 1945 SSU Austria decided to name all Vienna-controlled operations after New York City department stores, all Salzburg-controlled projects after NYC nightclubs, and all Trieste-based operations after NYC theaters.

91. Initially, the Allies prohibited the provisional government from maintaining diplomatic relations with any country. Hungarian diplomatic missions remained in legal and financial limbo, a problem compounded by the fact that many of the personnel had ambivalent feelings toward the new regime in Budapest.

92. For the creation of KALOT and Nagy's early contacts with Soviet officers, see Töhötöm Nagy, *Jesuitas y Masones* (Buenos Aires, 1963), chapters 5–6.

93. Ibid., 184–185.

94. Father Nagy and the larger Jesuit organization in early postwar Hungary have been portrayed as eager to seek an accommodation with the Soviets and the Hungarian Communist Party in contrast to the rejectionist position of Cardinal József Mindszenty, the Catholic primate of Hungary, and most of the Hungarian hierarchy. Nagy's connection to American intelligence suggests that this portrayal may require revision. Email from Christopher Adam, 6 October 2004.

95. Duncan Bare, "The Curious Case of Aradi Zsolt: Tracking the Distinguished Career of an OSS, SSU and CIA Central European Asset," *Journal for Intelligence, Propoganda and Security Studies* 8, no. 1 (2014): 120.

96. Ulmer to Commanding Officer, OSS Austria, 2 October 1945, subject: "Progress Report for September 1945," RG 226, Entry 108B, box 76; Ulmer to Command-

ing Officer, SSU Austria, 1 February 1946, subject: "Progress Report for January 1946," ibid.

97. SSU Austria, Original Report LA-298, 25 January 1946, ibid.

98. Bare, "The Curious Case of Aradi Zsolt," 120.

99. Ulmer to Penrose and Tofte, 23 January 1946, subject: "Progress Report: Central Europe and Balkan Areas," RG 226, Entry 108B, box 76.

100. Washington to Budapest, 16 September 1946, RG 226, Entry 213, box 1.

101. In 1950 Solyom would be arrested and executed as part of the "Generals' Trial." It is interesting that the indictment did not charge him with espionage for a foreign power. Tamas Meszerics, e-mail message to David Alvarez, 12 August 2005.

102. Tamas Meszerics, e-mail messages to David Alvarez, 10 August 2005 and 12 August 2005; Washington to Budapest, 16 September 1946, RG 226, Entry 213, box 1.

103. SSU Austria, Report LA-111, 19 October 1946, RG 226, Entry 108, box 168.

104. SSU, A-62416: "Armed Units of Communists and Social Democrats in Budapest," disseminated 25 October 1945, 226/108/168; The Representative in Hungary to the Secretary of State, 17 October 1945, *Foreign Relations of the United States, 1945*, vol. 4: *Europe*, 892.

105. SSU, A-62896: "Attitude of Hungarian Industrialists," disseminated 13 November 1945, RG 226, Entry 108, box 168. For an example of embassy coverage of the same topic, see The Representative in Hungary to the Secretary of State, 6 October 1945, *Foreign Relations of the United States, 1945*, vol. 4: *Europe*, 881–883.

106. Compare, for example, SSU, LA-388: "War of Nerves in Hungary," 11 March 1946, with The Minister in Hungary to the Secretary of State, 6 March 1946, *Foreign Relations of the United States, 1946*, vol. 6: *Eastern Europe, the Soviet Union*, 271.

107. James McCargar, interview by Eduard Mark, 19 March 1993.

108. Christopher Felix [James McCargar], *A Short Course in the Secret War*, 4th ed. (Lanham, MD, 2001), 171–174.

109. Ibid., 185–189.

110. Franklin Roosevelt to Cordell Hull, 7 March 1942, RG 59, Central Decimal File, 740.0011 EW/19908; The Acting Secretary of State to the Ambassador to the Polish Government-in-exile, 4 April 1942, *Foreign Relations of the United States, 1942*, vol. 3: *Europe* (Washington, DC: Government Printing Office, 1961), 136–137. For the American position at the Moscow Conference, see the undated exchange of notes between Ambassador to the Soviet Union Averell Harriman and Assistant Secretary of State James Dunn at the conference in Library of Congress, Washington, DC, W. Averell Harriman Papers, Box 170, folder "October 29–31."

111. Memorandum of conversation by H. Freeman Matthews, 17 April 1944, RG 59, Central Decimal File, 761.00/4-1744.

112. Memorandum of a conversation with Eduard Benes by Louis Fischer, 17 May 1943, Princeton University, Seelye G. Mudd Manuscript Library, Louis Fischer Papers, Box 39; Paraphrase of cable, W. Averell Harriman to Franklin Roosevelt and Cordell Hull, 20 December 1943, Papers of W. Averell Harriman, Box 171; Arthur Schoenfeld to Cordell Hull, 13 April 1944, RG 59, Central Decimal File, 860F.01/534.

113. Memorandum by the Division of Central European Affairs, 11 January 1945, *Foreign Relations of the United States, 1945,* vol. 4: *Europe,* 420; Charles Katek to William Donovan, 24 March 1945, RG 226, Washington Director's Office, microfilm roll 82.

114. The Ambassador in France to the Secretary of State, 5 June 1945, *Foreign Relations of the United States, 1945,* vol. 4: *Europe,* 455–457, enclosing Alfred Klieforth to the Department of State, 3 June 1945.

115. The two men may have clashed when both served together in the U.S. embassy in Moscow in the early months of the war, Steinhardt as ambassador and Thayer as third secretary.

116. Obituary of Charles Katek, *Washington Post,* 21 November 1971, 66.

117. Whitney Shephardson to William Donovan, 3 July 1944, RG 226, Entry 210, box 361; Frank Wisner to Charles Katek, 7 December 1945, RG 226, Entry 108B, box 70.

118. 971 to Frank Wisner, et al., 9 July 1945, RG 226, Entry 108B, box 75.

119. James Kronthal to Lester Houck, 14 December 1945, RG 226, Entry 215, box 8; SSU (AMZON) to Lester Houck, 21 January 1946, RG 226, Entry 216, box 1.

120. Charles Cheston to President Harry S. Truman, 18 May 1945, RG 226, Entry 180, reel 125.

121. Research and Analysis Branch, "Situation Report: USSR," 16 June 1945, National Archives microfilm publication M-1221, "Intelligence Reports 1941–1961," Report 1785.46.

122. OSS Prague, Original Report LC-160, 4 August 1945, RG 226, Entry 108, box 170; OSS Prague, Original Report LC-193, 19 August 1945, ibid.; OSS Prague, Original Report LC-202, 29 August 1945, ibid.; OSS Prague, Original Report LC-95, 9 July 1945, RG 226, Entry 108, box 169; X-2 Branch, "SSU/X-2 Counter-Intelligence Summary," 1 July 1946, RG 226, Entry 210, box 329.

123. OSS dissemination report, A-61151, 19 September 1945, RG 226, Entry 108E, box 2; OSS Prague, Original Report LC-319, 10 October 1945, RG 226, Entry 108, box 170; SSU Prague to Washington, London, and Vienna, 31 October 1945, RG 226, Entry 210, box 554.

124. Lieutenant Colonel Woldike's reports can be found in RG 319, Entry 1041, "Formerly Top Secret Intelligence Documents," box 15. During the war Woldike had served as military attaché in Finland and then held a similar position with regard to several of the governments-in-exile in London, including the Czech.

125. 1083 to Frank Wisner and Harry Rositzke, 10 August 1945, RG 226, Entry 108B, box 75.

126. Igor Lukes, "The Czechoslovak Special Services and Their American Adversary during the Cold War," *Journal of Cold War Studies* 9 (Winter 2007): 6.

127. Igor Lukes, *On the Edge of the Cold War: American Diplomats and Spies in Postwar Prague* (Oxford: Oxford University Press, 2012), 144, 152–153; Gordon Stewart to Whitney Shepardson and S. B. J. Penrose, 20 February 1946, RG 226, Entry 214, box 4.

128. Frank Wisner to Whitney Shepardson, 30 August 1945, RG 226, Entry 108B,

box 75; Gordon Stewart to Whitney Shepardson and S. B. J. Penrose, 20 February 1946, RG 226, Entry 214, box 4.

129. OSS Prague, Report A-56054,19 May 1945, RG 226, Entry 108, box 167; OSS Prague, Report LC-26, 15 June 1945, ibid.; OSS Prague, Report LC-42/a, 20 June 1945, ibid.

130. Lukes, *On the Edge of the Cold War*, 130.

131. Ibid., 134–135.

132. Donald Greer to Lester Houck, 10 June 1946, RG 226, Entry 210, box 477.

133. Lukes, *On the Edge of the Cold War*, 143–144.

134. Ibid.

135. Ibid., 146, 152.

136. Ibid., 147–149.

137. Ibid., 158; Crosby Lewis to Richard Helms, 18 September 1946, RG 226, Entry 214, box 4; Igor Lukes, "A Failure of Intelligence: Czechoslovakia, 1945–1948," 31–32. The authors would like to thank Professor Lukes for sharing this paper and other observations from his extensive research into American intelligence operations in Czechoslovakia. It was uncommon in early 1946 for the State Department to grant SSU intelligence officers official cover inside an embassy, although Ambassador Steinhardt may have been especially accommodating in this regard. It is possible that Spencer Taggart worked for the U.S. Army's Special Service Branch (the Pond), with which the State Department had an arrangement, but this seems unlikely since Taggart was certainly responsible to the SSU mission in Germany and SSU headquarters had control over his assignment and recall. Despite Crosby Lewis's recommendation, Taggart was still operating in Prague into 1948.

Chapter 6. The Nearer Shore: France and Italy

1. War Department (Strategic Services Unit History Project), *The Overseas Targets: War Report of the OSS* (New York: Walker, 1976), 2:141.

2. Ibid., 231–232; Bradley Smith, *The Shadow Warriors: O.S.S. and the Origins of the C.I.A.* (New York: Basic Books, 1983), 221–222.

3. War Department, *The Overseas Targets*, 180–181.

4. W. J. Casey to Colonel Gable, 11 July 1945, National Archives and Records Administration, College Park, Maryland, Record Group (RG) 226 (Records of the Office of Strategic Services), Entry 215, box 2; "SI Activities Projected for France," 9 May 1945, RG 226, Entry 210, box 435.

5. Philip Horton to Whitney Shepardson, 6 August 1945, RG 226, Entry 215, box 2.

6. Smith, *The Shadow Warriors*, 292.

7. "SI Activities Projected for France," 9 May 1945, RG 226, Entry 210, box 435.

8. W. J. Casey to Colonel Gable, 11 July 1945, RG 226, Entry 215, box 2.

9. "Report of SSU/France for October 1945," 30 November 1945, RG 226, Entry 210, box 208; "Monthly Progress Report for December 1945," 15 January 1946, RG 226, Entry 210, box 208.

10. Smith, *The Shadow Warriors*, 219.

11. "Individual Surveys of SSU Branches," RG 226, Entry 210, box 329.

12. Ibid., 218–219.

13. Whitney Shepardson to John Magruder, 4 February 1946, RG 226, Entry 210, box 475; "Individual Surveys of SSU Branches," RG 226, Entry 210, box 329; PANCHO to Elton, 14 May 1946, RG 226, Entry 210, box 147.

14. B. S. Carter to E. W. Gamble, 12 April 1945, RG 226, Entry 215, box 2.

15. Philip Horton to Frank Wisner, 29 June 1945, subject: "Exchange of Intelligence between OSS and DGER," RG 226, Entry 108B, box 17; on Dewavrin's anticipation of war with Russia, see the memoir by a senior officer in the DGER and SDECE, Philippe Thyraud de Vosjoli, *Lamia* (Boston: Little Brown, 1970), 145.

16. Ibid.; Philip Horton to Whitney Shepardson, 6 August 1945, RG 226, Entry 215, box 2.

17. Douglas Porch, *The French Secret Services: A History of French Intelligence from the Dreyfus Affair to the Gulf War* (New York: Farrar, Straus, and Giroux, 1995), 269, 272–273. For a perspective on the political battles that characterized the early postwar French services, see Sébastien Laurent, "Les services secrets gaullistes à l'épreuve de la politique (1940–1947)," *Politix: Revue des sciences sociales du politique* 14, no. 54 (2001): 150–153, and Philippe Bernert, *Roger Wybot et la bataille pour la DST* (Paris: Presse de la Cité, 1975). Wybot (aka Roger Warin) was the chief of the Direction de la Surveillance du Territoire (DST), a service within the Interior Ministry responsible for internal security.

18. See, for example, Philip Horton to SI Branch, Washington, 18 August 1945, RG 226, Entry 215, box 2, and Philip Horton to Colonel Quinn, 11 June 1946, subject: "SDECE Proposal Concerning Tripartite Collaboration," RG 226, Entry 210, box 418. There is no evidence in American intelligence records to sustain the claim made by some French authors that in 1945–1946 American intelligence was pushing its French counterparts to organize for a clandestine war against the Soviet Union. The available records suggest that it was the French who were pushing the Americans. For the claim, see Claude Faure, *Aux Services de la République: Du BCRA à la DGSE* (Paris: Fayard, 2004), 207.

19. [Lewis Gable], Covering Report, 1–31 January 1946, RG 226, Entry 210, box 208; Porch, *The French Secret Services*, 270; Bernert, *Roger Wybot et la bataille pour la DST*, 105; Thyraud de Vosjoli, *Lamia*, 159.

20. Faure, *Aux Services de la République*, 209.

21. SSU Paris to SSU Bern, 3 December 1945, RG 226, Entry 210, box 470.

22. Lester Houck to Philip Horton, 15 October 1945, RG 226, Entry 210, box 512.

23. John Magruder to the Chief, French Mission, 3 December 1945, RG 226, M1642, reel 73.

24. Some of SI Paris's French sources, code-named YORK or DORSET, are listed in "Paris Background Data," 27 March 1946, RG 226. Entry 210, box 329.

25. Faure, *Aux Services de la République*, 187.

26. Chief, SI/Switzerland to Chief, SI/Washington, 15 November 1945, RG 226, Entry 210, box 191.

27. Homer Hall to C. G. Gilpatric, 26 April 1946, RG 226, Entry 210, box 435.

28. Alton Childs to Henry Hyde, 9 July 1945, RG 226, Entry 210, box 432.

29. The date of ICARUS's recruitment remains unknown, but the source is first mentioned in a report from early October 1945. Alton Childs to Homer Hall, 9 October 1945, RG 226, Entry 210, box 512.

30. A collection of ICARUS reports can be found in RG 226, Entry 210, box 470.

31. David Alvarez, *Secret Messages: Codebreaking and American Diplomacy, 1930–1945* (Lawrence: University Press of Kansas, 2000), 184–185; Army Security Agency, "List of Cryptanalytic Short Titles," RG 457 (Records of the National Security Agency), Historic Cryptographic Collection, box 935.

32. David Alvarez, "Trying to Make the MAGIC Last: American Diplomatic Codebreaking in the Early Cold War," *Diplomatic History* 31, no. 5 (November 2007): 869.

33. William Donovan to Franklin Roosevelt, 3 April 1944, enclosing "Report from Argus to Regis on Conversations with French Resistance Leader," RG 226, Entry 190, reel 50; Charles Cheston to the Secretary of State, 9 August 1944, enclosing "France: Comité National," RG 226, Entry 190, reel 86.

34. Philip Horton to 209, 27 March 1946, RG 226. Entry 210, box 329.

35. Cable MA-173, USMILATTACHE AMEMBASSY Paris, 23 March 1948, RG 319 (Records of the Army Staff), Entry 58, TS G-2 Cables 1942–1952, box 114; Cable MA 216, USMILATTACHE AMEMBASSY Paris, 6 April 1948, ibid.

36. Report F-7264, 30 May 1946, RG 226, Entry 108A, box 8.

37. SSU Report F-6424 (disseminated as A-67320), 16 March 1946, RG 226, Entry 108A, box 6.

38. Commanding General USFET to War Department G-2, 9 March 1946, RG 319, Assistant Chief of Staff G-2, Top Secret Cables 1942–1952, box 68; U.S. Military Attache London to War Department G-2, 14 March 1946, RG 319, Assistant Chief of Staff G-2, Top Secret Cables, 1942–1952, box 67; Diary of James V. Forrestal, 4 May 1946, Papers of James V. Forrestal, Seeley G. Mudd Manuscript Library, Princeton University.

39. See, for example, SSU France, Report F-7241, 1 June 1946, RG 226, Entry 108A, box 8; James Angleton to GSI(b) Headquarters, No. 2 District, 3 April 1946, RG 226, Entry 108A, box 270; SAINT BB8 to SAINT JJ2, 28 June 1946, RG 226, Entry 108A, box 230; Susan Tully, Iberia Desk, X-2 to Miss Tenney, Iberia Desk, SI, 13 May 1946, RG 226, Entry 92, box 622.

40. Vincent Auriol, *Journal du Septennat, 1947–1954* (Paris: Librairie Armand Colin, 1970), 1:485–486.

41. James Townshend to Lester Houck, 2 August 1945, subject: "Background Data of Durham Sources," RG 226, Entry 210, box 329; Philip Horton to 209, 27 March 1946, ibid.

42. SSU Paris, Original Report F-6463, 20 March 1946, RG 226, Entry 108A, box 6; SSU Paris, Original Report F-6537, ibid.

43. See, for example, The Ambassador in France to the Department of State, 6 May 1946, *Foreign Relations of the United States, 1946*, vol. 5: *British Commonwealth,*

Western and Central Europe (Washington, DC: Government Printing Office, 1969), 438–440.

44. For an overview of American intelligence operations in Italy, see Max Corvo, *The O.S.S. in Italy, 1942–1945: A Personal Memoir* (New York: Praeger, 1990). The scope of operations is suggested by the fact that in April 1945 there were forty-six OSS teams operating in northern Italy. Smith, *The Shadow Warriors*, 299.

45. Vincent Scamporino to James Montante, 1 October 1944, RG 226, Entry 210, box 386; Vincent Scamporino to William Maddox, 2 October 1944, subject: "Established Contacts in Rome Area," ibid.

46. Chief, Italian and Albanian Section, SI, to the Director, n.d. [late summer 1945], subject: "Italy and Albania: Report on Operational Activities and Political and Economic Intelligence," RG 226, Entry 210, box 349.

47. Rescued by German commandos from the mountaintop hotel where he had been incarcerated after his removal from office on 25 July 1943, Benito Mussolini rallied diehard fascists around the Italian Social Republic, a rump government also known as the Republic of Salo from the small town on the Lago di Garda that housed some of its ministries.

48. Chief, Italian and Albanian Section, SI, to the Director, n.d. [late summer 1945], subject: "Italy and Albania: Report on Operational Activities and Political and Economic Intelligence," RG 226, Entry 210, box 349.

49. Ibid.

50. Quoted in Corvo, *The O.S.S. in Italy, 1942–1945*, 274.

51. Ibid., 270, 278–279.

52. Timothy Naftali, "ARTIFICE: James Angleton and X-2 Operations in Italy" in *The Secrets War: The Office of Strategic Services in World War II*, ed. George C. Chalou (Washington, DC: National Archives and Records Administration, 1992), 218–219.

53. BB8 to JJ1, 22 October 1945, subject: "Activity Report SCI/Z Units, 1–30 September 1945," RG 226, Entry 108A, box 259. SCI/Z was the designation for the X-2 field unit in Italy.

54. Ann Bray, *History of the Counter Intelligence Corps*, vol. 15: *Occupation of Austria and Italy* (Fort Holabird, MD: U.S. Army Intelligence Center, 1960), 54–58.

55. James Angleton to Director, SSU, 18 March 1946, subject: "Consolidated Progress Report for November, December 1945 and January 1946," RG 226, Entry 108A, box 268.

56. Ibid.

57. Richard Lamb, *War in Italy, 1943–1945* (New York: St. Martin's Press, 1993), 195–197.

58. Ambrogio Viviani, *Servizi Segreti Italiani, 1815–1985*, 2nd ed. (Rome: Adnkronos Libri, 1986), 276–277.

59. Naftali, "ARTIFICE: James Angleton and X-2 Operations in Italy," 225 and n36.

60. James Angleton to Director, SSU, 18 March 1946, subject: "Consolidated

Progress Report for November, December 1945, and January 1946," RG 226, Entry 108A, box 268.

61. Naftali, "ARTIFICE: James Angleton and X-2 Operations in Italy," 219 and nn.11 and 12.

62. Originally, VESSEL was the codename for the middleman, but eventually the designation was applied to the source and his product. VESSEL and DUSTY were probably the same person, Fillippo Setaccioli.

63. Quotes in David Alvarez, *Spies in the Vatican: Espionage and Intrigue from Napoleon to the Holocaust* (Lawrence: University Press of Kansas, 2002), 268–269.

64. For a discussion of the myth of Vatican intelligence, see David Alvarez, "The Best Information Service in Europe? Vatican Intelligence and the Final Solution," in *Secret Intelligence and the Holocaust*, ed. David Bankier (New York: Enigma Books, 2006), 187–211.

65. Alvarez, *Spies in the Vatican*, 246–247. Though not accredited as the American ambassador, Myron Taylor acted like a diplomatic representative and was treated as such by the Vatican. Despite the state of war between Italy and the United States, the Fascist government allowed Taylor to travel between Washington and Vatican City.

66. Ibid., 263–264.

67. Ibid., 255–257.

68. Ibid., 259.

69. Magruder and Shepardson to Caserta Station, 17 February 1945, RG 226, Entry 90, box 6; Magruder to Caserta Station, 3 March 1945, ibid.

70. "Analysis of VESSEL Cables," 8 June 1945, RG 226, Entry 210, box 437.

71. Vincent Scamporino to James Montante, 22 January 1945, RG 226, Entry 210, box 386. SSU ran most agent operations at the Vatican out of the Vienna station, where an officer named Zsolt Aradi specialized in Vatican affairs.

72. In January 1945, in the wake of a scandal that implicated senior army intelligence officers in the prewar assassination of an anti-Mussolini exile, the name of the Italian army intelligence service was changed to Ufficio Informazioni dello Stato Maggiore Generale. Despite the change, Italians and American intelligence officers continued to refer to army intelligence by its previous acronym, SIM.

73. SAINT, BB8 to SAINT, JJ1, 6 November 1945, subject: "Report of Activities of the Italian Mission from 1–31 October 1945," RG 226, Entry 108A, box 260.

74. Ibid.

75. Naftali, "ARTIFICE: James Angleton and X-2 Operations in Italy," 228–230.

76. Albert Materazzi, e-mail message to David Alvarez, 25 May 2006. In the spring of 1945 Al Materazzi was a member of an OSS team working with the partisans behind German lines. After the war, several Red Army officers were active in POW and repatriation missions in north Italy. They operated with the knowledge and permission of American and British authorities, although these authorities complained that the Russian officers sometimes went about in civilian dress rather than the prescribed uniforms. Alexander Kirk to the Secretary of State, 22 June 1945, NARA, RG 84 (Records of Foreign Service Posts), box 94.

77. SAINT, BB8 to SAINT, JJ1, 6 November 1945, subject: "Report of Activities of the Italian Mission from 1–31 October 1945," RG 226, Entry 108A, box 260.

78. Earl Brennan to William Donovan, 17 November 1944, subject: "Operational Activities, Political and Economic Intelligence for Italy and Albania for the Period 1 to 15 November 1944," RG 226, Entry 190, reel 60.

79. Unsigned and unaddressed memorandum, 27 March 1945, RG 226, Entry 125, box 51.

80. AFHQ G-2, "Appreciation of the Current Situation in Italy," 26 August 1945, RG 331, Film R-250 B.

81. G-2 Rome Allied Command, 7 October 1945, subject: "Rome Area Allied Command Security Report," RG 226, Entry 108A, box 259.

82. London to G2 AFHQ, 30 August 1945, RG 226, Entry 88, box 96.

83. Elena Aga-Rossi and Victor Zaslavsky, *Togliatti e Stalin: il PCI e la politica estera staliniana negli archive di Mosca* (Bologna: Il Molino, 1997), 81–82. Despite their strong insistence on purging fascist sympathizers from all aspects of Italian political, cultural, and economic life, the PCI accepted former members of the Fascist Party so long as their membership in that party preceded the downfall of Mussolini.

84. Ibid., 75; Elena Aga-Rossi and Victor Zaslavsky, "The Soviet Union and the Italian Communist Party, 1944–8," in *The Soviet Union and Europe in the Cold War, 1943–1945*, ed. Francesca Gori and Silvio Pons (New York: St. Martin's Press, 1996), 162–163.

85. Aga-Rossi and Zaslavsky, *Togliatti e Stalin*, 75–76; Roberto Gualtieri, *Togliatti e la politica estera italiana: dalla Resistenza al Tratto di pace, 1943–1947* (Rome: Editori Riuniti, 1995), 56–57.

86. Aga-Rossi and Zaslavsky, *Togliatti e Stalin*, 95. On the basis of documentation from Soviet archives, Elena Aga-Rossi and Victor Zaslavsky conclude that in the early postwar period Soviet control over the PCI was strong and that the Italian party took no important initiative without authorization from Moscow. On some issues, such as Moscow's insistence that the PCI support Yugoslav territorial claims concerning Trieste and Fiume, territories over which Italy asserted claims, the subservience compelled the party to adopt positions that alienated rather than attracted their fellow citizens. Aga-Rossi and Zaslavsky, "The Soviet Union and the Italian Communist Party, 1944–8," 170, 175.

87. Gualtieri, *Togliatti e la politica estera italiana*, 53–55; Silvio Pons, *L'impossibile egemonia: l'URSS, il PCI e le origini della Guerra fredda (1943–1948)* (Rome: Carocci, 1999), 158–160, 167.

88. Aga-Rossi and Zaslavsky, "The Soviet Union and the Italian Communist Party, 1944–8," 164.

89. Aga-Rossi and Zaslavsky, *Togliatti e Stalin*, 131–132.

90. For a useful summary of what American intelligence in Italy thought about the intentions of the PCI at the end of 1945, see Joint Intelligence Committee, AFHQ, "JIC Standing Appreciation on Italy," JIC(AF)/3/7(Final), 29 December 1945, RG 84, box 82.

91. James E. Miller, *The United States and Italy, 1940–1950: The Politics and Di-*

plomacy of Stabilization (Chapel Hill: University of North Carolina Press, 1986), 139, 157.

92. SAINT BB8 to SAINT JJ1, 12 November 1945, subject: "Rome Security Summary No. 17," RG 226, Entry 108A, box 260.

93. Ibid.; Asst. Chief of Staff, G-2, Rome Area Allied Command, Security Summary No. 20, 1–31 January 1946, RG 226, Entry 108A, box 265.

94. SAINT BB8 to SAINT JJ1, 9 January 1946, subject: "GSI Headquarters, No. 2 District Intelligence Summaries," RG 226, Entry 108A, box 263.

95. Angleton to the Director, SSU, 18 March 1946, subject: "Consolidated Progress Report for November, December 1945 and January 1946," RG 226, Entry 108A, box 268.

96. Ibid.

97. X-2 Italy to Washington, 30 October 1945, subject: "Slav penetration in Italy," RG 226, Entry 108A, box 260; X-2 Italy to Washington, 7 March 1946, subject: "JK23 Weekly Report," RG 226, Entry 108A, box 267. JK23 was the cryptonym for Italian army intelligence (SIM).

98. SAINT BB8 to SAINT JJ1, 6 November 1945, subject: "Report of Activities of the Italian Mission from 1–31 October 1945," RG 226, Entry 108A, box 260.

99. X-2 Italy to Washington, 9 October 1945, subject: "Albanian Activity in Italy," RG 226, Entry 108A, box 259; X-2 Italy to Washington, 3 January 1946, subject: "Anti-Hoxha Committee," RG 226, Entry 108A, box 262.

100. SAINT BB8 to SAINT DB1, 18 February 1946, subject: "Georgian Nationalists," RG 226, Entry 108A, box 265.

101. "SI Operations in Italy," [April 1946], RG 226, Entry 210, box 435; Frank Wisner to Whitney Shepardson, 6 November 1945, ibid.

102. SAINT BB8 to SAINT JJ1, 17 April 1946, subject: "Monthly Report on Balkan Activity," RG 226, Entry 108A, box 270.

103. Angleton to AC of S (G-2), AFHQ, 23 November 1945, subject: "Socialist Party Directives," RG 226, Entry 108A, box 261; X-2 Italy to Washington, 7 February 1946, subject: "Italian Proposals for War Reparations," RG 226, Entry 108A, box 265; SAINT BB8 to SAINT JJ1, 4 April 1946, RG 226, Entry 213, box 1.

104. See, for example, X-2 Italy to Washington, 15 March 1946, subject: "Yugoslav Political Report," RG 226, Entry 108A, box 268.

105. Report JZX-5928, 28 January 1946, subject: "Russian Embassy Activities in Rome," RG 226, Entry 108A, box 263.

106. X-2 Italy to Washington, 28 January 1946, subject: "Cable sent by Russian Embassy Rome to Moscow," RG 226, Entry 108A, box 263.

107. X-2 Italy to Washington, 30 January 1946, subject: "Recent Views of Father Leiber," RG 226, Entry 108A, box 263.

108. Ibid.

Chapter 7. Conclusion

1. See, for example, David F. Rudgers, *Creating the Secret State: The Origins of the Central Intelligence Agency, 1943–1947* (Lawrence: University Press of Kansas, 2000).

2. Among many examples of such assertions, see Jeffrey Burds, "The Early Cold War in Soviet East Ukraine, 1944–1948," Carl Beck Papers in Russian and East European Studies, No. 1501 (January 2001): 11–12; Richard Aldrich, *The Hidden Hand: Britain, America and Cold War Secret Intelligence* (London: John Murray, 2001), 36.

3. Christopher Andrew and Vasili Mitrokhin, *The Sword and the Shield: The Mitrokhin Archive and the Secret History of the KGB* (New York: Basic Books, 1999), 104–106; Allen Weinstein and Alexander Vassiliev, *The Haunted Wood: Soviet Espionage in America—The Stalin Era* (New York: Random House, 1999), 32–37.

4. Army Security Agency, *European Axis Signal Intelligence in World War II as Revealed by TICOM Investigations and by Other Prisoner of War Interrogations and Captured Materials, Principally German*, vol. 9: *German Traffic Analysis of Russian Communications*, Introduction, n.p., www.ticomarchive.com.

5. "Final Report on the Visit of TICOM Team 5 to the Schliersee Area," 31 October 1945, 9, www.ticomarchive.com.

6. For a particularly frank internal appraisal of SSU's Soviet operations, see Harry Rositzke to S. B. L. Penrose, 11 July 1946, subject: "Current Status of the Procurement of Intelligence on the USSR by SSU and Major Foreign Secret Intelligence Services," National Archives and Records Administration, Record Group (RG) 226, Entry 210, box 329.

7. Jonathan M. House, *A Military History of the Cold War, 1944–1962* (Norman: University of Oklahoma Press, 2012), 35.

8. Ibid., 42.

9. "Soviet Military Roundup," No. 1, 14 September 1945, RG 319, Entry 1041, box 17.

10. "Soviet Military Roundup," No. 4, 5 October 1945, ibid.; "Soviet Military Roundup," No. 8, 2 November 1945, ibid.

11. Compare "Soviet Military Roundup," No. 1, 14 September 1945, and "Soviet Military Roundup," No. 8, 2 November 1945, RG 319, Entry 1041, box 17.

12. "Protocol of the Proceedings of the Berlin Conference," 1 August 1945, *Foreign Relations of the United States 1945: The Conference of Berlin* (Washington, DC: Government Printing Office, 1960), 2:1481.

13. David Alvarez, *Secret Messages: Codebreaking and American Diplomacy, 1930–1945* (Lawrence: University Press of Kansas, 2000), 238–241.

14. "Soviet Military Roundup," No. 1, 14 September 1945, RG 319, Entry 1041, box 17.

15. Robert Patterson to John Magruder, 18 December 1945, RG 226, M1642, reel 29.

16. Karel Stiassni to Gordon Stewart and Crosby Lewis, 18 January 1946, RG 226, Entry 108B, box 75; "Distribution and Dissemination of SSU/SI Material, 1 January–31 May 1946," RG 226, Entry 210, box 182. This document suggests how

much SSU had been forced by demobilization and budget reductions to reduce its operational tempo. In May 1946 SSU sent 899 intelligence reports to the State Department, but a year earlier, in May 1945, OSS had distributed to State 1,320 reports. Comparable figures for distribution to MID and ONI in May 1946/May 1945 are: MID 992/1,922 and ONI 915/1,900.

17. See, for example, Secret Intelligence Branch (SSU) to James Riddleberger, Chief, Division of Central European Affairs, 22 May 1946, RG 226, Entry 210, box 477.

18. John Magruder to the Assistant Secretary of War, 25 October 1945, RG 226, Entry 21, box 142.

19. "Individual Surveys of SSU Branches: State Department Evaluation of SSU Services," 2, RG 226, Entry 210, box 329.

20. Karel Stiassni to Gordon Stewart and Crosby Lewis, 18 January 1946, RG 226, Entry 108B, box 75.

21. John Davies to Alfred Ulmer, 15 May 1946, RG 226, Entry 108B, box 75.

22. Alvarez, *Secret Messages*, 240.

23. Ibid., 243.

24. Woodrow Kuhns, ed., *Assessing the Soviet Threat: The Early Cold War Years* (Washington, DC: Central Intelligence Agency, Center for the Study of Intelligence, 1997), 9–10.

Unpublished Documents

National Archives and Records Administration, College Park, Maryland
  Record Group 38. Chief of Naval Operations
  Record Group 59. Department of State
  Record Group 84. Foreign Service Posts
  Record Group 218. U.S. Joint Chiefs of Staff
  Record Group 226. Office of Strategic Services
  Record Group 260. U.S. Occupation Headquarters, World War II
  Record Group 319. Army Staff
  Record Group 457. National Security Agency
Clemson University Library
  James F. Byrnes Papers
Library of Congress, Washington, D.C.
  W. Averell Harriman Papers
Seelye G. Mudd Manuscript Library, Princeton University
  Louis Fischer Papers

Published Documents

Foreign Relations of the United States, 1942. Vol. 3: *Europe.* Washington, DC: Government Printing Office, 1961.

Foreign Relations of the United States, 1944. Vol. 3: *The British Commonwealth and Europe.* Washington, DC: Government Printing Office, 1965.

Foreign Relations of the United States, 1944. Vol. 4: *Europe.* Washington, DC: Government Printing Office, 1966.

Foreign Relations of the United States, 1945: The Conferences at Malta and Yalta. Washington, DC: Government Printing Office, 1955.

Foreign Relations of the United States, 1945: The Conference of Berlin. 2 vols. Washington, DC: Government Printing Office, 1960.

Foreign Relations of the United States, 1945. Vol. 4: *Europe.* Washington, DC: Government Printing Office, 1963.

Foreign Relations of the United States, 1945. Vol. 5: *Europe.* Washington, DC: Government Printing Office, 1967.

Foreign Relations of the United States, 1945. Vol. 3: *European Advisory Commission, Austria, Germany.* Washington, DC: Government Printing Office, 1968.

Foreign Relations of the United States, 1946. Vol. 5: *The British Commonwealth, Western and Central Europe.* Washington, DC: Government Printing Office, 1969.

Foreign Relations of the United States, 1946. Vol. 6: *Eastern Europe, the Soviet Union.* Washington, DC: Government Printing Office, 1969.

Foreign Relations of the United States, 1945–1950: Emergence of the Intelligence Establishment. Washington, DC: Government Printing Office, 1996.

Benson, Robert Louis, and Michael Warner, eds. *Venona: Soviet Espionage and the American Response, 1939–1957.* Washington, DC: National Security Agency and Central Intelligence Agency, 1996.

Kuhns, Woodrow, ed. *Assessing the Soviet Threat: The Early Cold War Years.* Washington, DC: Central Intelligence Agency, Center for the Study of Intelligence, 1997.

Ruffner, Kevin C., ed. *Forging an Intelligence Partnership: CIA and the Origins of the BND, 1945–1949.* Langley, VA: Central Intelligence Agency, Center for the Study of Intelligence, 1999.

Steury, Donald, ed. *On the Front Lines of the Cold War: Documents on the Intelligence War in Berlin, 1946–1961.* Langley, VA: Central Intelligence Agency, Center for the Study of Intelligence, 1999.

Warner, Michael, ed. *The CIA under Harry Truman.* Washington, DC: Central Intelligence Agency, Center for the Study of Intelligence, 1994.

Books and Articles

Abt, Karl W. *A Few Who Made a Difference: The World War II Teams of the Military Intelligence Service.* New York: Vantage Press, 2004.

Aga-Rossi, Elena, and Victor Zaslavsky. "The Soviet Union and the Italian Communist Party." In *The Soviet Union and Europe in the Cold War, 1943–1945,* ed. Francesca Gori and Silvio Pons, 161–184. New York: St. Martin's Press, 1996.

———. *Togliatti e Stalin: il PCI e la politica estera staliniana negli archivi di Mosca.* Bologna: Il Mulino, 1997.

Aid, Matthew M. "The Anglo-American Signals Intelligence Effort against Russia, 1945–1950." Paper presented at the annual meeting of the Society for Historians of American Foreign Relations, 6 June 2003, Washington, DC.

———. "The National Security Agency and the Cold War." In *Secrets of Signals Intelligence during the Cold War and Beyond,* ed. Matthew Aid and Cees Wiebes, 27–66. London: Frank Cass, 2001.

———. *The Secret Sentry: The Untold History of the National Security Agency.* New York: Bloomsbury Press, 2009.

———. "Stella Polaris and the Secret Code Battle in Postwar Europe." *Intelligence and National Security* 17, no. 3 (Autumn 2002): 17–86.

Aldrich, Richard J. *The Hidden Hand: Britain, America and Cold War Secret Intelligence.* London: John Murray, 2001.

Alvarez, David. "Behind Venona: American Signals Intelligence in the Early Cold War." *Intelligence and National Security,* 14, no. 2 (Summer 1999): 179–186.

———. "The Best Information Service in Europe? Vatican Intelligence and the Final Solution." In *Secret Intelligence and the Holocaust*, ed. David Bankier, 187–211. New York: Enigma Books, 2006.

———. *Secret Messages: Codebreaking and American Diplomacy, 1930–1945*. Lawrence: University Press of Kansas, 2000.

———. *Spies in the Vatican: Espionage and Intrigue from Napoleon to the Holocaust*. Lawrence: University Press of Kansas, 2002.

———. "Tempest in an Embassy Trash Can." *World War II* 22, no. 9 (January–February 2008): 55–59.

———. "Trying to Make the MAGIC Last: American Diplomatic Codebreaking in the Early Cold War." *Diplomatic History* 31, no. 5 (November 2007): 865–882.

Andrew, Christopher. *For the President's Eyes Only: Secret Intelligence and the American Presidency from Washington to Bush*. New York: Harper Collins, 1995.

Andrew, Christopher, and Oleg Gordievsky. *KGB: The Inside Story of Its Foreign Operations from Lenin to Gorbachev*. New York: Harper Collins, 1990.

Andrew, Christopher, and Vasili Mitrokhin, *The Sword and the Shield: The Mitrokhin Archive and the Secret History of the KGB*. New York: Basic Books, 1999.

Angevine, Robert G. "Gentlemen Do Read Each Other's Mail: American Intelligence in the Interwar Era." *Intelligence and National Security* 7, no. 2 (April 1992): 1–29.

Army Security Agency. *European Axis Signal Intelligence in World War II as Revealed by TICOM Investigations and by Other Prisoner of War Interrogations and Captured Materials Principally German*. Vol. 9: *German Traffic Analysis of Russian Communications*. www.ticomarchive.com.

Auriol, Vincent. *Journal du Septennat, 1947–1954*. Paris: Librairie Armand Colin, 1970.

Bader, William B. *Austria between East and West, 1945–1955*. Stanford, CA: Stanford University Press, 1966.

Bare, Duncan. "The Curious Case of Aradi Zsolt: Tracking the Distinguished Career of an OSS, SSU and CIA Central European Asset." *Journal for Intelligence, Propaganda and Security Studies* 8, no. 1 (2014): 111–126.

Barlow, Jeffrey G. *From Hot War to Cold: The U.S. Navy and National Security Affairs, 1945–1955*. Stanford, CA: Stanford University Press, 2009.

Beer, Siegfried. "Target Central Europe: American Intelligence Efforts Regarding Nazi and Early Postwar Austria." Working Paper 97-1, Center for Austrian Studies, University of Minnesota.

Benson, Robert Louis, and Cecil Phillips. *History of Venona*. Fort George Meade, MD: National Security Agency, 1995.

Bernert, Philippe. *Roger Wybot et la bataille pour la DST*. Paris: Presse de la Cité, 1975.

Biddiscombe, Perry. "Operation Selection Board: The Growth and Suppression of the Neo-Nazi 'Deutsche Revolution.'" *Intelligence and National Security* 11, no. 1 (January 1996): 59–77.

———. "The Problem with Glass Houses: The Soviet Recruitment and Deployment of SS Men as Spies and Saboteurs." *Intelligence and National Security* 15, no. 3 (Autumn 2000): 131–145.

————. *Werwolf! The History of the National Socialist Guerrilla Movement, 1944–1946*. Toronto: University of Toronto Press, 1998.

Bidwell, Bruce W. *History of the Military Intelligence Division, Department of the Army General Staff: 1775–1941*. Frederick, MD: University Publications of America, 1986.

Bischof, Günter. *Austria in the First Cold War, 1945–55: The Leverage of the Weak*. New York: St. Martin's Press, 1999.

Blum, John Morton, ed. *From the Morgenthau Diaries: Years of War*. Boston: Houghton Mifflin, 1967.

Borhi, László. *Hungary in the Cold War, 1945–1956*. New York: Central European University Press, 2004.

Bray, Ann. *History of the Counter Intelligence Corps*. Vol. 15: *Occupation of Austria and Italy*. Fort Holabird, MD: U.S. Army Intelligence Center, 1960.

Bray, Ann, John Finnegan, and James Gilbert. *In the Shadow of the Sphinx: A History of Army Counterintelligence*. Fort Belvoir, VA: Department of the Army, 2005.

Brown, Ralph W., III. "Making the *Third Man* Look Pale: American-Soviet Conflict in Vienna during the Early Cold War in Austria, 1945–1950." *Journal of Slavic Military Studies* 14, no. 4 (December 2001): 81–109.

Burds, Jeffrey. "The Early Cold War in Soviet East Ukraine, 1944–1948." Carl Beck Papers in Russian and East European Studies, no. 1501 (January 2001), University Center for International Studies, University of Pittsburgh.

Carafano, James Jay. *Waltzing into the Cold War: The Struggle for Occupied Austria*. College Station: Texas A&M University Press, 2002.

Chodakiewicz, Marek Jan. *Between Nazis and Soviets: Occupation Politics in Poland, 1939–1947*. Lanham, MD: Lexington Books, 2004.

Clay, Lucius D. *Decision in Germany*. Westport, CT: Greenwood Press, 1970 reprint.

Clemens, Diane Shaver. *Yalta*. Oxford: Oxford University Press, 1970.

Clemente, Jonathan D. "OSS Medical Intelligence in the Mediterranean Theater: A Brief History." *Journal of Intelligence History* 2 (Summer 2002): 1–28.

Corvo, Max. *The O.S.S. in Italy, 1942–1945: A Personal Memoir*. New York: Praeger, 1990.

Cronin, Audrey Kurth. *Great Power Politics and the Struggle over Austria, 1945–1955*. Ithaca, NY: Cornell University Press, 1986.

Cutler, Richard. *Counterspy: Memoirs of a Counterintelligence Officer in World War II and the Cold War*. Washington, DC: Brassey's, 2004.

Davis, Lynn Etheridge. *The Cold War Begins: Soviet-American Conflict over Eastern Europe*. Princeton, NJ: Princeton University Press, 1974.

Delattre, Lucas. *A Spy at the Heart of the Third Reich: The Extraordinary Story of Fritz Kolbe, America's Most Important Spy in World War II*. New York: Atlantic Monthly Press, 2005.

Dessants, Betty Abrahamsen. "Ambivalent Allies: OSS' USSR Division, the State Department, and the Bureaucracy of Intelligence Analysis, 1941–1945." *Intelligence and National Security* 11, no. 4 (October 1996): 722–753.

Dorwart, Jeffrey M. *Conflict of Duty: The U.S. Navy's Intelligence Dilemma, 1919–1945*. Annapolis, MD: Naval Institute Press, 1983.

Eisenberg, Carolyn. *Drawing the Line: The American Decision to Divide Germany, 1944–1949.* Cambridge: Cambridge University Press, 1996.

Faure, Claude. *Aux Services de la République: Du BCRA à la DGSE.* Paris: Fayard, 2004.

Felix, Christopher [James McCargar]. *A Short Course in the Secret War.* 4th ed. Lanham, MD: Madison Books, 2001.

Gaddis, John Lewis. *The United States and the Origins of the Cold War, 1941–1947.* New York: Columbia University Press, 1972.

Greene, Harris. "Cloak and Dagger in Salzburg." In *The Cold War: A Military History,* ed. Robert Cowley, 14–22. New York: Random House, 2005.

Gualtieri, Roberto. *Togliatti e la politica estera italiana: dalla Resistenza al Tratto di pace, 1943–1947.* Rome: Editori Riunti, 1995.

Hansen, Peer Henrik. *Second to None: U.S. Intelligence Activities in Northern Europe, 1943–1946.* Dordrecht: Republic of Letters, 2011.

Haynes, John Earl, and Harvey Klehr. *Venona: Decoding Soviet Espionage in America.* New Haven, CT: Yale University Press, 1999.

Heideking, Jürgen, and Christof Mauch, eds. *American Intelligence and the German Resistance to Hitler.* New York: Westview, 1996.

Helms, Richard (with William Hood). *A Look over My Shoulder: A Life in the Central Intelligence Agency.* New York: Random House, 2003.

Hersh, Burton. *The Old Boys: The American Elite and the Origins of the CIA.* New York: Charles Scribners, 1992.

Holloway. David. *Stalin and the Bomb: The Soviet Union and Atomic Energy, 1939–1956.* New Haven, CT: Yale University Press, 1994.

House, Jonathan M. *A Military History of the Cold War, 1944–1962.* Norman: University of Oklahoma Press, 2012.

Kahn, David. *Hitler's Spies: German Military Intelligence in World War II.* New York: Macmillan, 1978.

Kent, Peter. *The Lonely Cold War of Pope Pius XII.* Montreal: McGill-Queen's University Press, 2002.

Krisch, Henry. *German Politics under Soviet Occupation.* New York: Columbia University Press, 1974.

Kuniholm, Bruce R. *The Origins of the Cold War in the Middle East: Great Power Conflict and Diplomacy in Iran, Turkey, and Greece.* Princeton, NJ: Princeton University Press, 1980.

Lamb, Richard. *War in Italy, 1943–1945.* New York: St. Martin's Press, 1993.

Lane, Arthur Bliss. *I Saw Poland Betrayed: An American Ambassador Reports to the American People.* New York: Bobbs-Merrill Co., 1948.

Laurent, Sébastien. "Les services secrets gaullistes à l'épreuve de la politique (1940–1947)." *Politix: Revue des sciences sociales du politique* 14, no. 54 (2001).

Leffler, Melvyn P. *A Preponderance of Power: National Security, the Truman Administration, and the Cold War.* Stanford, CA: Stanford University Press, 1992.

Lowenhaupt, Henry S. "On the Soviet Nuclear Scent." *Studies in Intelligence* 11, no. 4 (Fall 1967): 13–29.

Lukes, Igor. "The Czechoslovak Special Services and Their American Adversary during the Cold War." *Journal of Cold War Studies* 9, no. 1 (Winter 2007): 3–28.

———. "A Failure of Intelligence: Czechoslovakia, 1945–1948." Unpublished paper.

———. *On the Edge of the Cold War: American Diplomats and Spies in Postwar Prague.* Oxford: Oxford University Press, 2012.

Mahnken, Thomas C. *Uncovering Ways of War: U.S. Intelligence and Foreign Military Innovation, 1918–1941.* Ithaca, NY: Cornell University Press, 2002.

Mark, Eduard. "American Policy toward Eastern Europe and the Origins of the Cold War, 1941–1946." *Journal of American History* 68 (September 1981): 313–336.

———. "The OSS in Romania, 1944–45: An Intelligence Operation of the Early Cold War." *Intelligence and National Security* 9, no. 2 (April 1994): 320–344.

———. "Revolution by Degrees: Stalin's National Front Strategy for Europe, 1941–1947." Working Paper 31, Cold War International History Project, February 2001.

———. "The War Scare of 1946 and Its Consequences." *Diplomatic History* 21, no. 3 (July 1997): 383–415.

Mauch, Christof. *The Shadow War against Hitler: The Covert Operations of America's Secret Intelligence Service.* Trans. Jeremiah Riemer. New York: Columbia University Press, 1999.

Milano, James, and Patrick Brogan. *Soldiers, Spies, and the Rat Line.* Washington, DC: Brassey's, 1995.

Miller, James E. *The United States and Italy, 1940–1950: The Politics and Diplomacy of Stabilization.* Chapel Hill: University of North Carolina Press, 1986.

Mueller, Wolfgang. "Stalin and Austria: New Evidence on Soviet Policy in a Secondary Theatre of the Cold War, 1938–53/55." *Cold War History* 6, no. 1 (February 2006): 63–84.

Murphy, David, Sergei Kondrashev, and George Bailey. *Battleground Berlin: CIA vs KGB in the Cold War.* New Haven, CT: Yale University Press, 1997.

Murphy, Robert. *Diplomat among Warriors.* New York: Doubleday and Co., 1964.

Naftali, Timothy. "ARTIFICE: James Angleton and X-2 Operations in Italy." In *The Secrets War: The Office of Strategic Services in World War II*, ed. George C. Chalou, 218–245. Washington, DC: National Archives and Records Administration, 1992.

———. "Reinhard Gehlen and the United States." In *U.S. Intelligence and the Nazis*, ed. Richard Breitman, Norman J.W. Goda, Timothy Naftali, and Robert Wolfe, 375–418. Washington, DC: National Archives Trust Fund Board, 2004.

Nagy, Töhötöm. *Jesuitas y Masones.* Buenos Aires: Safian, 1966.

Naimark, Norman M. *The Russians in Germany: A History of the Soviet Zone of Occupation, 1945–1949.* Cambridge, MA: Belknap Press, 1995.

O'Donnell, Patrick. *Operatives, Spies, and Saboteurs: The Unknown Story of the Men and Women of World War II's OSS.* New York: Free Press, 2004.

Packard, Wyman H. *A Century of U.S. Naval Intelligence.* Washington, DC: Department of the Navy, 1996.

Paczkowski, Andrzej. "The Leading Force: The Communist Party and the Security Apparatus in Poland, 1944–1956." Paper prepared for the conference on "The

Communist Security Apparatus in East Central Europe, 1945–1989," Warsaw, 16–18 June 2005.

Pash, Boris T. *The ALSOS Mission.* New York: Award House, 1969.

Paterson, Thomas G. *Soviet-American Confrontation: Postwar Reconstruction and the Origins of the Cold War.* Baltimore: Johns Hopkins University Press, 1973.

Pons, Silvio. *L'impossibile egemonia: l'URSS, il PCI e le origini della Guerra fredda (1943–1948).* Rome: Carocci, 1999.

Porch, Douglas. *The French Secret Services: A History of French Intelligence from the Dreyfus Affair to the Gulf War.* New York: Farrar, Straus, and Giroux, 1995.

Quinn, William W. *Buffalo Bill Remembers: Truth and Courage.* Fowlerville, MI: Wilderness Adventure Books, 1991.

Reynolds, Quentin. *The Curtain Rises.* New York: Random House, 1944.

Rezabek, Randy. "The Russian Fish with Caviar." *Cryptologia* 38, no. 1 (January 2014): 61–76.

Rositzke, Harry. *The KGB: The Eyes of Russia.* New York: Doubleday & Co., 1981.

Rudgers, David F. *Creating the Secret State: The Origins of the Central Intelligence Agency, 1943–1947.* Lawrence: University Press of Kansas, 2000.

Ruffner, Kevin C. "Cold War Allies: The Origins of the CIA's Relationship with Ukrainian Nationalists." *Central Intelligence Agency.* Library, Electronic Reading Room. www.foia.cia.gov/document/519697e8993294098d50c281.

———. "Draft Working Paper. Chapter 5: Long Experience in the Anti-Soviet Game." 5. *Central Intelligence Agency.* Library, Electronic Reading Room. www .foia.cia.gov/document/519697e8993294098d50c29a.

———. "Project SYMPHONY: U.S. Intelligence and the Jewish *Brichah* in Postwar Austria," *Studies in Intelligence* 51, no. 1 (2007): 33–46.

———. "You Are Never Going to Be Able to Run an Intelligence Unit: SSU Confronts the Black Market in Berlin." *Journal of Intelligence History* 2, no. 2 (Winter 2002): 1–20.

Sandford, Gregory. *From Hitler to Ulbricht: The Communist Reconstruction of East Germany, 1945–1946.* Princeton, NJ: Princeton University Press, 1983.

Schwab, Gerald. *OSS Agents in Hitler's Heartland: Destination Innsbruck.* New York: Praeger, 1996.

Silver, Arnold. "Questions, Questions, Questions: Memories of Oberursel." *Intelligence and National Security* 8, no. 2 (April 1993): 199–213.

Smith, Arthur L. *Kidnap City: Cold War Berlin.* Westport, CT: Greenwood Press, 2002.

Smith, Bradley. *The Shadow Warriors: O.S.S. and the Origins of the CIA.* New York: Basic Books, 1983.

———. *Sharing Secrets with Stalin: How the Allies Traded Intelligence, 1941–1945.* Lawrence: University Press of Kansas, 1996.

Stephan, Robert W. *Stalin's Secret War: Soviet Counterintelligence against the Nazis, 1941–1945.* Lawrence: University Press of Kansas, 2004.

Stirling, Tessa, Daria Nałęcz, and Tadeusz Dubicki, eds. *Intelligence Cooperation between Poland and Great Britain during World War II.* London: Valentine Mitchell, 2005.

Stout, Mark. "The Pond: Running Agents for State, War, and the CIA." *Studies in Intelligence* 48, no. 3 (2004): no pagination.

Taylor, Frederick. *Exorcising Hitler: The Occupation and Denazification of Germany.* New York: Bloomsbury Press, 2011.

Thomas, Evan. *The Very Best Men: Four Who Dared: The Early Years of the CIA.* New York: Simon & Schuster, 1995.

Thyraud de Vosjoli, Philippe. *Lamia.* Boston: Little Brown, 1970.

Trogdon, Gary. "A Decade of Catching Spies: The United States Army's Counter-intelligence Corps, 1943–1953." PhD diss., University of Nebraska, 2001.

Troy, Thomas. *Donovan and the CIA: A History of the Establishment of the Central Intelligence Agency.* Frederick, MD: University Publications of America, 1981.

Viviani, Ambrogio. *Servizi Segreti Italiani, 1815–1985.* 2nd ed. Rome: Adnkronos Libri, 1986.

Waller, Douglas. *Wild Bill Donovan: The Spymaster Who Created OSS and Modern American Espionage.* New York: Free Press, 2011.

War Department (Strategic Services Unit, History Project). *The Overseas Targets: War Report of the OSS.* New York: Walker, 1976.

Warner, Michael. "Prolonged Suspense: The Fortier Board and the Transformation of the Office of Strategic Services." *Journal of Intelligence History* 2 (Summer 2002): 65–76. "Salvage and Liquidation: The Creation of the Central Intelligence Group." *Studies in Intelligence* 39, no. 5 (1996): no pagination.

———. "Salvage and Liquidation: The Creation of the Central Intelligence Group." *Studies in Intelligence* 39, no. 5 (1996): no pagination.

Webb, G. Gregg. "The FBI and Foreign Intelligence: New Insights into J. Edgar Hoover's Role." *Studies in Intelligence* 48, no. 1 (2004): 45–58.

Weinstein, Allen, and Alexander Vassiliev. *The Haunted Wood: Soviet Espionage in America—The Stalin Era.* New York: Random House, 1999.

West, Nigel, and Oleg Tsarev. *The Crown Jewels: The British Secrets at the Heart of the KGB Archives.* London: Harper Collins, 1998.

Whitnah, Donald R., and Edgar L. Erickson. *The American Occupation of Austria: Planning and Early Years.* Westport, CT: Greenwood Press, 1985.

Willoughby, John. *Remaking the Conquering Heroes: The Social and Geopolitical Impact of the Post-War American Occupation of Germany.* New York: Palgrave, 2001.

Wnuk, Rafal. "Operations of the Communist Security Apparatus against Armed Resistance in Poland in [the] 1940s and 1950s." Paper prepared for the conference on "The Communist Security Apparatus in East Central Europe, 1945–1989," Warsaw, 16–18 June 2005.

Ziemke, Earl. *The U.S. Army in the Occupation of Germany, 1944–1946.* Washington, DC: Center of Military History, 1975.